65

The Rehnquist Court

ABC-CLIO SUPREME COURT HANDBOOKS

The Burger Court, Tinsley E. Yarbrough
The Chase Court, Jonathan Lurie
The Fuller Court, James W. Ely Jr.
The Hughes Court, Michael E. Parrish
The Rehnquist Court, Thomas R. Hensley
The Stone Court, Peter G. Renstrom
The Taft Court, Peter G. Renstrom
The Taney Court, Timothy S. Huebner
The Vinson Court, Michal R. Belknap
The Waite Court, Donald Grier Stephenson Jr.
The Warren Court, Melvin I. Urofsky
The White Court, Rebecca S. Shoemaker

Forthcoming:
The Jay/Ellsworth Court, Matthew P. Harrington
The Marshall Court, Robert L. Clinton

Peter G. Renstrom, Series Editor

ABC-CLIO SUPREME COURT HANDBOOKS

The Rehnquist Court

Justices, Rulings, and Legacy

Thomas R. Hensley

With
Kathleen Hale
Auburn University
Carl Snook
Michigan State University

ABC-CLIO

Santa Barbara, California • Denver, Colorado • Oxford, England

Library of Congress Cataloging-in-Publication Data
Hensley, Thomas R.
    The Rehnquist court : justices, rulings, and legacy / Thomas R. Hensley with Kathleen Hale, Carl Snook.
        p. cm. — (ABC-CLIO Supreme Court handbooks)
    Includes bibliographical references and index.
    ISBN 1-57607-200-2 (hardcover : alk. paper) — ISBN 1-57607-560-5 (ebook)
1. United States. Supreme Court—History.   2. Rehnquist, William H., 1924-2005.
3. Constitutional history—United States.   4. Conservatism—United States.
I. Hale, Kathleen.   II. Snook, Carl.   III. Title.   IV. Series.

    KF8742.H46 2006
    347.73'26—dc22

                                    2006011011

09 08 07 06   10 9 8 7 6 5 4 3 2 1

This book is also available on the World Wide Web as an e-book. Visit http://www.abc-clio.com for details.

ABC-CLIO, Inc.
130 Cremona Drive, P.O. Box 1911
Santa Barbara, California 93116–1911

This book is printed on acid-free paper ∞ .
Manufactured in the United States of America

To my parents, Earl and Ada Hensley,
and my in-laws, Ralph and Lois Robertson,
whose love and support have made all the difference.

Contents

Series Foreword

T here is an extensive literature on the U.S. Supreme Court, but it contains discussion familiar largely to the academic community and the legal profession. The ABC-CLIO Supreme Court series is designed to have value to the academic and legal communities also, but each volume is intended as well for the general reader who does not possess an extensive background on the Court or American constitutional law. The series is intended to effectively represent each of fourteen periods in the history of the Supreme Court with each of these fourteen eras defined by the chief justice, beginning with John Marshall in 1803. Each Court confronted constitutional and statutory questions that were of major importance to and influenced by the historical period. The Court's decisions were also influenced by the values of each of the individual justices sitting at the time. The issues, the historical period, the justices, and the Courts' decisions in the most significant cases will be examined in the volumes of this series.

ABC-CLIO's Supreme Court series provides scholarly examinations of the Court as it functioned in different historical periods and with different justices. Each volume contains information necessary to understand each particular Court and an interpretative analysis by the author of each Court's record and legacy. In addition to representing the major decisions of each Court, institutional linkages are examined as well—the political connections among the Court, Congress, and the executive branch. These relationships are important for several reasons. Although the Supreme Court retains some institutional autonomy, all the Court's justices are selected by a process that involves the other two branches. Many of the significant decisions of the Court involve the review of actions of Congress or the president. In addition, the Court frequently depends on the other two branches to secure compliance with its rulings.

The authors for the volumes in this series were selected with great care. Each author has worked extensively with the Court, the period, and the personalities about which he or she has written. ABC-CLIO wanted each of the volumes to examine several common themes, and each author agreed to work within certain guidelines. Each author was free, however, to develop the content of each volume, and many of the volumes advance new or distinctive conclusions about the Court under examination.

Each volume contains four substantive chapters. The first chapter introduces the Court and the historical period in which it served. The second chapter examines each of the justices who sat on the particular Court. The third chapter represents the most significant decisions rendered by the particular Court. Among other things, the impact of the historical period and the value orientations of the individual justices are developed. A fourth and final chapter addresses the impact of each particular Court on American constitutional law—its doctrinal legacy.

Each volume contains several features designed to make it more valuable to those whose previous exposure to the Supreme Court and American constitutional law is limited. Each volume has a reference section that contains brief entries on some of the people, statutes, events, and concepts introduced in the four substantive chapters. Entries in this section are arranged alphabetically. Each volume also contains a glossary of selected legal terms used in the text. Following each of the four chapters, a list of sources used in the chapter and suggestions for further reading appears. Each volume also has a comprehensive annotated bibliography. A listing of Internet sources is presented at the end of the bibliography. Finally, there is a comprehensive subject index and a list of cases (with citation numbers) discussed in each volume. ABC-CLIO is delighted with the quality of scholarship represented in each volume and is proud to offer this series to the reading public.

Permit me to conclude with a personal note. This project has been an extraordinarily rewarding undertaking for me as series editor. Misgivings about serving in this capacity were plentiful at the outset of the project. After tending to some administrative business pertaining to the series, securing authors for each volume was the first major task. I developed a list of possible authors after reviewing previous work and obtaining valuable counsel from several recognized experts in American constitutional history. In virtually every instance, the first person on my list agreed to participate in the project. The high quality of the series was assured and enhanced as each author signed on. I could not have been more pleased. My interactions with each author have been most pleasant, and the excellence of their work will be immediately apparent to the reader. I sincerely thank each author.

Finally, a word about ABC-CLIO and its staff. ABC-CLIO was enthusiastic about the project from the beginning and has done everything necessary to make this series successful. I am very appreciative of the level of support I have received from ABC-CLIO. Alicia Merritt, senior acquisitions editor, deserves special recognition. She has held my hand throughout the project. She has facilitated making this project a reality in every conceivable way. She has encouraged me from the beginning, provided invaluable counsel, and given me latitude to operate as I wished while keeping me on track at the same time. This project would not have gotten off the ground without Alicia, and I cannot thank her enough.

Peter G. Renstrom
Series Editor

Preface and Acknowledgments

This book is organized around the question of whether the U.S. Supreme Court under the leadership of William Rehnquist engaged in a conservative constitutional counterrevolution by creating major new precedents supporting the government against claims of individuals that their civil rights and liberties had been violated. This question is also raised in regard to the Rehnquist Court's decisions in cases centering on the topics of federalism and government powers. This topic has been raised in various forms by numerous scholars, journalists, and political activists, and the answer has varied widely, based in part upon the time period when the question was raised. With the passing of Chief Justice Rehnquist in September 2005, we now have closure on this important era of Supreme Court history, and we can now be somewhat more confident in our assessment of the Rehnquist Court. Although others may disagree, the conclusion offered in this book is that the Rehnquist Court did not engage in a conservative constitutional counterrevolution.

An analysis of the Rehnquist Court must include an examination of the two preceding Court periods of the Warren Court (1953–1969 terms) and the Burger Court (1969–1986 terms). A widespread consensus exists that the Warren Court was the most liberal in U.S. history and did indeed engage in a liberal constitutional revolution. With six liberal justices, three moderates, and no conservatives by the end of the Warren Court era, the Court under Earl Warren created major new liberal precedents in regard to the Establishment Clause; the Free Exercise Clause; freedom of expression, including libel and obscenity; the guarantees of the criminally accused; and the Equal Protection Clause, especially regarding race.

A similar consensus exists that the Burger Court did not engage in a conservative constitutional revolution despite efforts of Republican presidents to nominate and appoint conservative jurists to the Court. Republican President Richard Nixon had the greatest impact on the Court's membership because he appointed four new justices in his first term as president: Chief Justice Warren Burger and Associate Justices Harry Blackmun, Louis Powell, and William Rehnquist. Republican President Gerald Ford was able to add one new member, John Paul Stevens, who succeeded the noted liberal William Douglas. The only other new Burger Court appointment was made by Republican President Ronald Reagan when he named Sandra Day O'Connor as the first woman justice in Supreme Court history, replacing moderate Justice Potter Stewart.

These changes certainly had an impact on the direction of the Court's decision making, but these changes did not produce a constitutional counterrevolution. Three considerations support this conclusion. First, quantitative voting data reveal that although in civil rights and liberties cases the Burger Court (56 percent conservative) was more conservative than the Warren Court (32 percent conservative), the Burger Court was moderately, not radically, conservative. Second, the Burger Court did not overturn a single major precedent of the Warren Court. Third, the Burger Court justices created several important liberal precedents by recognizing a woman's constitutional right to make the abortion decision, elevating gender to heightened scrutiny under the Equal Protection Clause, extending the scope of the Warren Court's jurisprudence regarding achieving racially equal schools, and providing support for most affirmative action programs.

By the time Warren Burger announced his retirement, the Court was equally divided, with four conservative justices (Burger, Rehnquist, White, and O'Connor), four liberal justices (Brennan, Marshall, Blackmun, and Stevens), and a key swing vote of Justice Powell. Conservatives thought that they were close to achieving a clear majority on the Court, and Republican Presidents Ronald Reagan and George H. W. Bush had significant opportunities to realize this long-sought goal.

Burger's resignation did not create a new realignment on the Court because the new chief justice, William Rehnquist, was a member of the conservative alignment, and Antonin Scalia, Rehnquist's replacement as an associate justice, was viewed as certain to maintain the four-person conservative coalition. However, Justice Powell's resignation from the Court in 1997 held the potential for a dramatic realignment, a fact that all sides recognized. After a long and bitter struggle, President Reagan was successful in nominating and appointing Anthony Kennedy to Powell's seat. It appeared in his first two terms that Kennedy was solidly in the conservative camp, creating a majority of conservative voices on the Court.

The situation soon became even more favorable for the conservatives when the Court's two leading liberals, William Brennan and Thurgood Marshall, resigned in 1990 and 1991, respectively. President Bush appointed a little-known New Hampshire jurist, David Souter, and Clarence Thomas replaced Thurgood Marshall. It appeared to most Court watchers that the conservatives now had a 7–2 advantage over the liberals, and the conservative argument would prevail even if two of the Republican-appointed justices would vote liberally.

The only other appointments to the bench during the Rehnquist Court era were made by Democratic President William Clinton, who named Ruth Bader Ginsburg to replace Justice White and Stephen Breyer to succeed Harry Blackmun. These two new justices were not viewed as threatening to the conservative control of the Court.

Despite the seeming predominance of the conservative majority, the argument is made in this book that the Rehnquist Court did not engage in a conservative constitutional counterrevolution, and the reasons for this assessment are remarkably similar to the analysis of the Burger Court. First, the voting data show identical records in regard to civil rights and liberties cases, with both Courts voting liberally in 44 percent of the cases. Second, the Rehnquist Court did not overturn any of the major decisions of the Warren and Burger Courts, although the justices of this era modified the jurisprudence of the earlier Courts in regard to such areas as the free exercise of religion, the Establishment Clause, affirmative action, and abortion. Third, the Rehnquist Court issued several liberal decisions that overturned previous conservative precedents in such fields as the death penalty as well as the privacy and equal protection rights of homosexuals.

In the effort to study the issue of whether a conservative constitutional counterrevolution has occurred under the Rehnquist Court, two different methodological techniques have been employed. One important method is quantitative in nature where the "Spaeth data" are utilized to compare the three Court eras as well as to examine the individual voting behavior of the Rehnquist Court justices in each major issue area facing the Court. As valuable as quantitative data can be, this form of analysis has its limitations, particularly a lack of consideration of the reasoning behind the justices' votes. A second method thus involves the qualitative approach of reading the opinions of the justices to determine the reasoning of the Court and the extent to which the Court sees itself as following, modifying, or overturning existing precedent.

Underlying these two methodological approaches are theories of Supreme Court decision making. The quantitative approach is associated with the attitudinal model of Supreme Court decision making, which asserts that justices vote consistently with their underlying political and social values and attitudes. The qualitative approach places more emphasis on the legal model of Supreme Court decision making, which argues that the Court bases its decision making primarily on the analysis of legal criteria. The position taken in this book is that the attitudinal model best explains Supreme Court behavior; but this process is extremely complex, and legal criteria certainly affect the justices as do such other factors as strategic bargaining among the justices, considerations of the interests of Congress and the executive branch, the activities of interest groups, and public opinion.

Many people who assisted with the completion of this book need to be recognized. Kathleen Hale wrote the initial draft of the Part II section on "Key People, Laws, and Events" as well as the initial draft of the "Chronology," and Carl Snook wrote the initial draft of chapter 2, "The Justices," as well as initial draft sections in chapter 3 on federalism and government powers. The importance of the work by Kathleen and Carl is reflected in their being listed as contributing authors of the book. Special thanks go to Peter Renstrom of Western Michigan University, who flattered me by asking me to author this book as part of a fourteen-volume series on the U.S. Supreme Court. Pete's insights and patience during this process were remarkable. Alicia Merritt, senior acquisitions editor of ABC-CLIO, provided both guidance and support throughout this project. Mim Jackson contributed significantly to the book by her research on the annotated bibliography in Part Two of the book. Sarah DePaul and Chris Bellas also made valuable contributions to the book. Several people played important roles in regard to the data set used throughout this project. The data set was originally created by Harold Spaeth of Michigan State University. This data set is now being handled by Kirk Randazzo of the University of Kentucky, and his assistance is appreciated. Janice Winchell of Kent State University provided excellent service in dealing with the technological issues that arose in using the Spaeth data. I also want to recognize the word processing assistance of Kathy Loughry of Kent State. Finally, I certainly want to thank my wife, Jane, who remained tolerant and supportive throughout the long process of producing this book.

PART ONE

Justices, Rulings, and Legacy

1

The Rehnquist Court and the Period

Introduction and Overview

William Hubbs Rehnquist served as chief justice of the U.S. Supreme Court from 1986 to 2005, a period of American history that has involved intense struggles over cultural values. Conservative voices have argued that Supreme Court liberal activists have undermined traditional American values and weakened American society, while liberal advocates have argued that conservatives are committed to an agenda that would radically undercut the freedom and equality of minority groups and the politically powerless. Battles have flared over such controversial issues as flag burning, pornography and obscenity, government regulation of the Internet, government-supported religious activities in public schools, warrantless searches by police, the *Miranda* warnings, the death penalty, affirmative action, and the rights of homosexuals.

The terms *liberal* and *conservative* are important ones and need careful definition. Although many definitions of these terms exist, the approach of Kenneth Janda, Jeffrey M. Berry, and Jerry Goldman (2003) will be used in this book. These authors argue that American society has historically confronted two major conflicts in competing values, an original dilemma involving the conflict between the values of freedom and order and a modern dilemma involving a conflict between the values of freedom and equality. In the original dilemma of American democracy, conservatives tend to favor order over freedom, and liberals tend to support freedom over order. Thus, in civil rights and liberties cases involving claimed violations of individual rights by the government, the conservative position would favor the government, while the liberal position would favor the individual. These approaches are typically reversed, however, in regard to the modern dilemma because liberals tend to support government programs favoring equality, whereas conservatives oppose such government activities; affirmative action programs are a good example of this.

The Supreme Court has been deeply involved in this cultural struggle between liberal and conservative forces. The 1996 case of *Romer v. Evans* provides a good example. This case involved a challenge to the constitutionality of a referendum approved by Colorado voters in 1991 that prohibited either state or local governments from adopting policies to protect persons based upon sexual orientation. A six-person majority ruled the referendum unconstitutional as a violation of the Fourteenth Amendment Equal Protection Clause. In dissent, Justice Scalia, joined by Justices Rehnquist and Thomas, emphasized throughout his opinion the American culture war, arguing vehemently that the majority justices were wrong "to take sides in this culture war" because they represented an elite attitude that was contrary to both majoritarian democracy and Court precedent (517 U.S. at 652).

Many conservatives argue that the foundations of this cultural conflict can be traced to the liberal decisions of the Court under Earl Warren (1953–1969) and Warren Burger (1969–1986). Conservatives hoped that membership changes during the Rehnquist Court era would produce a majority on the Court that would take a decisive stand in this cultural struggle, engaging in a conservative constitutional counterrevolution that would reverse the liberal precedents of the Warren and Burger Courts.

A widespread consensus exists that the Supreme Court under the leadership of Chief Justice Earl Warren was the most liberal in American history. For example, in First Amendment freedom of expression cases, the Warren Court created major new liberal precedents in several areas, including obscenity, libel, and incitement. The Court under Warren's leadership also created new liberal precedents in regard to the religious guarantees of the First Amendment, creating high levels of protection for religious minorities under the Free Exercise Clause and calling for a strong separation of church and state under the Establishment Clause. Similarly, in the area of the rights of the criminally accused, the Warren Court created dramatic new liberal precedents, including nationalizing most of the criminal rights guarantees and establishing the *Miranda* warnings. In addition, the Warren Court ruled in *Brown v. Board of Education* (1954) and subsequent civil rights cases that state-sponsored racial segregation violated the Equal Protection Clause of the Fourteenth Amendment.

These decisions of the Warren Court were highly controversial in American society, and in the 1968 presidential election, Republican candidate Richard Nixon promised if elected to appoint justices to the Supreme Court who would stop and hopefully reverse the pattern that conservatives saw as inappropriate judicial activism and bad public policy. During his first term in office, Nixon did have the opportunity to remake the composition of the Court by appointing four conservative justices: Chief Justice Warren Burger and Associate Justices Harry Blackmun, Lewis Powell, and William Rehnquist.

Although the majority of its decisions were more conservative than the Warren Court's, the Burger Court did not engage in the conservative counterrevolution that President Nixon and his fellow conservatives had hoped would occur. The Burger Court did not overturn any of the major liberal precedents of the Warren Court, and the justices of the Burger Court era created several major new liberal precedents that were strongly opposed by conservatives. The most publicized of these decisions came in *Roe v. Wade* (1973), in which the Court recognized the abortion decision as being an aspect of the constitutional right to privacy. The Burger Court also created new constitutional protections in the area of gender discrimination and established new liberal precedents supporting affirmative action programs.

Republican presidents Ronald Reagan (1981–1989) and George H. W. Bush (1989–1993) made determined efforts to succeed where Nixon had failed. Although Reagan had the opportunity in his first term to appoint only one member to the Court— Sandra Day O'Connor, the first woman in Court history—he was able to appoint two new justices in his second term. When Chief Justice Burger retired after the 1985–1986 term, Reagan elevated William Rehnquist from associate justice to chief justice and then nominated conservative Antonin Scalia to take Rehnquist's position. One year later, Reagan had another opportunity to remake the Court when Lewis Powell, the key swing justice on a closely divided Court, decided to retire. Reagan initially nominated ultraconservative Robert Bork, but this nomination was defeated in a bitter Senate confirmation hearing. After another unsuccessful attempt involving Douglas Ginsburg, a Harvard law professor, Reagan eventually settled on a less-controversial conservative, Anthony M. Kennedy, who was approved overwhelmingly by the Senate.

Kennedy's appointment to the Court seemed to assure that a conservative majority now controlled the Court, but Reagan's successor, George H. W. Bush, had the opportunity to create a seven-person conservative majority that could move Supreme Court precedents in radically conservative directions. During Bush's presidency, the Court's two most liberal justices—William Brennan and Thurgood Marshall—resigned, in 1990 and 1991, respectively. Bush was successful in nominating a relatively unknown New Hampshire jurist, David Souter, to replace Brennan. The next year Bush was able to place Clarence Thomas on the Court to replace Marshall, although not without one of the most bitter and controversial confirmation hearings in American history.

A twelve-year period of Republican control of the White House ended with William Clinton's election in 1992, but it appeared to be a case of too little, too late for those opposing a conservative counterrevolution by the Rehnquist Court. Clinton's first opportunity occurred in 1993, when Byron White stepped down and was replaced by the Court's second woman jurist, Ruth Bader Ginsburg, a leading attorney in the struggle for women's equality in the seventies. The next change in the Court's membership occurred a year later, in 1994, when Harry Blackmun resigned and was replaced by Stephen Breyer. Although Ginsburg was projected to be a more liberal justice than White had been, Blackmun had been a leading liberal in his later years on the Court, and thus Breyer's addition to the Court was not viewed as weakening the conservative dominance of the Court.

Did these carefully orchestrated and sometimes bitterly contested membership changes result in a conservative counterrevolution by the Rehnquist Court? This is the central question throughout this book. The answer offered is a qualified no. The Rehnquist Court has produced a real but limited conservative change in certain areas of the law. However, most of the Warren and Burger Courts' liberal precedents remain, and the Rehnquist Court has even extended constitutional protections in a few areas. Thus, the Rehnquist Court period has been characterized by continuity rather than change, and radical change has certainly not occurred. This chapter presents a more detailed history of the period, focusing upon the legacies of the Warren and Burger Courts, the political struggles involved in nominating and confirming new justices during the period of the Rehnquist Court, and the changes in voting patterns and major precedents that can be traced to each successive change in membership on the Supreme Court.

The Warren Court, 1953–1969

The Rehnquist Court cannot be understood without some attention being given to the era of the Warren Court, from 1953 to 1969. As its membership changed over the years, the Warren Court became increasingly liberal, but its precedent-setting liberal decisions spanned the entire period of the Court.

The first major new precedent under Earl Warren's leadership was *Brown v. Board of Education* (1954) as well as the implementing decision in *Brown v. Board of Education* (1955). In *Brown I*, in 1954, the Court overturned the 1896 case of *Plessy v. Ferguson*, in which the Court set forth the separate but equal doctrine in approving laws that allowed segregation by race. Writing for a unanimous Court, Chief Justice Warren rejected the separate but equal doctrine as being inconsistent with the requirements of the Fourteenth Amendment and the country's commitment to the principle of racial equality. After waiting a year for passions to cool and to consider fully the difficult issues of implementation, the Court in *Brown II* set forth three major implementation guidelines: a prompt and reasonable start must be made, the process should then proceed with all deliberate speed, and the process should be overseen by federal district judges. The aftermath of *Brown* was to occupy a substantial amount of attention by the Warren, Burger, and Rehnquist Courts.

The Warren Court also created major new liberal precedents in regard to First Amendment freedom of expression guarantees. One important area involved sexual expression. Prior to the Warren Court, the obscene was considered to be beyond any constitutional protection, and any form of sexual expression that could lead to "impure thoughts" by the youngest members of society could be made illegal. In *Roth v. United States* (1957) and subsequent cases, including *Memoirs v. Massachusetts* (1966), the Warren Court created dramatically heightened standards for finding sexual expression obscene, requiring that materials appeal to a prurient interest in sex, be patently offensive by community standards, and lack any redeeming social quality.

Another important area involved libel law. Prior to the Warren Court, written materials could be found libelous if they were false and defamatory. In *New York Times v. Sullivan* (1964), the Court expanded the definition of the libelous for public officials to include "actual malice," that is, written statements that were done with knowledge that they were false or with a reckless disregard for the truth. This and subsequent decisions regarding libel had the effect of substantially increasing protection for the press from libel suits.

Yet a third important area where the Warren Court significantly increased freedom of expression involved the area of incitement, expression that provokes individuals into lawless action. The Court had developed a "clear and present danger test" in the early part of the twentieth century, but this test had been applied in contradictory ways over the years by successive courts, typically depending upon the extent of perceived threats to the national security. In *Brandenburg v. Ohio* (1969), the Warren Court essentially abandoned the clear and present danger test and replaced it with a stronger, liberal standard that stated that political expression criticizing the government is protected under the First Amendment until the speech involves a direct incitement to imminent lawless action.

The Court under Warren's leadership also created major new liberal precedents in the area of the guarantees of the criminally accused involving the Fourth, Fifth, Sixth, and Eighth Amendments. The most important line of cases involved decisions nationalizing or incorporating many of these Bill of Rights guarantees. These cases included *Mapp v. Ohio* (1961), nationalizing the exclusionary rule; *Malloy v. Hogan* (1964), making the Fifth Amendment protection against self-incrimination applicable to the states; *Benton v. Maryland* (1969), incorporating the Fifth Amendment Double Jeopardy Clause; *Gideon v. Wainwright* (1963), which nationalized the right to counsel guarantee of the Sixth Amendment; *Pointer v. Texas* (1965), involving the Sixth Amendment Confrontation Clause; *Washington v. Texas* (1967), incorporating the Compulsory Process Clause of the Sixth Amendment; *Klopfer v. North Carolina* (1967), nationalizing the Sixth Amendment guarantee of a speedy trial; *Duncan v. Louisiana* (1968), which applied the Jury Trial Clause to the states; and, finally, *Robinson v. California* (1962), which nationalized the Eighth Amendment guarantee against cruel and unusual punishments.

In addition to the evidence provided by an examination of some of the Court's landmark new liberal precedents, the revolutionary nature of the Warren Court's decision making can also be seen in the analysis of systematic quantitative data provided by Harold J. Spaeth in his *United States Supreme Court Judicial Database, 1953–2004 Terms.*[1] The Warren Court decided liberally in 68 percent of its civil rights and liberties cases from 1953 to 1969, and the Court became increasingly liberal as Democratic presidents had the opportunities in the 1960s to add new members to the Court. By the end of the Warren Court era, the ideological alignment was six liberal justices and three moderate justices. In the words of Thomas Walker and Lee Epstein, two leading scholars of the Supreme Court, "[Chief Justice Warren] presided over what can only be described as a constitutional revolution, generated by a group of justices who were perhaps the most liberal in American history" (Walker and Epstein 1993, 19).

The Burger Court, 1969–1986

The conservative reaction against the Warren Court was intense, and the Court's activities became a major issue in the 1968 presidential campaign. Republican candidate Richard Nixon argued that the liberal activists of the Warren Court had substituted their own values and attitudes for a careful interpretation of the Constitution, and he pledged if elected to nominate Supreme Court justices who would exercise proper judicial restraint by basing their decisions purely upon legal criteria.

Nixon won the election and had the opportunity to remake the Court dramatically by appointing four new justices to the Court in his first term. Each new appointee promised to be far more conservative than his predecessor. Nixon's first nomination, in 1969, was the most publicized because it involved Warren Burger replacing Earl Warren as chief justice. The next change, in 1970, involved another leading liberal justice, Abe Fortas, being replaced by Harry Blackmun, a good friend of Warren Burger. Finally, Nixon was able to make two appointments in 1971. Lewis Powell, a moderately conservative southern Democrat from Virginia, replaced Hugo Black, another leading voice of the Warren Court. The most controversial Nixon appointee was William Rehnquist, who replaced the moderate John Marshall Harlan.

After the rapid membership change that occurred during Nixon's first term in office, the Court's membership was reasonably stable during the remainder of Burger's tenure as chief justice. Only two more justices were appointed from 1972 to 1985, and both of those were relatively uncontroversial. In 1975, John Paul Stevens, a moderate Republican who was a circuit court judge, was named by President Gerald Ford to replace William Douglas, a leading liberal force on the Court since his appointment by President Franklin Delano Roosevelt in 1937. In 1981, President Ronald Reagan selected Sandra Day O'Connor, a Republican from Arizona, to be the Court's first woman, replacing Eisenhower appointee Potter Stewart, a moderate Republican.

The transformation in membership from the Warren Court to the Burger Court clearly had the potential to change dramatically the interpretation of American constitutional law. As was noted earlier, the ideological composition of the late Warren Court consisted of six liberals, three moderates, and no conservatives. With the membership changes that occurred during the Burger Court era, the potential existed for a solid conservative majority that could reinterpret the liberal decisions of the Warren Court. The four Nixon appointees—Burger, Blackmun, Rehnquist, and Powell—were expected to be the core of this conservative bloc. White, although appointed by liberal Democrat President John F. Kennedy, had become increasingly conservative. In addition, both Stevens and O'Connor were expected to be at least moderately conservative. Brennan and Marshall were the only liberal holdovers from the Warren Court era.

Did the Burger Court engage in a conservative constitutional counterrevolution? Scholars have given an extraordinary amount of attention to this question, and the uniform answer has been no (e.g., Yarbrough 2000; Lamb and Halpren 1991; Blasi 1983). The Burger Court was certainly more conservative than the Warren Court, but the Burger Court did not overturn any of the major liberal precedents of the Warren Court, and, indeed, the Burger Court established several major new liberal precedents.

A comparative analysis of the voting patterns of the Warren and Burger Courts provides important insights into the more conservative orientation of the Burger Court. Overall, the Burger Court was decidedly more conservative than the Warren Court, with the Warren Court ruling liberally in 68 percent of all civil rights and liberties cases compared to the Burger Court's 44 percent liberal voting. This record of the Burger Court represents a moderately conservative rather than radically conservative Court, however, and the Burger Court did not become significantly more conservative with the addition of Stevens and O'Connor.

As valuable as quantitative data are for providing insights into the decision-making patterns and philosophies of the Supreme Court, such data can paint only part of the picture. It is also important to examine the Court's treatment of important precedents because overturning past precedents and creating new precedents can have an especially profound impact on American constitutional law and American society.

The Burger Court did not overturn any of the major liberal precedents of the Warren Court. This does not mean that all of the Burger Court justices happily accepted the jurisprudential legacy of the Warren Court. Several members of the Burger Court worked diligently to reject various liberal precedents created or extended during the Warren Court era. Chief Justice Burger, for example, sought to create a majority to reject the exclusionary rule, but he was unsuccessful.

It is important to recognize that although the Burger Court did not reject outright any of the leading liberal precedents of the Warren Court era, the Court under Burger's leadership did modify some areas of constitutional law. Examples can be cited in regard to obscenity, the exclusionary rule, and the *Miranda* warnings. The Burger Court in *Miller v. California* (1973) modified in several ways the *Roth/Memoirs* test of the Warren Court, most importantly by replacing the old requirement that sexual material had to be "utterly without redeeming social value" (354 U.S. at 484–485) with a new requirement that sexual material was obscene if the material "taken as a whole, lacks serious literary, artistic, political or scientific value" (413 U.S. at 24). In the area of the exclusionary rule, the Burger Court introduced several exceptions, most notably the good faith exception in *U.S. v. Leon* (1984) and the inevitability of discovery exception in *Nix v. Williams* (1984). The *Miranda* warnings were modified in several cases by the Burger Court justices, including the creation of a public safety exception to *Miranda* in *New York v. Quarles* (1984).

The conclusion that the Burger Court did not engage in a conservative constitutional counterrevolution is supported not only by systematic quantitative data and the absence of decisions overturning Warren Court precedents but also by the Burger Court's creation of new liberal precedents in such areas as abortion, gender equality, affirmative action, and racial equality in public education. In perhaps the single most controversial decision of the Burger Court era, a 7–2 majority in *Roe v. Wade* (1973) created a major new liberal precedent by establishing that a woman's decision over whether to have an abortion comes within the constitutionally protected right of privacy of the Fourteenth Amendment. The Burger Court also blazed new constitutional paths in the area of gender discrimination. In *Reed v. Reed* (1971) the Court by a 9–0 vote found a state law unconstitutional for the first time because it violated a woman's right to equal protection under the Fourteenth Amendment. The Court used minimal scrutiny to reach its decision in *Reed*, but the Court created a new, heightened standard of intermediate scrutiny for gender discrimination cases in *Craig v. Boren* (1976). The Warren Court did not hear any cases involving affirmative action, but the Burger Court drafted several opinions supporting affirmative action programs. The most famous case was *Regents of the University of California v. Bakke* (1978), in which a closely divided Court rejected the use of a rigid quota system regarding admitting racial minorities into medical school but ruled that race was one of many legitimate factors that could be considered in the admissions decision. A final example of precedent-setting liberal decision making by the Burger Court involved racial equality in public education. The justices of the Burger Court went far beyond their Warren Court counterparts in interpreting *Brown* by giving approval to court-ordered busing in *Swann v. Charlotte–Mecklenburg County Board of Education* (1971) and extending *Brown* from the southern and border states to the entire country in *Keyes v. School District No. 1, Denver* (1973).

In conclusion, the Burger Court did not engage in the conservative constitutional counterrevolution that conservatives had sought and liberals had feared. Although the Burger Court justices voted substantially more conservatively than the Warren Court, this was a moderate not a radical conservatism. And although the Burger Court did modify some Warren Court precedents, the jurisprudential legacy of the Warren Court remained intact. Finally, the Burger Court created some of its own major liberal precedents.

By the end of the Burger Court era, in 1986, it was a closely divided institution with no bloc in control. Recognizing the dangers of oversimplification, the Court can be accurately characterized as divided 4–1–4. Justices Rehnquist and Burger were strongly conservative and were frequently joined by moderate conservatives O'Connor and White. Balancing the four conservatives were four liberals, with Brennan and Marshall as the strongly liberal justices who were usually supported by the moderate liberal pair of Blackmun and Stevens. Powell was frequently the key swing vote on the Burger Court, although he was more likely to support a conservative outcome than a liberal one.

The Rehnquist Court and the Reagan Appointments

This analysis of the Burger Court provides the background for a more detailed analysis of the Rehnquist Court period that can be dated from 1986 with Warren Burger's resignation as chief justice and William Rehnquist assuming the leadership of the Court. The Supreme Court during this period was a major front in the culture war of this era of American history, with each new appointment potentially affecting the ongoing struggle.

The analysis of this period is divided into four parts. The first period covers from 1986 to 1990, when President Reagan was able to elevate Rehnquist from associate justice to chief justice and then appoint two new justices, Antonin Scalia and Anthony M. Kennedy, to the Court. The second period, from 1990 to 1992, involved President George H. W. Bush replacing the Court's two leading liberals, William Brennan and Thurgood Marshall, with more conservative justices David Souter and Clarence Thomas. The third period, covering 1993 and 1994, saw Democratic President William Clinton having the opportunity to appoint moderate liberals Ruth Bader Ginsburg and Stephen Breyer to replace Byron White and Harry Blackmun. The final period involves the lengthy era from 1994 to June 2005, when the Court's membership did not change, which we call a natural court period.

The argument is made that the Rehnquist Court period has been an unpredictable one characterized by some intense confirmation hearings reflecting the issues and arguments in the country's cultural battles, but the overall decision making by the Court has involved much more continuity than change. The initial period, from 1986 to 1990, involving Reagan's appointments did seem to mark the beginning of a profound period of conservative constitutional counterrevolution. It appeared that the second period, from 1990 to 1992, would consolidate and strengthen this counterrevolution because of the resignation of the Court's two leading liberals, Brennan and Marshall, but unexpectedly this did not occur. The election of Clinton in 1992 was a critical event because it was to result in moderately liberal justices joining the Court, further blunting the possibility of a controlling conservative majority. In the period from 1994 to June 2005, the Court was moderately conservative, with complex voting alignments, a commitment to existing precedent, and the creation of some major liberal precedents.[2] We now examine each of these themes in greater detail.

Although President Reagan's appointment during his first term of Sandra Day O'Connor did not have a significant impact on the direction of the Court's decision making, Reagan had the opportunity to make two additional appointments during his second term that had the promise to achieve the conservative constitutional counterrevolution that had been sought for many years. In 1986, Chief Justice Warren Burger resigned, and then a year later, in 1987, the Court's key swing justice, Lewis Powell, stepped down from the Court. Reagan and his advisors were determined to take advantage of these opportunities to create a Court that would be fully supportive of their conservative agenda.

The resignation of Burger as chief justice did not provide a real opportunity to affect the voting pattern of the Court because Burger had been a consistently conservative vote, but it did create the possibility to have more effective conservative leadership on the Court. Burger had not been successful as either a social or task leader on the Court. Although he certainly looked the part with his impressive size, flowing silver hair, and deep voice, he seemed to lack the intellectual depth and vision to control the Court effectively.

Reagan and his close associates saw in Associate Justice William Rehnquist the person with the ideal characteristics to serve as chief justice. Rehnquist was experienced but relatively young, he had articulated effectively a conservative judicial philosophy consistent with the views of the White House, and he was respected for his intellect and his personality by the other members of the Court. Thus, Reagan's strategy was to elevate Rehnquist from associate justice to chief justice and then to nominate conservative Circuit Court Judge Antonin Scalia to assume Rehnquist's former seat on the Court as associate justice.

The Democratic majority in the U.S. Senate did not necessarily share the same view of Rehnquist that was held by the Reagan administration. On the one hand, opposition Democrats grudgingly admitted that Rehnquist did possess the qualities that were attractive to Reagan, but these characteristics meant that Rehnquist might be far more effective than Burger in achieving a revolution to the Right. On the other hand, Senate Democrats emphasized issues in Rehnquist's record that Republican supporters tried to minimize.

One issue was Rehnquist's opposition to major liberal precedents such as *Roe v. Wade* (1973). Critics of Rehnquist hoped that his stated philosophy of judicial self-restraint would lead him to uphold well-established precedents, but they feared the social and political consequences of major liberal precedents being overturned if Rehnquist's leadership took judicial activism to the Right instead.

Another issue was concern over Rehnquist's personal commitment to principles of racial equality. A problem that arose during his original confirmation hearing resurfaced in 1986 when he was questioned about writing a memo as a law clerk for Justice Robert Jackson in which he advocated maintaining *Plessy v. Ferguson* (1896), the case in which the Court had permitted strict racial segregation by law under the principle of "separate but equal." Rehnquist asserted that he took this position because Justice Jackson instructed him to do so, but critics were not convinced. Another problem for Rehnquist involved allegations that he had been involved in activities in the 1960s in Arizona that deprived minorities of their right to vote.

These types of issues and concerns led to a long, partisan confirmation fight for Rehnquist, but eventually he prevailed by a vote of 65–33. This was the closest vote for a chief justice in American history.

Once Rehnquist's lengthy battle was completed, the confirmation process for Scalia went quickly and without controversy. Scalia was viewed as being eminently qualified, and he did not have to defend himself against allegations of racial discrimination like those Rehnquist faced. Furthermore, liberal Democrats did not view Scalia's confirmation as upsetting the delicate 4–1–4 balance on the Court. Scalia was in effect replacing Burger, and thus the conservative coalition would remain at four justices. Scalia received a unanimous vote from the Senate.

Intense as the confirmation battle over Rehnquist had been, it proved to be the quiet before the storm. At the end of the 1986–1987 term, the Court's centrist swing justice, Lewis Powell, announced his resignation. As noted previously, Powell was in an exceptionally powerful position as the key vote on a closely divided Court, and his resignation offered the Reagan administration the opportunity to create a solid, five-person conservative majority.

Federal Circuit Court Judge Robert Bork was the controversial nominee of President Reagan to replace Justice Powell. Bork's credentials and experience were impressive. A law professor, Bork had published extensively on a wide variety of legal issues. In addition to his experience on the federal bench, he also had served in important positions in the executive branch, including leading the attorney general's office during the Nixon administration.

The controversy surrounding Bork thus did not stem from his credentials or experience but rather from his conservative views on American law and especially some of the major issues of constitutional law. Bork had developed a thorough and sophisticated philosophy of constitutional interpretation that he labeled as "original understanding." This approach to decision making emphasized the plain language of the Constitution, the original intent of the writers of the Constitution, and the general understanding of the document in American society when the Constitution was created. If none of these criteria provided clear guidance, then a justice should defer to the majoritarian branches of government. Bork argued that this was the only approach to constitutional adjudication that could lead to impartial, objective decision making and the avoidance of the subjective, liberal, and activist decision making that he saw as characteristic of the Warren and Burger Courts (Bork 1990).

Applying this judicial philosophy to contemporary areas of constitutional law, Bork typically advocated strongly conservative positions that favored the government over the rights of the individual. The single most controversial issue involved abortion, where Bork's earlier writings had strongly criticized *Roe v. Wade* (1973) as a flagrant abuse of judicial power where the Court majority created a new constitutional right based upon the justices' personal ideologies rather than objective criteria. The controversy over Bork's views was certainly not limited to the issue of abortion but rather extended widely to such topics as the exclusionary rule, the *Miranda* warnings, racial and gender equality, affirmative action, the separation of church and state, and freedom of expression issues such as obscenity and libel.

Given what was potentially at stake, it is perhaps not surprising that liberal interest groups engaged in a massive campaign to defeat Bork in the Senate. In a long, partisan, and extremely nasty confirmation process, liberal forces eventually succeeded in defeating Bork's nomination by a decisive margin of 58–42. The confirmation hearing was so intense that a new verb was introduced into American society; to "bork" someone was to launch an all-out, no-holds-barred attack on someone you desperately want to defeat.

The Reagan administration was not only outraged at the attacks on Bork but also bitterly disappointed in the defeat of a person they had thought could help produce profound change in the Court's interpretations of American law. Determined to nominate and appoint a dependable conservative voice to the Court, President Reagan rather quickly named Harvard law professor Douglas Ginsburg to replace Powell. The Republican administration may have moved too quickly, however. Ginsburg was confronted immediately with various ethical issues, and he withdrew his name from consideration when it was discovered that he had smoked marijuana with some of his Harvard Law School students.

At this point in the long and extremely partisan battle over Powell's successor, the Reagan administration decided to nominate a less-controversial person but someone who they thought could provide a consistently conservative vote on the Court. They selected Circuit Court Judge Anthony M. Kennedy, and Kennedy proved to be a popular choice with members of the Senate. Senate Democrats were not in a mood to continue the damaging fight over the confirmation process, and they grudgingly acknowledged that Reagan would get his conservative appointment this time. Kennedy's record was impeccable, and his writings and Senate testimony suggested that he would not bring a strongly ideological orientation to the Court. Kennedy received a unanimous vote of 97–0 after only three days of hearings, and he took his seat on the Court in February 1988.

What impact did President Reagan's appointments of Rehnquist, Scalia, and Kennedy have on the Court? To answer this question, we need to examine both systematic quantitative data as well as the language of the major precedents of the Court before and after the three Reagan appointments. The evidence reveals that Reagan's appointees did indeed succeed in creating the conservative majority that could fundamentally change American constitutional law.

Quantitative data presented in table 1.1 reveal that the Court became decidedly more conservative in civil rights and liberties cases once Kennedy joined the Court. In the 1986–1987 and 1987–1988 terms, the Rehnquist Court had voted liberally 46 percent and 49 percent, respectively. In Kennedy's first full term on the Court, in 1988–1989, the Court's liberal voting in civil rights and liberties cases fell to 36 percent, and then in the 1989–1990 term, the Rehnquist Court justices ruled liberally in only 33 percent of the civil rights and liberties cases.

Kennedy's role was clear and decisive. He voted liberally in only 36 percent of the civil rights and liberties cases in the 1988 term and then voted even more conservatively in the 1989 term, with only a 22 percent liberal voting record. Furthermore, the conservatives now had a majority voting bloc. Kennedy joined with Rehnquist, Scalia, O'Connor, and White to form a five-person bloc that had an average voting agreement of 80 percent in the 1988 term and 86 percent in the 1989 term.

The dramatic increase in conservative voting was accompanied by even more dramatic changes in the Rehnquist Court's treatment of liberal precedents. The new conservative majority overturned or modified numerous liberal decisions of the Warren

Table 1.1: Liberal/Conservative Voting Records of the
Rehnquist Court in Civil Rights/Liberties Cases, 1986–1989 Terms

Terms of the Rehnquist Court	Outcomes	
	Liberal	Conservative
1986–1987	46%	54%
1987–1988	49%	51%
1988–1989	36%	64%
1989–1990	33%	67%

Source: Harold J. Spaeth, *United States Supreme Court Judicial Database, 1953–2004 Terms* (Ann Arbor, MI: Inter-University Consortium for Political and Social Research, 2005).

and Burger Court eras, and they gave every indication that a massive conservative constitutional counterrevolution was under way. This assault on liberal precedents extended to many constitutional fronts, including the Free Exercise Clause, the Establishment Clause, the Fourth Amendment, affirmative action, and abortion.

One of the most controversial and highly criticized cases during this period was *Employment Division, Department of Human Resources of Oregon v. Smith* (1990), involving the Free Exercise of Religion Clause. Prior to the *Smith* case, the Supreme Court had generally adhered to a strict scrutiny approach to free exercise issues based upon a test set forth in *Sherbert v. Verner* (1963). Under the *Sherbert* test, a government law or action that imposed an undue burden on a person's religious rights could only be sustained if the government could show that it had a compelling interest and that this interest was being achieved by narrowly tailored means. Under this test, various exemptions from the law could be granted to individuals acting upon their religious beliefs. Writing for a five-person majority in *Smith*, Scalia argued that *Sherbert* was not the controlling precedent. Instead, Scalia maintained, the Court's precedents required that all religious practices must conform to valid secular laws, and thus no religious exemptions can ever be made, even when individuals are required by the law to violate their deeply held religious beliefs.

Affirmative action was another area in which the Rehnquist Court turned sharply right in the 1988–1990 period. Both the Burger Court and the Rehnquist Court had generally been supportive of affirmative action programs, but in *City of Richmond v. J. A. Croson Co.* (1989) the Court ruled unconstitutional a minority set-aside program for construction bids established by the city of Richmond, Virginia. The *Croson* decision was especially radical because a Court majority for the first time agreed that the strict scrutiny equal protection test should apply to state affirmative action programs, requiring such policies to serve a compelling government interest achieved by narrowly tailored means. In her controlling opinion, O'Connor made it clear that state governments could rarely meet this test because a compelling interest required proof of specific past discriminatory treatment, and the remedy had to be limited to those persons against whom the discrimination had occurred.

Warrantless searches under the Fourth Amendment were yet another area of civil rights and liberties that saw significant conservative changes during the 1988 and 1989 terms of the Rehnquist Court. During the Warren and Burger Court eras, government searches without warrants were generally permissible if they were based upon probable cause or reasonable suspicion. In the companion cases of *Skinner v. RLEA* (1989) and *National Treasury Employee Union v. Von Raab* (1989), the conservative majority on the Rehnquist Court gave a somewhat novel interpretation to the Fourth Amendment. The justices argued that the last half of the Fourth Amendment, which requires a warrant based upon probable cause, was no longer central in interpreting this amendment. Rather, the Fourth was to be interpreted based upon the first part of the amendment prohibiting unreasonable searches, and reasonableness was to be determined by a balancing test weighing a suspect's privacy rights against police and society's interests in safety and order.

The conservative movement of the Rehnquist Court majority extended into the controversial area of abortion. In *Webster v. Reproductive Health Services* (1989), the five-person majority of Rehnquist, Scalia, White, O'Connor, and Kennedy upheld several provisions of a Missouri law placing restrictions on abortions, including a preamble that stated that "life begins at conception" and "unborn children have protectable interests in life, health, and well-being." Although the conservative justices rejected the federal government's request to overturn *Roe v. Wade* (1973) and could not agree on a majority opinion, the decision undermined the basic principles of *Roe* and led Blackmun, the author of *Roe*, to conclude: "I fear for the future. I fear for the liberty and equality of the millions of women who have lived and come of age in the 16 years since *Roe* was decided. I fear for the integrity of, and public esteem for, this Court" (492 U.S. at 538).

Yet another facet of civil rights and liberties that felt the direct impact of Kennedy's appointment was the Establishment Clause. The Burger Court had been deeply divided over the proper interpretation of this clause, but in a series of decisions in 1985, the Burger Court justices embraced a liberal orientation that stressed the importance of government neutrality involving church-state relations and supported the *Lemon* test that emphasized that the primary purpose and effect of government policies must neither advance nor inhibit religion. In two 1989 companion cases involving public holiday displays with religious elements present—*Pittsburgh v. ACLU* and *County of Allegheny v. ACLU*—Kennedy wrote an opinion joined by fellow conservatives Rehnquist, Scalia, and White in which he argued strongly against the neutrality approach and the *Lemon* test. He advocated instead a more conservative accommodationist approach that would allow much more substantial church-state involvement. Although the Court as a whole was fractured and divided in these decisions, upholding one display and rejecting another, Kennedy gave the conservative accommodationists another vote and a strong additional voice for rejecting past liberal policies.

The significant impact of Kennedy was widely recognized. A leading constitutional law expert, Erwin Chemerinsky, offered the following assessment in the *Harvard Law Review:*

> Justice Kennedy's first full term on the Court produced a clear and resounding initial answer to his ideology and impact. Joining Chief Justice Rehnquist and Justices White, O'Connor, and Scalia, Justice Kennedy supplied the critical fifth vote in a series of conservative 5–4 decisions in cases involving abortion, capital punishment, civil rights, and criminal procedure. The Reagan legacy of a conservative court seems secure for many years to come. For liberals, it is a time of despair. The 1988–1989 term was devastating for civil rights and civil liberties (1989, 44–45).

The Rehnquist Court and
the Bush Appointments

If the situation looked bright for conservatives and dismal for liberals because of Kennedy's immediate impact on the Court, then these perspectives became even more heightened in the next two years, when the Court's leading liberal voices—William Brennan and Thurgood Marshall—resigned, in 1990 and 1991, respectively, allowing Republican President George H. W. Bush to replace them with far more conservative justices. Brennan had voted liberally in 86 percent of civil rights and liberties cases during his time on the Rehnquist Court, and Marshall's liberal voting record was even higher, at 88 percent. Bush now had the unique opportunity to solidify the conservative grip on the Court by adding two additional votes to the existing conservative majority of Rehnquist, Scalia, White, O'Connor, and Kennedy, creating a seven-person conservative bloc that could fundamentally alter American constitutional law. In this section of this chapter, an analysis is presented of the nomination and confirmation process of Bush's two appointees, David Souter and Clarence Thomas, and then an analysis is undertaken of the impact of these two justices on the Court's decision making.

When William Brennan announced his resignation, in 1990, the Bush administration vividly recalled the intense fight over Bork's nomination to replace Powell. They did not want a repeat performance in the democratically controlled Senate. After substantial debate, Bush settled on David Souter, a former state supreme court justice from New Hampshire who was serving on the U.S. Court of Appeals for the First Circuit in Boston. Souter had impressive credentials. He graduated from Harvard with honors, was a Rhodes Scholar, earned his law degree from Harvard Law School, and rose rapidly through the legal ranks in New Hampshire. Souter was also virtually unknown outside of his home state, and this worked to his advantage in being nominated and confirmed. Souter's views on the host of controversial issues before the Court were largely unknown, and his testimony before the Senate revealed little about either his general philosophy or his positions on specific issues. Liberal senators thus had little to criticize. Souter, called the "stealth candidate," was confirmed by a vote of 90–9.

Bush's nomination of Clarence Thomas, in 1991, did not go nearly as smoothly. Unlike Souter, Thomas's conservative views on the hot-button issues of American law were well known from his work in the Reagan administration, and the Bush administration knew his nomination would attract intense liberal opposition. Bush and his advisors felt they had a trump card, however, because of race. Marshall had been the first African American ever to serve on the Court, and liberals would find it difficult to oppose an African American replacement in Thomas, even if he did hold much more conservative views than Marshall. The Senate hearings on Thomas were intense and controversial, and they became even more inflamed when Anita Hill, a college professor and former assistant of Thomas, testified that Thomas had subjected her to various forms of sexual harassment. The lengthy, bitter, and ugly confirmation process eventually concluded with Thomas being approved by the narrowest of margins, 52–48.

What impact did the appointments of Souter and Thomas have on the Court? The answer to this question is both complex and surprising. On the one hand, substantial evidence can be cited regarding the distinctively more conservative voting records of Souter and Thomas, and some landmark cases seemed to signal that a full-fledged conservative constitutional counterrevolution was at hand. On the other hand, a more accurate characterization of the impact of Souter and Thomas is that the Court not only stopped short of a dramatic conservative redirection but actually became more liberal with the addition of Souter and Thomas. This seeming paradox needs some detailed discussion.

As was predicted, both Souter and Thomas were significantly more conservative in their initial term than their predecessors, Brennan and Marshall. As mentioned above, Brennan had an average liberal voting record of 86 percent per term in civil rights and liberties cases on the Rehnquist Court, but Souter voted liberally in only 35 percent of the civil rights and liberties cases in his first term, in 1990–1991. Furthermore, Souter formed a voting bloc with Rehnquist, Scalia, O'Connor, and Kennedy in his initial term. In Thomas's first term, in 1991–1992, he voted liberally in civil rights and liberties only 26 percent of the time compared to Marshall's liberal average of 88 percent. In addition, Thomas formed a conservative voting bloc with Rehnquist and Scalia in the 1991–1992 term.

The potential for a major conservative revolution was evident not only in the initial voting records of Souter and Thomas but also in the language of some key opinions. *Payne v. Tennessee* (1991) was especially noteworthy. This case involved the constitutionality of victim impact statements during the sentencing phase of murder cases whereby family members could testify regarding the impact of the victim's death in their lives. The Rehnquist Court had ruled victim impact statements unconstitutional in *Booth v. Maryland* (1987) and *South Carolina v. Gathers* (1989), but a six-person majority of Souter, Rehnquist, Scalia, White, Kennedy, and O'Connor explicitly overturned these decisions in *Payne*.

In his majority opinion, Rehnquist made an argument that seemingly laid the groundwork for a full-scale conservative attack on the liberal precedents of the Warren and Burger Courts. Raising the question of whether the Court should follow the principle of *stare decisis* and thus not overturn *Booth* and *Gathers*, Rehnquist wrote that "when governing decisions are unworkable or badly reasoned, 'this Court has never felt constrained to follow precedent'" (*Payne v. Tennessee*, 501 U.S. at 827). Rehnquist went on to argue: "*Stare decisis* is not an inexorable command; rather it 'is a principle of policy and not a mechanical formula of adherence to the latest decision.'

This is particularly true in constitutional cases, because in such cases 'correction through legislative action is practically impossible'" (501 U.S. at 828).

Justice Marshall wrote an impassioned dissent, harshly criticizing the new conservative majority and their seeming intention to engage in a conservative constitutional counterrevolution.

> Power, not reason, is the new currency of this Court's decision making. In dispatching *Booth* and *Gathers* to their graves, today's majority ominously suggests that an even more extensive upheaval of this Court's precedents may be in store. The implications of this radical new exception to the doctrine of *stare decisis* are staggering. The majority today sends a clear signal that scores of established constitutional liberties are now ripe for reconsideration (*Payne v. Tennessee*, 501 U.S. at 844).

Compelling as the evidence seems regarding the impact of Souter and Thomas in solidifying conservative control of the Court and propelling it into profound constitutional change, the reality is quite different. The Rehnquist Court's voting record was actually much *less* conservative in the successive terms after Souter and Thomas joined the Court, and the conservative bloc diminished rather than expanded. Both of these perhaps surprising statements are examined in some detail, and then an effort is made to explain the reasons for these unexpected patterns.

Despite the replacement of Brennan by Souter in the 1990 term and the assumption of Marshall's seat by Thomas in the 1991 term, the Court was decidedly less conservative in the 1990 and 1991 terms than it had been in the 1988 and 1989 terms. As reported above, the Court decided only 36 percent of its civil rights and liberties cases liberally in the 1988 term, and this figure fell to 33 percent in the 1989 term. In Souter's first term, in 1990, however, the Court decided 43 percent of its civil rights and liberties decisions liberally; and then with both Souter and Thomas on the Court in the 1991 term, the Court ruled liberally in 51 percent of these cases.

In addition, the controlling five-person conservative bloc of the early Rehnquist Court years disappeared in the 1990 and 1991 terms. In the 1990 term, a four-person conservative bloc emerged consisting of Rehnquist, O'Connor, Kennedy, and Souter, but Scalia and White were not associated with it. Then in the 1991 term, the conservative bloc shrank to only Rehnquist, Scalia, and Thomas.

The question that demands to be answered from this prior discussion is why the Rehnquist Court became more liberal in the 1990 and 1991 terms when Souter replaced Brennan and Thomas took Marshall's seat. The answer to this question and to this fascinating and important development is complex and nuanced.

The 1990 term of the Court was a somewhat unique one because of the issues before it. Seven of the eight returning justices voted substantially more liberally than they had in previous terms, and the eighth—Marshall—was at his usual high level of liberal voting. Thomas R. Hensley and Christopher E. Smith (1995) argue that during this term the Court accepted a large number of ultraconservative decisions from the lower courts, which had become increasingly conservative over the years with Reagan and Bush appointees. Thus, in the 1990 term, 89 percent of the liberal decisions favored the petitioning party, thus reversing the conservative decision of the lower court. In contrast, in the 1988 term, only 56 percent of the liberal decisions favored the petitioners, and this figure was an even lower 48 percent in the 1989 term. Thus, the Court's relatively moderate voting in the 1990 term may have been prompted by the unusual issues presented to the Court that stimulated more liberal reactions from all of the justices.

The reason for the Rehnquist Court's surprising liberal voting in the 1991 term seems to involve another explanation and one of a more long-lasting nature: more moderate voting by O'Connor, Kennedy, and Souter. All three justices engaged in significantly more liberal voting in the 1991 term than in the three prior terms of 1988, 1989, and 1990. O'Connor's liberal average for 1988–1990 was 32 percent, but for the 1991 term it was 58 percent liberal. Kennedy's liberal voting record increased from 28 percent in 1988–1990 to 49 percent in the 1991 term. Finally, Souter voted liberally 35 percent in the 1990 term, but his liberal voting record for the 1991 term was 54 percent.

We do not know why these three justices changed their voting patterns so dramatically, but a critical factor may have been a deep concern about the future direction of the Court stemming from Rehnquist's opinion in *Payne*, in which he argued that the Court was not going to be constrained by the principle of *stare decisis*. The 1992 case of *Planned Parenthood of Southeastern Pennsylvania v. Casey* seems to have been especially important. This case presented a direct challenge to the controversial Burger Court decision of *Roe v. Wade* (1973). Pennsylvania had passed a law containing provisions similar to ones the Court had struck down previously: informed consent, parental consent for minors, a twenty-four-hour waiting period, spousal notification, and public reporting and disclosure requirements. Sensing that the timing was right with the new conservative justices, the Bush administration filed an amicus brief asking the Court to overturn *Roe*. However, in a complex and multifaceted decision, the Court upheld all of the provisions except the spousal notification requirement, and Rehnquist, Scalia, White, and Thomas called for *Roe* to be overturned.

O'Connor, Kennedy, and Souter, however, broke ranks from their more conservative colleagues. In a most unusual development, they coauthored a joint opinion announcing the judgment of the Court, upholding the precedent of *Roe*, and emphasizing the importance of the principle of *stare decisis*. In a key passage, the three justices stated: "A decision to overrule *Roe*'s essential holding under the existing circumstances would address error, if error there was, at the cost of both profound and unnecessary damage to the Court's legitimacy, and to the Nation's commitment to the

rule of law. It is therefore imperative to adhere to the essence of *Roe*'s original decision, and we do so today" (505 U.S. at 869). O'Connor, Kennedy, and Souter did modify *Roe* by introducing an "undue burden standard" that modified the original trimester
formulation, but the critical point in their opinion was their adherence to the core of
Roe and the principle of *stare decisis*.

The Rehnquist Court and the Clinton Appointments

Although President William Clinton's two appointments to the Supreme Court—Ruth
Bader Ginsburg, in 1993, and Stephen Breyer, in 1994—were somewhat anticlimactic
given the significant moderation of the Court in the 1990 and 1991 terms, these
appointments did serve to undermine further the possibility of a conservative constitutional counterrevolution during the Rehnquist Court era. Ginsburg's replacement of
White was especially important because a conservative justice was replaced with a
moderate liberal. The assumption of Blackmun's seat by Breyer had relatively little
impact although Breyer has been slightly less liberal than Blackmun. A more detailed
examination of the appointments of Ginsburg and Breyer and their effect on the Court
develops each of these themes.

The elections of 1992 proved to be of critical significance for the future directions of the Court. Democrat William Clinton defeated incumbent Republican President George H. W. Bush largely on the issue of the national economy and on a significant margin of support by women, reacting in part to the Clarence Thomas nomination
battle. These same factors contributed to continued Democratic control of both
houses of Congress in the 1992 election. Thus, White's resignation, in 1993, and Blackmun's resignation, in 1994, occurred when Democrats controlled both the White
House and Senate, allowing them considerable freedom to nominate, confirm, and
appoint new Supreme Court justices.

White's resignation, in 1993, was an important development. Appointed in 1962
by Democratic President John Kennedy, White became increasingly conservative over
the years and was part of the five-person conservative bloc of the 1988 and 1989 terms.
Although he moderated his voting in the 1990–1992 terms and was not a member of
the conservative bloc in any of these terms, his resignation meant that only Rehnquist,
Scalia, and Thomas constituted the Court's conservative coalition.

Ginsburg was in many ways an ideal choice for Clinton and the Democrats. She
was eminently qualified. She attended Harvard and Columbia Law Schools, she was a
professor at both Rutgers and Columbia Law Schools, she led the movement in the
seventies to gain greater constitutional protection for women in several major gender
cases, and she had served since 1980 on the U.S. Court of Appeals for the District of

Columbia Circuit. She had a strong appeal to the liberals because of her leadership in the American Civil Liberties Union Women's Rights Project in the seventies, and Clinton characterized her as the Thurgood Marshall of the women's movement. And although the Republicans lacked the votes to stop her appointment, Ginsburg portrayed herself as a judicial moderate, believing in the principle of judicial restraint and bringing neither a liberal nor a conservative philosophy to the bench. Her Senate confirmation hearing was uneventful, and she received a 96–3 vote.

Ginsburg has delivered what she promised. She has been moderately liberal in civil rights and liberties cases, with a mean liberal support score of 66 percent through the 2004–2005 term of the Court. She has voted most frequently with Souter and Breyer, and in several terms she has formed a voting bloc with these justices. Her replacement of White has thus had an important influence on the overall alignment of the Court, reducing the conservative coalition from four to three justices and providing a somewhat predictable fourth liberal vote. Ginsburg's replacement of White has been especially important in Establishment Clause and abortion cases.

Although a Democratic president had not been able to nominate and appoint a Supreme Court justice for more than a quarter of a century before Ginsburg, Clinton had his second opportunity one year later when Harry Blackmun announced his resignation in April 1994. Justice Blackmun's career was in many ways a mirror image of Justice White's, who had resigned the year before. White was appointed by a liberal Democratic president, but he became increasingly conservative during his long service on the Court. In contrast, Blackmun was appointed by Republican President Richard Nixon, but Blackmun became increasingly liberal during the later years of the Burger Court and throughout the Rehnquist Court era.

Clinton initially expressed his desire to fill Blackmun's seat with an experienced politician with a "big heart"; but the leading candidate, Secretary of Interior Bruce Babbitt, seemed likely to generate intense conservative opposition, and memories of the Bork and Thomas confirmation battles remained vivid. Clinton eventually went the safer route, selecting Stephen Breyer, a highly qualified candidate whom the Republicans would find quite acceptable. A graduate of Stanford and Oxford Universities as well as Harvard Law School, Breyer's record was exemplary. He clerked for Supreme Court Justice Arthur Goldberg; served briefly in the Justice Department; joined the faculty of Harvard Law School, where he specialized in the relatively abstract areas of administrative law, antitrust law, and economic regulation, authoring several books; and was named by President Carter in 1980 to the U.S. Court of Appeals for the First Circuit, eventually becoming chief judge.

Breyer's nomination sailed through the Senate. He portrayed himself as an experienced, pragmatic jurist who was more interested in solutions than theories. He sought to address concerns that he was an Ivy League technocrat by emphasizing that the judicial role requires a person to use both the head and the heart. He expressed support for the idea of judicial restraint and stated his support for the precedent of *Roe v. Wade* (1973), but he was generally noncommittal about other areas of the law. The vote in the Senate in support of Breyer was an overwhelming 87–9.

Breyer's record on the Supreme Court has not provided many surprises. He has been a moderate liberal in civil rights and liberties cases, voting 62 percent liberal through the 2004–2005 term. He has been most likely to vote with the Court's other moderate liberals, Souter and Ginsburg. Breyer's replacement of Blackmun has therefore not had a significant impact on the direction of the Court, although Blackmun was somewhat more liberal in every major area of civil rights and liberties.

The Rehnquist Court, 1994–2005

With Breyer's appointment, in 1994, the period of rapid changes in the Court's membership came to a halt. The composition of the Court did not change until O'Connor's resignation, in July 2005, and Rehnquist's death, in September 2005, making this the second-longest natural court era in U.S. history. It is therefore appropriate to conclude this chapter's analysis of the Rehnquist Court by examining this unique time span as contrasted with the earlier years of the Rehnquist Court. The argument that is made is that the potential of a conservative constitutional counterrevolution that seemed so certain at the end of the 1990 term failed to materialize; instead, the Rehnquist Court since 1994 has been moderately conservative, with Justice O'Connor frequently serving as the key swing vote determining the outcome of cases.

We can first examine a variety of voting data to support this characterization of the Court as moderately conservative. One important perspective can be gained from examining the comparative voting records of the Warren, Burger, and Rehnquist Court eras, which are presented in table 1.2. The Warren Court decided 68 percent of its civil rights and liberties cases liberally, whereas the Burger Court decided 44 percent of these cases liberally. This was a distinctively conservative shift but hardly constituted a conservative revolution. The Rehnquist Court's voting record of 44 percent liberal has been identical to that of the Burger Court, and thus the Rehnquist Court cannot be considered to have made a major conservative shift. Furthermore, the Rehnquist Court has become slightly more liberal over time. Comparing the 1986–1993 terms with the 1994–2004 terms, the liberal voting was 42 percent in the former and increased to 45 percent in the latter period.

Bloc voting analysis for the period from 1994 to 2004 provides further support for the characterization of the Court as a moderately conservative one in which O'Connor has had exceptional power.[3] As seen in table 1.3, three blocs can be identified for this period. One bloc consists of the Court's three most conservative jurists—Scalia, Thomas, and Rehnquist—who have an average interagreement score of 88 percent. A

Table 1.2: A Comparison of the Liberal/Conservative
Voting Records of the Warren, Burger, and Rehnquist Courts in
Civil Rights/Liberties Cases, 1953–2004 Terms

Court Eras	Outcomes	
	Liberal	Conservative
Warren Court	68%	32%
Burger Court	44%	56%
Rehnquist Court	44%	56%

Source: Harold J. Spaeth, *United States Supreme Court Judicial Database, 1953–2004 Terms* (Ann Arbor, MI: Inter-University Consortium for Political and Social Research, 2005).

second bloc involving Rehnquist and Kennedy (85 percent interagreement) is also con-servative, but Kennedy's alignments with Scalia and Thomas are not strong enough to include Kennedy. The Rehnquist Court's four liberal justices—Breyer, Ginsburg, Souter, and Stevens—also form a bloc with an interagreement average of 85 percent. O'Connor is the only justice who does not belong to any bloc, and she has thus been able to exercise extraordinary power over the outcome of cases.

Yet another perspective on the key role played by O'Connor can be seen in table 1.4, which presents the rank-ordered success rates of the Rehnquist Court justices dur-ing the natural court period of the 1994–2004 terms. The success rate shows the per-centage of time that a justice was on the winning side of civil rights and liberties cases. The data show that O'Connor has been the most successful, joining the winning side in 89 percent of the decisions. Kennedy's role as a key swing justice can also be seen with his 85 percent success rate.

In addition to examining voting data during the natural court period since 1994, we can also examine the Rehnquist Court's treatment of existing precedent during this era. As we have done throughout this chapter, we draw upon the Spaeth data. Specif-ically, we are interested in identifying those cases in which the Rehnquist Court dur-ing the natural court era from 1994 to 2005 explicitly altered existing precedents. We are also interested in cases of major importance, as measured by their identification in the annual survey of the Court's term by the *New York Times* and other authorita-tive sources on the Court.

During the natural court period of the Rehnquist Court from 1994 to 2005, eight civil rights and liberties cases qualified as ones of major importance that involved the explicit alteration of existing precedent by a majority of the Court. Three of them involved a conservative change of precedent, but five of the cases were liberal

Table 1.3: Bloc Voting Patterns of the Rehnquist Court Justices in Civil Rights/Liberties Cases, 1994–2004 Terms (Percent Agreement Rates)

	Scalia	Thomas	Rehnquist	Kennedy	O'Connor	Breyer	Ginsburg	Souter	Stevens
Scalia	—	93	86	80	72	52	50	52	43
Thomas	93	—	86	80	73	52	49	50	43
Rehnquist	86	86	—	85	79	59	55	56	48
Kennedy	80	80	85	—	79	64	61	61	56
O'Connor	72	73	79	79	—	72	66	68	60
Breyer	52	52	59	64	72	—	87	85	82
Ginsburg	50	49	55	61	66	87	—	89	85
Souter	52	50	56	61	68	85	89	—	84
Stevens	43	43	48	56	60	82	85	84	—

Court Mean = 68

Significance Level (Sprague Criterion) = 84

Conservative Blocs:

Scalia, Thomas, Rehnquist = 88

Rehnquist, Kennedy = 85

Liberal Bloc:

Breyer, Ginsburg, Souter, Stevens = 85

Source: Harold J. Spaeth, *United States Supreme Court Judicial Database, 1953–2004 Terms* (Ann Arbor, MI: Inter-University Consortium for Political and Social Research, 2005).

Table 1.4: Rank Ordering of the Justices of the
Rehnquist Court in Terms of Percentage of Cases on the
Winning Side in Civil Rights/Liberties Cases, 1994–2004 Terms

Justice	Percentage on the Winning Side
O'Connor	89%
Kennedy	85%
Rehnquist	79%
Breyer	77%
Souter	75%
Ginsburg	74%
Scalia	74%
Thomas	74%
Stevens	68%

Source: Harold J. Spaeth, *United States Supreme Court Judicial Database, 1953–2004 Terms* (Ann Arbor, MI: Inter-University Consortium for Political and Social Research, 2005).

alterations of existing precedent, thus providing additional support to the argument that the Rehnquist Court has not been radically conservative. The three cases in which the Court created new conservative precedents were *Adarand Constructors, Inc. v. Pena* (1995), in which the strict scrutiny standard was applied to federal affirmative action cases; *Agostini v. Felton* (1997), an Establishment Clause case in which the Court rejected a 1985 precedent and allowed public school teachers to give classes in parochial schools to disadvantaged children; and *Mitchell v. Helms* (2000), in which the Court approved federal government support for parochial students regarding a variety of nonreligious teaching materials.

The most remarkable feature of the Rehnquist Court's treatment of existing precedent in the natural court period from 1994 to 2005 is that the majority of cases involved the liberal alteration of existing precedent. Two of the decisions were Eighth Amendment death penalty cases. In *Atkins v. Virginia* (2002), the Rehnquist Court overruled one of its own precedents by finding that capital punishment cannot be imposed on the mentally retarded. Similarly, in the 2005 case of *Roper v. Simmons*, the Court overruled another of its own precedents in finding that it is unconstitutional to give the death penalty to anyone sixteen or seventeen at the time of the crime. Two additional cases involving new liberal precedents were Sixth Amendment cases. In *Ring v. Arizona* (2002), the Rehnquist Court ruled that juries, not judges, must make decisions on the presence of aggravating factors in murder cases, and *Crawford v. Washington* (2004) emphasized the requirement that an accused must be able to confront a hostile witness directly in the courtroom. The final new liberal precedent decided by the Rehnquist Court was *Lawrence v. Texas* (2003), in which a majority ruled unconstitutional a Texas law that criminalized homosexual activity.

Conclusion

The central question we have been examining in this chapter is whether the Rehnquist Court has engaged in a conservative constitutional counterrevolution. The answer is no, although important conservative change has occurred in a few areas. The voting record of the Rehnquist Court in civil rights and liberties cases has been 44 percent liberal, a moderately conservative pattern identical to that of the Burger Court. In the early terms of the Rehnquist Court, after Kennedy assumed his seat, the justices did create new conservative precedents in regard to the Free Exercise Clause and affirmative action, and significant conservative interpretations of precedent occurred in several areas, including the death penalty and abortion. In the long natural court period after 1994, when Breyer joined the Court, however, the justices have made several major liberal changes in precedent.

Given the intensity of the struggle over America's cultural values during the Rehnquist Court era, it may seem surprising that the Court has taken a relatively moderate position on so many of the controversial issues to come before it. Neither liberals nor conservatives have been pleased with the decision making of the Court. Liberals think the Court has shifted too far to the Right, and conservatives criticize the Court both for not being conservative enough and also for engaging in liberal activism.

Perhaps an answer to this puzzle lies in a recognition that the American public is deeply divided and fragmented over these issues and over politics more generally, and, as history reveals, the U.S. Supreme Court is generally reflective of and responsive to the dominant cultural values of American society. The divided and fragmented nature of American politics can be seen in many indicators. Throughout the period since 1986, power in the federal government has frequently been split between Republican and Democratic control. The same party has controlled the presidency and both houses of Congress only from 1993 to 1994 and since 2003, and the former involved Democratic control, while the latter is Republican control. In addition, neither the Republican nor Democratic parties can claim the allegiance of a majority of the American population. Americans identify almost equally as Republicans, Democrats, and Independents (Patterson 2001, 222). Furthermore, in terms of ideological identification, nearly one-half of American citizens identify themselves as political moderates; and of the remainder, conservatives are much more predominant than liberals (Patterson 2001, 177). Given these divisions in the American public, it is perhaps not surprising that the Court has stopped short of the conservative counterrevolution that seemed so imminent in 1990. Despite its removal from the electoral process and public opinion, the Court has been and remains in touch with the views of the American public.

Having provided an overview of the Rehnquist Court and the period, we turn in chapter 2 to a detailed examination of each of the fourteen justices who have sat on the bench during the years of the Rehnquist Court. Chapter 3 involves an in-depth analysis of the Rehnquist Court's decisions in each of the major areas of American constitutional law. Finally, chapter 4 consists of an analysis of the impact of the Rehnquist Court both in terms of a summary of its major decisions and a discussion of its jurisprudential legacy.

Notes

1. The Spaeth data being used in this book extend from the 1953–1954 term of the Supreme Court to April of the Court's 2004–2005 term.

2. This book was finalized in early 2006. Justice O'Connor announced her resignation in July 2005, and Circuit Court Judge John Roberts was nominated by President George W. Bush to replace O'Connor. However, when Chief Justice Rehnquist passed away, in September 2005, Bush shifted Roberts's nomination to chief justice. After an ill-fated attempt to nominate Harriet Meiers to replace O'Connor, Bush successfully nominated Samuel Alito to take O'Connor's seat.

3. See Hensley, Smith, and Baugh for a detailed discussion of bloc voting: Thomas R. Hensley, Christopher E. Smith, and Joyce A. Baugh, *The Changing Supreme Court: Constitutional Rights and Liberties* (Minneapolis/St. Paul: West/ Wadsworth, 1997), 869–870.

References

Blasi, Vincent, ed. *The Burger Court: The Counter-Revolution That Wasn't.* New Haven, CT: Yale Univ. Press, 1983.

Bork, Robert H. *The Tempting of America: The Political Seduction of the Law.* New York: Free Press, 1990.

Chemerinsky, Erwin. "The Vanishing Constitution." *Harvard Law Review,* 103 (1989): 43–73.

Hensley, Thomas R., and Christopher E. Smith. "Membership Change and Voting Change: An Analysis of the Rehnquist Court's 1986–1991 Terms." *Political Research Quarterly,* 48 (1995): 837–856.

Janda, Kenneth, Jeffrey M. Berry, and Jerry Goldman. *The Challenge of Democracy: Government in America.* Boston: Houghton Mifflin, 2003.

Lamb, Charles C., and Stephen Halpren, eds. *The Burger Court.* Urbana, IL: Univ. of Chicago Press, 1991.

Patterson, Thomas E. *The American Democracy.* 5th ed. Boston: McGraw-Hill, 2001.

Spaeth, Harold J. *United States Supreme Court Judicial Database, 1953–2004 Terms.* Ann Arbor, MI: Inter-University Consortium for Political and Social Research, 2005.

Walker, Thomas G., and Lee Epstein. *The Supreme Court of the United States: An Introduction.* New York: St. Martin's Press, 1993.

Yarbrough, Tinsley. *The Burger Court: Justices, Rulings, Legacy.* Denver: ABC-CLIO, 2000.

2

The Justices

Introduction and Overview

Fourteen people were justices during the period of Supreme Court history known as the Rehnquist Court, covering the years from 1986 to 2005. Although white males dominated the Court during this era, the social forces recognizing and promoting gender and racial diversity were evident on the Rehnquist Court; the only two African Americans as well as the only two women ever to serve on the Court were members of the Rehnquist Court. Perhaps surprisingly, however, the presence of African Americans and women on

The Rehnquist Court from 1986 to 1988: (left to right, front row) Thurgood Marshall, William J. Brennan Jr., William H. Rehnquist, Byron R. White, and Harry A. Blackmun; (left to right, back row) Sandra Day O'Connor, Lewis F. Powell Jr., John Paul Stevens, and Antonin Scalia. (National Geographic Society, Collection of the Supreme Court of the United States)

the Court did not directly result in the movement of the Court toward more liberal decisions regarding gender and racial discrimination.

The Rehnquist Court was composed of justices nominated by eight presidents, five Republicans and three Democrats. The most senior justice was William Brennan, appointed by Republican President Dwight Eisenhower in 1956. Democratic President John Kennedy named Byron White to the Court in 1962, and Kennedy's successor, Lyndon Johnson, appointed Thurgood Marshall as the Court's first African American justice in 1967. Republican President Richard Nixon had a significant impact by not only appointing Rehnquist to the Court in 1971 but also naming Harry Blackmun in 1970 and Lewis Powell in 1971. Nixon's successor, President Gerald Ford, had the opportunity to make one Supreme Court appointment, John Paul Stevens, in 1975.

Republican President Ronald Reagan had a huge impact on the composition of the Rehnquist Court, appointing Sandra Day O'Connor in 1981, elevating Rehnquist from associate justice to chief justice in 1986, naming Antonin Scalia to Rehnquist's associate seat in 1986, and appointing Anthony M. Kennedy in 1988. President George H. W. Bush, Reagan's successor, named two new Court members, David Souter, in 1990, and Clarence Thomas, in 1991. A twenty-five-year period of Republican control of appointing Supreme Court justices ended during the first term of

The Rehnquist Court from 1988 to 1990: (left to right, front row) Thurgood Marshall, William J. Brennan Jr., William H. Rehnquist, Byron R. White, and Harry A. Blackmun; (left to right, back row) Antonin Scalia, John Paul Stevens, Sandra Day O'Connor, and Anthony Kennedy. (Larry D. Kinney, National Geographic Society, Collection of the Supreme Court of the United States)

The Rehnquist Court from 1990 to 1991: (left to right, front row) Harry A. Blackmun, Byron R. White, William H. Rehnquist, Thurgood Marshall, and John Paul Stevens; (left to right, back row) Anthony Kennedy, Sandra Day O'Connor, Antonin Scalia, and David Souter. (Joseph Bailey, National Geographic Society, Collection of the Supreme Court of the United States)

The Rehnquist Court from 1991 to 1993: (left to right, front row) John Paul Stevens, Byron R. White, William H. Rehnquist, Harry A. Blackmun, and Sandra Day O'Connor; (left to right, back row) David Souter, Antonin Scalia, Anthony Kennedy, and Clarence Thomas. (Joseph Bailey, National Geographic Society, Collection of the Supreme Court of the United States)

The Rehnquist Court from 1993 to 1994: (left to right, front row) Sandra Day O'Connor, Harry A. Blackmun, William H. Rehnquist, John Paul Stevens, and Antonin Scalia; (left to right, back row) Clarence Thomas, Anthony Kennedy, David Souter, and Ruth Bader Ginsburg. (Richard Strauss, Smithsonian Institution, Collection of the Supreme Court of the United States)

The Rehnquist Court from 1994 to 2005: (left to right, front row) Antonin Scalia, John Paul Stevens, William H. Rehnquist, Sandra Day O'Connor, and Anthony Kennedy; (left to right, back row) Ruth Bader Ginsburg, David Souter, Clarence Thomas, and Stephen Breyer. (Richard Strauss, Smithsonian Institution, Collection of the Supreme Court of the United States)

Democratic President William Clinton, who appointed the Court's second woman justice—Ruth Bader Ginsburg—in 1993 and then named Stephen Breyer to the Court in 1994. The Court's membership did not change from 1994 to 2005. This natural court period—an era when the Court's membership is the same—from the 1994–1995 term through the 2004–2005 term has been the second longest in Supreme Court history. A new natural court era occurred in the 2005–2006 term, when John Roberts replaced William Rehnquist as chief justice, and it will change yet again as Samuel Alito replaces O'Connor.

This chapter contains an in-depth analysis of each of the fourteen members of the Rehnquist Court. They are discussed in the order of their appointment to the Court. Three tables are provided to supplement the analysis of the justices. Table 2.1 contains a variety of factual information about the justices, including their birth year, the year they were appointed to the Court, their age when appointed, the president who appointed them, their predecessors, and the justices who replaced them. Table 2.2 shows the overall liberal and conservative voting records of the justices in civil rights and liberties cases during their years on the Rehnquist Court. Table 2.3 breaks their voting records into the areas of criminal procedure, civil rights, and First Amendment cases.

Table 2.1: Information on the Rehnquist Court Justices

Justice	Birth Year	App't Year	App't Age	App't President	Predecessor	Replacement
Blackmun	1908	1970	61	Nixon	Fortas	Breyer
Brennan	1906	1957	50	Eisenhower	Minton	Souter
Breyer	1938	1994	56	Clinton	Blackmun	
Ginsburg	1933	1993	60	Clinton	White	
Kennedy	1936	1988	51	Reagan	Powell	
Marshall	1908	1967	59	Johnson	Clark	Thomas
O'Connor	1930	1981	51	Reagan	Stewart	Alito
Powell	1907	1971	64	Nixon	Black	Kennedy
Rehnquist	1924	1986	61	Reagan	Burger	Roberts
Scalia	1936	1986	50	Reagan	Rehnquist	
Souter	1939	1990	51	G. H. W. Bush	Brennan	
Stevens	1920	1975	55	Ford	Douglas	
Thomas	1948	1991	43	G. H. W. Bush	Marshall	
White	1917	1962	44	Kennedy	Whittaker	Ginsburg

Table 2.2: Liberal/Conservative Voting Records of Rehnquist Court
Justices in Civil Rights/Liberties Cases, 1986–1987 to 2004–2005 Terms
(Percent Liberal Voting, Ranked from Lowest to Highest)

Justice	Percent Liberal Voting
Thomas	23
Rehnquist	24
Scalia	27
White	34
Kennedy	35
O'Connor	38
Powell	39
Breyer	62
Souter	63
Ginsburg	66
Blackmun	71
Stevens	71
Brennan	87
Marshall	88

Source: Harold J. Spaeth, *United States Supreme Court Judicial Database, 1953–2004 Terms*
(Ann Arbor, MI: Inter-University Consortium for Political and Social Research, 2005).

Eisenhower Appointment

William J. Brennan

William J. Brennan came to the U.S. Supreme Court in 1956, having earned a reputation for integrity and skill both on the New Jersey State Supreme Court and in his earlier effort to reform the New Jersey state court system. New Jersey political leaders from both major political parties supported Brennan. Because President Dwight D. Eisenhower was seeking bipartisan support in his 1956 reelection effort, Brennan—a Democrat and the son of an immigrant Irish-Catholic trade unionist—appeared a natural choice for the Court after Justice Sherman Minton resigned, in 1956. On the Court, Brennan came to be a hero of liberals and social reformers, who regarded him as one of the great justices in Supreme Court history, but his service was a bitter disappointment to President Eisenhower and many of the socially conservative ethnic Democrats whose support Eisenhower solicited by nominating him.

Born on April 25, 1906, Brennan was the second of eight children and was to a significant extent the product of his environment. Brennan's father, who came to the

Table 2.3: Liberal/Conservative Voting Records of the Justices of the Rehnquist Court in Major Civil Rights/Liberties Issue Areas, 1986–1987 to 2004–2005 Terms (Percent Liberal Voting, Ranked from Lowest to Highest)

Criminal Procedure		Civil Rights		First Amendment	
Justice	*Percent*	*Justice*	*Percent*	*Justice*	*Percent*
Rehnquist	20	Thomas	23	Rehnquist	21
Thomas	21	Rehnquist	29	Scalia	27
Scalia	26	Scalia	29	White	28
White	28	Kennedy	39	Thomas	28
Kennedy	30	O'Connor	42	Kennedy	43
O'Connor	30	Powell	42	O'Connor	46
Powell	30	White	44	Powell	46
Souter	53	Ginsburg	69	Breyer	62
Breyer	53	Souter	70	Stevens	72
Ginsburg	60	Stevens	70	Blackmun	74
Blackmun	62	Breyer	73	Souter	76
Stevens	70	Blackmun	85	Ginsburg	77
Brennan	87	Brennan	92	Brennan	87
Marshall	89	Marshall	94	Marshall	88

Source: Harold J. Spaeth, *United States Supreme Court Judicial Database, 1953–2004 Terms* (Ann Arbor, MI: Inter-University Consortium for Political and Social Research, 2005).

United States from Ireland in 1890, was an activist for democratic causes in labor unions and subsequently became the business manager for several labor organizations. Brennan learned to respect the intrinsic value of all people from his father, a person who would eventually leave the labor movement to become the director of public safety for Newark. Brennan's father taught his children the value of hard work, and the future justice worked various odd jobs in his youth to earn extra money. Although the family was financially secure as well as Roman Catholic, Brennan attended Newark public schools during his high school years. After high school, Brennan left home to attend the prestigious Wharton School of Finance and Commerce at the University of Pennsylvania, where he graduated with honors in 1928. Next, Brennan attended Harvard Law School, where he graduated in the top 10 percent of his class.

Brennan's connections and academic record made him an attractive job candidate after his graduation from law school. From 1932 until the start of World War II, he worked as a labor law litigator at a top Newark law firm, where he eventually became a partner. With America's entry into the war, Brennan was commissioned as

William J. Brennan (Ken Heinen, Collection of the Supreme Court of the United States)

an officer and given responsibility for military procurement. By the end of the war, he had become a colonel.

Following the war, Brennan turned his attention to reforming the New Jersey judicial system. In 1947, New Jersey was in the process of overhauling its state constitution, and the state court system was a primary target of reformers' zeal. Because Brennan was the associate editor of the *New Jersey Law Review*, he was asked to testify before the state constitutional convention's judiciary committee. Through his reform efforts, he came to the attention of the leaders of New Jersey's political establishment, especially the reform-minded Republican governor Alfred E. Driscoll. This attention began a process that culminated in Brennan's appointment to the U.S. Supreme Court. Although Brennan made no secret of his ties to the Democratic Party, Driscoll appointed Brennan to three different state court positions between 1949 and 1952, culminating in his appointment to the New Jersey Supreme Court in 1952 at the request of New Jersey Chief Justice Arthur T. Vanderbilt.

Despite clear indications from the New Jersey Supreme Court that Brennan was an activist liberal, Eisenhower gave Brennan a recess appointment to the Court in October 1956, allowing Brennan to assume a seat on the Court because the Senate was not in session. Eisenhower believed that the recess appointment was necessary to avoid deadlocked results on the Court. However, Brennan still had to be confirmed by the Senate. Senators tend to guard jealously their advice and consent prerogatives. Brennan's initial service on the Court caused him a few problems as senators asked him questions about cases that he could not discuss because they were under consideration. After a personal conflict with Senator Joseph McCarthy, who resented attacks that Brennan had made on the senator's largely unsuccessful and constitutionally dubious search for Communists in government, Brennan was confirmed, with only Senator McCarthy voting against him.

During his thirty-four years on the Court, Brennan contributed greatly to our modern understanding of constitutional jurisprudence. As the ideological pendulum on the Court swung during his years on the Court first to the Left, then back toward the Right, Justice Brennan was a consistent, activist voice for liberal egalitarianism, expanded individual freedoms, and an evolutionary interpretation of the "living" Constitution. Through his philosophical force, intellectual strength, and political savvy, Justice Brennan was largely responsible for the Court's direction on civil rights and liberties issues during those years.

If the Supreme Court has created an environment conducive to significant liberal, social, and political change in America during the past fifty years, then Brennan should receive much of the credit for that change. A reformer who was skeptical of majoritarian principles and the efficacy and fairness of the other elective branches of government, Brennan once wrote in dissent from a Rehnquist Court Fourth Amendment

opinion approving sobriety checkpoints on public roadways, "Consensus that a particular law enforcement technique serves a laudable purpose has never been the touch-
stone of constitutional analysis" (*Michigan Department of State Police v. Sitz*, 496
U.S. at 459, 1990). Instead, Brennan viewed the court system as the chief guardian of
equity and equality.

During the Warren Court years—when a majority of the justices generally shared
his interpretation of the Constitution—Brennan wrote landmark decisions that established Court doctrine in such significant areas as guaranteeing the "one person, one
vote" model of equal representation for all state residents in legislative redistricting
(*Baker v. Carr*, 1962), broadening the application of the Free Exercise Clause to protect workers who refused to work on their holy days (*Sherbert v. Verner*, 1963), allowing the government a very limited ability to prohibit obscene materials (*Roth v. United
States*, 1957), and granting the press sweeping protection from libel laws (*New York
Times v. Sullivan*, 1964).

Brennan frequently found himself in dissent during the years of the Burger
Court, but on occasions Brennan was successful in creating liberal majorities. An
especially important area involved gender discrimination. Brennan, in a plurality opinion in *Frontiero v. Richardson* (1973), argued that gender cases should be considered
under the Court's highest standard, strict scrutiny. Although he was not successful in
gaining majority support for this standard, he did write for a six-person majority in
Craig v. Boren (1976) that established a new standard of intermediate scrutiny. More
frequently, Brennan was in dissent on the Burger Court. For example, he dissented
from the Burger Court's majority opinion in *Miller v. California* (1973), which gave
the government more power to regulate obscene materials. Brennan was a leading
proponent of the rights of those accused of crimes. Brennan's opposition to the death
penalty on Eighth Amendment and moral grounds was absolute, but his view of the
death penalty was always in the minority.

During his four years on the Rehnquist Court, Brennan spent much of his time in
dissent. In his last year on the Court, a five-justice majority in *Oregon v. Smith* (1990)
cast aside Brennan's *Sherbert* test providing strict scrutiny protection for those claiming government violations of their right to the free exercise of religion. In 1989, the
Court gave its first clear indication that most state affirmative action plans might be
unconstitutional, a position that Justice Brennan rejected from the time of *Regents of
the University of California v. Bakke* (1978), the Court's first examination of affirmative action. In *Bakke*, Brennan—writing a four-justice opinion that concurred with part
of the decision and dissented in part—found that the clear implication of the Court's
split ruling was "government may take race into account when it acts not to demean or
insult any racial group, but to remedy disadvantages cast on minorities by past racial
prejudice" (438 U.S. at 325). Justice O'Connor's controlling opinion in *City of Richmond v. J. A. Croson, Co.* (1989) rejected an underlying premise of Brennan's *Bakke*

opinion: "Absent searching judicial inquiry . . . there is simply no way of determining what classifications are 'benign' or 'remedial' and what classifications are in fact motivated by illegitimate notions of racial inferiority or simple racial politics" (488 U.S. at 493). However, Brennan did achieve a victory in his final year on the Court in an affirmative action case. In *Metro Broadcasting, Inc. v. FCC* (1990), the Court found that the judiciary must give more deference to federal affirmative action plans than state plans. After Brennan left the Court, however, *Adarand Constructors, Inc. v. Pena* (1995) overturned the *Metro Broadcasting* precedent and set the same standard for both federal and state programs. Finally, the Rehnquist Court modified liberal Fourth Amendment doctrine in several cases near the end of Brennan's tenure (*National Treasury Employee Union v. Von Raab*, 1989; *Skinner v. Railway Labor Executives' Association*, 1989; and *Michigan Department of State Police v. Sitz*, 1990).

Next to Justice Marshall, who was Brennan's closest ally on the Court, Brennan was the most liberal member of the Rehnquist Court in every area of constitutional law. Brennan had an 87 percent liberal voting record in civil rights and liberties cases during the Rehnquist Court era, and he and Justice Marshall formed a two-person voting bloc during Brennan's four years on the Rehnquist Court.

Brennan's legacy as one of the most influential liberal members of the Supreme Court seems secure. His landmark opinions in such cases as libel law, censorship, and gender discrimination are deeply ingrained in America's legal culture. Brennan feared that his legacy might be severely undercut by his resignation at age eighty-four, but failing health left him with no choice. Before he died, in 1997, however, Brennan had the opportunity to observe his replacement, David Souter, assume the role as a moderate liberal on the Court, helping to preserve much of Brennan's legacy.

Kennedy Appointment

Byron White

When his longtime friend and political ally John F. Kennedy nominated Byron White to the Supreme Court in 1962, White brought to the Court a firm belief in the efficacy and authority of the federal government to solve the problems that faced society. White's earlier role as deputy attorney general in the forceful implementation of civil rights decisions and laws also enhanced his reputation as a liberal crusader. However, White did not see the judiciary as a major actor in solving those problems, as many of his fellow liberals did. White's minimalist view of the Court's role put him at odds with liberals throughout his long tenure and made him a frequent ally of the Court's conservative wing. When White retired in 1993, President Clinton replaced him with Ruth Bader Ginsburg, a more reliable liberal vote.

Byron R. White (Joseph Bailey, National Geographic Society, Collection of the Supreme Court of the United States)

Born on June 8, 1917, in Fort Collins, Colorado, White spent his early years in the small town of Wellington, Colorado. White's father was the manager of a local lumber company and served for a time as mayor of Wellington. As a youth, White supplemented the family income picking sugar beets, the leading local product. He credited the fact that he was paid by the speed at which he picked the beets for helping to build his impressive strength. Although neither of his parents had graduated from high school, they encouraged their son to succeed academically. Fortunately, the University of Colorado offered an academic scholarship to the valedictorian of every high school in the state, and White was the top student in a class of five at his high school.

While in college, White's exceptional academic performance was overshadowed by an athletic career that made him famous across America. White—nicknamed "Whizzer" by the media—was a college All-American football player who led the nation in scoring and yards gained. He was also a leading member of the school's nationally ranked basketball team. His renown on the football field led to numerous offers to play professional football. In 1938, White signed a contract to play one year in the National Football League for more than $15,000, the highest in the league at the time.

White's academic success was typical of other Rehnquist Court justices. He was a member of Phi Beta Kappa at the University of Colorado. When he graduated, in 1938, he was offered a Rhodes Scholarship. While a student at Oxford, White met John F. Kennedy—the son of the American ambassador to England. The two quickly struck up a friendship that would last for the rest of Kennedy's life. White studied at Oxford for one year before the start of World War II in Europe forced him to return to the United States. White enrolled at Yale Law School, where he excelled. In his first year at Yale Law School, White had the highest grades in his class and was offered the editorship of the law review, which he rejected to play professional football.

White joined the U.S. Navy in 1942 and became an intelligence officer, serving in the Pacific. One of White's assignments was to write the official report concerning the sinking of *PT-109*, John F. Kennedy's torpedo boat. His report exonerated his friend of any wrongdoing and helped create a heroic image that Kennedy would use to great advantage during his political career.

White returned to Yale Law School after the war and received his law degree in 1946, graduating magna cum laude. After his graduation, Chief Justice Fred Vinson appointed White to serve as his law clerk from 1946 to 1947. Following his clerkship at the High Court, White returned to practice law for the next fourteen years in Denver.

When Kennedy decided to run for president in 1960, White was one of his earliest supporters, especially in Colorado. White's stock with the Kennedy campaign rose when he helped deliver Colorado to the Massachusetts senator. After Kennedy won the election in November, he appointed White deputy attorney general, where he served under the president's brother, Robert. More seasoned and pragmatic than Robert Kennedy, White won plaudits for his administrative capability and his toughness at the

Department of Justice. As deputy attorney general, White's responsibilities included conducting investigations of potential judicial nominees and supervising the federal marshals and deputies who were charged with protecting the "Freedom Riders"—civil rights activists who traveled across the South attempting to desegregate interstate buses and bus terminals. In May 1961, White went to Alabama, along with 600 National Guardsmen, to help make the point that the government was serious about protecting the riders after several attacks on them had occurred.

When Charles Whittaker resigned from the Supreme Court following the 1961–1962 term, President Kennedy jumped at the opportunity to place his friend and ally on the Court. Although White had no experience as a judge or law professor and had served only one and a half years in the Justice Department, Kennedy thought that White had unique qualities of intellect, ability, and dedication along with liberal political values. White was given a strong endorsement by the American Bar Association and was confirmed by the U.S. Senate by a voice vote on April 11, 1962. White would serve on the Court for thirty-one years, until 1993.

Although White had gained his reputation as an ally of President Kennedy, he was a frequent supporter of conservative outcomes throughout his tenure on the Court. Many of these decisions were based on pragmatic concerns. He broke with the Warren Court majority in several major criminal procedure cases, most notably *Miranda v. Arizona* (1966), arguing that the Court's new requirement to inform arrested suspects of their right to remain silent and right to an attorney would allow guilty offenders to avoid legal punishment. In *United States v. Leon* (1984), a Burger Court case, White wrote the opinion that established the "good faith" exception to the exclusion of evidence discovered under an improper search warrant.

White based his judicial philosophy on four tenets. First, White believed that the federal government's role in the constitutional structure should be supreme, with few limits on the power of the central government to act in the best interest of the people. Second, White believed that the chief responsibility of the federal government is to protect individual rights, although his early support for affirmative action during the Burger Court did not extend into his time on the Rehnquist Court. Third, White believed that the executive and legislative branches hold the primary responsibility and authority to enact policy. More than any other factor, White was separated philosophically from the Rehnquist Court's liberal justices by his commitment to judicial restraint and resistance to overturning congressional acts. Because he opposed the invention or extension of previously unrecognized constitutional rights, White never accepted the Court's creation of a right to abortion. White and Rehnquist were the two dissenters in *Roe*, and White never supported abortion rights in subsequent cases. In *Bowers v. Hardwick* (1986), White noted America's long history of antisodomy legislation in explaining why the Court had not created a privacy exception for sodomy laws. Fourth, White was extremely impatient with philosophical and theoretical arguments that did not have a basis in empirical reality.

White served seven terms on the Rehnquist Court. During that time, he was the fourth most conservative justice in civil rights and liberties cases with a liberal support score of 34 percent. During his seven terms, White's support for liberal outcomes in civil rights and liberties cases ranged from 26 percent to 44 percent. In only one term, 1990–1991, did his liberal support score exceed the Court average. White's conservative voting record extended to most civil rights and liberties cases; however, he did vote for a liberal outcome in a small majority of cases involving Equal Protection Clause claims that did not involve affirmative action. Next to Chief Justice Rehnquist and Justice Scalia, White was the most conservative justice in freedom of expression cases.

An analysis of White's bloc voting patterns reveals his important role regarding the extent to which a conservative majority controlled the Rehnquist Court in its early years. White was a member of the five-person conservative bloc of the 1988 and 1989 terms, joined by Rehnquist, Scalia, Kennedy, and O'Connor. These were the years when the Court was successful in altering some major precedents in constitutional law. In the 1990, 1991, and 1992 terms, however, White was not a member of the conservative bloc, which shrank to a plurality in each of these terms, and few liberal precedents were altered. Thus, White played an important role not only in creating a conservative coalition that was partially successful in instituting a conservative counterrevolution but also in limiting the scope of this movement.

Byron White died of pneumonia on April 15, 2002, at the age of eighty-four. As a Kennedy Democrat who came to be considered a bedrock conservative, he illustrated the principle that presidents are not always successful in selecting justices who will adhere closely to their ideological views. Indeed, White was a crucial member of the early Rehnquist Court that engaged in significant conservative change.

Johnson Appointment

Thurgood Marshall

Thurgood Marshall, the first African American to serve on the Supreme Court, was a member of the Warren Court, the Burger Court, and the Rehnquist Court. By the time he retired from the Court, in 1991, Marshall's role on the Rehnquist Court had become primarily that of vocal dissenter. Occasionally, he and Justice Brennan were able to secure a majority to uphold a Warren Court or Burger Court precedent regarding civil liberties or civil rights. Most often, however, an outvoted Marshall could only chastise

Thurgood Marshall (Joseph Lavenburg, National Geographic Society, Collection of the Supreme Court of the United States)

the Rehnquist Court majority for what he perceived as its insensitivity to the needs of the oppressed and disadvantaged in society. Most ironically, Marshall was replaced by Clarence Thomas, an African American who has frequently advocated policies directly opposite those supported by Marshall.

Thurgood Marshall was born into a middle-class black family on July 2, 1908, in Baltimore, Maryland, at that time a city segregated by law. Baltimore, a city at the crossroads of the North and South, provided Marshall with the opportunity to view race relations in both sections of the country. However, Marshall's convictions and the faith to fight for them probably came from his family. The Marshall family owned the only black house in what had previously been an all-white neighborhood. The future justice was the great-grandson of a slave, but three of his grandparents were free, literate, and socially active in Maryland before the start of the Civil War. Marshall's father, William, worked as a railroad porter, a relatively high-paying and respected job for an African American in the early 1900s. Later, William Marshall would be placed in charge of the all-black staff of waiters at an exclusive all-white country club. His mother, Norma Williams, graduated from Coppin State with a teaching degree, but she stayed home to raise her children.

Thurgood Marshall's family stressed education, and his academic career reflects an early aptitude that was later supplemented by meticulous effort. He was educated in Baltimore public schools, including Frederick Douglass High School, the only high school for African Americans in Baltimore. At Frederick Douglass, Marshall was a popular student and captain of the debate team, even when he was forced to work because his father was ill during this period.

After high school, Marshall attended Lincoln University in Oxford, Pennsylvania, where he graduated with honors in 1930. He made enough money working for his father at the country club to pay his expenses at Lincoln, despite the economic difficulties that his family had faced while he was in high school. Early in his academic career, Marshall gravitated to fraternity membership and social activities; but starting in his junior year, he became a serious and respected student. Once again, he gained a reputation as an outstanding debater.

Originally, Marshall applied to law school at the University of Maryland, but he was rejected on racial grounds. He attended law school at Howard University in Washington, D.C., graduating first in his class in 1933. At Howard, Marshall became the protégé of Charles Houston, the dean of the law school and a man with whom he would later collaborate to lead the legal battle against racial segregation. In fact, one of Marshall's first major cases involved the University of Maryland School of Law. Marshall, working with Houston, convinced the Maryland Court of Appeals to order the law school to admit blacks in 1935.

After receiving his LL.B. from Howard, Marshall returned to Baltimore, where he started a private practice and became associated with the local branch of the National

Association for the Advancement of Colored People (NAACP), first as a volunteer, then as counsel. In 1936, Charles Houston named him special assistant legal counsel to the NAACP, and two years later, following an illness, Houston resigned and Marshall became special counsel in charge of litigation. He remained in the position until 1950, when he became director-counsel of the NAACP's Legal Defense and Education Fund Inc., the organization that led the attack on racial segregation in the United States. Marshall argued thirty-two cases before the Supreme Court and won twenty-nine. He was the lead counsel in one of the most significant civil rights case ever decided by the Supreme Court, *Brown v. Board of Education of Topeka, Kansas* (1954), which outlawed public school segregation.

Marshall, in addition to being the leading African American attorney in the nation, had been a vocal supporter of Kennedy's election in 1960 and felt that he had earned an appeals court nomination. When President Kennedy's brother, Attorney General Robert Kennedy, offered him a district court nomination as an "all or nothing" proposition in 1961, Marshall heatedly rejected the nomination. After botching the nomination of another African American, Robert Carter, to the court of appeals, the Kennedy administration saw a conjunction between doing the right thing and political advantage, giving Marshall a recess appointment to the U.S. Court of Appeals for the Second Circuit. The recess appointment allowed Marshall to begin serving immediately, while the Senate considered his nomination. Because of Marshall's status as a black civil rights attorney and because they were angered by President Kennedy's use of the recess appointment, southern Democrats delayed his confirmation for nearly a year before the Senate finally voted 54–16 to approve him. Marshall served on the Second Circuit until 1965, when President Lyndon Johnson appointed him as solicitor general.

President Johnson indicated several times during his presidency that he wished to appoint an African American to the Supreme Court. Justice Tom Clark's retirement from the Court, in 1967, presented Johnson with such an opportunity, and Marshall was the clear choice. He had a distinguished record, with service both on the court of appeals and as solicitor general. Once again, senators from the Deep South sought unsuccessfully to derail Marshall's confirmation. Nominated on June 13, 1967, Marshall was confirmed on August 30, 1967, by a 69–11 vote.

During his five terms on the Rehnquist Court, Marshall was its most liberal member. He voted for a liberal outcome in 88 percent of civil rights and liberties cases. In each major area of constitutional interpretation from the First Amendment's Establishment Clause to the Fourteenth Amendment's Equal Protection Clause, Marshall was a reliable liberal vote. Marshall's dissent in *Gregg v. Georgia* (1976), the Burger Court decision that allowed the reintroduction of the death penalty in the United States, illustrates Marshall's attitude that the Court should serve as an enlightened protector of human dignity: "The American people are largely unaware of the information critical to a judgment on the morality of the death penalty, . . . and . . . if they were better informed they would consider it shocking, unjust, and unacceptable" (428 U.S. at 232).

Marshall's judicial philosophy had at its core a belief that the Bill of Rights and the Civil War Amendments must be used expansively, particularly to protect the powerless, the disadvantaged, and the despised in society. Broad phrases such as "due process," "equal protection," "freedom of speech," and "cruel and unusual punishments" should be applied "to protect those outside the political mainstream" (Goldman and Gallen 1992, 210). Related to this was a conviction that the Supreme Court is responsible for giving meaning to constitutional rights. Furthermore, as his opinions indicated, Marshall thought the Court's responsibility was to protect people from intrusive and abusive governmental action, whether such action involved legislators, law enforcement officers, administrative officers in government agencies, or other executive branch officials.

Marshall's strident liberal philosophy left him with few allies on the Rehnquist Court. For its first three terms, only Justice Brennan voted with Marshall regularly. Increasingly, Justices Stevens and Blackmun voted with Marshall during his last two terms, but neither justice was the reliable ally that Brennan had been. In his years on the Rehnquist Court, Marshall found himself in the role of a dissenter.

Health problems forced Marshall to retire from the Court in 1991, following twenty-four years of service. Conservative African American Circuit Court Judge Clarence Thomas replaced him on the Court after a contentious confirmation process. Marshall died on January 24, 1993, at the age of eighty-four.

Marshall's life—before and during his service on the Supreme Court—helped change America in fundamental and permanent ways. Marshall was at the forefront of the fight to broaden the concepts of freedom and equality in the United States and to secure those rights for all Americans. Thurgood Marshall was one of the most important Americans of the twentieth century.

Nixon Appointments

Harry A. Blackmun

When President Richard Nixon nominated Harry A. Blackmun to the Supreme Court in 1970, most observers expected Blackmun to be an ally of his childhood friend, Chief Justice Warren Burger. Instead, Justice Blackmun surprised everyone as he evolved into one of the Court's most liberal voices during the latter part of his tenure. By the first year of the Rehnquist Court, Blackmun had become a frequent ally of liberal Justices William Brennan and Thurgood Marshall in civil rights and liberties cases. After the retirement of Justices Brennan and Marshall, Blackmun and Justice John Paul

Stevens became the two most liberal members of the Court. Despite serving on the Court for twenty-four years (1970–1994), Blackmun will be remembered most for the results of his opinion in a single case, *Roe v. Wade* (1973), which recognized a right for a woman to obtain an abortion prior to the viability of the fetus. To the day he retired in 1994, Blackmun recognized and accepted the burden of his controversial opinion and defended his reasoning.

Harry Andrew Blackmun was born on November 12, 1908, in the tiny community of Nashville, Illinois. However, Blackmun spent most of his youth in St. Paul, Minnesota, where his father owned a grocery and hardware store in a working-class neighborhood. Although Blackmun attributed his concern for the disadvantaged to his childhood memories, Warren Burger—who grew up in the same neighborhood under harsher circumstances—had a much more conservative record on the Supreme Court.

Following an exceptional high school career, Blackmun received a scholarship to Harvard University from the Harvard Club of Minnesota. At Harvard, Blackmun continued his academic success. He was elected to Phi Beta Kappa and graduated summa cum laude in 1929. After receiving his bachelor's degree in mathematics, Blackmun attended Harvard Law School, graduating in 1932. Following law school, Blackmun served for a year as a law clerk to Judge John B. Sanborn on the U.S. Court of Appeals for the Eighth Circuit. Next, he taught at the St. Paul College of Law in Minnesota before being hired by a respected law firm in Minneapolis. Blackmun spent sixteen years in private practice before becoming the general counsel for the Mayo Clinic.

In 1959, President Eisenhower nominated Blackmun to the Eighth Circuit Court to replace Judge Sanborn on the recommendation of Hubert Humphrey, the powerful Democratic senator from Minnesota. Although a Republican, Blackmun had a good relationship with both political parties in Minnesota. Over the next eleven years, Blackmun developed a reputation as a strong law-and-order judge who respected precedent and did not let his personal opinions guide his decisions.

Under ordinary circumstances, Blackmun—already sixty-one years old in 1970—would have remained a little-noted appeals court judge, but events in Washington were soon to place him on the Supreme Court. Justice Abe Fortas was forced to resign from the Supreme Court in 1969 after revelations that he had accepted a $20,000 per year honoraria from a foundation controlled by a political ally who had recently been convicted of fraud. Although Fortas returned the honoraria after the man was convicted, many observers questioned Fortas's judgment and integrity for accepting money from someone under investigation. At first President Nixon attempted to replace Fortas—a prominent liberal who had nearly become chief justice only a year earlier—with a southern conservative. However, the Senate blocked Nixon's first two choices, Clement Haynsworth and Harrold Carswell. This led Nixon to seek a compromise candidate. Nixon chose Blackmun, whose leading supporters were former vice-president and 1968 Democratic Party presidential nominee, Hubert Humphrey, and Chief Justice

Harry A. Blackmun (Joseph Lavenburg, National Geographic Society, Collection of the Supreme Court of the United States)

Warren Burger, his childhood friend. Blackmun was a popular compromise, and the Senate gave him unanimous approval. When Blackmun took the oath of office, on June 9, 1970, his seat on the Court had been vacant for more than a year.

Justice Blackmun was never known as a great writer, as dissenters to his majority opinions sometimes mentioned. His opinions took longer to draft than those of other justices and often contained personal observations. Early in his career, liberals complained that his decisions seemed superficial or poorly reasoned. *Roe* was a popular decision with civil libertarians, but it received critical reviews across the ideological spectrum because Blackmun did not tie abortion and privacy rights to any specific constitutional provision. Liberals had hoped abortion rights would receive a stronger foundation in the law. Conservative disdain for *Roe* was inevitable, but Blackmun's reliance on social and psychological references and an inferred privacy right provided ample material for Justice White's and Justice Rehnquist's dissents. Later, conservatives would complain that Blackmun's decisions were based more on personal feelings than either case law or the Constitution.

During Blackmun's early years on the Court, he was viewed as a moderate conservative. However, a closer examination shows a justice who was nonideological but also pro-government early in his career before becoming more critical of the elected branches. Blackmun's basic trust of federal government institutions at the start of his tenure led him to accord deference to the other branches. Also, several early decisions suggest particular support for the war effort in Vietnam. He was one of three justices to dissent from the Court's decision not to grant an injunction against printing secret government documents in a newspaper in *New York Times v. United States* (1971)— the *Pentagon Papers* case. Also, Blackmun's dissent in *Cohen v. California* (1971) rejected the free speech claims of an individual who wore an offensive and disruptive antiwar slogan into a courtroom, noting "the Court's agonizing over First Amendment values seems misplaced and unnecessary" given "Cohen's absurd and immature antic" (403 U.S. at 27). Until his last year on the Court, Blackmun provided nominal support for the death penalty, despite a personal aversion. Even Blackmun's support for affirmative action in *Regents of the University of California v. Bakke* (1978) can be seen as supportive of governmental actions to remedy past discrimination.

Later in his career, Blackmun became more cynical about the role of government and less likely to defer to the elective branches. Starting with *Roe*, Blackmun became a champion of abortion rights. He was also an active proponent of equal rights before the law for women, African Americans, and homosexuals. Blackmun claimed to oppose all ideologies on the Court, asserting that his views had not changed as much as the Court had changed around him. Still, Blackmun's voting record shifted dramatically from his first years on the Court to his last on almost every issue. Increasingly, Blackmun began to base his decisions on his personal notions of fairness. In his dissent in *Bowers v. Hardwick* (1986), a gay rights case that involved enforcement of Georgia's antisodomy law, Blackmun wrote, "A necessary corollary of giving individuals freedom to choose how they conduct their lives is acceptance of the fact that different individuals will make different choices" (478 U.S. at 205–206). In one of his last written opinions, a dissent from an unsigned order rejecting the final appeal of a death row inmate in Texas, Blackmun stated that he was now opposed to the death penalty. Blackmun's personal decision no longer to vote to enforce the death penalty was based on his conclusion that no consistent, infallible, and equitable imposition of the death penalty was possible.

By the start of the Rehnquist Court, Justice Blackmun was a fairly reliable liberal vote in most areas of civil rights and liberties. Blackmun voted for a liberal outcome in 71 percent of those cases between the start of the 1986–1987 term and end of the 1993–1994 term. Blackmun was most liberal in cases involving privacy and abortion and in cases involving the Equal Protection Clause. Blackmun had a 100 percent pro–abortion rights voting record, and in twenty-one cases involving equal protection and race, gender, and/or affirmative action, Blackmun voted for the liberal result twenty times. Blackmun voted for the liberal outcome in only 54 percent of Establishment Clause cases while serving on the Rehnquist Court. However, Blackmun was far more liberal in other types of First Amendment cases. After voting for a liberal outcome in only 51 percent of Free Speech Clause cases during the Burger Court, Blackmun supported the liberal side in 73 percent of Rehnquist Court freedom of expression cases. In cases that involved the rights of the accused, Blackmun had a conservative voting record (61 percent conservative) in Fourth Amendment cases and moderate in Fifth Amendment cases (46 percent conservative), but he was notably liberal in Sixth Amendment cases (29 percent conservative). In Eighth Amendment cases, he voted for a liberal outcome 90 percent of the time.

Despite Blackmun's liberal voting patterns during the Rehnquist Court years, he was typically not part of a liberal bloc. Brennan and Marshall were so extreme in their liberal voting that Blackmun did not vote with them frequently enough to qualify as a bloc member. However, Blackmun and Stevens did form a liberal bloc in three of Blackmun's last four terms on the Rehnquist Court, reflecting the changing nature of the Court's liberal wing with the retirements of Justices Brennan and Marshall.

Although Blackmun resisted efforts to label his judicial philosophy, his voting record shows that he was a liberal member of the Rehnquist Court. Certainly, Blackmun opposed efforts by the Rehnquist Court's conservative members to change Court doctrine before his retirement, in 1994. However, Blackmun will not be most remembered for his ideological migration or his struggles to promote fairness in Supreme Court decision making but as the author of one of the most controversial decisions in modern Supreme Court history—*Roe v. Wade*.

Lewis F. Powell Jr.

Lewis F. Powell Jr., who served only one term on the Rehnquist Court, will be remembered as the swing vote on the Burger Court. Widely admired by both colleagues and Court experts, Powell's support was usually necessary to achieve a majority throughout the Burger Court years. Powell's moderately conservative record, especially in criminal justice cases, helped distinguish the Burger Court from the liberal activism of the Warren Court. However, Powell broke with his conservative colleagues in some of the most high-profile civil rights and liberties cases to reach the Burger Court, including *Roe v. Wade* (1973), *Regents of the University of California v. Bakke* (1978), and *Wallace v. Jaffree* (1985). Although Powell had little direct impact on the Rehnquist Court, his resignation created a firestorm because of his important place as the key swing vote on a closely divided Court.

Powell was born in Suffolk, Virginia, on September 19, 1907, and experienced success in many areas before coming to the Court. Although Powell's relatives had lived in Virginia since the original Jamestown settlement, his parents were not affluent. However, Powell's father, the manager of a Richmond furniture and wooden-box-making company, was able to provide his son with exceptional educational opportunities. Powell attended a local college preparatory academy before enrolling at Washington and Lee University, where he majored in commerce. While at Washington and Lee, Powell was student body president and a member of Phi Beta Kappa. Powell received his bachelor's degree in 1929 and his law degree from Harvard University in 1931. After turning down an offer in New York, Powell took a position at a Richmond law firm in 1932. In 1936, Powell began his sixty-year marriage to Josephine Pierce Rucker, the daughter of a local doctor. After becoming a partner at his law firm in 1938, Powell would remain in that position until his appointment to the Supreme Court, eventually becoming one of America's top corporate lawyers.

Powell was the only member of the Rehnquist Court without prior judicial or executive branch experience. Powell's unique qualifications to serve on the Court derived from the wide variety of positions that he held and the quality of his service. Powell was an intelligence officer with the rank of colonel in the U.S. Army Air Corps during World War II. As president of the American Bar Association, he successfully lobbied for the creation of a legal services program for the poor. Powell also served as the president of the American College of Trial Lawyers and the American Bar Foundation. As the president of the Richmond School Board, Powell defused the controversy between the state Democratic machine and civil libertarians over court-ordered desegregation by agreeing to implement a largely cosmetic desegregation plan.

At the time of his appointment, in 1971, Powell had every qualification that President Richard Nixon desired in finding a replacement for Justice Hugo Black. In the 1968 campaign, Nixon had promised to nominate a southerner to the Court. In the early

Lewis F. Powell Jr. (Joseph Bailey, National Geographic Society, Collection of the Supreme Court of the United States)

1970s, Nixon and his allies sought to build a competitive Republican Party in the South by appealing to disaffected Democrats with a call for a less-activist approach by the federal government to mandated desegregation. Nixon's unsuccessful Supreme Court nominations of southerners Harrold Carswell and Clement Haynsworth had been popular with his supporters, despite their rejection by the Senate. In Powell, the first Supreme Court justice from Virginia since the Civil War, Nixon saw the opportunity to nominate a southerner who would win easy approval. Unlike Carswell and Haynsworth, Powell had compromised on desegregation, making him acceptable to liberal Senate Democrats. Plus, the American Bar Association gave its highest rating to its former president. Powell, already sixty-four when nominated, was a reluctant nominee, but Nixon persisted until he agreed. Following an uneventful confirmation hearing, Powell was approved 89–1 by the Senate. He took the oath of office on January 7, 1972.

Powell's one term on the Rehnquist Court, 1986–1987, was unremarkable. The Court was moderately conservative, deciding 46 percent of the civil rights and liberties cases in a liberal manner. Powell voted liberally in 39 percent of these cases. He was not a member of any voting bloc in this term.

Powell's impact on the Rehnquist Court was minimal. He will be most remembered for his critical role on the Burger Court, where he was frequently a key swing vote on a closely divided Court. His role in the 1978 *Bakke* case best illustrates this point where he sided with four conservative justices in opposing a quota system for medical school admissions but agreed with four liberals that race could be one of many factors considered in the admissions process. Powell died in August 1998, eleven years after retiring from the Court, and he was appropriately eulogized for his extraordinary qualities on and off the bench.

William Hubbs Rehnquist

President Richard Nixon's nomination of William Hubbs Rehnquist to serve on the U.S. Supreme Court fulfilled a campaign promise to reshape what many conservative Americans perceived to be a pro-criminal and pro-leftist Court. Nixon had promised to select nominees who placed law and order and traditional values ahead of the rights of criminals. Alone among Nixon's four confirmed nominees, Rehnquist became the type of "strict constructionist" envisioned by Nixon's conservative supporters. From the first, Rehnquist brought a new perspective to the Court—authoring fifty-four lone dissents in the period between 1972 and his nomination to be chief justice. As the leading conservative voice on the Court in the mid-1980s, Rehnquist's nomination to serve as chief justice by President Reagan was no surprise. As both an associate justice and chief justice, Rehnquist provided a consistent, vigorous, and cogent voice for conservative constitutional interpretation for more than thirty years until his death, in September 2005.

William H. Rehnquist (Dane Penland, Smithsonian Institution, Collection of the Supreme Court of the United States)

Rehnquist was born on October 1, 1924, in Milwaukee, Wisconsin. Rehnquist's father was a successful wholesale paper salesman who had not graduated from college. The Rehnquist family lived in the Milwaukee suburb of Shorewood, where the future justice attended public elementary and high schools. Accepted at Kenyon College in Ohio, Rehnquist left college just after his eighteenth birthday to enlist in the U.S. Army. Attached to the U.S. Air Corps as a weather observer, Rehnquist served in both the United States and Northern Africa from 1943 to 1946, rising in rank to sergeant. After the war, Rehnquist attended Stanford University, where he was a member of Phi Beta Kappa. Rehnquist received his B.A. and M.A. degrees in political science, in 1948 and 1949, respectively. After graduating from Stanford, Rehnquist attended Harvard University, where he received a master's degree in political science before returning to Stanford for law school. In 1952, he graduated first in his law school class, which included future Supreme Court Justice Sandra Day O'Connor.

Following law school, Rehnquist began a law career that impressed even those senators who would eventually vote to reject his Supreme Court nomination. He was a law clerk to Supreme Court Justice Robert H. Jackson from February 1952 until June 1953. In 1953, Rehnquist—newly married—moved to Phoenix, Arizona, where he practiced law for the next sixteen years and became deeply involved in Republican Party politics. Considered one of the most respected young attorneys in Arizona in 1969, Rehnquist had already served as counsel for the Arizona House of Representatives during several impeachment hearings and had served briefly as a junior partner in a major Arizona law firm before starting his own. Rehnquist's successes in Arizona brought him to Washington, D.C., and eventually the Supreme Court.

In 1969, Rehnquist left Arizona to become an assistant U.S. attorney general and director of the Office of Legal Counsel in the Department of Justice, a key advisory position on legal questions facing the government that do not involve litigation. As assistant attorney general, Rehnquist became embroiled in several controversies as the Nixon administration attempted to change Johnson administration legal policy—including the unsuccessful nomination of Harrold Carswell to the Supreme Court, the reinstitution of federal wiretaps as an investigational tool, and even touchy investigations of state responses to antiwar protests and riots. Still, the American Bar Association noted that Rehnquist had won the respect of his colleagues in every position that he had held.

President Nixon nominated Rehnquist on October 21, 1971, to replace Justice John Marshall Harlan. As a relatively young, strident conservative, Rehnquist suffered somewhat in comparison to Justice Powell, a former president of the American Bar Association and pro-desegregation southerner, who was considered at the same time as a replacement to Justice Hugo Black. Concerns about Rehnquist's ideology mounted when a memo—written by Rehnquist when he was Justice Jackson's law clerk—surfaced that opposed using *Brown v. Board of Education* (1954) to overturn the separate but equal doctrine. Rehnquist and his supporters argued that Jackson, who struggled with the *Brown* decision, had asked Rehnquist to draft possible arguments for conference in the event Jackson decided to oppose desegregation. Because Justice Jackson died in 1954, he was unable to confirm Rehnquist's story. Consequently, most civil rights organizations opposed his nomination. Still, Rehnquist was confirmed by a 68–26 vote with the support of southern Democrats in the Senate.

From January 7, 1972, until the end of the 1985–1986 term, Rehnquist served as the Court's most conservative justice. When he was nominated to be chief justice, many senators noted that he had written the most lone dissents in the history of the Supreme Court—fifty-four. Rehnquist's record had always provided very few opportunities to attack his qualifications, but his track record on the Court gave senators many opportunities to attack his philosophy as extremist in 1986. Because the Republican Party controlled the Senate, Rehnquist's conservative record on the Court could not derail his nomination. The only serious opposition to Rehnquist resulted from reports about his role in poll watching in Arizona, which opponents suggested was designed to intimidate minority voters. Rehnquist was confirmed on September 26, 1986, by a vote of 65–33.

In the years since William Rehnquist became chief justice, his views on constitutional law have become part of the Court's mainstream. As an associate justice, Rehnquist was a lone supporter of state sovereignty federalism, the most strident advocate for exceptions to the Fourth Amendment's Warrants Clause, a proponent of limiting the reach of the Free Exercise Clause, the most avid supporter of state accommodation of religion in Establishment Clause cases, and a bitter opponent of affirmative action. Rehnquist was also one of two Burger Court justices to oppose *Roe v. Wade* (1973), White being the other dissenter.

Much of Rehnquist's increased influence derived from the conservative nature of several justices who joined the Court following his confirmation. None of Rehnquist's three most frequent allies as chief justice served on the Burger Court. Justice Antonin Scalia was appointed by President Reagan to replace Rehnquist as associate justice in 1986, Justice Kennedy joined the Court in 1988, and Justice Clarence Thomas was appointed by President George H. W. Bush to replace Justice Marshall in 1991. Justice Kennedy voted with Rehnquist nearly as often as Justices Thomas and Scalia in civil rights and liberties cases that did not involve free speech or abortion. Other than in abortion law and free speech cases, the Supreme Court moved toward Rehnquist's decision-making doctrine in most areas of constitutional law, because Justice O'Connor frequently allied herself with Rehnquist.

Rehnquist's judicial philosophy was based on the principles of majoritarianism, moral relativism, and original intent (Davis 1989, 1991). In a 1969 speech, Rehnquist attacked the culture of protest in American society, stating, "the minority, no matter how disaffected or disenchanted, owes an unqualified obligation to obey a duly enacted law" (Irons 1994, 52). Rehnquist viewed lawmaking as a function of the elective branches. However, Rehnquist's search for original meaning often created a tension between his support for majoritarianism—as expressed through the elective branches of government—and his strong support for states' rights federalism. Rehnquist's frequent support for deference to Congress disappeared in federalism cases, as he supported the use of judicial power to prevent Congress from taking power from states.

According to Rehnquist's philosophy, the limited mandate of the Constitution's enumerated powers protects liberty far more than such individual rights as might be indirectly inferred from the document's spirit. Unlike the Court's civil libertarians of the past, such as Justice Douglas and Justice Brennan, Rehnquist did not seek to use the Constitution to empower individuals but as a series of rules designed to regulate and balance the competing interests of government and individuals equally. As such, governments have rights and powers in the same manner as individuals; and while Rehnquist envisioned a federal government with few unenumerated powers, likewise he seldom inferred individual rights not specifically set forth in the Constitution's text.

Typically, Rehnquist supported the power of state legislatures and Congress to enact legislation that restricts the activities of individuals, but he had little hesitation about using the power of the federal judiciary to overturn congressional acts that limit state power. As expressed in *United States v. Lopez* (1995), Rehnquist viewed federalism as a "constitutionally mandated division of authority" designed to protect liberty (514 U.S. at 552). Rehnquist saw the enumerated powers as an exhaustive list of congressional powers in cases that do not involve the Bill of Rights or the Civil War Amendments. Rehnquist joined the Court's majority in each case in which it overturned a federal law for violating the Tenth Amendment or the Eleventh Amendment.

An analysis of voting records in civil rights and liberties cases shows that Rehnquist was one of the most conservative members of the Court during the Rehnquist Court era. Rehnquist voted for the conservative position in 76 percent of civil rights and liberties cases since 1986, second only to Thomas. Since he became chief justice, Rehnquist was never lower than the third most conservative member of the Court in any term. Rehnquist formed a strongly conservative voting bloc with Justices Scalia and Thomas in the natural court period since 1994; the three justices had an average agreement of 88 percent. Perhaps equally important for a justice who set a record for the most lone dissents during the Burger Court, Rehnquist formed a voting bloc with at least one other justice in every term except 1987–1988.

Rehnquist's voting record was solidly conservative across the spectrum of constitutional law. In the period since he became chief justice, Rehnquist was the most conservative justice in First Amendment cases. Similarly, Rehnquist voted for a conservative outcome in 80 percent of cases involving the rights of the criminally accused, the most conservative record of any member of the Rehnquist Court. In the area of civil rights, Rehnquist was tied with Scalia as the second most conservative justice, at 29 percent liberal.

When Rehnquist passed away in September 2005, he was recognized as one of the most significant justices in the history of the U.S. Supreme Court. As a measure of the important change in Supreme Court decision making during Rehnquist's service, the justice who wrote fifty-four lone dissents between 1972 and 1986 was in the majority in 79 percent of the cases decided between 1994 and 2005. For more than thirty years, he was the most conservative justice on the U.S. Supreme Court. A substantial amount of modern conservative jurisprudence owes its formulation to Rehnquist's lone dissents on the Burger Court. As chief justice, he helped to create a majority in favor of conservative doctrinal change in several areas of constitutional interpretation from affirmative action to the Free Exercise Clause. However, Rehnquist was not successful in moving the Court as far to the Right as he had hoped.

Ford Appointment

John Paul Stevens

Like Gerald Ford, the president who nominated him, John Paul Stevens secured his position by being acceptable to the heavily Democratic Congress that controlled the American government in the aftermath of Watergate. Stevens's reputation as an honest, nonpartisan, moderate Republican served him well when Justice William O. Douglas resigned from the Supreme Court, in 1975. Given his lack of ideology and his experience on the court of appeals, Stevens did not present a target for Democratic senators. With President Ford eager to avoid controversy less than a year before the presidential election, Stevens was a natural choice. On the Court, Stevens has been variously described as a maverick and a moderate; but after the retirement of Justice Thurgood Marshall, in 1991, Stevens was the Rehnquist Court's most consistent liberal in civil rights and liberties cases.

Stevens was born on April 20, 1920, in Chicago, Illinois, into a prominent family. Stevens's father, Ernest James Stevens, was one of Chicago's most prominent citizens, both in the insurance industry and as the owner of one of the city's landmark hotels. Stevens's mother was an English teacher. As might be expected of a son of a wealthy family, Stevens began to follow in his father's academic footsteps at an early age. The University of Chicago—Ernest Stevens's alma mater—operated the prestigious Laboratory School, which Stevens attended at both the elementary and secondary level. Next, he attended the University of Chicago, where he majored in English literature and edited the student newspaper. Stevens graduated first in his class in 1941.

John Paul Stevens (Joseph Bailey, National Geographic Society, Collection of the Supreme Court of the United States)

After the United States declared war on Japan, Stevens joined the U.S. Navy. He was assigned to the Communication Intelligence Organization as a watch officer. Although Stevens did not engage in combat during his stay in the U.S. Navy, from 1942 until 1945, he played a significant role in America's war effort. Stevens was one of several officers responsible for deciphering Japanese codes. For his meritorious service, Stevens was awarded the Bronze Star.

Unsure about his future plans following his discharge from the U.S. Navy, in 1945, Stevens returned to Chicago. Family and friends encouraged Stevens to forgo his initial inclination to become an English teacher in favor of attending law school. Again, Stevens followed his father's lead and attended Northwestern University Law School, in nearby Evanston, Illinois. In 1947, Stevens graduated first in his class and served as coeditor of the law review. Following law school, Supreme Court Justice Wiley B. Rutledge selected Stevens to serve as his law clerk.

Stevens was admitted to the bar in Illinois in 1949 and began a long, successful career in private practice and academics, mixed with several forays into government to help fight monopolies. Stevens taught antitrust law at Northwestern University Law School from 1950 until 1954 before moving to the University of Chicago Law School, where he taught from 1955 until 1958. During the fifties, Stevens advised numerous federal and state committees investigating monopolies or drafting antitrust regulations. In 1969, Stevens would serve as chief counsel to a committee investigating judicial corruption in Illinois.

When President Richard Nixon nominated Stevens to serve on the U.S. Court of Appeals for the Seventh Circuit, in 1970, Stevens's role as a judicial reformer and the very nominal nature of his Republican affiliation eased his confirmation process. When William Douglas retired in 1975, Gerald Ford was looking for a justice with a moderate reputation and a track record for integrity to avoid a confrontation. In addition to the political advantages of nominating an unassailable but little-known judge, a quick confirmation would fill a need on the Court. Douglas's long illness had left the Court essentially short one member for almost an entire term. Stevens was officially nominated on December 1, 1975, confirmed unanimously on December 17, and took his seat on December 19, 1975—a remarkably rapid series of events compared to the modern confirmation process.

Scholars who have studied Stevens express varying views about the coherence of Stevens's judicial philosophy, but Stevens's foremost biographer, Robert J. Sickels, argues that Stevens does have a logical and consistent philosophy guiding his judicial decision making. Sickels posits that Stevens does not adhere to any grand theory of judicial interpretation but rather has several principles that interrelate and support each other. One important concept is judicial restraint. Stevens recognizes that the courts have a limited role to play in American society because of major constraints of time, expertise, legitimacy, and constitutional authority. The elected branches of government, in contrast, have more expertise and legitimacy in most areas of public policy, and the courts therefore should be deferential to the other branches. Another important component of Stevens's judicial philosophy involves the need to balance carefully both guiding rules and principles as well as the facts of individual cases; "a decision deficient in principle is ad hoc and arbitrary; a decision deficient in fact is unrealistic and mechanical—a 'mere formula'" (Sickels 1988, 31). Finally, Stevens's judicial philosophy has a pragmatic element to it because he emphasizes that justices must be concerned about the consequences of their decisions in terms of their impacts not only on the parties to the case and other courts but also on other branches of the government and American society. This latter concern may have played a part in Stevens's increased liberalism during the era of the Rehnquist Court.

Stevens's voting record has shown substantial variation during his nearly three decades of tenure on the High Court. Stevens was a moderate liberal in civil rights and liberties cases during the Burger Court, supporting a liberal outcome in 59 percent of the cases. During the Rehnquist Court era, however, Stevens has voted liberally 71 percent of the time. Furthermore, in the long natural court era since the 1994 term when Breyer joined the Court, Stevens has consistently served as its leading liberal. Stevens has been remarkably consistent across the various areas of civil rights and liberties, voting liberally in 70 percent of criminal cases, 70 percent liberal in civil rights decisions, and 72 percent liberal in First Amendment cases.

Stevens has consistently been a member of the liberal voting bloc of the Rehnquist Court, and he frequently formed voting blocs with Marshall, Brennan, and Blackmun in the terms of the late eighties and early nineties. In the natural court era from 1994 to 2005, Stevens joined Ginsburg, Souter, and Breyer to form a four-person liberal bloc.

As the Rehnquist Court's leading liberal during the last decade, Stevens has also been the least effective in terms of being on the winning side in cases. His record of 68 percent was the lowest winning score of any recent member of the Rehnquist Court.

Stevens has been strongly liberal in the First Amendment areas of the Establishment Clause and freedom of expression, but rather unexpectedly, he has taken a conservative stance in free exercise cases. Stevens has been a consistent advocate of the separation of church and state; for example, he agreed with the majority in *Lee v. Weisman* (1992) that prayer at graduation ceremonies violated the Establishment Clause, and he opposed the Cleveland school voucher system in *Zelman v. Simmons-Harris* (2002) that allowed public funds to support parochial schools. In freedom of expression cases, Stevens's role has been significant. Because Chief Justice Rehnquist frequently dissents from the Court's liberal free speech decisions, Stevens—as the senior associate justice—is usually in position to assign the majority opinion. Stevens tends to support freedom of expression in cases involving artistic or commercial speech as well as in cases where the government has applied broad restrictions on adult access to indecent materials in an effort to protect minors. Writing for the majority in *Reno v. American Civil Liberties Union* (1997), Stevens argued that an act that outlawed the distribution of pornographic images on the Internet, if those images might be seen by minors, "is unacceptable if less restrictive alternatives would be at least as effective in achieving the legitimate purpose that the statute was enacted to serve" (521 U.S. at 874).

Despite his liberal orientation in Establishment Clause and freedom of expression cases, Stevens has been conservative in the area of the free exercise of religion. Stevens provided the critical fifth vote in *Oregon v. Smith* (1990), in which the Court rejected the liberal strict scrutiny test of *Sherbert v. Verner* (1963) and instead ruled that religious practices must conform to universally applicable laws that are nonreligious in nature.

Stevens's record is consistently liberal in other areas. He was the most liberal member of the Rehnquist Court in the area of criminal procedure. He has supported the liberal side in 70 percent of the cases, with the next most liberal justice in criminal cases being Blackmun, at 62 percent liberal. He has supported affirmative action programs, he opposes governmental regulation of abortion, and he is a predictable vote in equal protection cases involving minorities and women. Stevens has also taken a consistently liberal stance in the Court's federalism cases.

Stevens joins White and Blackmun as a justice who has performed quite differently than expected by the president who appointed him to the Court. Considered a moderate when he joined the Burger Court, Stevens has been the leading advocate for a liberal interpretation of civil rights and liberties since the retirements of Justices Brennan and Marshall. Although not as liberal as these two justices, Stevens has worked diligently and successfully to preserve many of the liberal precedents of the Warren and Burger Courts.

Reagan Appointments

Sandra Day O'Connor

Sandra Day O'Connor is the first woman to sit on the U.S. Supreme Court, serving twenty-four years until her retirement announcement at the end of the Court's 2004–2005 term. Arguably, Justice O'Connor will be remembered more for her role on the Rehnquist Court than her historical first, however. Appointed by President Ronald Reagan, who hoped she would be a dependable conservative vote, an empirical analysis of Justice O'Connor's votes in civil rights and liberties cases demonstrates that she has defined a center position on the Court since 1990. O'Connor's moderate positions have disappointed both conservative and liberal Court watchers; but like Justice Powell

Sandra Day O'Connor (Dane Penland, Smithsonian Institution, Collection of the Supreme Court of the United States)

during the Burger Court, O'Connor used her position on the Rehnquist Court to create the winning coalition on many of the leading issues that have come before it.

O'Connor was born into a prosperous cattle-ranching family on March 26, 1930, in El Paso, Texas. As a youth, the future justice spent summers at her family's ranch on the Arizona–New Mexico border, where she learned self-sufficiency; but starting at age six, she spent most of her time with her grandparents in El Paso, where she attended the prestigious and exclusive Radford School for Girls and Austin High School. O'Connor excelled in school, skipping her final year at Radford, completing an honors program at Austin High School, and enrolling at Stanford University by the age of sixteen. This was only the beginning of her academic success. Within six years, she had earned her bachelor's degree and law degree from Stanford, where she finished third in her class in 1952 behind future Chief Justice William Rehnquist. Upon finishing her law degree, she married John Jay O'Connor III, a law school classmate, whom she met while working on the *Stanford Law Review.*

Despite her impressive credentials, O'Connor had difficulty finding employment as an attorney because few private firms hired women in the 1950s. Therefore, the third-ranking graduate of Stanford Law School was forced to accept a position as a legal secretary. Frustrated by her efforts to find private employment, O'Connor became a deputy county attorney before following her husband to Germany, where she worked as a civilian attorney in the U.S. Army Quartermaster's Corps. Between 1957 and 1962, she gave birth to three sons and worked in community and volunteer organizations.

Beginning in 1964, O'Connor began her work in government that would eventually lead to her appointment to the U.S. Supreme Court. Following her involvement in Arizona Senator Barry Goldwater's campaign for president, O'Connor served as an Arizona assistant attorney general from 1965 to 1969. In 1969, she was appointed to fill a vacant state senate seat. O'Connor spent five years as a state senator, and during her final term she was the senate majority leader. In 1974, she left the legislature to run for a Maricopa County (Phoenix) Superior Court judgeship. From there, Democratic Governor Bruce Babbitt appointed O'Connor to the Arizona Court of Appeals in 1979. Some speculated that Governor Babbitt appointed O'Connor to this position so she would not run against him for governor.

These legislative and judicial positions would not typically have led to a Supreme Court appointment. As of 2003, six of O'Connor's colleagues had been U.S. Court of Appeals judges, one served on a state supreme court and as a state attorney general, four were former law professors, and five had been high-ranking U.S. Justice Department attorneys. However, other factors worked in O'Connor's favor. During the 1980 campaign, Ronald Reagan promised, if he was elected, to nominate a woman to the Supreme Court. At the same time, President Reagan had promised his supporters that he would nominate conservatives and strict constructionists to the Court. Also, the

Reagan administration hoped that a justice with a background in state government would give deference to state governmental activities. Ironically, O'Connor's difficulty in finding employment in 1952 worked in her favor in 1981. William French Smith, a partner in the law firm that had hired O'Connor to work as a legal secretary, was Reagan's attorney general. Years later, O'Connor would quip, "I immediately guessed he was planning to offer me a secretarial position . . . Secretary of Labor or Secretary of Commerce" (Maveety 1996, 14). Although she refused to answer any questions regarding cases that might come before the Court—including abortion—she was confirmed on September 21, 1981, by a 99–0 vote.

During her time on the Rehnquist Court, O'Connor's voting record was moderately conservative. Her support score of liberal positions in civil rights and liberties cases during the Rehnquist era was 38 percent, roughly a mirror image of moderately liberal Justice Ruth Bader Ginsburg's 66 percent score. During the early years of the Rehnquist Court, O'Connor voted with the conservative bloc; but in recent years, she moved away from the most conservative justices toward a more centrist position. In the natural court period from 1994 to 2005, O'Connor was the only justice who was not a member of a voting bloc. Befitting her reputation as a key swing justice on the Rehnquist Court, O'Connor was on the winning side of 89 percent of all civil rights and liberties cases since 1994, the highest success rate of any member of the Rehnquist Court.

Naturally, the justice whose vote is necessary to form a majority is the justice whose philosophy strongly affects the direction of the Court. O'Connor has written many of the Rehnquist Court's most significant opinions. Arguably, O'Connor's most conservative opinions have been in the arena of race relations. Justice O'Connor wrote the opinion of the Court in *Adarand Constructors, Inc. v. Pena* (1995), a case that subjected all affirmative action programs to the strict scrutiny standard. This rejection of race-based policies extended to a series of equal protection voting rights opinions written by O'Connor, including *Shaw v. Reno* (1993):

> A reapportionment plan that includes in one district individuals who belong to the same race, but who are otherwise widely separated by geographical and political boundaries, and who may have little in common with one another but the color of their skin, bears an uncomfortable resemblance to political apartheid. It reinforces the perception that members of the same racial group—regardless of their age, education, economic status, or the community in which they live—think alike, share the same political interests, and will prefer the same political candidates at the polls (509 U.S. at 647).

O'Connor has not identified closely with either the separationists or the accommodationists in Establishment Clause cases, and her vote has typically been critical to the outcome of these decisions. O'Connor wrote the Court's opinion in *Agostini v. Felton* (1997), a case that allowed public school employees to provide instruction in parochial school classrooms to underprivileged children. *Agostini* altered the Court's long-standing *Lemon v. Kurtzman* (1971) three-prong test that required an act's purpose to be secular, required its effect to be neutral with regard to advancing or inhibiting religion, and required that its result not lead to excessive entanglement between government and religion. Instead, O'Connor—expanding on Chief Justice Rehnquist's reasoning in *Zobrest v. Catalina Foothills School* (1993)—proposed a simpler test that no longer appeared to worry about entanglements between government and religion, so long as government programs use neutral, secular criteria.

Justice O'Connor's key role on the Court can be seen distinctly in the controversial area of abortion. Justice O'Connor's undue burden test from *Planned Parenthood of Southeastern Pennsylvania v. Casey* (1992) protected a woman's right to an abortion while allowing greater leeway for governmental regulation. Notably, O'Connor's opinion in *Casey* paid considerable homage to precedent—defending *Roe*'s continued existence primarily because of its prior existence. O'Connor also joined a majority in the *Stenberg v. Carhart* case of 2000 in ruling against Nebraska's partial-birth ban because it imposed an undue burden on a woman.

Justice O'Connor's Free Exercise Clause interpretations have been more liberal than the Court's prevailing majority, but Justice Stevens's support for governmental restrictions on the practice of religion has created a rare area of constitutional law in which conservatives do not need her support. O'Connor's concurrence in *Oregon v. Smith* (1990) and her dissent in *City of Boerne v. P. F. Flores* (1997) actually showed support for Justice Brennan's liberal reasoning in *Sherbert v. Verner* (1963).

Justice O'Connor generally voted in favor of the Rehnquist Court's reinterpretation of the Fourth Amendment, although her vote has not been needed. Her opinions in *Michigan v. Sitz* (1990) and *Florida v. Bostick* (1991) permitted law enforcement officers to conduct random searches without prior suspicion. However, in dissenting from the Court's decision in *Vernonia School District 47J v. Acton* (1995) that allowed school districts to use urinalysis to test student athletes for drug use, she argued that blanket searches have been historically impermissible unless minimally intrusive under the Constitution, whether applied evenhandedly or not.

As President Reagan hoped, Justice O'Connor has been a consistent vote in favor of Tenth and Eleventh Amendment states' rights federalism. Her opinion in *New York v. United States* (1992)—which prevented the federal government from compelling states to take part in a waste disposal plan—gave a preview of the Court's later decisions. Because the Rehnquist Court was divided 5–4 on this issue, with each side rejecting the premises of the other, O'Connor's vote has been critical to state sovereignty decisions.

Scholars have struggled to define Justice O'Connor. On some issues, she has shown a strong commitment to a conservative philosophy. However, she has disappointed conservatives on several issues that they find important. Whenever a divisive case reached the Court—from abortion to school vouchers to election recounts—Court watchers searched for even the most minute indications of how she would vote. Although she was the first woman to serve on the Court, O'Connor seems more likely to be remembered for her role as a key swing justice on the Rehnquist Court along with Justice Kennedy. Her moderate conservatism played a major role in preventing Rehnquist, Scalia, and Thomas from creating radically conservative change on the Court, and her important place in history seems secure.

Antonin Scalia

By the time President Ronald Reagan nominated Antonin Scalia to the U.S. Supreme Court in 1986 to take William Rehnquist's associate justice position, Scalia had already provided clear evidence that he supported a reexamination of the Warren and Burger Courts' liberal decisions. As a longtime law professor and court of appeals judge, Scalia was on record as an advocate for limiting the role of the judiciary in public policy, for empowering state governments, and for a narrow textual interpretation of the Constitution. As a frequent ally of the chief justice throughout the Rehnquist Court era, Scalia fulfilled the hopes and expectations of the Reagan administration.

Scalia was born in Trenton, New Jersey, on March 11, 1936, into a family whose values became an important part of Scalia's character. Scalia's father, an immigrant from Sicily, was a professor of romance languages at Brooklyn College. His mother was an elementary school teacher. Scalia's parents were devout Roman Catholics and proud Italians, who passed their faith and heritage on to their only child.

Scalia excelled throughout his academic years. After starting his education at a public elementary school, Scalia attended St. Francis Xavier Academy, a respected Jesuit prep school in lower Manhattan. Even in a strict Jesuit high school atmosphere, Scalia had a reputation for his staunch Catholic views and cultural conservatism. He was also the best student in the class; a noted thespian, playing the title role in a high school production of *Macbeth;* and a leader in the school band. After graduating first in his class, Scalia attended Georgetown University in Washington, D.C., as well as the University of Fribourg, in Switzerland, as an exchange student. Scalia graduated from Georgetown in 1957 as the class valedictorian. Next, Scalia attended Harvard Law School, where he was the note editor of the *Harvard Law Review* and graduated magna cum laude in 1960.

In 1960, Scalia accepted a Sheldon Fellowship, which allowed him to travel through Europe. Also in 1960, Scalia married Maureen McCarthy, an Irish-Catholic Radcliffe College student, whom he had met while attending Harvard. Together, they would have nine children.

Antonin Scalia (Joseph Lavenburg, National Geographic Society, Collection of the Supreme Court of the United States)

Scalia had a variety of legal experiences prior to his appointment to the Supreme Court. After his year as a Sheldon Fellow, Scalia moved to Ohio, where he accepted a job with Jones, Day, Cockney, and Reavis, a leading law firm in Cleveland, practicing law from 1961 to 1967. Passing on a chance to become a partner, Scalia moved from private practice into academia, becoming a professor at the University of Virginia Law School. Scalia taught contracts, commercial law, and comparative law for the next four years before taking a leave of absence to work for a year in the Nixon administration as general counsel to the Office of Telecommunications Policy in the Executive Office of the President.

In 1972, Scalia became chairman of the Administrative Conference of the United States, an administrative law and procedure advisory group. Scalia's success in this position led President Nixon to make Scalia the assistant attorney general in charge of the Department of Justice's Office of Legal Counsel in 1974, which advises the executive branch on issues that do not involve pending lawsuits. This is the same position that William Rehnquist had held two years earlier before Nixon nominated him to the Supreme Court.

Scalia, a political appointee, was forced to seek other employment following President Gerald Ford's defeat in 1976, so he accepted a Visiting Scholar position with the American Enterprise Institute, a public policy think tank located in Washington, D.C. Between 1977 and 1982, Scalia taught law at the University of Chicago, with brief stints as a visiting professor at Stanford Law School and Georgetown Law School. From 1979 until 1982, he was editor of *Regulation* magazine.

Scalia earned a reputation as a brilliant and conservative legal theorist during his years as a law professor and government official. Ronald Reagan had run for president in 1980 on a platform calling for more conservative judges on the federal courts. Young, conservative, and objectively well qualified, Scalia fit the Reagan administration's profile of an ideal judicial nominee. President Reagan nominated Scalia to the U.S. Court of Appeals for the District of Columbia in 1982. For the next four years, Scalia would serve on what many consider to be the second-highest court in the nation behind the Supreme Court.

In 1986, President Reagan nominated William Rehnquist to be chief justice, replacing Warren Burger. Because Rehnquist was a sitting associate justice, Reagan appointed Scalia to take Rehnquist's place, provided Rehnquist was confirmed. President Reagan announced Scalia's nomination on June 17, 1986. Three circumstances combined to make Scalia's confirmation inevitable. First, Republicans controlled the Senate by a small margin, so little or no Democratic support was needed. Second, Democrats chose to concentrate their efforts against Rehnquist, a controversial figure and known quantity from his years as associate justice and Nixon Justice Department official. Third, Scalia was the first Italian American nominated to the Supreme Court, a fact that made many Italian American groups (and senators from both parties) very supportive of him. After only two days of hearings, Scalia received unanimous support from the Judiciary Committee, and the full Senate confirmed him on September 17, 1986. On September 26, 1986, Scalia took the oath of office.

Scalia bases his judicial philosophy on five tenets. First, Scalia espouses support for original intent, often citing legal texts, natural law philosophy, and dictionary definitions from the time of the nation's founding to support decisions by the Court. Second, Scalia believes that the Court should defer to the elected branches of government whenever possible. Third, Scalia believes that interpretations of statutory language should be derived from the plain meaning of the text. Fourth, Scalia supports both the traditional rights and the policy effectiveness of state governments in conflict with the federal government. Fifth, Scalia has few qualms about overturning previous Court decisions if he believes they involved clear error (Brisbin 1993, 1997).

Scalia's voting record on the Rehnquist Court has reflected these components of his judicial philosophy. In civil rights and liberties cases, he has a 27 percent liberal voting record, ranking him a close third behind Rehnquist and Thomas as the Court's most conservative justices. Not surprisingly, Scalia, Rehnquist, and Thomas formed a three-person conservative bloc with an average interagreement score of 88 percent. Scalia and Thomas have been an especially close voting pair; their mean agreement score in the Rehnquist Court years has been 93 percent, and they have been part of a voting bloc every term. Scalia has been consistently conservative across issue areas, voting conservatively in 74 percent of the criminal procedure cases, 71 percent conservative in civil rights decisions, and 73 percent conservative in First Amendment cases.

Although he was a frequent ally of Chief Justice Rehnquist, Scalia's style and role on the Court were very different. While sharing Rehnquist's reputation as a brilliant jurist and conservative icon, his acerbic opinions and controversial remarks at speaking engagements prevented Scalia from matching the chief justice as a consensus builder among the Court's conservative and moderate members. Scalia once compared his colleagues' use of the *Lemon* test to a "ghoul in a late night horror movie that repeatedly sits up in its grave and shuffles abroad, after being repeatedly killed and buried . . . frightening the little children and school attorneys" (*Lamb's Chapel v. Center Moriches Union Free School District*, 508 U.S. at 398, 1993). This was a concurrence. Scalia's harangues of his colleagues sometimes seem more consistent with a justice who is actually in dissent rather than one who usually votes with the majority.

Except in freedom of expression cases, in which Scalia has been a frequent ally of the Court's moderates, Scalia has been a rather reliable and quotable member of the Court's conservative wing. Scalia wrote the opinion that set a new precedent in the area of free exercise of religion. In upholding a state law against sacramental drug use by American Indians, Scalia asserted that restricting religious practices was "an unavoidable consequence of democratic government [and preferable] to a system in which each conscience is a law unto itself"(*Oregon v. Smith*, 494 U.S. at 890, 1990). Scalia's opinion replaced the *Sherbert* test, which allowed for some religious exemptions from laws, with a new test that provided no religious exemptions to neutral, generally applicable laws.

Scalia's support for freedom of expression has been most pronounced in cases that involve government efforts to keep the peace or promote fairness through limitations on political speech. In *R.A.V. v. City of St. Paul, Minnesota* (1992), Scalia wrote an opinion that overturned the conviction of a youthful cross burner, noting, "The point of the First Amendment is that majority preferences must be expressed in some fashion other than silencing speech on the basis of its content" (505 U.S. at 392) In *Republican Party of Minnesota v. White* (2002), a case that overturned restrictions on the right of judges to state issue positions in campaign advertising, Scalia wrote: "The notion that the special context of electioneering justifies an abridgment of the right to speak out on disputed issues sets our First Amendment jurisprudence on its head" (536 U.S. at 781).

In the Court's affirmative action cases, Scalia has joined Justice Thomas in a position to the Right of the Court's conservative majority. Since the time of *Johnson v. Transportation Agency of Santa Clara County, California* (1987), Scalia has questioned the Court's acceptance of affirmative action. Joined by Justice Thomas in *Adarand Constructors, Inc. v. Pena* (1995), Scalia wrote: "In my view, government can never have a 'compelling interest' in discriminating on the basis of race in order to 'make up' for past racial discrimination in the other direction" (512 U.S. at 239). Scalia has voted against affirmative action in each of the eight cases heard by the Rehnquist Court, including the Court's two Michigan affirmative action cases of 2003.

As would be expected of a conservative textualist, Scalia is one of the Court's strongest proponents of states' rights. In *Printz v. United States* (1997), Scalia wrote: "Residual state sovereignty was . . . implicit . . . in the Constitution's conferral upon Congress of not all governmental powers, but only discrete, enumerated ones, which implication was rendered express by the Tenth Amendment" (521 U.S. at 919).

Scalia certainly has been the most entertaining and quotable member of the Rehnquist Court, but his effectiveness can be questioned. The Rehnquist Court has been moderately conservative, which should mean that Scalia would have an impressive record of being on the winning side in cases; however, only Stevens, the Court's leading liberal, has been on the losing side more than Scalia, with a 74 percent success rate. Scalia has defined the Court's most extreme conservative positions in several areas, such the free exercise of religion and affirmative action, but his strident style may have been in part responsible for the movement toward the center by the more moderately conservative justices, Kennedy and O'Connor.

Anthony M. Kennedy

Following two unsuccessful attempts to replace Justice Lewis F. Powell, the Reagan administration was determined to select a less-controversial—but still conservative—Supreme Court nominee. Anthony M. Kennedy, an enigmatic, longtime U.S. Appeals Court judge from California, appeared to meet President Ronald Reagan's criteria. Kennedy was one of the most conservative judges on the otherwise rather liberal Court of Appeals for the Ninth Circuit; however, both Kennedy's liberal and conservative colleagues considered him fair and conscientious. Liberals respected Kennedy's pattern of coming to his decisions on a case-by-case basis. Conservatives noted that his written opinions were based on constitutional text and precedents rather than social analysis. Kennedy was given unanimous approval by the Senate, and he has developed a reputation for well-written and internally cogent opinions coupled with a nonideological, moderate conservative jurisprudence. Kennedy occupied a position of extraordinary influence on the Rehnquist Court because his vote was generally necessary for the conservatives to prevail, but he frequently joined the Court's liberal wing in major, controversial cases. With a record of being on the winning side in 85 percent of the Court's decisions, a score exceeded only by Justice O'Connor, it is not an exaggeration to state that Kennedy was a key swing justice on the Rehnquist Court.

Kennedy was born on July 23, 1936, in Sacramento, California, into comfortable circumstances. Kennedy's father was a politically active and well-connected attorney in the state capital. When Kennedy was ten years old, his parents allowed him to take a year off school to serve as a page for the California State Senate. Otherwise, Kennedy's academic career was like that of most Supreme Court justices: impressive. He attended Stanford University from 1954 to 1958, with a one-year break to attend the renowned London School of Economics. In 1958, Kennedy was a Phi Beta Kappa graduate from Stanford. Three years later, Kennedy received his law degree from Harvard Law School.

Kennedy's years before joining the federal judiciary involved successful work in academic life as well as both private and public legal activity. After law school, Kennedy joined a leading San Francisco law firm. In 1963, he married Mary Davis. By all accounts, Kennedy was well positioned to become a successful corporate lawyer, but he was forced to return to Sacramento after his father's death to save the family's law practice. From 1963 until his appointment to the U.S. Court of Appeals in 1975, Kennedy was a private practice attorney and lobbyist with several prominent clients, including a major liquor distillery and Capitol Records. In 1965, Kennedy became a professor of constitutional law at the McGeorge School of Law at the University of the Pacific in Sacramento, a position he held until his nomination to the Supreme Court in 1987. True to his pattern, students reported that Kennedy was a tough but fair grader.

Anthony Kennedy (Joseph Bailey, National Geographic Society, Collection of the Supreme Court of the United States)

At the behest of Governor Ronald Reagan, Kennedy wrote a California ballot proposition designed to cut taxes in 1973. Although the proposition was unsuccessful, this work helped bring Kennedy to the attention of Edwin Meese, who would serve as attorney general during President Reagan's second term. In 1975, President Gerald Ford appointed Kennedy to the U.S. Court of Appeals.

Kennedy was President Reagan's third choice to serve on the Supreme Court to replace Justice Powell, but he had been on the White House's short list on previous occasions, so his nomination was not a surprise to Court watchers. After the bitter battles over the previous nominees, both sides were looking to end the divisive struggle to fill Justice Powell's seat. Only the National Organization for Women voiced any opposition. In marked contrast to the Bork debacle, Kennedy's confirmation hearings were nonconfrontational and brief. The Senate Judiciary Committee voted unanimously to recommend him following only three days of hearings. After a brief floor debate consisting of universal acclaim, Kennedy was approved by a 97–0 vote on February 3, 1988. Kennedy took his seat on the Court on February 18, 1988—slightly more than halfway into the 1987–1988 term.

In his testimony before the Senate, Kennedy stated that he did not adhere to any overall theory of constitutional interpretation, and his opinions on the Supreme Court have supported this position. Kennedy has expressed certain key principles that tend to guide his decision making, however; they are the closely related concepts of *stare decisis* and judicial self-restraint.

Kennedy has stated in both his Senate testimony and his opinions that *stare decisis,* or closely following precedent, is a critically important principle in the judicial process. The courts must operate in an impartial manner, and reliance upon precedent is a key element in controlling personal values and ensuring that legal criteria determine the outcomes of cases. This in turn serves to enhance the legitimacy of the courts, which is crucial to the implementation of judicial decisions.

Closely related to the principle of *stare decisis* for Kennedy is the idea of judicial self-restraint. He views the courts as third in line in regard to America's governing system because the legislative and executive branches not only are given primacy in the Constitution but also are the popularly elected branches. An additional facet of Kennedy's conception of self-restraint is that Court decisions should be decided on the narrowest grounds possible, including deciding cases on statutory rather than constitutional grounds whenever possible. Finally, Kennedy seeks to give a literal reading to statutory and constitutional language.

Kennedy's judicial philosophy has translated into moderately conservative voting behavior on the Rehnquist Court. In civil rights and liberties cases through the 2004–2005 term, Kennedy voted liberally in 35 percent of the cases. This made him the fourth most conservative justice on the Rehnquist Court, trailing Scalia (27 percent liberal), Rehnquist (24 percent liberal), and Thomas (23 percent liberal), but making him more conservative than O'Connor (38 percent liberal). Kennedy's support for civil rights and liberties claimants varies from area to area. He is most liberal in First Amendment cases at 43 percent, compared to 39 percent liberal in civil rights cases, and only 30 percent liberal in criminal procedure decisions.

Kennedy's bloc voting record is interesting and important in terms of understanding the history of the Rehnquist Court. Early in his tenure, Kennedy was a critical member of the five-person conservative majority bloc that handed down numerous decisions creating important new conservative precedents. Thus, in the 1988–1989 and 1989–1990 terms, Kennedy joined with Rehnquist, Scalia, White, and O'Connor to form voting blocs with 88 percent and 86 percent interagreement rates, respectively. Just when it appeared that Souter and Thomas would expand this bloc to seven members, however, Kennedy began to move away from the conservative bloc, which never again reached a majority of five members. In the long natural court period from 1994 to 2005, Kennedy and Rehnquist constituted a two-person conservative bloc, but Kennedy's record differed significantly enough from Scalia and Thomas that he did not join them in a conservative alignment.

Kennedy's moderate conservatism made him a powerful force on the Rehnquist Court. In many cases, both the conservative and liberal justices needed Kennedy if they were to prevail, and Kennedy undoubtedly exercised influence on both the outcome and the reasoning of many cases. Trailing only Justice O'Connor, he was the second most successful justice on the Rehnquist Court, voting in the majority in 85 percent of all cases.

Turning to an analysis of Kennedy's decision making in various areas of the law, a pattern can be seen of a distinctively conservative justice; Kennedy is not a doctrinaire conservative, however, and he frequently has authored major liberal decisions. Kennedy's conservatism is more notable in criminal, federalism, and affirmative action cases.

Kennedy joined Rehnquist, Scalia, Thomas, and O'Connor in voting predominantly conservative in criminal procedure cases. Kennedy authored the Court's controversial 1989 decisions of *N.T.E.U. v. Von Raab* and *Skinner v. R.L.E.A.*, in which drug tests were approved for U.S. Customs personnel and railroad employees involved in train accidents, respectively, even though the Fourth Amendment requirements of a warrant and probable cause were absent. Kennedy argued that the meaning of the Fourth Amendment did not primarily involve the idea of obtaining a warrant based upon probable cause. Rather, the Fourth Amendment should be interpreted based upon the concept of reasonableness, with the Court balancing the interests of society and law enforcement against the privacy interests of individuals. For Kennedy and the majority, the government's interest prevailed in this case, and the principle was eventually extended into drug testing for junior high athletes in *Vernonia School District 47J v. Acton* (1995).

Kennedy has also been a consistent member of the conservative coalition in affirmative action programs. He supported the argument in *City of Richmond v. J. A. Croson Co.* (1989) that state affirmative action programs must meet the difficult standard of strict scrutiny, requiring the government to show it is promoting a compelling state interest by narrowly tailored means. Kennedy joined a five-person majority in extending this strict scrutiny test to federal affirmative action programs in *Adarand Constructors, Inc. v. Pena* (1995). Kennedy also voted against the University of Michigan's law school and undergraduate affirmative action admissions programs in 2003 (*Grutter v. Bollinger* and *Gratz v. Bollinger*).

Kennedy's opinions in the Rehnquist Court's federalism cases illustrate his conservative views but also his efforts to avoid dogmatic approaches. Although Kennedy's groundbreaking opinion in *Alden v. Maine* (1999) granted states a "sovereign immunity" from lawsuits under the Commerce Clause, Kennedy views the Court's role in government powers cases as a referee, preserving "the federal balance . . . interven[ing] when one or the other level of Government has tipped the scales too far" (*United States v. Lopez*, 514 U.S. at 578, 1995). This vision for state power decision making differs considerably from the more absolutist viewpoint of Justice Thomas, who has suggested that the Commerce Clause does not give the federal government any police power over the states.

Despite the predominantly conservative orientation of Kennedy, his vote and his reasoning are rarely predictable, and he has taken liberal positions in many important cases. For example, Kennedy authored the majority opinion in *Romer v. Evans*, the 1996 case that ruled unconstitutional Colorado's Amendment Two, which prevented local governments from developing ordinances to protect homosexuals from discrimination. This landmark case marked the first time the Court had ever used the Fourteenth Amendment's Equal Protection Clause to provide constitutional protection regarding sexual orientation. Kennedy also wrote the majority opinion in *Lawrence v. Texas* (2003), in which the Court ruled unconstitutional a Texas law that prohibited homosexual acts and explicitly overturned its earlier decision in *Bowers v. Hardwick* (1986). In another important and surprising majority opinion authored by Kennedy, he argued in *Lee v. Weisman* (1992) that school-sponsored prayers at public junior high graduation ceremonies violated the Establishment Clause, rejecting the argument by the Justice Department to uphold the practice and to overturn the liberal *Lemon* test in Establishment Clause cases. As a final example of Kennedy's willingness to support liberal causes, he sided with the majority in *Texas v. Johnson* (1989) in upholding a person's First Amendment right to burn the flag in political protest.

Kennedy was one of the most important members of the Rehnquist Court. His appointment in 1988 to replace swing Justice Lewis Powell promised to create a five-person majority that could engage in a conservative constitutional counterrevolution. In his initial terms on the Court, it appeared that this would indeed occur. Kennedy, however, became steadily more independent of the most conservative justices, and he did not align with the conservative bloc of Rehnquist, Scalia, and Thomas in the natural court period since 1994. Neither did he align with the moderate liberals. Kennedy occupied a critical role on the Rehnquist Court. In most closely decided cases, the key factor was how Kennedy, as well as O'Connor, decided.

George H. W. Bush Appointments

David H. Souter

Following Justice William Brennan's retirement, in 1990, many observers expected an intense struggle over his replacement. Republican Party conservatives saw this as an exceptional opportunity to add a sixth member to the five-person conservative majority (Rehnquist, Scalia, Kennedy, O'Connor, and White) controlling the Court. The Democratic Party controlled the Senate, however, and several liberal interest groups promised to resist any attempt to nominate a radical conservative to replace Brennan, the Court's leading liberal for the past four decades. Attempting to avoid conflict, President Bush nominated Judge David Hackett Souter, a virtually unknown New Hampshire Supreme Court Justice, who had joined the U.S. Court of Appeals for the First Circuit only weeks earlier. Souter's appointment turned out to be one of the most significant in Supreme Court history. Rather than expanding the conservative majority, Souter has become part of the moderate liberal wing of justices that has stymied the efforts of the most conservative justices to alter American constitutional law in fundamental ways.

Souter, an only child, was born on September 17, 1939, in Melrose, Massachusetts, into modest surroundings. The Souter family was middle class, his father having had a career as a banker in Massachusetts and later Concord, New Hampshire. As a young child, Souter spent his summers at the home of his maternal grandparents in rural Weare, New Hampshire. Souter's parents, who were uncomfortable with the fast-paced life in Massachusetts, moved into the family home in Weare following the death of his maternal grandparents. According to friends, the Souter family was austere, reclusive, and religious.

Souter was always an outstanding student. Because he was a gifted student and his local high school did not offer college preparatory classes, the village of Weare paid Souter's tuition to attend high school in Concord, a larger city eleven miles away. Souter was an exceptional student in high school, but he was unathletic and shy. After high school, Souter attended Harvard University, where he studied philosophy. In 1961, Souter graduated with honors from Harvard and accepted a Rhodes Scholarship.

David Souter (Joseph Bailey, National Geographic Society, Collection of the Supreme Court of the United States)

Souter spent two years in England at Oxford before returning to Harvard to attend law school, where he graduated in 1966.

Following law school, Souter, a lifelong bachelor, dedicated his life to his work, primarily in the public sector. Souter returned to New Hampshire, accepting a position at a law firm in Concord. However, Souter did not enjoy the tax cases, which he was assigned as a new lawyer at a small-town firm. At the first opportunity, Souter left private practice to become a deputy attorney general in New Hampshire. Within a year, Souter rose to head the criminal division of the New Hampshire attorney general's office. When future U.S. senator Warren Rudman became New Hampshire's attorney general, he made Souter his top assistant. Souter, just thirty-seven, replaced Rudman as state attorney general in 1976.

While serving as attorney general, Souter defended several controversial state policies, including a governor's order to fly flags at half-staff on Good Friday in observance of the Crucifixion and the decision to prosecute a man who covered the state's "live free or die" motto on his license plate. Souter also argued that antinuclear protestors who tried to stop construction of the Seabrook nuclear power plant should be sentenced to jail rather than probation. Later, Souter distanced himself from these decisions, observing that a state attorney general is required to enforce state laws and represent the state in court, regardless of personal opinions.

From 1978 until 1990, Souter served as an appointed state court judge, spending five years on the New Hampshire Superior Court and seven years on the New Hampshire Supreme Court. On these state courts, Souter had few opportunities to express opinions on important civil rights and liberties cases. Furthermore, Souter had not contributed to law journals, and he rarely gave public speeches that defined his judicial philosophy. In April 1990, the U.S. Senate confirmed Souter to the U.S. Court of Appeals for the First Circuit, and he was nominated to the Supreme Court only three months later.

Initially, liberal senators and interest groups were suspicious of Souter. President Bush's chief of staff, John Sununu, had promised conservative groups that the White House had found the perfect candidate to replace Justice Brennan. Many suspected Souter, or his mentor, Senator Warren Rudman, had made promises to Sununu in order to obtain the nomination. Because no one knew Souter's opinions on key issues before the Court, including affirmative action and abortion, civil rights and pro-abortion groups argued against his confirmation. Fortunately for Souter, the American Bar Association gave Souter its highest recommendation on the eve of his confirmation hearings. This recommendation was crucial for Souter because so little was known about him.

Souter's performance at his confirmation hearing ensured his approval by the Senate. His ability to summarize and discuss a wide range of Supreme Court cases and issues without referring to notes defused any worries that he was intellectually incapable of serving on the Supreme Court. Souter helped allay the doubts of Senate Judiciary Committee Democrats by denying that he had made promises to Chief of Staff Sununu about how he would vote on issues before the Court, especially abortion. He also praised Justice Brennan for his service on the Court and for being the nation's most outstanding defender of the Bill of Rights. Souter refused to answer any specific questions about how he would vote on issues before the Court. Without any specific reasons to reject Souter, the full Senate confirmed him by a vote of 90–9, with only a handful of liberal senators in opposition.

Souter's judicial philosophy is difficult to characterize. He gave few hints in his confirmation hearings about his adherence to any guiding philosophical principles, and he has not articulated a coherent, overarching philosophy in his years on the Court. Nonetheless, a number of important principles can be discerned in his voting and opinions, and, interestingly, several of these were mentioned by Souter in his Senate testimony.

Souter has a deep respect for the principle of *stare decisis*, maintaining existing precedent. This commitment was perhaps seen most clearly in his joint controlling opinion in the 1992 abortion case of *Planned Parenthood of Southeastern Pennsylvania v. Casey*, where Souter, O'Connor, and Kennedy wrote about the importance of *stare decisis* to the Court's reputation and legitimacy. Souter's commitment to the principle of *stare decisis* certainly helps to explain his moderately liberal voting record and especially his unwillingness to join the Court's most conservative justices' attempts to alter major Warren and Burger Court precedents.

Although Souter explicitly rejects the original understanding interpretation of the Constitution, he does view history as a valuable aid to a justice when the evidence seems relevant. Souter has produced especially impressive historical analyses regarding both the Free Exercise Clause and the Establishment Clause, but his opinions have not garnered much support from the other members of the Court.

Souter also views the Constitution as the source of protection of individual rights and liberties from excessive governmental exercises of power. Souter gave a clear indication of this liberal philosophy in his Senate confirmation hearings when he stated that he could not identify any Supreme Court decisions that had gone too far in recognizing constitutional rights. Although liberals were unconvinced at the time, Souter's record on the Court has supported his Senate testimony.

These components of Souter's judicial philosophy are reflected in his voting record on the Court, although his voting patterns have changed rather dramatically over time. Indeed, no member of the current Rehnquist Court has changed his or her voting pattern more dramatically than Souter. In Souter's first term on the Court, in 1990–1991, he voted liberally only 35 percent in civil rights and liberties cases, and he was a member of a five-person conservative bloc along with Rehnquist, Scalia, O'Connor, and Kennedy. In the next term, however, Souter had a 54 percent liberal voting record, and his score has since ranged from 56 percent to 82 percent liberal. His over-all voting in all of his terms on the Rehnquist Court has been 63 percent liberal, and he has been a member of a four-person liberal voting bloc with Justices Stevens, Ginsburg, and Breyer. Souter's support for liberal causes varies across issue areas. As seen in table 2.3, his liberal voting is highest in First Amendment (76 percent) and civil rights cases (70 percent) but lower in criminal cases (53 percent).

Souter's rather unique brand of moderate liberalism can be understood better by examining his opinions in selective areas. Souter has struggled to find a consistent position in cases involving the rights of homosexuals. In *Romer v. Evans* (1996), Souter joined Kennedy's majority opinion striking down an amendment to the Colorado Constitution that prevented local governments from adopting policies to protect individuals from discrimination based on their sexual orientation. He also sided, in dissent, with a homosexual respondent who was denied membership in the Boy Scouts because he was gay (*Boy Scouts of America v. Dale*, 2000). However, in *Hurley v. Irish-American Gay, Lesbian, and Bisexual Group of Boston* (1995), Souter authored a majority opinion interpreting the First Amendment to allow the organizers of a parade to ban homosexual rights groups from marching in a Saint Patrick's Day parade.

In Free Exercise Clause and Establishment Clause cases, Souter has distinguished himself as one of the Court's leading liberals. Although Souter, like most justices, advocates neutrality in interpreting the Establishment Clause, his interpretation of neutrality would prevent most programs and activities involving church-state interactions. In *Mitchell v. Helms* (2000), for example, a decision in which six justices voted to allow state governments to give educational equipment to parochial schools, Souter lectured the Court on the dangers of church-state interaction in education. Souter noted three reasons why the framers had created the Establishment Clause: "First, compelling an individual to support religion violates the fundamental principle of freedom of conscience. . . . Second, government aid corrupts religion. . . . Third, government establishment of religion is inextricably linked with conflict" (530 U.S. at 870–872).

Souter has been a leading opponent of enhanced states' rights in both Tenth Amendment and Eleventh Amendment cases. In these cases, Souter supports a broad reading of the Commerce Clause. In *United States v. Lopez* (1995), the Court rejected the substantive effects doctrine, which granted Congress the power to enact legislation whenever any activity affects interstate commerce. Souter argued that firearm possession near school buildings made learning dangerous, hampering education and thus damaging interstate commerce, because schoolchildren lost the opportunity to be educated. Souter ignored historical interpretations in his dissent from *Alden v. Maine* (1999), finding that the absence of constitutional language supporting sovereign immunity indicated individuals had a right to bring lawsuits against states, except where barred by the Eleventh Amendment.

When President George H. W. Bush nominated David Souter to serve on the Supreme Court, many liberals feared that he would help to overturn many of the precedents established with the help of his predecessor, William Brennan. Instead, Souter has proven to be a supporter of liberal causes on the Court, if somewhat more moderately than Justice Brennan, especially on criminal procedure cases. The second-youngest member of the Rehnquist Court, Souter stands a good chance to serve on the Court for many more years, but it is unclear if his shift from conservatism to liberalism has culminated or if he will continue to move in a more liberal direction.

Clarence Thomas

Clarence Thomas might be the most controversial nominee ever confirmed to the Supreme Court. As a leading African American conservative in the Reagan administration and advocate for administration policies, Thomas presented a stark ideological contrast to his predecessor on the Court, Justice Thurgood Marshall, the first African American to serve on the Supreme Court and one of the Rehnquist Court's most liberal justices along with William Brennan. Many observers felt that the addition of Thomas would provide Rehnquist Court conservatives with a solid majority on major issues of civil rights and liberties. Although the expected conservative majority committed to dramatic constitutional change did not materialize, Thomas has proven a reliable conservative vote on the Court and a strong voice for strict construction of the Constitution.

American history is replete with almost mythic stories of earnest and dedicated young people working their way from humble beginnings to honored positions in American society and government, but Clarence Thomas's triumph over abject poverty and aggressive racial discrimination enforced by the rule of law is unparalleled in the history of the U.S. Supreme Court. Thomas was born on June 23, 1948, in Pin Point, Georgia. This was the year after Jackie Robinson became the first African American to play major-league baseball, but even the first glimmers of equal opportunity had not yet reached Pin Point, a small black community near Savannah. Every aspect of life in southern Georgia was strictly segregated, and black Georgians had few opportunities for advancement. Thomas's family lived in a wooden shack with a dirt floor and no plumbing or electricity. After his father abandoned the family, Thomas went to live with his grandfather so his mother could work as a cleaning woman for wealthy white families in Savannah.

Thomas's grandfather, Myers Anderson, a hardworking black entrepreneur, was the single greatest influence on his life. Limited by discrimination, Anderson was successful in one of the few occupations open to him—fuel oil delivery. Thomas, who

Clarence Thomas (Joseph Bailey, National Geographic Society, Collection of the Supreme Court of the United States)

worked long hours after school helping his grandfather deliver fuel oil, credited Anderson with teaching him that hard work can lead to success even in the harshest environments. A proponent of self-help and generational advancement, Anderson determined that his grandson would use self-discipline and education to advance from poverty.

Thomas's grandfather sent him to strict parochial grade schools and a previously all-white boarding school for high school. At these schools, Thomas faced slights and insults from his white classmates, but he credited the nuns who taught him for providing him with an excellent education. Later, Thomas's early educational background led him to criticize the reliance on self-esteem programs at the expense of academics. Thomas would say that fear of his grandfather's wrath, rather than concern for his self-esteem from any teacher, was the impetus for his academic success.

Following high school, Thomas attended a previously all-white Catholic seminary, expecting to become a priest. Raised a Roman Catholic, Thomas would admit later that he fell away from his faith briefly in the late sixties and early seventies because of the tumultuous times, including the assassinations of Martin Luther King Jr. and Robert Kennedy and the Vietnam War. After leaving the seminary, Thomas enrolled at Holy Cross College, where he graduated with honors. He received his law degree from Yale Law School in 1974.

Following law school, Thomas worked for Missouri Attorney General John Danforth as an assistant attorney general. For the next decade and a half, Danforth would serve as Thomas's mentor and advisor. After Danforth was elected to the U.S. Senate in 1976, Thomas worked as an attorney for the Monsanto Company—a St. Louis–based agrochemical and biotechnology company—from 1977 to 1979. From 1979 to 1981, Thomas served as a legislative assistant to Senator Danforth. Senator Danforth, an ordained minister in the Episcopal Church, was an early supporter of Ronald Reagan's 1980 campaign for president, so it was no surprise that Thomas—as Danforth's protégé—received a position in the Reagan administration.

President Reagan first appointed Thomas the assistant secretary of education for civil rights and later the chairman of the Equal Employment Opportunity Commission. In these two positions, Thomas defended the Reagan administration's conservative interpretation of civil rights laws. As assistant secretary of education, Thomas was responsible for the Reagan administration's early efforts to combat the *Bakke* decision supporting affirmative action. In addition, Thomas's tenure on the EEOC was controversial, because civil rights groups and some members of Congress accused Thomas of reducing enforcement of antidiscrimination laws.

In 1990, President George H. W. Bush nominated Thomas for the U.S. Court of Appeals for the District of Columbia. Immediately, Court watchers speculated that Thomas was being prepared to replace Justice Marshall, whose health was failing. Many consider the Court of Appeals for the District of Columbia the second-highest court in the United States, and the position had served as a springboard to the Supreme Court in the past.

Following Marshall's retirement, Bush nominated Thomas to the Supreme Court on July 1, 1991. Thomas's confirmation hearings were acrimonious from the beginning as senators questioned him about the positions he took while at the EEOC and the Department of Education. His detractors were skeptical about his assertions that he had only been representing the viewpoints of the conservative administrations he served. As with most Supreme Court nominees, Thomas refused to answer direct questions about his opinions on controversial issues that might come before the Court, but his history as a lightening rod on important issues for the Reagan administration made his reluctance more difficult for Senate Democrats to accept.

Nonetheless, Thomas had weathered the Senate Judiciary Committee's questioning and appeared headed for confirmation until reports leaked that a former assistant, Anita Hill, claimed Thomas sexually harassed her while she worked for him at the Department of Education and the EEOC. A special prosecutor's report would later reveal that members of the Judiciary Committee had been aware of Professor Hill's accusations throughout the hearings process, but public disclosure of the charges forced the committee to reopen the confirmation hearings. As the entire nation watched, Hill—at the time a professor at the University of Oklahoma College of Law—accused Thomas of sexual harassment. In his defense, Thomas accused the committee of conducting a "high-tech lynching" and denied each of Hill's charges. Because Hill had no corroboration, Americans as well as the Senate were divided over the credibility of her testimony. Eventually, the Senate confirmed Thomas on October 15, 1991, by a nearly party-line vote of 52–48 with a group of seven southern Democrats and Democratic Senator Alan Dixon of Illinois providing the margin of victory for Thomas. Thomas took his seat on the Court on October 15, 1991.

Thomas's voting behavior on the Court has lived up to the expectations of both liberals and conservatives. He has been the most conservative member of the Rehnquist Court in civil rights and liberties cases; as can be seen in table 2.2, Thomas has voted liberally in only 23 percent of these cases. In the natural court period from 1994 to 2005, Thomas joined Rehnquist and Scalia to form a three-person conservative bloc, and Thomas's agreement level with Scalia was an extraordinary 93 percent. In cases involving the rights of the criminally accused, Thomas rivals Chief Justice Rehnquist as the most conservative justice; Thomas has been the most conservative Rehnquist Court justice in civil rights cases; and he has been the third most conservative in First Amendment cases, tied with Justice White. In addition, Thomas is the Court's foremost advocate of a states' rights interpretation of the Tenth and Eleventh Amendments—traditionally conservative causes.

Two distinct but interrelated ideas can be discerned in Thomas's judicial philosophy. Stemming from his childhood background and continuing in his years of government service, Thomas places great emphasis on individual initiative and personal responsibility, thus creating a narrow view on the role of government in protecting and promoting individual rights and liberties. Thomas made this point forcefully in his concurrence in *Adarand Constructors, Inc. v. Pena* (1995) when the Court ruled against a federal affirmative action program, asserting that the strict scrutiny test must apply in such cases: "Government cannot make us equal; it can only recognize, respect, and protect us as equal before the law" (512 U.S. at 240). Thomas has been consistently skeptical of the government's positive role in ameliorating the effects of discrimination. According to Thomas, the Equal Protection Clause prohibits most affirmative action programs. In *Adarand*, Thomas wrote that "there can be no doubt that the paternalism that appears to lie at the heart of this [federal affirmative action] program is at war with the principle of inherent equality that underlies and infuses our Constitution" (512 U.S. at 240). Predictably, Thomas voted against the University of Michigan's affirmative action programs for law school (*Grutter v. Bollinger*, 2003) and undergraduate school (*Gratz v. Bollinger*, 2003).

Another important component of Thomas's judicial philosophy is the concept of original intent, whereby a justice examines closely the historical record associated with a particular constitutional provision to attempt to determine exactly how the writers of the provision understood its meaning and intended it to be applied. Thomas's dissent in *Helling v. McKinney* (1998) illustrates his strong application of original intent. In *Helling*, the Court determined that a severe beating by prison guards violated a prisoner's Eighth Amendment protection against cruel and unusual punishments. However, Thomas disagreed. After a careful examination of the historical meaning of the word *punishment*, Thomas determined: "I believe that the text and history of the Eighth Amendment, together with the decisions interpreting it, support the view that judges or juries—but not jailers—impose 'punishment'" (509 U.S. at 40). Likewise, Thomas's support for original intent has informed his federalism opinions. In *United States v. Lopez* (1995), he argued in a concurrence that commerce—as the term was used at the time the Constitution was written—"consisted of selling, buying, and bartering, as well as transporting for these purposes." Using his *Lopez* reasoning, Thomas has consistently argued that the Commerce Clause, as modified by the Tenth Amendment, severely limits Congress's power to regulate the nonbusiness activities of individuals, except in the very narrow arena of civil rights and liberties cases—in which they can be sued only if they are governmental actors.

Clarence Thomas is no stranger to controversy. His Senate confirmation battle was one of the most intense in U.S. history, and a torrent of books have come out about him. As with other ideological justices in the modern era (e.g., Marshall, Brennan, Scalia, and Rehnquist), opinions about Thomas are often driven by the viewpoints of the analyst as much as the reasoning of the justice. Interestingly, Thomas's impact on the Rehnquist Court was less than his supporters anticipated and his opponents feared. Because of the movement of Justices Souter, O'Connor, and Kennedy to the center, Thomas found consistent support only from Scalia and Rehnquist.

Clinton Appointments

Ruth Bader Ginsburg

On June 14, 1993, President William Clinton nominated Ruth Bader Ginsburg to the Supreme Court to replace retiring Justice Byron White. Ginsburg's nomination marked the first opportunity in twenty-five years for a Democratic president to fill a Court vacancy, dating back to 1967, when President Lyndon Johnson chose Thurgood Marshall. In some respects, Ginsburg was very much like Justice Marshall; both were veteran plaintiff's attorneys in civil rights and liberties cases who had been appointed to their appeals court positions by a prior Democratic president. Like Thurgood Marshall's famed record attacking racial discrimination in the fifties, Ginsburg's briefs in leading gender discrimination cases in the seventies led the charge for gender equality in the United States. However, Ginsburg and Marshall proved to be different Supreme Court justices. Ginsburg's moderately liberal record on the Court has been far different from Justice Marshall's extreme liberal advocacy from the bench. Ginsburg's impact has been significant, however, because the conservative coalition lost a key ally when White retired, and a majority conservative bloc has not coalesced since Ginsburg's appointment to the Court.

Joan Ruth Bader Ginsburg was born into a lower-middle-class Jewish family on March 15, 1933, in Brooklyn, New York. Her father was a struggling furrier and later a haberdasher, while her mother was the center of the family. Although her parents struggled to provide for their daughter, tragedy touched the family. The future justice was the second child of Nathan and Celia Bader, but her older sister died before Ginsburg began school. Following her older daughter's death, Celia Bader began to save money so that her remaining daughter could go to college, as she wished that she had. From an early age, Ginsburg was encouraged to excel in academic pursuits. In high school, she was a leading student, a baton twirler, and an athletic booster whose enthusiasm for selling athletic tickets and organizing activities was termed pushy by some of her fellow students. However, Ginsburg's high school years were saddened by her mother's struggle with cancer. Although she graduated sixth in her high school class in 1950 and was chosen to speak at her high school honors convocation, she did not attend her graduation ceremony because her mother had died the previous day. When Celia Bader's estate was settled, it was determined that she had left $8,000 for her daughter to attend college; however, Ginsburg had earned several scholarships and did not need the money to be able to pursue higher education.

Ruth Bader Ginsburg (Richard Strauss, Smithsonian Institution, Collection of the Supreme Court of the United States)

Following high school, Ginsburg attended Cornell University, majoring in government. A member of Phi Beta Kappa, she graduated in 1954, receiving the distinction of being class marshall—the award for being the highest-ranking female student in her graduating class.

Following graduation, she married Martin Ginsburg, a former Cornell student who had graduated a year earlier and was attending Harvard Law School. In 1954, Martin Ginsburg was drafted and posted at Fort Sill, in Oklahoma. After two years at Fort Sill, where she worked as a clerk typist, the Ginsburgs returned to Harvard, where both enrolled in law school. Despite ranking among the top ten students at Harvard Law School and being a member of the prestigious *Harvard Law Review* staff after her second year, financial and family considerations forced Ginsburg to leave Harvard in 1958 after her husband was diagnosed with testicular cancer. Fortunately, Martin Ginsburg made a miraculous recovery and was able to land a job in New York later that year. Because her husband had accepted a promising position in a New York law firm, Ginsburg transferred to Columbia University School of Law, where she finished her degree. Despite juggling family life and law school, she tied for first in her class at Columbia Law School and was a member of its law review staff.

Ginsburg's impressive academic record did not translate into job offers from private law firms following her graduation. Spurned by private employers, Ginsburg took a law-clerk position with U.S. District Court Judge Edmund Palmieri. She worked for Palmieri from 1959 until 1961. Next, Ginsburg worked in Sweden on Columbia University's Project on International Procedure, first as a research assistant and later as an associate director. After returning to the United States, Ginsburg became the second female law professor at Rutgers School of Law. Ginsburg served on the Rutgers law faculty from 1963 until 1972, when she became a law professor at Columbia University, where she taught until she became an appeals court judge in 1980.

While at Rutgers, Ginsburg began to focus her attention on the impact of gender discrimination, both in her life and in American society. Learning from experience, she had hidden her second pregnancy from everyone at Rutgers, but she resented the need to do so. Deeply disturbed by the pervasive discrimination faced by women, she began working with the American Civil Liberties Union (ACLU), focusing on laws that treated men and women differently. Legal experts regard Ginsburg's brief in *Reed v. Reed* (1971) as one of the most significant legal arguments in the history of gender discrimination cases. *Reed* marked the first time that the Supreme Court ruled a state law unconstitutional on the grounds of gender discrimination. After her success in *Reed*, the ACLU made Ginsburg the first director of its Women's Rights Project, from 1972 to 1973. Later, Ginsburg served as general counsel of the Women's Rights Project, from 1973 until her appointment to the U.S. Court of Appeals. While working with the Women's Rights Project, Ginsburg participated in five gender discrimination cases, winning four. Ginsburg's single most significant accomplishment involved the Court's decision in *Craig v. Boren* (1976) to classify gender discrimination under the intermediate scrutiny test, thus making it significantly easier for those claiming gender discrimination to prevail.

In 1980, President Jimmy Carter nominated Ginsburg to the Court of Appeals for the District of Columbia, where she served with Robert Bork and future Supreme Court Justice Antonin Scalia. Considered a unifier on the court, Ginsburg joined and wrote opinions with both conservative and liberal judges.

Given Ginsburg's record both as a judicial moderate and a feminist hero, President Clinton's decision to nominate her to the Supreme Court on June 14, 1993, to replace Justice Byron White, was no surprise. Following a muted confirmation process, the Senate voted 96–3 to confirm Ginsburg on August 3, 1993.

Although Ginsburg was praised by President Clinton as the Thurgood Marshall of the women's movement, her judicial philosophy has been a more restrained form of judicial activism. Ginsburg views the courts as the third branch of government, with the Constitution establishing the legislative and executive branches as preeminent in determining public policy. However, Ginsburg maintains that the courts are a check on the other branches of government, especially when they fail to act to support the weak and powerless, and she recognizes that the courts must decide some controversial cases that clearly raise constitutional issues.

Ginsburg has not demonstrated the same expansive interpretation of constitutional guarantees of civil rights and liberties as such justices as Brennan and Marshall, but, with a few exceptions, she has applied a pragmatic liberal approach across the spectrum of civil rights and liberties cases. Predictably, Ginsburg has supported a broad interpretation of the Equal Protection Clause both in gender discrimination and affirmative action cases. As a member of a religious minority, it is not surprising that she is the Court's most liberal member in Establishment Clause cases, but she has not yet clearly expressed her views regarding the proper interpretation of the Free Exercise Clause. In criminal procedure and Due Process Clause cases, Ginsburg has been more moderate, but she remains one of the most liberal members of the Rehnquist Court.

As expected, Ginsburg has fought gender discrimination while on the Court. Drawing from *Frontiero v. Richardson* (1973), a Supreme Court case in which she participated, Ginsburg's majority opinion in *United States v. Virginia* (1996) established a historical explanation for the Court's activity in gender discrimination cases. In striking down Virginia Military Institute's male-only admission policy, Ginsburg noted, "Today's skeptical scrutiny of official action denying rights or opportunities based on sex responds to volumes of history. As a plurality of this Court acknowledged a generation ago (in *Frontiero*), 'our Nation has had a long and unfortunate history of sex discrimination'" (518 U.S. at 531).

Ginsburg does not accept the conservative view that the Fourteenth Amendment bars Congress from enacting affirmative action programs. In *Adarand Constructors*,

Inc. v. Pena (1995), Ginsburg wrote, "Large deference is owed by the Judiciary to Congress' institutional competence and constitutional authority to overcome historic racial subjugation" (512 U.S. at 271). Likewise, Ginsburg has supported race-conscious redistricting plans against Fourteenth Amendment challenges.

Ginsburg has been the Court's most consistent voice for separation of church and state, voting for a liberal outcome in every Establishment Clause case since she joined the Court. This opposition to entanglements between religion and government has extended even into symbolic interactions, such as Christmas decorations and invocations at high school graduations.

Ginsburg's voting record reflects her commitment to a moderate judicial activism. Her overall liberalism score in civil rights and liberties cases has been 66 percent. This makes her the second most liberal member of the Rehnquist Court since 1994, ranking behind Justice Stevens, at 71 percent liberal. Her support for liberal outcomes varies somewhat by issue area, with her highest support in First Amendment cases (77 percent liberal), followed by civil rights decisions (69 percent liberal), and then criminal cases (60 percent liberal). Ginsburg has joined Justices Stevens, Souter, and Breyer to form a four-person voting bloc, with an average interagreement score of 85 percent.

Like Thurgood Marshall, Ruth Bader Ginsburg came to the Court with a long history of successful and innovative legal arguments in favor of equal protection rights. However, Justice Ginsburg has been a moderate liberal during her service on the Court rather than an extreme liberal, like Marshall. Ginsburg's replacement of Justice White had a dramatic effect on the Court, however; White's resignation deprived the conservatives of an important vote they needed, and Ginsburg strongly opposed the conservative agenda of Justices Rehnquist, Scalia, and Thomas.

Stephen Breyer

The 1994 Supreme Court nomination of Stephen Breyer, a respected court of appeals judge and former Senate Judiciary Committee counsel, won immediate acclaim from both senators and Court watchers. However, Breyer was not President Clinton's first choice. When Justice Harry Blackmun announced his retirement in early 1994, President Clinton was embroiled in the controversy surrounding his ultimately unsuccessful effort at health care reform. Because 1994 was an election year and Clinton wanted to avoid another major controversy, he decided to forgo his initial desire to nominate a liberal political figure to help steer the Court to the left. Instead, Clinton turned to Breyer, a respected moderate with an extensive background in both Washington and on the court of appeals. Breyer's nomination brought little of the controversy that any well-known politician would have. Best known for his expertise in administrative law,

Stephen Breyer (Richard Strauss, Smithsonian Institution, Collection of the Supreme Court of the United States)

international law, regulation reform, and the intersection between law and science, Breyer has maintained his low profile, moderate liberal image through his tenure on the Court.

Breyer was born on August 15, 1938, in San Francisco, California, into a family that belonged to San Francisco's large, middle-class Jewish community. Breyer's father was an attorney who worked for the San Francisco public school system for forty-two years, while his mother was active in the local Democratic Party.

Typical of Supreme Court justices, Breyer was an excellent student whose parents encouraged him to excel in school. He attended a well-regarded public high school that numbered two Nobel laureates among its alumni. Breyer was voted "most likely to succeed" by his high school graduating class in 1955. Breyer attended Stanford University, where he received only one B grade and was a member of Phi Beta Kappa. He received his bachelor of arts degree in 1959. After failing to receive a Rhodes Scholarship because he did not letter in a varsity sport although he tried various sports from soccer to crew, Breyer accepted a Marshall Scholarship and attended Magdalen College at Oxford University, where he received another bachelor of arts degree. After Oxford, Breyer returned to the United States to attend Harvard Law School. This began an association with Harvard that would last until he was appointed to the Supreme Court. At Harvard, Breyer was a distinguished student and was voted a member of the *Harvard Law Review* staff. He received his law degree in 1964.

After completing his law degree at Harvard, Breyer began a career in public service by serving for a year as a law clerk to Supreme Court Justice Arthur Goldberg. In 1965, Breyer became a special assistant to the assistant attorney general for Antitrust. Breyer remained a Department of Justice attorney until 1967, when he became a professor at Harvard Law School. That same year, Breyer married Joanna Hare, the tennis-playing daughter of a British viscount and later a noted clinical psychologist. Over the next several years, Breyer taught at both Harvard Law School and the Kennedy School of Government. In 1973, Breyer became an assistant special prosecutor, investigating Watergate. After Watergate, Breyer worked for the Senate Judiciary Committee from 1974 to 1975 and from 1979 to 1980. In 1980, President Carter appointed Breyer to the Court of Appeals for the First Circuit. Breyer spent the next fourteen years on the court of appeals, the last four as chief judge, until President Clinton nominated him to the Supreme Court.

Although Breyer was Clinton's first and only nominee to replace Blackmun, Clinton reportedly gave serious thought to nominating a candidate with a strong background of active involvement in national politics. However, Senate Majority Leader George Mitchell took himself out of the running, and Clinton did not have the political strength to nominate his next choice, Interior Secretary Bruce Babbitt. Of Clinton's choices with judicial experience, Breyer was not only eminently qualified but also promised the easiest confirmation. Although several senators and several newspaper editorials expressed concern over Breyer's risky investments with the English insurance syndicate Lloyds of London, his confirmation was never really in doubt. In three days of hearings, senators from both parties praised Breyer's experience and moderate judicial philosophy. The Judiciary Committee voted unanimously to recommend Breyer on July 19, 1994. On July 29, 1994, the Senate voted 87–9 to confirm him. Stephen Breyer took his seat on the Court on August 3, 1994.

Breyer's judicial philosophy does not lend itself to easy description and analysis. Breyer's academic background was rooted in the areas of administrative law and economic regulation. These are somewhat technical areas not associated with overall theories of the law, and the Court decides few cases each term in these areas. Breyer provided little insight during his Senate confirmation hearings because he gave no indication of possessing a distinctive judicial philosophy to guide his Supreme Court decision making.

Commentators frequently use the term *pragmatist* to describe Breyer's decision making. This means that he is more interested in workable solutions than in grand theories. An important aspect of this pragmatic approach involves the balancing of arguments involving competing rights, with a heavy reliance upon the unique facts of each case.

Nonetheless, Breyer does have a liberal orientation to his judicial philosophy, but it is a moderate liberalism. One the one hand, as he testified at his Senate hearings, he recognizes Brennan and Marshall as great justices and adheres to their view that the Constitution must be read as a living document to be adapted to the needs of a changing society. On the other hand, Breyer's liberal orientation is tempered by his commitment to precedent and to the view that the popularly elected branches have the primary responsibility for creating public policy.

Breyer's voting record on the Court reflects these elements of his judicial philosophy. His overall liberalism score in civil rights and liberties cases is 62 percent. Breyer has been relatively consistent throughout his years on the Rehnquist Court. Breyer's liberalism scores vary somewhat across issue areas of civil rights and liberties, with his support highest in civil rights cases, at 73 percent liberal; he has voted liberally in 62 percent of the First Amendment cases and 53 percent liberally in criminal procedure cases. Breyer has been in strongest agreement with Justices Stevens, Ginsburg, and Souter, forming a voting bloc with an 85 percent average agreement score in the natural court period from 1994 to 2005.

In terms of more specific areas of the law, Breyer has been generally supportive of liberal values in First Amendment cases, but this pattern has not been consistent across all issues. Breyer has been a reliable liberal vote and voice in freedom of expression cases. He has also taken a liberal stance in regard to the free exercise of religion, calling in *City of Boerne v. P. F. Flores* (1997) for the overturn of the conservative *Smith* test. Breyer has been more of a moderate in Establishment Clause cases, however, supporting a middle ground between the Court's more liberal justices and the accommodationist philosophy of the more conservative members of the Court.

Breyer's moderate liberalism can also be seen in the abortion controversy, where he has taken a position close to that of O'Connor's. In *Stenberg v. Carhart* (2000), Breyer utilized the Court's undue burden test to overturn a law that outlawed one form of abortion because an improper interpretation of that law could have led to prosecution of abortion providers.

In Fourteenth Amendment cases involving racial and gender discrimination and in the related area of affirmative action, Breyer has been a more traditional liberal. Although his liberal voting record has been consistent, he has written few opinions in these areas. Breyer has joined in dissents against the Court's conservative decisions in affirmative action and voting rights cases.

Although he is a moderate liberal in civil rights and liberties cases, Breyer's judicial philosophy differed markedly from the Rehnquist Court conservatives on the role of the national government. Breyer was the leading critic of the Court's federalism reasoning. Breyer has come close to rejecting the very premise of dual sovereignty that the Rehnquist Court majority viewed as inherent in federalism.

Although a moderate liberal, Breyer played a key role on the Rehnquist Court since he was appointed in 1994. Breyer replaced one of the Court's leading liberals, Harry Blackmun, and Breyer's record has been somewhat similar to Blackmun's, with the most important differences being in the areas of the Establishment Clause and abortion, where Blackmun took stronger liberal stances. Breyer, however, has been consistently associated with Justices Stevens, Ginsburg, and Souter in the liberal bloc that placed considerable constraints on the conservative agenda of Chief Justice Rehnquist and his close allies, Justices Scalia and Thomas.

References

Brisbin, Richard. "Antonin Scalia, William Brennan, and the Politics of Expression: A Study of Legal Violence and Repression." *American Political Science Review*, 87, no. 4 (1993): 912–927.

———. *Justice Antonin Scalia and the Conservative Revival.* Baltimore: Johns Hopkins Univ. Press, 1997.

Davis, Sue. *Justice Rehnquist and the Constitution.* Princeton, NJ: Princeton Univ. Press, 1989.

———. "Justice William H. Rehnquist: Right Wing Ideologue or Majoritarian Democrat?" In *The Burger Court: Political and Judicial Profiles*, edited by C. M. Lamb and S. C. Halpern, 315–342. Urbana: Univ. of Illinois Press, 1991.

Goldman, Roger, and David Gallen. *Thurgood Marshall: Justice for All.* New York: Carroll and Graf,, 1992.

Irons, Peter. *Brennan vs. Rehnquist: The Battle for the Constitution.* New York: Knopf, 1994.

Maveety, Nancy. *Justice Sandra Day O'Connor: Strategist on the Supreme Court.* Lanham, MD: Rowman and Littlefield, 1996.

Sickels, Robert J. *John Paul Stevens and the Constitution: The Search for Balance.* University Park: Pennsylvania State Univ. Press, 1988.

3

The Rulings

T
he central theme of this book is whether the Rehnquist Court engaged in a conservative constitutional counterrevolution. As mentioned previously, the answer to this question is no; although the Rehnquist Court created a few major new conservative precedents, most of the leading Warren Court and Burger Court precedents remain in place, and the Rehnquist Court even created some major new liberal precedents. The purpose of this chapter is to provide systematic evidence to support this position. This includes an examination of the Rehnquist Court's decision making in major areas of American law, including civil rights and liberties issues—the religious guarantees, freedom of expression, the constitutional guarantees of the criminally accused, equal protection and privacy, and the Takings Clause—as well as the topics of federalism and government powers.

This chapter utilizes both quantitative and qualitative approaches, and a few words of explanation are necessary regarding the methods associated with these approaches. Quantitative data involve the researcher in reading carefully the decisions of the Court and then recording the outcomes of the cases, typically as liberal or conservative, as well as the vote of each justice. This information, and much more, is contained in Harold J. Spaeth's *United States Supreme Court Judicial Database, 1953–2004 Terms* (2005). With these data, we can look at each area of constitutional law to compare the voting records of the Warren, Burger, and Rehnquist Courts, and we can analyze the voting records of each member of the Rehnquist Court. The results of these analyses can provide considerable insight into the question of whether the Rehnquist Court has decided cases in a fundamentally different way than the Warren and Burger Courts.[1]

Valuable as quantitative methods are in understanding the Rehnquist Court, however, this approach has important limitations. First, it treats all cases as being of equal importance, and it is clearly the reality that Supreme Court cases vary greatly in their importance. Second, coding the decisions of the Court and the votes of the justices as dichotomies (liberal or conservative) can oversimplify a complex reality. Third, quantitative techniques disregard the legal reasoning of the justices, and it is the legal reasoning that provides the meaning to constitutional provisions and the guidelines for public policy.[2] Given these limitations to quantitative methods of analysis, qualitative analysis is also an important approach in analyzing the decisions of the Rehnquist Court. This involves interpreting the relative importance of cases and assessing the legal reasoning of the Court's controlling opinion. An especially important concern is whether the Rehnquist Court created new conservative precedent; if in a given area of the law the Rehnquist Court did not hand down at least one decision overturning a prior liberal precedent and replacing it with a new conservative decision, then it cannot be concluded that the Rehnquist Court engaged in a conservative counterrevolution.

Establishment Clause

The First Amendment states: "Congress shall make no law respecting an establishment of religion, or prohibiting the free exercise thereof." This seemingly simple language has been the basis for some of the Supreme Court's most difficult and contentious cases. In regard to the Establishment Clause, the Court has been confronted with such controversial issues as prayer in public schools, government aid to parochial schools, and religious displays on public property. The Free Exercise Clause has been the basis of many disputes that have typically raised the question of whether exemptions can be made from government policies that unintentionally require people to act contrary to their religious beliefs. In this section, the Establishment Clause is examined initially, and then the Free Exercise Clause is analyzed.

The Supreme Court has struggled with interpreting the Establishment Clause since its first major case involving the clause, *Everson v. Board of Education*, in 1947, and the Rehnquist Court has been no exception. The justices of the Rehnquist Court modified Establishment Clause jurisprudence in important ways, allowing substantial accommodations between church and state, and the Rehnquist Court explicitly modified two previous liberal decisions. Nonetheless, the Rehnquist Court did not have a clear majority committed to one distinctive approach to Establishment Clause cases, and hence it is not possible to conclude that a conservative constitutional counterrevolution has occurred. Instead, a comment by Justice Thomas seems to characterize accurately this complex and highly controversial area of constitutional law: "Our Establishment Clause jurisprudence is in hopeless disarray" (*Rosenberger v. Rector and Visitors of the University of Virginia*, 515 U.S. at 861, 1995).

The Vinson Court Period

Before examining in greater detail the Establishment Clause decisions of the Rehnquist Court, it is necessary to discuss briefly the Establishment Clause jurisprudence of earlier Court eras. This history begins in 1947 with the *Everson* case, in which the Vinson Court nationalized the Establishment Clause, making it applicable to the states, and upheld a New Jersey program that allowed financial reimbursement to parents of parochial students who sent their children to school on public buses.

The Court discussed and to some extent embraced three competing visions of the Establishment Clause in *Everson:* strict separation, neutrality, and accommodation. Writing for the majority, Justice Black forcefully stated the strict separation approach: "The First Amendment has erected a wall between church and state. That wall must be kept high and impregnable" (330 U.S. at 18). Neutrality is a more moderate interpretation of the Establishment Clause, requiring that the government remain neutral regarding religion, neither advancing nor inhibiting religion. According to this approach, which Black also discussed, the Constitution only requires "the state be neutral in its relations with groups of religious believers and non-believers; it does not require the state to be their adversary" (330 U.S. at 18). The dissenters in *Everson* thought the program was unconstitutional and argued that the majority had argued for strict separation or neutrality but had actually taken an accommodationist approach that allowed an extensive amount of support by the government for religion by subsidizing the transportation of children to parochial schools. The first major Establishment Clause case decided by the Supreme Court thus provided the basis for future justices to support any of three competing approaches to the Establishment Clause, and this is exactly what happened.

The Warren Court Period

The Warren Court heard relatively few Establishment Clause cases; and although the justices embraced contrasting approaches in different cases, the Warren Court can best be characterized as supporting a neutrality approach. In the Court's first major case involving state-sponsored religious activities in public schools, *Engel v. Vitale* (1962), the Court majority used strong, strict separationist language in ruling 6–1 that an optional, nondenominational prayer policy in the state of New York violated the Establishment Clause. Several years later, however, in *Board of Education v. Allen* (1968), the Warren Court used more accommodationist language in approving a New York State parochial aid program that allowed the state to loan secular textbooks to parochial school students. The single case that seems to characterize the Warren Court most accurately, however, is *School District of Abington Township v. Schempp* (1963). Reacting in part to the intense public outcry and criticism against the *Engel* decision, the Court ruled 8–1 that Pennsylvania's law requiring Bible reading in public schools to begin each day violated the Establishment Clause. Writing for the majority, Justice Tom Clark avoided the harsh, strict separationist language of *Engel* and instead articulated a neutralist approach to the Establishment Clause. Clark extended this reasoning by developing a two-pronged test for Establishment Clause cases, requiring that any government policy must (1) have "a secular legislative purpose" and (2) have "a primary effect that neither advances nor inhibits religion" (347 U.S. at 222).

The Burger Court Period

Cases involving the proper relationship of church and state occupied a significant portion of the time and energy of the Burger Court, whose Establishment Clause cases are not easy to summarize. The Burger Court decided thirty-seven Establishment Clause cases, compared to only seven for the Warren Court. The Burger Court justices engaged in an intense struggle over the proper approach to the clause, with the conservatives arguing strongly in favor of an accommodationist approach and liberals advocating the neutrality orientation. The Burger Court initially embraced the neutrality approach, then seemingly shifted to accommodation, and finally utilized neutrality in a series of major cases in the mideighties.

The landmark case of *Lemon v. Kurtzman* (1971) best characterizes the Burger Court's early interpretation of the Establishment Clause. In an 8–0 decision penned by Chief Justice Burger, the Court ruled unconstitutional a Pennsylvania law that provided various forms of financial aid to parochial schools, including teacher's salaries. The Burger Court expanded the two-part *Schempp* test into a three-part *Lemon* test by adding to the purpose and effect prongs a third part that stated that a government law must not foster an excessive entanglement with religion, which the Pennsylvania law did.

Burger and other conservative justices grew increasingly disenchanted with the *Lemon* test in the seventies because few challenged government programs were found to be constitutional, and with the addition of Justice O'Connor to the Court, in 1981, the conservative accommodationists began to prevail on a regular basis. The Burger Court approved tax breaks to the parents of parochial students in *Mueller v. Allen* (1983), the practice of state legislative prayer in *Marsh v. Chambers* (1983), and the sponsorship by a city of a Christmas display that included a nativity scene in *Lynch v. Donnelly* (1984). In each of these cases, the majority embraced an accommodationist approach and also sharply criticized or made no reference to the *Lemon* test.

Surprisingly, however, the Burger Court in a series of cases in 1985 returned to the neutrality approach and the *Lemon* test. The lead case of *Wallace v. Jaffree* (1985) saw a challenge to an Alabama law that permitted silent prayer at the beginning of each day in state public schools. The Court ruled the law unconstitutional in a 6–3 vote. Writing for the majority, Justice Stevens paid no attention to the Court's previous support of accommodation and instead simply asserted "the established principle that government must pursue a course of complete neutrality toward religion" (472 U.S. at 60). Stevens also asserted that any analysis of the Establishment Clause must begin with the *Lemon* test, and he stated the Alabama law failed the first prong because it did not have a secular purpose. The guiding principles of neutrality and the *Lemon* test were supported further in the 1985 parochial aid cases of *Grand Rapids School District v. Ball* and *Aguilar v. Felton,* in which the Court ruled unconstitutional state programs that provided secular classes to parochial students in their church-affiliated classrooms.

The Rehnquist Court Period

The Rehnquist Court thus inherited an ambiguous jurisprudential legacy from both the Warren and Burger Courts because ample precedents existed to support almost any approach and any decision upon which five justices could agree. The dominant approach, however, was neutrality, and the controlling doctrine seemed to be the three-pronged *Lemon* test.

Did the Rehnquist Court engage in a conservative constitutional counterrevolution in regard to the Establishment Clause? The answer is no, but this is a qualified no. Quantitative data show that the Rehnquist Court was significantly more conservative than the Warren and Burger Courts. These data also suggest a conservative voting bloc of five justices, but this conservative majority has only agreed on the outcome of cases and not upon distinctively conservative doctrinal guidelines. The Rehnquist Court created modified versions of both the neutrality approach and the *Lemon* test, but these were modest rather than radical changes. Two Burger Court Establishment Clause precedents were overturned, but they were narrow decisions affecting limited areas of the law and American society.

Looking initially at the quantitative data, table 3.1 reveals that the Rehnquist Court was distinctively more conservative than the Warren and Burger Courts in Establishment Clause cases, deciding only 32 percent of twenty-eight decisions liberally, that is, opposing various forms of governmental support and involvement with religious activities. This figure contrasts rather sharply with the 57 percent liberal record of the Warren Court and the even more liberal 68 percent of the Burger Court.

Table 3.2 shows the voting record of each justice who has served on the Rehnquist Court, and the sharp divisions on the Court are clearly apparent. Looking initially at all fourteen justices and using a range of 40–60 percent liberal as indicating moderate voting, not one of the fourteen justices of the Rehnquist Court can be classified as moderate in Establishment Clause cases. If we focus on the nine justices who occupied the Court during the natural court period from 1994 to 2005, we can observe the exact alignments of a closely divided Court. Rehnquist, Thomas, and Scalia occupy the conservative end of the continuum, having voted conservatively in almost

Table 3.1: Liberal/Conservative Voting in Establishment Clause Cases by the Warren, Burger, and Rehnquist Courts, 1953–1954 to 2004–2005 Terms

Court Era	Liberal Decisions	Conservative Decisions	Total Cases
Warren Court (1953–1968 Terms)	57% (4)	43% (3)	7
Burger Court (1969–1985 Terms)	68% (25)	32% (12)	37
Rehnquist Court (1986–2004 Terms)	32% (9)	68% (19)	28
Total	53% (38)	47% (34)	72

Source: Harold J. Spaeth, *United States Supreme Court Judicial Database, 1953–2004 Terms* (Ann Arbor, MI: Inter-University Consortium for Political and Social Research, 2005).

Table 3.2: Liberal/Conservative Voting Records of the Justices of the Rehnquist Court in Establishment Clause Cases, 1986–1987 Term to 2004–2005 Term (Justices Ranked from Most Conservative to Most Liberal)

Justices	Liberal Decisions	Conservative Decisions	Total Cases
Scalia	0% (0)	100% (28)	28
Thomas	0% (0)	100% (16)	16
Rehnquist	4% (1)	96% (27)	28
White	14% (2)	86% (12)	14
Kennedy	24% (6)	76% (19)	25
Powell	33% (1)	67% (2)	3
O'Connor	36% (10)	64% (18)	28
Blackmun	71% (12)	29% (5)	17
Breyer	73% (8)	27% (3)	11
Brennan	75% (9)	25% (3)	12
Marshall	75% (9)	25% (3)	12
Stevens	93% (26)	7% (2)	28
Souter	94% (15)	6% (1)	16
Ginsburg	100% (14)	0% (0)	14

Source: Harold J. Spaeth, *United States Supreme Court Judicial Database, 1953–2004 Terms* (Ann Arbor, MI: Inter-University Consortium for Political and Social Research, 2005).

every Establishment Clause decision. Ginsburg, Souter, and Stevens are at the other extreme, having voted liberally in almost every Establishment Clause decision. Breyer is also distinctively liberal at 73 percent, thus creating a predictable four-person liberal coalition. Justices Kennedy and O'Connor are not extreme conservatives but do have predominantly conservative voting records at 76 percent and 64 percent, respectively. Thus, a five-person conservative coalition typically prevailed in the Establishment Clause decisions of the Rehnquist Court. Kennedy and O'Connor, however, held the balance of power in these cases, and they frequently used it either to give the liberals the vote they needed to prevail or to moderate the language of the Court's opinion.

Quantitative data can provide important insights into the decision-making patterns of the Court, but they also have limitations that we have previously discussed. The generalizations offered above thus need to be examined more closely by analyzing in detail the written opinions of the justices in the major Establishment Clause cases of the Rehnquist Court.

The Rehnquist Court overturned two earlier Establishment Clause precedents, but in both of these cases the changes were of a somewhat limited scope. *Agostini v. Felton* was a 1997 decision in which Justice O'Connor wrote a majority opinion joined by Rehnquist, Scalia, Thomas, and Kennedy overturning the Burger Court decision of *Aguilar v. Felton* (1985). In *Agostini*, the Court approved the practice of allowing public school teachers to instruct in parochial schools under Title I of the 1965 Elementary and Secondary Education Act, which focused on remedial education for disadvantaged children, a practice the Burger Court ruled unconstitutional in *Aguilar*. O'Connor's majority opinion adhered closely to neutrality and the questions of *Lemon*, however, and its practical effect was limited to Title I programs.

The Rehnquist Court also modified precedent in *Mitchell v. Helms* (2000), but this case had a limited impact as well. In *Mitchell* the same 5–4 majority of Rehnquist, Scalia, Thomas, Kennedy, and O'Connor approved of a federal parochial aid program that provided both public and private schools with a variety of secular educational equipment and materials, including computer hardware and software. In reaching its decision in *Mitchell*, the Rehnquist Court modified two Burger Court Establishment Clause precedents, *Meek v. Pittenger* (1975) and *Wolman v. Waters* (1977). *Mitchell's* impact is limited, however, because the controlling opinion by Thomas did not command majority support. O'Connor joined with Stevens, Breyer, Ginsburg, and Souter in rejecting Thomas's radically conservative interpretation of the Establishment Clause, which is discussed below.

Another important perspective on the Rehnquist Court's Establishment Clause jurisprudence involves the interpretations that have been given to the neutrality approach and the *Lemon* test, which the Burger Court left as legacies. Both neutrality and *Lemon* remain, but they have undergone many alterations and certainly have different and more conservative meanings than they did at the beginning of the Rehnquist Court.

In the Court's first major Establishment Clause case, *Edwards v. Aguillard* (1987), the seven-person majority used both the neutrality approach and the three-part *Lemon* test to invalidate Louisiana's Creationism Act, which forbid the teaching of evolution in the public schools unless creation science, based upon a biblical interpretation of the origins of Earth, was also taught.

The next major Establishment Clause case was *Lee v. Weisman* (1992), a case that involved the constitutionality of public school–sponsored prayers at graduation ceremonies. Many Court experts thought that both neutrality and the *Lemon* test might be rejected by a conservative majority in this case. Rehnquist, Scalia, and White had long been critical of neutrality and the *Lemon* test; Kennedy had expressed strong support for an accommodationist approach; and the Court's two leading liberals were gone, with Souter replacing Brennan and Thomas replacing Marshall. The Bush administration sensed the timing was right for radical change and filed an amicus brief calling for the Court to rule the practice constitutional and overturn the *Lemon* precedent. Surprisingly, Kennedy wrote a majority opinion joined by Blackmun, O'Connor, Souter, and Stevens finding the policy unconstitutional. Kennedy's opinion did not reject the *Lemon* test, but it did not use the test either, relying instead on the principle of coercion, which Kennedy argued the Establishment Clause forbids.

The Rehnquist Court justices continued to struggle with both the proper approach and the appropriateness of the *Lemon* test. *Lemon* was used in some cases, typically with efforts being made to refine the test. The neutrality-versus-accommodation debate all but disappeared, but the liberal and conservative justices were in sharp disagreement about the proper interpretation of neutrality. The Court's recent cases of *Mitchell v. Helms* (2000) and *Zelman v. Simmons-Harris* (2002) reveal the Court's struggle over the proper principles for interpreting the Establishment Clause.

As discussed previously, *Mitchell* was a parochial aid case that saw a 5–4 majority approve a federal program that provided secular educational materials and equipment—for example, computer hardware and software—to both public and religious elementary and secondary schools. Thomas wrote a plurality opinion that was joined by Rehnquist, Scalia, and Kennedy that set forth highly accommodationist principles for interpreting the Establishment Clause, arguing that a parochial aid program is constitutional as long as it is offered on a neutral basis and is secular in nature. O'Connor and Breyer agreed that the program was constitutional, but they disagreed with Thomas's statement of Establishment Clause principles. Writing a strong dissent, Souter was joined by Stevens and Ginsburg in rejecting Thomas's plurality opinion, arguing that "the plurality would break with the law" and that "there is no mistaking the abandonment of doctrine that would occur if the plurality were to become a majority" (530 U.S. at 911).

Zelman was one of the Rehnquist Court's last Establishment Clause cases and one of the most important. The case involved the constitutionality of the Cleveland, Ohio voucher program that provides tuition payments for children attending parochial schools. The Court found the program to be constitutional in a 5–4 majority opinion written by Rehnquist and joined by Scalia, Thomas, Kennedy, and O'Connor. Rehnquist utilized the first two prongs of the *Lemon* test, arguing that the program had a secular purpose and that the primary effect of the program was neutral, neither advancing nor inhibiting religion. In a concurrence, O'Connor argued quite correctly that the Court's approach was similar to the test originally set forth by the Warren Court in the 1963 *Schempp* case. Souter wrote a stinging dissenting opinion joined by Stevens, Ginsburg, and Breyer. The liberals accused the conservative majority of reaching "doctrinal bankruptcy" and ignoring the clear meaning of the principle of neutrality.

The Rehnquist Court's last major Establishment Clause cases involved the display of the Ten Commandments on public property. *Van Orden v. Perry* (2005) involved a challenge to the placement of a six-foot-high monolith containing the Ten Commandments on the grounds of the Texas state capitol. In *McCreary County v. ACLU* (2005), the posting of the Ten Commandments in public courthouses was challenged as a violation of the Establishment Clause. The Rehnquist Court found the display of the Ten Commandments on the state capital grounds to be constitutional but ruled unconstitutional the posting of the Ten Commandments in courthouses. The Court not only reached opposite conclusions in these cases but also set forth in the controlling opinions diametrically opposed ideas regarding the proper interpretation of the Establishment Clause, thus muddying the waters even more.

In the *McCreary County* case, Souter's majority opinion, joined by Justices Stevens, O'Connor, Breyer, and Ginsburg, utilized the *Lemon* test and the neutrality approach to find unconstitutional the display of the Ten Commandments in public courthouses. Souter's opinion argued that the county's activities violated the first prong of the *Lemon* test because the purpose of the display was religious in nature. Souter also stressed that neutrality is the key principle in Establishment Clause analysis.

Scalia authored a dissenting opinion that was joined in its entirety by Rehnquist and Thomas and in part by Kennedy. Scalia made three major arguments. First, he rejected the neutrality argument of the majority, arguing that the United States has a long and continuous history of government accommodation of religion. Kennedy did not join this part of Scalia's dissent, but he did join the rest of Scalia's opinion. Scalia's second argument was that the majority used *Lemon* in a manner that both modified the test and increased the Court's hostility toward religion. Scalia's third major argument was that even under the *Lemon* test, the posting of the Ten Commandments in courthouses was constitutional because the displays had a valid secular purpose.

Scalia and his fellow accommodationists prevailed in *Van Orden*, where a 5–4 majority found the six-foot-high monolith containing the Ten Commandments on the grounds of the state capitol of Texas to be constitutional. Rehnquist wrote the controlling opinion, but it was joined by only Scalia, Thomas, and Kennedy. Breyer supplied the critical fifth vote to find the display constitutional, but he concurred only with the judgment and did not join any of Rehnquist's plurality opinion.

The conservative accommodationists agreed that *Lemon* was not an appropriate test for this type of case, but they were badly fragmented regarding the proper test to apply. Rehnquist's plurality opinion argued the Court should rely on "the monument's nature and the Nation's history" in deciding the case. Scalia, in a concurring opinion, indicated he could support Rehnquist's opinion, but he called for a more strongly accommodationist approach for interpreting the Establishment Clause. Thomas also wrote a concurring opinion, calling for a coercion approach to Establishment Clause analysis. Breyer, who did not join any of these opinions, argued that a case like this requires an "exercise of legal judgment." The dissenting group of Stevens, Ginsburg, Souter, and O'Connor produced three separate opinions in *Van Orden*, with a common theme being that the proper general approach to Establishment Clause cases is neutrality.

We can conclude this examination of the Rehnquist Court's Establishment Clause jurisprudence by summarizing briefly the public policy contours that the Court set forth. Several major cases involved religion and the schools. The Rehnquist Court handed down several liberal decisions, including rulings that found unconstitutional a requirement to teach creation science, in *Edwards v. Aguillard* (1997); rejected school-sponsored prayers at public graduation ceremonies, in *Lee v. Weisman* (1992); and declared unconstitutional school-sponsored prayers before high school football games, in *Santa Fe v. Doe* (2000). In a more conservative ruling, the Rehnquist Court ruled 5–4 in *Good News Club v. Milford Central School* (2001) that the Establishment Clause is not violated by allowing a private Christian organization for children to use public school facilities after school. The Rehnquist Court was supportive of parochial aid programs, overturning two prior cases that had banned various forms of parochial assistance and giving approval to the controversial Cleveland school-voucher program. Finally, the Court drew some close lines in regard to religious displays on public property, but these cases typically involved plurality opinions with minimal value as precedents.

To conclude this analysis of the Establishment Clause, the answer to the question of whether the Rehnquist Court engaged in a conservative constitutional counterrevolution must be negative, but it is a close call. Three justices—Rehnquist, Scalia, and Thomas—clearly favored such a revolution, thus allowing a high degree of government involvement with religion. Four liberal justices—Stevens, Souter, Ginsburg, and Breyer—were committed to stronger principles separating church and state. Kennedy and O'Connor's views were critical and were not easily predictable, but they served as a check on the efforts of the conservative justices to interpret the Establishment Clause in a radically conservative manner.

Free Exercise of Religion

The First Amendment's Free Exercise Clause reads: "Congress shall make no law . . . prohibiting the free exercise [of religion]." This simple pronouncement suggests a profound affirmation and clear codification of religious tolerance in the United States, but the Court's interpretation of the text has been far more ambiguous than the constitutional language would suggest. Although Free Exercise Clause cases have been far less frequent than Establishment Clause cases, and the Court has often found the free exercise right subsidiary to concerns over a governmental establishment of religion, the Free Exercise Clause places limits on the government's ability to burden both religious belief and practice.

During the Warren and Burger Court eras, the Court utilized a compelling government-interest test developed in *Sherbert v. Verner* (1963) for laws that presented a substantial burden to the free exercise of religion. Under this test, the Court was willing to protect individuals from laws interfering with their religious liberty by granting exemptions from government laws unless the government could show that it was pursuing a compelling government interest by narrowly tailored means.

In *Employment Division, Department of Human Resources of Oregon v. Smith* (1990) (henceforth *Oregon v. Smith*), however, the Rehnquist Court dramatically altered the liberal *Sherbert* test by ruling that no religious exemptions can be allowed to government laws that have a secular purpose and that apply generally to the population. The difference between the logic in *Sherbert* and *Smith* reveals that the Rehnquist Court produced a conservative revolution within the confines of Free Exercise Clause jurisprudence, but a much deeper examination of the evidence is necessary to support this argument.

The Pre–Warren Court Period

We begin with *Reynolds v. United States* (1879), the Court's first major free exercise case. *Reynolds* involved doctrines of the Church of Jesus Christ of Latter-day Saints promoting polygamy for Mormon males. Polygamy within the Mormon Church was very unpopular in the United States, and it led to conflict between Mormons and the general population. Laws were passed specifically to counteract Mormon polygamy in federal territories in the West. Although polygamy violated federal law, church leaders asserted that their right to marry multiple women was integral to their religious beliefs. The Supreme Court, however, unanimously rejected religious arguments in favor of polygamy, creating a distinction between religious beliefs and religious practices. The Court held that Congress could enact laws that impinged on religious practices that were overt criminal acts. Chief Justice Waite wrote for the Court, "To permit [religious practices that are contrary to the law] would be to make professed doctrines of religion superior to the law of the land" (98 U.S. at 166–167). Thus, the Court's initial Free Exercise Clause case established the nonexemption principle: individuals must conform to valid laws even if it means they must violate their religious beliefs.

Following *Reynolds*, Court doctrine remained unchanged until the New Deal era. In the forties, the Court decided several major cases involving the religious practices of Jehovah's Witnesses. In *Cantwell v. Connecticut* (1940), the Court applied the Free Exercise Clause to a state law for the first time.

Following *Cantwell*, the Court decided two major cases involving salutes to the American flag and the free exercise of religion. Both cases involved Jehovah's Witnesses, who are forbidden by their faith to salute the flag. In *Minersville School District v. Gobitis* (1940), the Court ruled 8–1 that children who violated the flag salute law could be expelled from school. In a decision seemingly influenced by threats to national security as Europe and Asia were enveloped by war, Justice Felix Frankfurter summarized the Court's reasoning by noting: "National unity is the basis of national security" (310 U.S. at 595). However, Justice Jackson considered national aspirations instead of national security three years later, as the Court explicitly overturned *Gobitis* in *West Virginia Board of Education v. Barnette* (1943). Writing for a 6–3 majority, Jackson argued:

> The freedom to differ is not limited to things that do not matter much. That would be a mere shadow of freedom. The test of its substance is the right to differ as to things that touch the heart of the existing order (310 U.S. at 642).

The Warren Court Period

The Warren Court thus inherited an ambiguous record in regard to free exercise cases. On the one hand, *Barnette* was a strong precedent supporting the exemption approach. On the other hand, *Reynolds* stood for a nonexemption philosophy and had not been overruled.

In some ways, the early years of the Warren Court showed less deference to religious practice than the New Deal courts. In 1961, in *Braunfeld v. Brown*, for example, the Court ruled that laws forcing businesses to close on Sundays did not violate the Free Exercise Clause because they did not compel people to act against their religious beliefs. However, the Warren Court eventually became more favorable toward an expansive view of the Free Exercise Clause and is most notable for developing the rationale of the doctrinal test that would govern free exercise cases until 1990.

In *Sherbert v. Verner* (1963), the Court ruled 7–2 in favor of a woman who lost her job because she refused to work on Saturdays, establishing a strict scrutiny test that allowed for limited exemptions from government laws. The state of South Carolina had determined that Sherbert, a Seventh-day Adventist, was fired for just cause and denied her unemployment benefits. However, Sherbert felt that the compulsory Saturday work violated her Free Exercise Clause rights because she was forced into violating her religious faith or losing her benefits. Justice Brennan's opinion applied a three-prong strict scrutiny test to the Free Exercise Clause. First, the Court must determine whether a law or government action imposes a burden on the free exercise of religion. If a burden exists, the second element is that the law must promote a compelling government interest. Brennan intended this to be a difficult test for the government to meet, with few governmental interests being sufficiently compelling to justify interference with religious freedom. Furthermore, even if a compelling interest exists, the third consideration of the test is whether the government is using narrowly tailored means to achieve its compelling interests. Justice Brennan determined that South Carolina had burdened Sherbert's religious practice and further that South Carolina could show no compelling interests in denying Sherbert's benefits. Although the Warren Court decided only five free exercise cases, the *Sherbert* test became the accepted doctrinal test for this issue area until 1990.

The Burger Court Period

For the most part, the Burger Court continued the Warren Court's adherence to the *Sherbert* test, strict scrutiny, and the exemption approach. In *Wisconsin v. Yoder* (1972), the Court ruled 6–1 that members of Amish communities were exempt from compulsory education statutes, because education beyond eighth grade violated three-century-old religious traditions of their faith. Despite Chief Justice Burger's assertion that education is a critical responsibility of government, he wrote for the majority that the faith community's religious considerations took priority over the state's interest, especially in light of the Amish community's long tradition of supporting its own members.

After *Yoder,* the Burger Court continued to utilize the *Sherbert* test, overturning a Tennessee law against allowing ministers to serve in elected office (*McDaniel v. Paty,* 1978) and voting 8–1 to require the payment of unemployment benefits to a person who quit his job for religious reasons (*Thomas v. Review Board of Indiana Employment Security Division,* 1981).

However, the justices became more willing to recognize the existence of a compelling government interest in upholding federal laws in the last years of the Burger Court. In *United States v. Lee* (1982), the Court ruled unanimously that Amish employers could be compelled to pay Social Security taxes for Amish employees, notwithstanding claims that the Amish faith required a community-based support system for its destitute members. In *Bob Jones University v. United States* (1983), the Court by an 8–1 vote upheld a federal decision to deny educational benefits to a private college that discriminated against African Americans because the founder's religious beliefs called for a separation of the races. Chief Justice Burger wrote that the government's interest in eradicating racial discrimination in education was compelling, and the denial of tax benefits to the university was a narrowly tailored means to that objective.

In the Burger Court's final year, two conservative decisions foreshadowed the eventual demise of the *Sherbert* test, although this was far from clear at the time. First, the Court voted 5–4 to uphold federal regulations that prohibited the wearing of a yarmulke by a Jewish member of the U.S. Air Force in *Goldman v. Weinberger* (1986). Justice Rehnquist's five-person majority decision noted that "courts must give great deference to the professional judgment of military authorities" in cases that involve a military issue (475 U.S. at 507). In *Bowen v. Roy* (1986), the Court rejected the claim of a Native American who felt that his free exercise rights were violated by a federal law that required him to obtain a Social Security card for his daughter if he was to seek government benefits for her. Despite Roy's claims that providing information about his two-year-old daughter to the government robbed the girl's spirit, a Court plurality determined that requirements for governmental benefits are reasonable "absent proof of an intent to discriminate against particular religious beliefs or against religion in general," provided the requirement is "neutral and uniform in application" (476 U.S. at 708). To a significant degree, Burger's test in *Bowen v. Roy* is the same as the *Smith* test. Thus, although the justices were divided in *Bowen*, some members of the Court were poised to revisit the strict scrutiny test when William Rehnquist became chief justice in 1986.

The Rehnquist Court Period

In examining the free exercise cases of the Rehnquist Court era, quantitative analyses provide relatively little insight because so few cases were decided in this area of constitutional law; indeed, the Court decided only three free exercise cases in the natural court period from 1994 to 2005. Table 3.3 shows that the Rehnquist Court was somewhat more conservative than either the Warren Court or the Burger Court, but the differences are not large enough to support a conclusion that the Rehnquist Court engaged in a conservative constitutional counterrevolution. A careful qualitative examination of major cases does support this conclusion, however.

Table 3.3: Liberal/Conservative Voting in Free Exercise of Religion Cases by the Warren, Burger, and Rehnquist Courts, 1953–1954 to 2004–2005 Terms

Court Era	Liberal Decisions	Conservative Decisions	Total Cases
Warren Court (1953–1968 Terms)	60% (3)	40% (2)	5
Burger Court (1969–1985 Terms)	50% (5)	50% (5)	10
Rehnquist Court (1986–2004 Terms)	42% (5)	58% (7)	12
Total	48% (13)	52% (14)	27

Source: Harold J. Spaeth, *United States Supreme Court Judicial Database, 1953–2004 Terms* (Ann Arbor, MI: Inter-University Consortium for Political and Social Research, 2005).

The Rehnquist Court's initial free exercise cases did not suggest that profound constitutional change was imminent. In *Hobbie v. Unemployment Appeals Commission of Florida* (1987), for example, the Court heard another case involving the denial of unemployment compensation to a woman who quit her job for religious reasons. This case raised a new type of issue because she developed her religious beliefs after she took her job. An 8–1 majority ruled that the *Sherbert* precedent controlled and that Hobbie's free exercise rights had been violated.

The Rehnquist Court's attack on the strict scrutiny test of *Sherbert* began with the 1988 case of *Lyng v. Northwest Indian Cemetery Protective Association.* The U.S. Forest Service sought to pave a road between two towns, but a federal government study reported that building the road "would cause serious and irreparable damage to the sacred areas which are an integral and necessary part of the belief systems and lifeway of Northwest California Indian peoples" (485 U.S. at 442). Despite this report, the Forest Service decided to build the road, and Native Americans brought suit in federal district court. The court ruled in favor of the Native Americans, and the Ninth Circuit Court of Appeals used the *Sherbert* test to affirm the lower court decision.

The Supreme Court, however, reversed the Ninth Circuit in a remarkable decision that rejected the strict scrutiny test of *Sherbert.* Writing for a five-person majority, O'Connor acknowledged that building the road could "virtually destroy . . . the Indians' ability to practice their religion" (485 U.S. at 451), but she nonetheless said their First Amendment freedom of religion would not be violated. Introducing a new coercion test, O'Connor argued that if government programs do not coerce individuals into violating their religious beliefs, then such programs are constitutional. Brennan wrote a bitter dissent joined by Marshall and Blackmun in which he argued that the Court's coercion test lacked any basis in either the text of the Constitution or the Court's free exercise precedents.

Lyng appeared to be a major new free exercise precedent, but its effects proved to be limited. In terms of public policy, Congress passed a law in 1990 making the disputed area protected wilderness territory, thus ensuring the road would not be built. In addition, *Lyng* has rarely been cited in subsequent free exercise of religion cases, and in the Court's next three religious freedom cases, the strict scrutiny approach was utilized: *Frazee v. Illinois Department of Employment Security* (1989), *Hernandez v. Commissioner of Internal Revenue Service* (1989), and *Jimmy Swaggart Ministries v. Board of Equalization of California* (1990). Thus, although *Lyng* did not prove to be a major new conservative precedent for the Rehnquist Court, it did signal that a majority of the justices were unhappy with the *Sherbert* test, and in *Oregon v. Smith* (1990), a five-person majority rejected the *Sherbert* strict scrutiny test and adopted a minimal scrutiny approach.

Clearly, the most important free exercise case during the Rehnquist Court era was *Oregon v. Smith* (1990). In *Smith*, a member of the Native American Church lost his job as a drug and alcohol counselor with a private treatment center because he used peyote as part of his church sacraments. Peyote is a hallucinogenic drug that was illegal in Oregon at that time, although some states had laws allowing members of the Native American Church to use it in religious ceremonies. Smith had signed an agreement not to use drugs while working in the treatment program. When Oregon's Department of Human Services, Employment Division, determined that drug use was an appropriate reason to terminate the employment of a drug and alcohol abuse counselor, he was denied unemployment compensation.

Attorneys for both Smith and the state of Oregon assumed that the strict scrutiny test of *Sherbert* was controlling in this unemployment compensation case. The debate between the two sides thus focused on the question of whether Oregon had a compelling interest in denying unemployment compensation to Smith. In a surprising and unexpected decision, however, the Rehnquist Court in ruling for Oregon severely undermined—without explicitly overturning—the *Sherbert* strict scrutiny test and instead substituted a minimal scrutiny or nonexemption test that requires all persons to conform to valid, religiously neutral, generally applicable laws, even if this requires one to violate his religious beliefs.

Justice Scalia wrote the five-person majority decision in *Smith* that undermined the *Sherbert* test, asserting that the Court since *Reynolds v. United States* (1879) has recognized that the Free Exercise Clause does not prevent the application of "an otherwise valid law prohibiting conduct that the state is free to regulate" (494 U.S. at 879). Scalia asserted that the Court's seemingly liberal line of cases, including *Cantwell* and *Yoder*, could all be explained by recognizing that they involved the "Free Exercise Clause in conjunction with other constitutional provisions, such as freedom of speech and of the press" (494 U.S. at 879). Additionally, Scalia noted that the Court had never invalidated state actions under the *Sherbert* test in stand-alone free exercise cases, except in cases involving state unemployment compensation concerning religious objections to work requirements. Scalia also argued that applying the compelling interest test generally to free exercise cases "would be courting anarchy" (494 U.S. at 888), while allowing such constitutional outliers as the *Sherbert* and related unemployment cases was inconsistent with recent cases and sound judicial practice. Finally, Scalia acknowledged that "leaving accommodation to the political process will place at a relative disadvantage those religious practices that are not widely engaged in, . . ." but this was an "unavoidable consequence of democratic government" (494 U.S. at 890).

Four justices—Brennan, Marshall, Blackmun, and O'Connor—were outraged at what they saw as an unjustified departure from the Court's long-standing commitment to the *Sherbert* test of strict scrutiny. Joined by her liberal colleagues, O'Connor argued that "today's holding dramatically departs from well-settled First Amendment jurisprudence, appears unnecessary to resolve the question presented, and is incompatible with our Nation's fundamental commitment to individual religious liberty" (494 U.S. at 890). Interestingly, O'Connor did think that Oregon met the burden of the compelling interest test, and thus she joined the judgment of the Court in favor of Oregon.

The Court's decision in *Oregon v. Smith* was criticized not only by Brennan, Marshall, Blackmun, and O'Connor but also by Court scholars, religious leaders, and political figures. One concern focused on the Court's treatment of precedent, with some critics arguing that the Court misinterpreted precedent and other critics contending that the majority badly distorted precedent. Another criticism involved the charge that the validity of the *Sherbert* test was not raised in either the written briefs or oral argument, and therefore it was improper for the Court to consider—let alone reject—the strict scrutiny test. The strongest criticism involved concerns that the new *Smith* test would seriously harm religious minorities, who could now experience significant encroachments on their religious practices with no effective way of challenging these governmental actions.

In response to these concerns, Congress passed in 1993 the Religious Freedom Restoration Act (RFRA). In this remarkable law, Congress was openly critical of the Court's decision in *Oregon v. Smith* and sought to replace the *Smith* minimal scrutiny test with the *Sherbert* strict scrutiny test.

The Court rejected this challenge to its authority in *City of Boerne v. P. F. Flores* (1997), ruling the RFRA unconstitutional. The Court did not treat this as a free exercise case but rather saw it as a separation of powers case. Writing for the majority, Kennedy argued that Congress had vastly exceeded its powers in RFRA, and therefore the obligation of the Court was to declare the law unconstitutional. Thus, the attempt by Congress to override the *Smith* decision was rejected sharply by the Rehnquist Court.

The only significant free exercise case decided by the Court since *Smith* was *Church of the Lukumi Babalu Aye v. City of Hialeah* (1993). This case reaffirmed the

Smith test, but it also revealed that government laws could be found unconstitutional even under the minimal scrutiny standards of *Smith*.

Members of the Church of the Lukumi Babalu Aye are Santerians, an Afro-Caribbean religious sect that combines elements of the Roman Catholic faith and Yoruban ethnic religious customs as passed down among slaves on the Caribbean islands. One controversial element of Santerian religious practice is animal sacrifice. This controversy became an issue in Hialeah, Florida, after the Santerians purchased land and announced plans to build a church within Hialeah. Faced with the prospect of animal sacrifice and concerns over cruelty to animals within the city, Hialeah passed an ordinance that outlawed the practice. Although Hialeah argued that the law was neutral and generally applicable, inasmuch as it applied to anyone who would sacrifice an animal, the residents' panicked reaction and the close proximity of the emergency passage of the ordinance with the announcement of the church's plans made the purpose of the ordinance clear.

The Supreme Court was unanimous in deciding to overturn the Hialeah ordinance, but the reasoning varied. Justice Kennedy, joined by Rehnquist, White, Stevens, Scalia, and Thomas, applied the *Smith* test and found that the Santerian practice was protected because Hialeah's ordinance was not neutral. Instead, the ordinance was aimed at a specific religious group and was not neutral in its intent or application. Kennedy argued that such laws were still subject to the compelling government interest test. Justices Souter, Blackmun, and O'Connor concurred with the judgment of the Court, but Blackmun (joined by O'Connor) and Souter wrote separate opinions questioning the rationale in *Smith*.

Hialeah was the Rehnquist Court's last major free exercise case, although the Court did decide a minor religious freedom case in 2004, *Locke v. Davey*. In this case, Joshua Locke won a college scholarship from the state of Washington, but he was subsequently denied the award because the state did not allow the scholarship to be utilized to major in devotional theology. Davey claimed that this was a violation of his rights under the Free Exercise Clause, but a 7–2 majority rejected his claim. Chief Justice Rehnquist's brief majority opinion gave little attention to the proper standard of review. Instead, he argued that this case could be distinguished from *Hialeah* because the state imposed only a minor burden on Davey and the state had a substantial interest in not supporting the pursuit of devotional degrees under state sponsorship. It seems doubtful that *Locke* will prove to be a significant free exercise precedent.

The *Smith* test stands in sharp contrast to the *Sherbert* test. In *Smith* the Court rejected strict scrutiny in favor of a minimal scrutiny approach that basically allows for no religious exemptions to secular, neutral laws. This is a clear example of a significant conservative doctrinal change that has rendered the Supreme Court a secondary player in protecting religious liberty in the United States. Since *Smith*, both Congress and the executive branch—under both Republican and Democratic leadership—have acted to extend religious freedom to minority religious groups, including American Indians. Meanwhile, the Court has maintained its silent adherence to *Smith* for more than a decade.

Freedom of Expression

Having analyzed the two religion clauses of the First Amendment, we now turn our attention to the remaining clauses of the amendment, the freedom of expression guarantees. The language of the First Amendment specifies four forms of expression: "Congress shall make no law . . . abridging the freedom of speech, or of the press; or the right of the people peaceably to assemble, and to petition the government for a redress of grievances." The Court has never viewed the First Amendment freedom of expression guarantees as being limited to speech, press, assembly, and petition, however. Individuals can communicate ideas in a wide variety of ways, and the Court has been generous in recognizing these activities as coming within the protection of the First Amendment; for example, the Court has stated that the Constitution protects such diverse activities as tenting, when it is done to protest the plight of the homeless, and nude dancing.

In this section of chapter 3, we examine the record of the Rehnquist Court in the important and frequently controversial area of freedom of expression. One area—obscenity and pornography—is reserved for a separate section, however, because this area has been an extremely busy one for the Court, it is a highly controversial subject of constitutional law, and it has its own unique line of precedents and doctrines.

Did the Rehnquist Court engage in a conservative constitutional counterrevolution in regard to the First Amendment freedom of expression guarantees? The answer to this question is clear and unequivocal: no. Quantitative data in table 3.4 reveal that the Rehnquist Court decided a majority—62 percent—of its freedom of expression cases liberally, a somewhat more liberal record that the Burger Court, which had a 48 percent liberal record. Furthermore, the Rehnquist Court adhered consistently to the liberal precedents of the Warren and Burger Courts; the Rehnquist Court did not create a single new conservative precedent in any major freedom of expression case.

The Pre–Warren Court Period

An understanding of the Rehnquist Court's freedom of expression policies requires some historical perspective. Given the magnificent language of the Declaration of Independence and the Bill of Rights, it is easy to assume that American society and the U.S. Supreme Court have always been deeply committed to freedom of expression principles. The reality, however, is quite different. Reflecting the values of American society, the Court has over time provided varying levels of protection to these First Amendment ideas, and it has only been in the last fifty years that the Court has provided consistently high levels of protection to most forms of freedom of expression.

A useful way of thinking historically about the Court's general approach to interpreting the expression guarantees of the First Amendment is to contrast the balancing and preferred freedoms ideas. The balancing approach provides only minimal protection for expression, weighing First Amendment claims against competing government interests, which are viewed as equally valid with freedom of expression interests. In actual application, the balancing approach almost always results in the government prevailing because the arguments of the government typically carry greater weight than the reasoning of the individual. In contrast, the preferred position approach views First Amendment freedom of expression values as critically important to American democracy and therefore deserving of a high level of protection from government interference. Under the preferred freedoms theory, the individual claiming a First Amendment violation can be expected to prevail unless the government can show exceptionally strong interests in limiting expression.

The Supreme Court generally used the balancing approach throughout the nineteenth century and the first half of the twentieth century. The Court heard very few freedom of expression cases until the twenties because these guarantees were not nationalized, that is, made applicable to the states, until *Gitlow v. New York*, in 1925. In the few cases the justices did decide, they typically used a conservative balancing approach to decide in favor of the government. Thus, in *Schenck v. United States* (1919), the Court ruled unanimously that Charles Schenck's First Amendment rights were not violated when he was arrested and convicted under the 1917 Espionage Act for mailing fifteen thousand brochures to young American males, criticizing U.S. involvement in World War I and urging them to resist the draft.

The Court's support for freedom of expression values varied in the period from the twenties to the fifties, but the balancing approach tended to prevail over the preferred position orientation. The Court did establish some important liberal precedents during this period, especially as Democratic President Franklin Delano Roosevelt was able to appoint new justices to the Court. For example, in *West Virginia Board of Education v. Barnette* (1943), the Court ruled unconstitutional a requirement that schoolchildren must at the beginning of each school day stand and salute the flag while reciting the Pledge of Allegiance. Children of members of the Jehovah's Witnesses refused to participate, were expelled from school, and ultimately appealed to the Supreme Court on First Amendment grounds. Justice Robert Jackson authored one of the most eloquent opinions in Supreme Court history: "If there is any fixed star in our constitutional constellation, it is that no official, high or petty, can prescribe what shall be orthodox in politics, nationalism, religion, or other matters of opinion or force citizens to confess by word or act their faith therein. If there are any circumstances which permit an exception, they do not now occur to us" (310 U.S. at 642).

Despite the stirring language of *Barnette* and decisions in other cases where the Court used the preferred freedoms approach, the preponderance of the Court's freedom of expression decisions during the period from the twenties to the early fifties were based upon the conservative balancing approach. For example, in *Dennis v. United States* (1951), the Court ruled 6–2 against ten leaders of the Communist Party of the United States who had been arrested under the 1940 Smith Act that made it a crime to organize or join any group advocating violent revolution against the United States. Justice Hugo Black in dissent argued that the preferred freedom approach should have been used: "There is hope, however, that in calmer times, when present pressures, passions and fears subside, this or some later Court will restore the First Amendment liberties to the high preferred place where they belong in a free society" (341 U.S. at 579).

The Warren Court Period

Black was a member of the Warren Court who fulfilled his hope that First Amendment freedom of expression cases would be analyzed through the lens of the preferred freedoms position. Although the Warren Court did not approach all freedom of expression cases from the preferred freedoms philosophy, the Warren Court justices revolutionized this important area of constitutional law by generally requiring the government to meet a high burden of proof before interfering with freedom of expression activities. Numerous examples can be cited. In *Yates v. United States* (1957), the Warren Court reached a dramatically different decision than in *Dennis* in finding that the First Amendment rights of American Communist Party officials had been violated by their arrests under the Smith Act. In another national security case in 1969—*Brandenburg v. Ohio*—the Warren Court set forth the liberal incitement test that stated that speech directed at revolutionary activities could be punished only when a speaker engages in direct incitement to imminent lawless action and the action is likely to occur. In the area of libel law, the Warren Court unanimously strengthened freedom of the press by requiring public officials to prove that a news story was not only false and defamatory—the previous standard—but also done with "actual malice," that is, with knowledge that a statement was false or with a reckless disregard for the truth. In *Roth v. United States*, in 1957, the Warren Court justices also provided vastly greater protection for sexual expression. A final example of the Warren Court's commitment to the preferred freedoms position can be seen in *Tinker v. Des Moines Independent Community School District* (1969), a case in which the Court applied a preferred freedom position in regard to schoolchildren in ruling 7–2 that the First Amendment was violated when school officials suspended children from public school for wearing black armbands containing a peace symbol during the Vietnam War era.

The Burger Court Period

The Burger Court was generally supportive of the preferred freedoms position of the Warren Court, but the Court under Chief Justice Burger was both less innovative and less supportive of freedom of expression claims than the Warren Court. As Tinsley Yarbrough observes, "The Burger Court's impact on [the] provisions of the First Amendment safeguarding freedom of expression and association was significant but more subtle than fundamental, elaborating upon Warren-era and earlier precedents while both narrowing and expanding their scope" (2000, 161).

Several important cases can be cited in which the Burger Court justices strongly supported freedom of expression values. *New York Times v. United States* (1971) involved an attempt by the Nixon administration to block the publication by the *New York Times* and *Washington Post* of *The Pentagon Papers*, a history of U.S. involvement in the Vietnam War. Rejecting government claims that national security was being compromised, the Court in a *per curiam* decision ruled in favor of the newspapers because the government had not met the strong burden necessary to justify censorship or prior restraint. In another 1971 case, the justices ruled in *Cohen v. California* that a young war protestor's freedom of expression rights were violated when he was arrested and convicted for wearing in a courthouse a jacket with the words "F**k the Draft" written on it. Justice Harlan's majority opinion spoke powerfully to the preferred freedom approach to the First Amendment:

> The constitutional right of free expression is powerful medicine in a society as diverse and populous as ours. It is designed and intended to remove governmental restraints from the arena of public discussion, putting the decision as to what views shall be voiced largely into the hands of each of us, in the hope that use of such freedom will ultimately produce a more capable citizenry and more perfect polity and in the belief that no other approach would comport with the premise of individual dignity and choice upon which our political system rests (403 U.S. at 24).

The Burger Court also expanded significantly constitutional protection for commercial speech—advertising—which had not been given any degree of First Amendment protection by the Warren Court or in any previous Court era. In *Bigelow v. Virginia* (1975), the Burger Court recognized that commercial speech does come within the meaning of freedom of expression, and then in *Central Hudson Gas v. Public Ser-*

vice Commission (1980), the Burger Court justices adopted a test that provided heightened scrutiny for commercial speech.

Despite these cases and others that revealed a liberal orientation toward freedom of expression guarantees, the Burger Court also handed down decisions that were distinctively conservative. In the area of obscenity, for example, Chief Justice Burger, writing for a five-person majority in *Miller v. California* (1973), modified the liberal standards of the Warren Court's *Roth* test with the intention of giving government greater power to regulate obscene materials. Another example of the Burger Court's more conservative orientation to freedom of expression can be seen in the public school case of *Bethel School District v. Fraser* (1986). Without overturning *Tinker*, Chief Justice Burger took a highly deferential position toward school authorities by approving disciplinary action against a high school student who used sexually suggestive language in a speech at a high school assembly.

The Rehnquist Court Period

This admittedly brief analysis of the historical treatment of the First Amendment freedom of expression guarantees provides the background for a more detailed analysis of the activities of the Rehnquist Court in this important area of constitutional law. The argument has already been made that the Rehnquist Court did not engage in a conservative constitutional counterrevolution in regard to the freedom of expression guarantees of the First Amendment, but little evidence has been produced to support this position. We turn, therefore, first to a quantitative analysis of the Rehnquist Court, comparing it to the Warren and Burger Courts, and then we will engage in a qualitative analysis of some of the major freedom of expression cases of the Rehnquist Court.

Looking initially at the quantitative data, table 3.4 contains important information comparing the overall voting records of the Warren, Burger, and Rehnquist Courts. The results show that the Warren Court, as expected, was distinctively liberal, deciding 74 percent of its freedom of expression cases liberally. The Burger Court was split almost equally between liberal and conservative outcomes, deciding 48 percent of its cases liberally. The Rehnquist Court, at 62 percent, was more liberal than the Burger Court, and this constitutes important evidence supporting the argument that the Rehnquist Court did not engage in a conservative constitutional counterrevolution in this major area of the Constitution.

Important insights into the behavior of the Rehnquist Court justices can be gained by extending the quantitative analysis to include an examination of the voting patterns of individual justices. Table 3.5 shows the voting behavior of the fourteen justices who served on the Rehnquist Court. The data in this table do not allow for easy

Table 3.4: Liberal/Conservative Voting in Freedom of Expression Cases by the Warren, Burger, and Rehnquist Courts, 1953–1954 to 2004–2005 Terms

Court Era	Liberal Decisions	Conservative Decisions	Total Cases
Warren Court (1953–1968 Terms)	74% (108)	26% (39)	147
Burger Court (1969–1985 Terms)	48% (74)	52% (81)	155
Rehnquist Court (1986–2004 Terms)	62% (66)	38% (41)	107
Total	60% (248)	40% (161)	409

Source: Harold J. Spaeth, *United States Supreme Court Judicial Database, 1953–2004 Terms* (Ann Arbor, MI: Inter-University Consortium for Political and Social Research, 2005).

Table 3.5: Liberal/Conservative Voting Records of the Justices of the Rehnquist Court in Freedom of Expression Cases, 1986–1987 Term to 2004–2005 Term (Justices Ranked from Most Conservative to Most Liberal)

Justices	Liberal Decisions	Conservative Decisions	Total Cases
Rehnquist	24% (24)	76% (78)	102
White	29% (16)	71% (40)	56
Thomas	32% (19)	68% (41)	60
Scalia	35% (36)	65% (67)	103
Kennedy	50% (46)	50% (47)	93
O'Connor	53% (55)	47% (49)	104
Powell	57% (4)	43% (3)	7
Breyer	60% (29)	40% (19)	48
Stevens	65% (68)	35% (36)	104
Ginsburg	62% (25)	38% (15)	40
Souter	72% (48)	28% (19)	67
Blackmun	75% (44)	25% (15)	59
Brennan	88% (35)	12% (5)	40
Marshall	89% (40)	11% (5)	45

Source: Harold J. Spaeth, *United States Supreme Court Judicial Database, 1953–2004 Terms* (Ann Arbor, MI: Inter-University Consortium for Political and Social Research, 2005).

interpretations. Although nine of the fourteen justices have voted liberally more than 50 percent of the time, the three leading liberals of the Rehnquist Court era—Blackmun, Brennan, and Marshall—retired from the Court in the early nineties. Focusing on the natural court that began in 1994, we can classify three justices as moderate liberals: Breyer (60 percent liberal), Ginsburg (62 percent liberal), and Stevens (65 percent liberal). Only Souter at 72 percent liberal falls into the classification as strongly liberal. Rehnquist was the only strongly conservative justice on the Court, with a 24 percent liberal voting record, while two justices can be considered moderate conservatives: Scalia (35 percent liberal) and Thomas (32 percent). O'Connor and Kennedy occupy the critical middle, with O'Connor voting liberally in 53 percent of the cases and Kennedy at exactly 50 percent. Thus, the Rehnquist Court was closely balanced in freedom of expression cases, making prediction very difficult in this area of constitutional law.

As we have already discussed, although quantitative analysis is valuable, it must be supplemented by various forms of qualitative analysis. This involves examining the Rehnquist Court's treatment of existing freedom of expression precedents, discussing the general doctrinal framework that the Rehnquist Court developed in the area of freedom of expression, and analyzing some of the major areas of freedom of speech and freedom of the press to assess the Court's policies regarding these First Amendment guarantees.

Looking initially at the Rehnquist Court's treatment of existing freedom of expression precedents, it is important to recall the argument that a conservative constitutional counterrevolution requires that the justices have overturned at least one major liberal precedent. This did not occur. The Rehnquist Court decided only 38 percent of its freedom of expression cases conservatively, and none of these involved overturning a major liberal precedent. The only conservative decision in which the Rehnquist Court justices modified precedent was a minor case, *Thornburgh v. Abbott* (1989), which involved the Court creating a reasonableness standard instead of a heightened scrutiny standard regarding the refusal of prison officials to forward mail to inmates.

The most effective way of understanding the Rehnquist Court's treatment of freedom of expression cases involves a description of the four-part doctrinal framework that is presented in table 3.6. The underlying principle in this approach is that expression can take numerous forms in American society, and different forms of expression deserve different levels of protection from the courts because of their importance to our democratic system of government. Two stark examples can help to clarify this point. The Court has ruled that both political opposition to war and nude dancing are forms of expression that come within the scope of the First Amendment. The Court has also recognized, however, that expression of opposition to U.S. involvement in a war is critically important in a democratic society, whereas nude dancing can claim at best only slight importance. Thus, the Court provides an extremely high level of protection

Table 3.6: The Rehnquist Court's Four-Level Doctrinal Framework for the Analysis of Freedom of Expression Cases

Test	Compelling Government-Interest Test	Important Government-Interest Test	Rational Basis Test	Incitement/Libel Obscenity/Fighting Words
Level of Scrutiny	Strict	Intermediate	Minimal	None
Types of Cases Where Applicable	Pure speech and press Censorship Content-based regulation Viewpoint-based regulation Traditional and designated public forums Internet	Symbolic speech Commercial speech Cable broadcasting	Students Prisoners Government employees Conflict with other rights Radio and TV broadcasting Nonpublic forums Content-neutral regulations Speech plus conduct	Libel Obscenity Fighting words Incitement
Questions Asked by the Court	(1) Is the government pursuing a compelling interest? (2) If so, are the means used by the government narrowly tailored to achieve the compelling interest?	(1) Is the government pursuing an important objective? (2) If so, are the means used by the government closely related to the important objective?	(1) Is the government pursuing a legitimate objective? (2) If so, are the means used by the government rationally related to the legitimate objective?	Unique test for each form of expression

for expression of political opposition to a war and only minimal protection for nude dancing.

We need to examine each level of the doctrinal framework in some detail, beginning with the approach that provides the highest level of protection, the strict scrutiny or compelling government-interest test. Because these forms of expression are so central to a democratic form of government, the government must meet extremely high standards to interfere with these types of expression. Specifically, the government must establish that it is pursuing a compelling interest and, if this is done, then the government must show that it is pursuing this compelling interest by narrowly tailored means. These standards make it exceptionally difficult—although not impossible—for the government to convince the justices that interference with freedom of expression does not violate the First Amendment.

What types of cases fall within the strict scrutiny category and why? As can be seen in table 3.6, cases involving pure speech and press are given this highest level of protection. This includes the street-corner orator and the editorials in the daily newspaper. Such forms of expression are viewed as central to the effective communication of ideas in a democratic society and as posing little inherent threat to public safety and order.

Other forms of expression receiving strict scrutiny include the closely related ideas of censorship, content-based regulations, and viewpoint-based regulations. Censorship, or the prior restraint of ideas, is viewed as antithetical to democratic government. Censorship means that ideas never get expressed, and this is a power of government associated with dictatorships, not democracies. Content-based regulation is closely related to censorship, but it does not go as far; it is a form of censorship that applies to the discussion of particular ideas or topics. Viewpoint-based regulation is similar to content-based regulation, but it involves prior restraint regarding a particular position regarding an idea or topic. An example might help to clarify the differences among censorship, content-based regulations, and viewpoint-based regulations. If a city prohibits the use of a city park for political discussion, this is censorship; if the city allows political discussion but prohibits the discussion of a war, this is content-based regulation; and if the city allows discussion of a war but only by proponents of a war, this is viewpoint-based regulation.

The Court has also applied the strict scrutiny test in cases involving traditional and designated public forums. A traditional public forum is a place like a city park that has been used for a long period of time as a gathering place where people have come to express their ideas on public issues. This long-standing tradition creates a high level of protection for such expression. A designated public forum is one that may not always be available for public discussions but is frequently used by governments for this purpose, for example, a city hall, and this area also receives strict scrutiny protection.

The Rehnquist Court has decided numerous cases using the strict scrutiny approach; several major examples are discussed here. *Florida Star v. B.J.F.* (1989) was a censorship case. Under Florida law, it was illegal to publish the name of any victim of a sex offense, but a newspaper printed the name of a rape victim. She sued and won both compensatory and punitive damages. In a 5–4 decision authored by Justice Marshall and joined by Justices Brennan, Blackmun, Stevens, and Kennedy, the Court ruled in favor of the newspaper by holding that imposing these damages constituted a form of censorship in violation of freedom of the press. Marshall argued that newspapers can be punished for publishing truthful, lawfully obtained information only if strict scrutiny standards are met, and in this case the state did not have a compelling governmental interest nor were the means narrowly tailored.

Texas v. Johnson (1989) involved the highly controversial topic of flag burning, and the Court used the strict scrutiny standard in finding a Texas law prohibiting flag burning to be unconstitutional. In an unusual coalition, Justice Brennan wrote a majority opinion joined by Justices Marshall, Blackmun, Kennedy, and Scalia. Brennan reasoned that the Texas law involved content-based regulation, triggering the Court's strict scrutiny approach. Texas argued that they had a compelling interest of promoting the cause of national unity, but Brennan's opinion rejected this position: "The way to preserve the flag's special role is not to punish those who feel differently about these matters. It is to persuade them that they are wrong" (491 U.S. at 419).

A final example of the Rehnquist Court's use of the strict scrutiny in freedom of expression cases can be found in *Reno v. American Civil Liberties Union* (1997), a case involving the presence of sexual expression on the Internet. As the Internet has grown in popularity, many individuals and groups have expressed concern about the availability of sexually oriented materials, and a special concern has been the availability of such materials to minors. In response, Congress passed the Communications Decency Act (CDA) of 1996. Two provisions of the CDA were especially controversial and were subjected to First Amendment challenges. An "indecency" provision stipulated that criminal fines and up to two years in prison could occur if a person was convicted of knowingly transmitting indecent messages to persons under eighteen years of age. The "patently offensive" section made it criminal to knowingly communicate about sexual or excretory activities in terms that were patently offensive under contemporary community standards.

This was the first case in which the Court considered the Internet, and the most important question for the Court was what standard to use in evaluating this new form of communication. In a 7–2 opinion, Justice Stevens argued that the Internet should receive the Court's highest level of protection, strict scrutiny. Stevens acknowledged that both radio and television receive lower levels of protection because of the presence of government regulation, the scarcity of available frequencies, and the invasive nature of radio and television, but none of these characteristics were associated with the Internet. In applying the two prongs of the strict scrutiny test, Stevens found that the government did have a compelling interest in protecting minors from potentially harmful materials, but the means utilized were not narrowly tailored to meet this government interest.

In addition to the strict scrutiny standard, the Court also has developed an intermediate scrutiny standard that provides heightened protection for individuals claiming a governmental violation of their freedom of expression rights, but this level of protection is not as strong as that provided by strict scrutiny. Intermediate scrutiny requires the government to prove that they are pursuing an important state interest (as opposed to a compelling interest under strict scrutiny) and that the means used are closely related to the important objective (as opposed to being narrowly tailored under strict scrutiny).

The intermediate scrutiny standard is used in a limited range of cases in which the Court has determined that these types of expression deserve more than minimal protection but less than the highest level of protection. Specifically, intermediate scrutiny applies in cases involving symbolic speech, commercial speech, and cable broadcasting.

Symbolic speech involves the use of symbols to communicate ideas, for example, burning a draft card. Symbolic speech can be an effective way of expressing ideas, but because symbols can trigger powerful emotions and reactions leading to disruptions and violence, the Court gives symbolic speech less protection that pure expression. Commercial speech or advertising is viewed by the Court as deserving heightened protection under intermediate scrutiny but not strict scrutiny because it is concerned with economic rather than political communication. Cable broadcasting is viewed as falling between the minimal scrutiny given to regular radio and television and the strict scrutiny afforded pure speech, pure press, and the Internet.

An example case involving the use of the intermediate scrutiny standard in a commercial speech case is *44 Liquormart v. Rhode Island* (1996). The case stemmed from a Rhode Island law that prohibited businesses from advertising the retail price of alcoholic beverages. In 1991, 44 Liquormart placed an ad in a newspaper that did not mention the exact price of certain alcoholic beverages but did use the word *WOW* in large letters by bottles of vodka and rum in the ad. Competitors of 44 Liquormart filed a complaint, and Rhode Island fined the establishment $400 for its ad. The store 44 Liquormart filed suit in federal district court alleging a violation of the owners' First Amendment freedom of expression rights. The district court found the law to be unconstitutional, but a federal circuit court reversed, upholding the law.

The Rehnquist Court unanimously found the law to be unconstitutional, but the justices split sharply in their reasoning. Justice Stevens authored the plurality opinion of the Court. He argued that the Court uses a less than strict scrutiny standard in commercial speech cases, but Rhode Island could not meet the lower standards of intermediate scrutiny or even the minimal scrutiny standard because no logical connection could be made between the state's goal of promoting temperance and its method of a complete ban on the price of alcoholic beverages. Stevens's language suggested that the strict scrutiny standard might be applied to truthful, nonmisleading ads, but a majority of the justices distanced themselves from this position.

Turner Broadcasting System v. Federal Communications Commission (1994) is an example case of the Court using the intermediate scrutiny standard in regard to cable broadcasting. This case centered on the constitutionality of a 1992 federal law, the Cable Television Consumer Protection and Competition Act. The specific sections that were challenged involved "must carry" provisions that required cable operators to include in their offerings a specified number of both commercial and educational local stations. This was the Supreme Court's first major case involving cable broadcasting. Attorneys for the federal government argued that the Court should use minimal scrutiny as it does in cases involving broadcast radio and television, whereas attorneys for Turner Broadcasting System argued that the Court should use strict scrutiny. The Court rejected both positions. Writing for an eight-person majority, Justice Kennedy argued instead that the proper test was that of intermediate scrutiny as long as the regulation was content-neutral. Kennedy's support diminished to a five-person majority when he argued that the regulations were content-neutral and that the government was pursuing important objectives. This complex opinion became even more fractured when only a four-person plurality existed to find the means used were not constitutionally permissible, thus nullifying the must carry provisions of the law.

In addition to the standards of strict and intermediate scrutiny, the Rehnquist Court also employed a minimal scrutiny standard in freedom of expression cases. The logic underlying this test is that various forms of expression are significant enough to come within the protection of the First Amendment, but for various reasons they do not rise to the level of importance that they deserve the higher levels of protection afforded by the intermediate and strict scrutiny tests. Thus, under the minimal scrutiny or rational basis test, the government needs only to establish that it is pursuing a legitimate government purpose and that the means being utilized have a rational relationship to this legitimate purpose. These are typically easy criteria for the government to meet, and thus the government usually prevails in cases involving the minimal scrutiny test.

As can be observed in table 3.6, the Rehnquist Court applied the minimal scrutiny or rational basis test in a wide variety of cases. These include cases involving elementary and secondary students, prisoners, government employees, conflicts involving freedom of expression and other rights, radio and television broadcasting, nonpublic forums; content-neutral regulations, and speech-plus-conduct cases. Two example cases can be discussed involving the Court's use of minimal scrutiny: *Hazelwood*

School District v. Kuhlmeier (1988), involving high school students, and *Rankin v. McPherson* (1987), involving public employees.

The *Hazelwood* case involved a high school principal, Robert Reynolds, censoring two articles scheduled to appear in the *Spectrum*, the student newspaper of Hazelwood East High School, in St. Louis County, Missouri. One article focused upon three students who were pregnant, and the other article dealt with the impact of divorce on Hazelwood students. Three students on the staff of the *Spectrum* filed suit against the principal, alleging that his actions violated their First Amendment freedom of expression rights. A federal district court ruled against the students, but a court of appeals reversed, finding in favor of the students.

Justice White authored a five-person majority opinion joined by Rehnquist, Scalia, O'Connor, and Stevens. White gave little credence to the students' argument that this case involved censorship triggering strict scrutiny. He also dismissed the students' argument that the *Spectrum* was a public forum, thus requiring the use of strict scrutiny. Instead, White emphasized the primacy of local school boards in setting and implementing school policy. Applying minimal scrutiny standards, Principal Reynolds's actions were determined by White to be reasonable under the circumstances.

The *Rankin* case began with comments by Ardith McPherson, an African American woman who was a clerical worker in the office of Walter Rankin, the constable of Harris County, Texas. McPherson and other public employees learned in March 1981 of the assassination attempt on the life of President Ronald Reagan. McPherson suggested that the gunman might have been African American because of the cutbacks Reagan was making on welfare programs benefiting African Americans, and she remarked: "If they go for him again, I hope they get him" (483 U.S. at 381). When Rankin learned of McPherson's remarks, he fired her. McPherson brought suit claiming a violation of her freedom of speech liberty under the First Amendment.

Justice Marshall wrote an opinion favoring McPherson for a five-person majority that included Justices Brennan, Blackmun, Stevens, and Powell. Marshall argued that this case involved a public employee, thus triggering a minimal scrutiny balancing approach. For Marshall and the majority, McPherson's First Amendment rights outweighed the government's interest because her remarks presented little threat to the effective functioning of the government office. The *Rankin* case thus represents the rather unusual situation in which the individual prevails even though minimal scrutiny is employed.

One final category of freedom of expression cases remains to be discussed. This category involves expression that is outside the parameters of the First Amendment and thus receives no protection from government regulation and punishment. Four specific types of expression can be identified—libel, obscenity, fighting words, and incitement. All four of these share the common characteristic that they are so lacking in social value as to be beyond the protection offered by the First Amendment. Libel involves the printing of false and defamatory words with knowledge that they are false or with reckless disregard of the truth. Obscenity is sexual expression that lacks a serious purpose and that violates acceptable community standards. Fighting words are those expressions that are so provocative that they are likely to cause an immediate, violent response from the listener. Finally, incitement involves expression that encourages others to engage in immediate, lawless action.

We examine in some detail two of the libel cases decided by the Rehnquist Court. Obscenity cases are discussed in the next section of this chapter because this is an especially controversial and highly litigated area of freedom of expression. In contrast, the Rehnquist Court heard few cases involving either fighting words or incitement.

The Warren Court set the modern standard for libel in the 1964 case of *New York Times v. Sullivan*. Before this case, courts could find a written statement libelous if it met two conditions: if it was false and if it was defamatory. The Court unanimously introduced a new third condition that had to be met for a statement involving public officials to be libelous: if the statement was made with knowledge that it was false or with a reckless disregard of the truth. This new, liberal standard was extended by the Warren Court to public figures in two 1967 cases, *Curtis Publishing Co. v. Butts* and *Associated Press v. Walker*.

Although the Rehnquist Court did not hear many libel cases, they adhered to the standards established by the Warren Court (and extended by the Burger Court). This can be seen in the 1991 case of *Masson v. New Yorker Magazine*. Janet Malcolm was a writer for the *New Yorker Magazine*, and she did a story on a prominent Freudian psychologist named Jeffrey Masson. Masson claimed that Malcolm used a number of direct quotes in her story that Masson did not make; he argued that the story was false, that it was defamatory, and that it was done with actual malice. Two lower federal courts ruled in favor of Malcolm, but the Supreme Court reversed. In a 7–2 decision authored by Justice Kennedy, the Court focused on the concept of falseness; Kennedy argued that although the mere changing of words is not sufficient to establish falseness, in this case Malcolm had changed the meaning of Masson's words significantly enough to make them false.

Hustler Magazine v. Falwell (1988) was undoubtedly the Rehnquist Court's most famous case relating to libel, in part because the case achieved national publicity when it was made into a film—*The People vs. Larry Flynt*—starring Woody Harrelson and Courtney Love. The case arose out of an advertising parody in *Hustler Magazine* published by Larry Flynt. Campari Liqueur had a national advertising campaign using the double entendre "the first time" to describe the experience of famous people when they experienced Campari for the first time. *Hustler* ran a series of parodies based upon the Campari ad about famous people experiencing their first sexual encounter. In one ad, Jerry Falwell, a famous minister and conservative political leader, was portrayed as having his first sexual encounter with his drunken mother in the family's backyard outhouse. Falwell sued for libel, invasion of privacy, and the intentional infliction of emotional distress, winning $150,000 in district court on the latter issue. The Rehnquist Court, however, found 8–0 in favor of *Hustler* and Flynt, ruling that the *New York Times* standard applied in this case. This meant that Falwell, a public figure, could not receive compensation for the intentional infliction of emotional distress unless proving that a false statement was made with actual malice, and this was not done because a parody could not be false. Speaking for a unanimous Court, Chief Justice Rehnquist authored a ringing endorsement of the preferred freedoms approach to the First Amendment:

> At the heart of the First Amendment is the recognition of the fundamental importance of the free flow of ideas and opinions on matters of public interest and concern. . . . We have therefore been particularly vigilant to ensure that individual expressions of ideas remain free from government imposed sanctions. The First Amendment recognizes no such thing as a "false" idea (485 U.S. at 50–51).

This review of the Rehnquist Court's freedom of expression cases has established that the Court under Rehnquist's leadership was distinctively liberal in this area of the First Amendment. Although less liberal than the Warren Court, the Rehnquist Court was more liberal than the Burger Court and certainly did not engage in a conservative counterrevolution in this important area of constitutional law. One area of freedom of expression—obscenity—has not yet been analyzed, however, and thus we now turn our attention to this controversial topic.

Obscenity

The Supreme Court's most controversial and difficult area of freedom of expression has involved obscenity. The Court has never viewed the obscene as coming within the protection of the First Amendment, but the Court has had enormous difficulty in trying to define that which is obscene and therefore beyond the First Amendment. Obscenity involves sexual expression that lacks social value and that violates acceptable community standards, and this means that most sexual expression is not obscene. A major problem for the Court and for American society has been where to draw the line in dealing with such vague concepts as "social value" and "community standards." Definitional problems are not the only ones confronting the Court in this difficult area, however. Another major controversy involves the question of whether obscene materials are harmful and, if they are harmful, to whom and to what extent. Yet another controversial issue associated with obscenity involves changing sexual values over the last half century in American society, which has become more tolerant and accepting of explicit sexual expression. These are formidable obstacles indeed for the Supreme Court, and they help to explain Justice Potter Stewart's frustration in the 1964 case of *Jacobellis v. Ohio* when he lamented that the Court was "faced with the task of trying to define what may be indefinable" (378 U.S. at 197). Stewart in the same opinion stated that he might not be able to define the obscene but observed that "I know it when I see it" (378 U.S. at 197).

Our central concern throughout this book is whether the Rehnquist Court engaged in a conservative constitutional revolution, and the answer to that question in regard to obscenity is no. The Warren Court did undertake a liberal revolution in this area, and the Burger Court responded with a limited conservative counterrevolution while adhering to many of the principles of the Warren Court. The Rehnquist Court remained committed to the basic principles guiding the Warren and Burger Courts although typically applying these principles to achieve conservative outcomes.

The Pre–Warren Court Period

A detailed understanding of the Rehnquist Court's obscenity decisions requires a brief overview of the proceeding eras of Supreme Court history. We will examine three periods: the pre-Warren Court era, the Warren Court, and the Burger Court.

Obscenity was not much of an issue in the initial 150 years of American society from the creation of the Bill of Rights to the post–World War II period. Indeed, the Court did not decide a single case in this era involving obscenity and the First Amendment. The Court did assume, however, that the obscene was beyond constitutional protection. In *Chaplinsky v. New Hampshire* (1942), for example, the Court observed that forms of expression lacking in social value were not protected from government regulation by the First Amendment, and such forms of expression included the obscene, the libelous, the profane, and fighting words.

American society changed dramatically in the decade following World War II in regard to sexual expression. Whatever the causes, and they were multiple, sexually oriented materials became increasingly prevalent, epitomized in this period by the beginning of the *Playboy* empire. In reaction to this rapid growth of sexual expression in American society, governments at all levels began to develop laws to control sexually oriented expression, and the sanctions of government—fines and arrests—became increasingly more frequent. Some individuals subject to these sanctions challenged them in court, frequently arguing that their First Amendment freedom of expression rights were being violated. It was thus only a matter of time before the Supreme Court would have to face the difficult issue of obscenity.

The Warren Court Period

Roth v. United States (1957) was the Warren Court's initial attempt to deal with obscenity and the First Amendment. Writing for a five-person majority, Brennan argued that although the obscene was beyond constitutional protection, the First Amendment's guarantees of freedom of expression must be observed to the maximum extent possible because they are so vital to American democracy. Drawing upon the efforts of American courts, Brennan argued that the obscene should be defined as follows: "whether to the average person, applying contemporary community standards, the dominant theme of the material taken as a whole appeals to prurient interests" (354 U.S. at 489). The *Roth* test eventually evolved into a three-part test, known as the *Roth/Memoirs* test, set forth in the 1966 case of *A Book Named "John Cleland's Memoirs of a Woman of Pleasure" v. Massachusetts*. To be found obscene, a work had to meet all of the following characteristics: (1) the material's dominant theme taken as a whole had to appeal to a prurient interest in sex, (2) the material had to present sex in a patently offensive manner based upon national standards, and (3) the material had to be utterly without redeeming social value.

Brennan and the Warren Court were clearly committed to a broad liberal interpretation of obscenity that provided constitutional protection for all but the most extreme forms of sexual expression. The data in table 3.7 show that this was a busy topic for the Warren Court, with twenty-two cases, and the Court decided 73 percent of these cases liberally, that is, in favor of the individual or organization claiming a First Amendment violation because of government regulation of sexually oriented

Table 3.7: Liberal/Conservative Voting in Obscenity Cases by the Warren, Burger, and Rehnquist Courts, 1953–1954 to 2004–2005 Terms

Court Era	Liberal Decisions	Conservative Decisions	Total Cases
Warren Court (1953–1968 Terms)	73% (16)	27% (6)	22
Burger Court (1969–1985 Terms)	30% (10)	70% (23)	33
Rehnquist Court (1986–2004 Terms)	33% (6)	67% (12)	18
Total	44% (32)	56% (41)	73

Source: Harold J. Spaeth, *United States Supreme Court Judicial Database, 1953–2004 Terms* (Ann Arbor, MI: Inter-University Consortium for Political and Social Research, 2005).

expression. The Warren Court justices were deeply divided over how to define *obscenity*, however, and no opinion after *Roth* was joined by a majority of the justices. By the end of the Warren Court period, the typical approach of the justices was simply to reverse summarily lower-court obscenity convictions without any attempt being made to define *obscenity*. The only areas where consensus seemed to exist involved the wide range of latitude the Court was willing to give to government efforts to prohibit child pornography and to protect citizens from being subjected to unwanted displays of sexual material, such as advertisements.

The Burger Court Period

The Nixon administration expressed strong opposition to the liberal orientation of the Warren Court regarding obscenity, and Nixon's four new appointees—Burger, Blackmun, Rehnquist, and Powell—shared this concern. In *Miller v. California* (1973), these four members of the Burger Court were joined by Justice White in an opinion authored by Chief Justice Burger that significantly modified the *Roth/Memoirs* test. Although the new *Miller* test contained many of the same provisions as the *Roth/Memoirs* test, two major innovations were introduced. First, the previous national standard was replaced with a new state and local standard, and second, the old standard—that works must be utterly without redeeming social value—was rejected and replaced by the new "LAPS test," under which a work could be found obscene if it lacked serious literary, artistic, political, or scientific value. Thus, a new three-part *Miller* test for obscenity emerged: "(1) whether 'the average person, applying contemporary community standards,' would find the work, taken as a whole, appeals to the prurient interest . . . ; (b) whether the work depicts or describes, in a patently offensive way, sexual conduct specifically defined by the applicable state law; and (c) whether the work, taken as a whole, lacks serious literary, artistic, political, or scientific value" (413 U.S. at 24).

The Burger Court's *Miller* decision had far-reaching effects. One important result was the introduction of more conservative standards for judging sexual expression, and the data in table 3.7 show clearly that the Burger Court (30 percent liberal) was much more conservative than the Warren Court (73 percent liberal). A second important effect of the *Miller* decision was to keep the issue of obscenity an active one for the Burger Court, which handed down written opinions in thirty-three cases, an average of two per term. A third effect, one that was unintended but not surprising, involved continued confusion over the definition of *obscenity*. Despite the Burger Court's efforts to achieve greater definitional clarity, ambiguity remained. The terms *prurient interest* and *patently offensive* had been retained from the *Roth/Memoirs* test but remained as ambiguous as ever. The new LAPS test proved to be difficult to apply because of the uncertainty associated with determining if a work has serious social value. In addition, the determination of contemporary local standards proved to be as difficult as assessing national community standards. A fourth and final effect, one that was both unintended and unexpected, was a dramatic rise during the Burger Court era from 1969 to 1985 in both the quantity of sexual expression and its explicitness, despite the tighter standards of the *Miller* test. This development seems to have been related both to the market system, in which a strong demand existed that meant high profits could be earned, and to evolving, more permissive community standards regarding what was acceptable in sexual expression.

One area where the Burger Court did have consensus involved the subject of child pornography. In *New York v. Ferber* (1982), a unanimous Court upheld a New York law that criminalized the production and distribution of materials depicting children under the age of sixteen engaging in sexual activities. The justices agreed that the evidence of harm associated with child pornography was so strong that it could be made illegal even if it was not obscene under *Miller.*

The Rehnquist Court Period

How did the Rehnquist Court approach the area of obscenity? In regard to the central concern of the book, the Rehnquist Court did not engage in a conservative constitutional counterrevolution. Instead, the Rehnquist Court followed closely the pattern of the Burger Court, supporting the three-prong *Miller* test and ruling conservatively in the vast majority of cases. Several differences from the Burger Court can also be observed, however. The Rehnquist Court heard substantially fewer sexual expression cases than the Burger Court; furthermore, most of the Rehnquist Court cases did not deal with obscenity per se but rather with government regulation of sexual expression within the protection of the First Amendment, and the Rehnquist Court surprised some Court experts by ruling liberally in regard to sexual expression over the Internet.

Quantitative data provide important insights into the decisional patterns of the Rehnquist Court in regard to the limits of sexual expression in American society. Table 3.7 compares the Warren, Burger, and Rehnquist Courts, and the table reveals two important characteristics. First, the Rehnquist Court has voted virtually identically (67 percent conservative) with the Burger Court (70 percent conservative), while the Warren Court was far less conservative, at 27 percent. Second, the Rehnquist Court was somewhat less active in this area, deciding only eighteen cases compared to thirty-three cases by the Burger Court and twenty-two by the Warren Court. Because the Court controls its agenda, it seems reasonable to conclude that the Rehnquist Court justices made decisions to limit their attention to cases of sexual expression raising the most significant social issues.

The voting records of the individual justices who have served on the Rehnquist Court are shown in table 3.8. Focusing upon the last natural court that existed from 1994 to 2005, we can observe a plurality conservative coalition consisting of Scalia, Rehnquist, O'Connor, and Thomas, with conservative voting patterns ranging from 83 percent by Scalia to 70 percent conservative by Thomas. A three-person liberal coalition can be observed, with Souter at 73 percent liberal, Ginsburg at 78 percent liberal, and Stevens voting 94 percent liberal. Kennedy and Breyer occupy the middle ground, with Kennedy voting 65 percent conservative and Breyer at 56 percent conservative. The data in table 3.8 thus show that the Court lacked a majority bloc in the area of obscenity, and the justices appeared to be deeply divided over these cases.

Useful as quantitative analysis is, we also need to engage in the qualitative examination of the decisions of the Rehnquist Court in cases involving sexual expression. This analysis will reveal that the Rehnquist Court was predominantly conservative in its decisions involving sexual expression, supporting both state and federal laws regulating and punishing those who go beyond the defined limits of sexual communication. The Rehnquist Court did not, however, create new conservative precedents in this area of constitutional law, adhering to the basic principles of the *Miller* test set

Table 3.8: Liberal/Conservative Voting Records of the Justices of the Rehnquist Court in Obscenity Cases, 1986–1987 Term to 2004–2005 Term (Justices Ranked from Most Conservative to Most Liberal)

Justices	Liberal Decisions	Conservative Decisions	Total Cases
Powell	0% (0)	100% (1)	1
Scalia	17% (3)	83% (15)	18
Rehnquist	22% (4)	78% (14)	18
O'Connor	24% (4)	76% (13)	17
Thomas	30% (3)	70% (7)	10
White	33% (3)	67% (6)	9
Kennedy	35% (6)	65% (11)	17
Breyer	44% (4)	56% (5)	9
Blackmun	56% (5)	44% (4)	9
Souter	73% (8)	27% (3)	11
Ginsburg	78% (7)	22% (2)	9
Stevens	94% (17)	6% (1)	18
Brennan	100% (7)	0% (0)	7
Marshall	100% (8)	0% (0)	8

Source: Harold J. Spaeth, *United States Supreme Court Judicial Database, 1953–2004 Terms* (Ann Arbor, MI: Inter-University Consortium for Political and Social Research, 2005).

forth by the Burger Court. Furthermore, the Rehnquist Court on occasion ruled liberally in favor of the individual or organization challenging existing governmental laws regulating sexual expression.

Beginning with the Court's liberal decisions, we can examine cases involving the interpretation of the *Miller* test, the regulation of sexual content over the Internet, government efforts to deal with "virtual child pornography," and government controls over sexual expression involving cable television. Despite the liberal outcomes of these cases, however, deep divisions characterized these decisions.

An early obscenity decision for the Rehnquist Court involved the interpretation of the third prong of the *Miller* test. In *Pope v. Illinois* (1987), the issue was whether state or national standards should apply to the third prong of the *Miller* test, which asks whether a work taken as a whole lacks serious literary, artistic, political, or scientific value (the LAPS test). Pope was arrested under an Illinois law for selling obscene magazines, he was convicted under all three prongs of *Miller*, and each of the three questions involved the use of the community standards of citizens of Illinois. In a majority opinion written by Justice White, the Rehnquist Court ruled that only the first two prongs of the *Miller* test involve state standards; the LAPS test requires a broader national standard. Although this central holding was supported by all members of the Court, the ubiquitous conflict in obscenity cases also existed in *Pope*. One point of contention was the decision of a conservative majority to return the case to the lower court, where the conviction could stand if the error was found to be harmless, whereas the liberals argued the conviction should be reversed. Another major point of contention was the opposition to the entire *Miller* test by Brennan, Marshall, and Stevens, who argued that *Miller* was bad constitutional law and that obscenity laws like those in Illinois were unconstitutional unless they focused on protecting minors or regulating objectionable displays to unconsenting adults.

The Internet is another area in which the Rehnquist Court ruled liberally in regard to sexual expression. *Reno v. ACLU* (1997) is the most important of the cases involving the federal government attempting to regulate sexual content over the Internet. This case involved challenges to two portions of the 1996 Communications Decency Act (CDA), which was concerned with controlling the availability of sexual materials over the Internet to persons under eighteen years of age. The American Civil Liberties Union (ACLU) challenged two provisions of the act, one prohibiting the knowing transmission of indecent messages to anyone under eighteen and the other criminalizing the sending of patently offensive communication to persons under eighteen. Both provisions provided for fines and prison sentences of up to two years. A three-judge district court panel ruled unanimously to enjoin enforcement of the provisions, and the Rehnquist Court agreed to hear the case.

This was a landmark case because it was the Court's first decision involving the Internet, and a seven-person majority in an opinion written by Justice Stevens gave strong constitutional protection to the Internet by applying the strict scrutiny test and finding both provisions unconstitutional. Stevens acknowledged that other media forms like radio, television, and cable had been given lower levels of constitutional protection by the Court, but he argued that the Internet was fundamentally different from radio, television, and cable. The Internet did not have an extensive history of government regulation, it did not have limited frequencies, and its presence in the home could be regulated more easily by parents. This strict scrutiny standard meant that the government needed to show a compelling interest achieved by narrowly tailored methods. Stevens acknowledged a strong governmental interest but argued that the means were not sufficiently narrow; in addition, the laws had problems of vagueness and overbreadth.

Reno was an important development in constitutional law because of the strong protection given by the Court to the Internet, but it did not result in Congress backing away from attempting to regulate sexual expression over the Internet. And, as is discussed shortly, the Court has given approval to other efforts by Congress to control sexual expression over the Internet.

In addition to handing down liberal decisions in regard to the third prong of the *Miller* test and the Internet, the Rehnquist Court also reached a liberal outcome in the 2002 case of *Ashcroft v. Free Speech Coalition*, a case involving virtual child pornography. At issue in this case was the constitutionality of the Child Pornography Prevention Act of 1996 (CPPA). This law criminalized depictions of child pornography that did not involve real children, including computer-generated images and visual depictions of young-looking adults over the age of eighteen. This law was challenged by the Free Speech Coalition, a California-based trade association representing adult film companies. Lower federal courts came to contradictory conclusions about the constitutionality of the CPPA, and the Rehnquist Court agreed to hear the case.

A majority of the Court ruled the act unconstitutional, with the three liberals in this area—Stevens, Ginsburg, and Souter—being joined by Breyer, Kennedy, and Thomas. Writing for the majority, Kennedy considered two key precedents of *Miller v. California* (1973) and *New York v. Ferber* (1982), and he argued that these precedents provided no support for Congress and the CPPA. *Miller* requires three conditions for material to be found obscene, and the CPPA did not require any of these three elements. For example, material banned under the CPPA did not have to appeal to a prurient interest in sex; the matter need not be patently offensive; and the depictions could have serious literary, artistic, political, or scientific value. In regard to the *Ferber* precedent that allowed for greater government control over child pornography, Kennedy argued that the CPPA could find no support in *Ferber*. The *Ferber* decision rested upon the assumption that child pornography is harmful in many ways, but because the CPPA is directed at virtual child pornography, where no actual child is involved, the harm argument cannot be considered persuasive. Kennedy thus concluded that the CPPA went well beyond the guidelines provided by *Miller* and *Ferber*, thus resulting in the suppression of constitutionally protected freedom of expression.

A final example of a liberal decision by the Rehnquist Court involving sexual expression is *United States v. Playboy Entertainment Group* (2000), a case dealing with government regulation of sexual content of cable programming. This case arose from concerns of the public and Congress about the transmission of sexually explicit material over cable television. Attempts were made to scramble such programming to prevent minors and unwilling adults from viewing it, but the technology did not prevent all visual and audio transmissions. Congress sought to deal with this issue by passing Section 505 of the Telecommunications Act of 1996, which required cable programmers either to scramble fully sexually explicit shows or to restrict such programming to the hours of 10 p.m. to 6 a.m., when children were less likely to watch television. Playboy Entertainment Group filed suit on First Amendment grounds, and a three-judge district court ruled in favor of Playboy.

The Rehnquist Court supported the district court ruling that the congressional enactment violated the First Amendment. Justice Kennedy wrote the majority opinion, joined by Stevens, Ginsburg, Souter, and Thomas. Kennedy reasoned that the law was a form of content-based regulation, thus requiring the strict scrutiny test. Kennedy agreed that the government did have a compelling interest in terms of preventing exposure of youth to such programming, but the methods used to achieve this interest were not sufficiently narrow. A more appropriate method was suggested involving individual households requesting the blockage of such programming.

These examples make clear that the Rehnquist Court was willing to rule unconstitutional various forms of government regulation of sexual expression, but the predominant approach of the Court was to give constitutional approval to governmental policies controlling sexually explicit materials. Several major decisions can be discussed to illustrate this conservative orientation of the Court. Specifically, we examine cases involving child pornography, public nudity, government funding of the arts, and the Internet.

The Warren, Burger, and Rehnquist Courts have been in agreement that the government can exercise broad control over child pornography, and *Osborne v. Ohio* (1990) illustrates the willingness of the Rehnquist Court to support government regulation and punishment of the use of children in sexual contexts. Clyde Osborne was arrested under an Ohio child pornography law for possessing in his home four sexually explicit photos of a nude fourteen-year-old male. This case presented the justices with a conflict between two leading precedents, *Stanley v. Georgia* (1969) and *New York v. Ferber* (1982). In *Stanley*, the Warren Court had ruled that persons could legally possess obscene materials in the privacy of their own homes, and in *Ferber*, the Burger Court had given the government extensive power to regulate child pornography. Writing for a six-person majority in *Osborne*, Justice White argued that *Ferber* not

Stanley controlled this case. The harm associated with child pornography was so great, White wrote, that the right to possess obscene materials in your own home does not extend to child pornography.

The conservative orientation of the Rehnquist Court can also be observed in two cases involving government bans on public nudity. The two leading cases are *Barnes v. Glen Theatre* (1991) and *City of Erie v. Pap's A.M.* (2000), with both cases involving nude dancing.

The *Barnes* case involved two South Bend, Indiana, businesses—the Kitty Kat Lounge and Glen Theatre—that wanted to offer nude dancing. This was prohibited, however, by an Indiana law requiring female dancers to wear pasties and G-strings. The establishments brought suit that the law violated the guarantees of the First Amendment. In a fractured decision, the Rehnquist Court voted 5–4 to uphold the Indiana statute. In a three-person plurality opinion, Chief Justice Rehnquist was joined by Justices Kennedy and O'Connor. He argued that nude dancing was protected by the First Amendment, even if "only marginally so" (501 U.S. at 566). He further argued that nude dancing was a form of symbolic expression triggering intermediate scrutiny and that Indiana's law met the requirements of this standard. Scalia and Souter agreed with the majority's judgment but not their reasoning. White, typically conservative in sexual expression cases, wrote a dissenting opinion joined by Blackmun, Marshall, and Stevens in which he argued that strict scrutiny should apply because the law involved content-based discrimination and that Indiana had neither a compelling interest nor narrowly tailored means.

The Rehnquist Court revisited *Barnes* in the 2000 case of *City of Erie v. Pap's A.M.* The *Erie* case was remarkably similar to *Barnes*. Pap's was a corporation operating a nude-dancing club called Kandyland, and dancers who wanted to perform nude were required by a Pennsylvania law to wear pasties and G-strings. The Court relied on *Barnes* to uphold the Pennsylvania law, but, as in *Barnes*, the justices could not reach a majority opinion. O'Connor wrote the plurality opinion joined by Rehnquist, Breyer, and Kennedy, reasoning that the intermediate scrutiny test should apply and that Pennsylvania met the requirements of the test.

Unlike the nude-dancing cases, the Rehnquist Court justices had less trouble in finding agreement in upholding by an 8–1 vote a federal government regulation requiring the National Endowment for the Arts (NEA) to take into account "general standards of decency" when awarding grants. This case—*National Endowment for the Arts v. Finley* (1998)—arose out of intense public controversy in the late eighties over grants awarded to photographers Andrew Serrano and Robert Mapplethorpe. Serrano was heavily criticized for "Piss Christ," a photo of a crucifix immersed in urine. Mapplethorpe similarly produced several controversial photographs, including one of a man urinating into the mouth of another man. In response to criticisms of these works, Congress considered abolishing the NEA but chose instead to write legislation requiring the NEA in judging grant applications to take into account general standards of decency as well as the values and beliefs of the American public. This was challenged in federal court and was ruled unconstitutional.

Although the 8–1 vote in the case suggested a high level of agreement among the Rehnquist Court justices, sharp differences could be found. Justice O'Connor's majority opinion rejected the arguments that the case involved censorship, viewpoint discrimination, or vagueness. According to O'Connor, Congress has wide latitude in regulating grants it finances, and this particular legislation was within the acceptable boundaries of the First Amendment. Scalia, joined by Thomas, took a much more conservative view, arguing that the case did involve viewpoint discrimination but that this was constitutional in regard to such funding decisions. In dissent, Souter wrote a lengthy opinion strongly rejecting the arguments of both O'Connor and Scalia.

We can conclude this analysis of the Rehnquist Court's decisions regarding obscenity and sexual expression by analyzing two recent cases involving regulation of the Internet. As was discussed earlier, the Rehnquist Court's first decision involving sexual expression and the Internet—*Reno v. ACLU* (1997)—found the Court ruling unconstitutional portions of the 1996 Communications Decency Act. This policy was concerned with protecting minors from inappropriate sexual materials over the Internet, and Congress was determined to try again despite the Court's position in *Reno*. These subsequent efforts gained the Court's approval in the cases of *Ashcroft v. ACLU* (2002) and *United States v. American Library Association* (2003), but the Rehnquist Court justices were deeply divided in both cases.

The *Ashcroft* case involved a challenge to the 1998 Child Online Protection Act (COPA). This was an attempt by Congress to avoid the problems in *Reno* by following closely the language of the three-part *Miller* test. A federal district court and an appeals court both found COPA to be unconstitutional based upon the *Reno* precedent, but the Supreme Court disagreed. The decision was a narrow one, however, focusing on the permissibility of the "community standards" provision of the first prong of the *Miller* test, and the Court could not reach a majority opinion. The case was sent back to the court of appeals to resolve several other issues, such as vagueness and the appropriate level of scrutiny.

The *American Library Association* (ALA) case of 2003 was similar in many ways to *Ashcroft*. The ALA case was also concerned with protecting children from inappropriate sexual communication over the Internet. Specifically, the case was a challenge to the constitutionality of the Children's Internet Protection Act of 2000. This congressional enactment withheld federal funds to libraries that did not utilize filtering software to block visual sexual images that could be harmful to minors. As in the *Ashcroft* case, lower federal courts rejected the law as unconstitutional, but the Rehnquist Court disagreed and upheld the law. Also as in *Ashcroft*, the Court was unable to reach a majority opinion, thus leaving this issue in considerable ambiguity.

We have now completed our examination of the First Amendment. In regard to the central question of whether the Rehnquist Court engaged in a conservative constitutional counterrevolution, an analysis of systematic, quantitative data as well as of the written opinions of the justices in leading cases leads to the conclusion that the Rehnquist Court has brought about fundamental change only in regard to the Free Exercise Clause. The Rehnquist Court justices moved away from the neutrality approach and the *Lemon* test in regard to the Establishment Clause, but the justices were not in consensus regarding new conservative standards in interpreting the Establishment Clause. Finally, although adhering to the conservative patterns of the Burger Court in obscenity cases, the Rehnquist Court was surprisingly liberal in other freedom of expression cases.

Guarantees of the Criminally Accused

Having examined in some detail the major constitutional guarantees within the First Amendment, we can now turn our attention to the rights of the criminally accused. Although a few criminal rights' guarantees are located in the main body of the Constitution—for example, the guarantee against bills of attainder, the prohibition on ex post facto laws, and the right of habeas corpus—the vast majority of the guarantees of the criminally accused are located in the Fourth, Fifth, Sixth, and Eighth Amendments.

The Fourth Amendment corresponds to the beginning of the criminal justice process, the investigatory and arrest stage. This amendment prohibits unreasonable searches and seizures, requiring that the issuance of a warrant be based upon probable cause.

The Fifth Amendment guarantees are varied, but they focus on the pretrial stage. The most important specific right is the protection against self-incrimination, but the Fifth Amendment also guarantees the right to a grand jury. In addition, the Fifth Amendment protects against double jeopardy and also contains a sweeping Due Process Clause ensuring that no person can be deprived of his or her rights to life, liberty, or property without due process.

The Sixth Amendment focuses upon the trial rights of the criminally accused. The most important of these is the guarantee of the right to counsel, but many other important constitutional provisions governing criminal trials are also found in the Sixth Amendment. These include the right to a speedy and public trial by an impartial jury, to confront one's accusers, to be notified of charges against you, and to have persons required to testify.

Finally, the Eighth Amendment focuses upon the penalty stage of the criminal justice process. The most litigated clause of the Eighth Amendment is the prohibition against cruel and unusual punishments. The Eighth Amendment also guarantees against excessive fines and bails.

The central theme of this book is whether the Rehnquist Court engaged in a constitutional counterrevolution. Given the differences among the constitutional guarantees within the Fourth, Fifth, Sixth, and Eighth Amendments, it certainly is necessary to examine separately the guarantees of each amendment to assess the extent of change in the decision making of the Rehnquist Court. The cases dealing with the rights of the criminally accused also have much in common, however, and therefore it makes sense to engage in a broad overview of the criminal rights area before undertaking an analysis of each specific amendment.

The Warren Court certainly engaged in a liberal constitutional revolution in regard to the rights of the criminally accused, but neither the Burger Court nor the Rehnquist Court achieved a conservative counterrevolution. The justices of the Warren Court had their most profound impact in the criminal justice field through their incorporation decisions, those cases that made many of the guarantees of the criminally accused applicable to the states. Specifically, the Warren Court nationalized the Fifth Amendment protection against self-incrimination (*Malloy v. Hogan*, 1964), the Fifth Amendment guarantee against double jeopardy (*Benton v. Maryland*, 1969), the Sixth Amendment right to counsel (*Gideon v. Wainwright*, 1963), the Sixth Amendment confrontation clause (*Pointer v. Texas*, 1965), the Sixth Amendment right to a speedy trial (*Klopfer v. North Carolina*, 1967), the compulsory process or subpoena power of the Sixth Amendment (*Washington v. Texas*, 1967), and the right to a trial by jury in the Sixth Amendment (*Duncan v. Louisiana*, 1968). In addition, the Warren Court made the exclusionary rule—banning from trial any evidence obtained illegally—applicable to the states in *Mapp v. Ohio* (1961). These cases revolutionized the American criminal justice system by now requiring all state and local law enforcement personnel to observe the guarantees of the U.S. Constitution and to meet federal standards of law enforcement.

The Warren Court's criminal rights revolution extended beyond the incorporation decisions into other important areas of the rights of the criminally accused. In *Miranda v. Arizona* (1966), for example, the Court introduced the requirement that law enforcement personnel must inform arrested suspects before questioning that they have the right to remain silent and the right to counsel. Yet another major innovation by the Warren Court in regard to criminal rights was to extend some of these guarantees to juveniles in *In re Gault* (1967).

These decisions by the Warren Court were highly controversial and were a major issue in the 1968 presidential election. Republican presidential candidate Richard Nixon strongly criticized Chief Justice Warren and the Court for what he viewed as their inappropriate judicial activism that allegedly "took the handcuffs off the criminals and put them on the police." Nixon promised that if he was elected he would appoint justices to the Court who would follow the language of the Constitution and restore a proper balance of power to the criminal justice system.

Nixon won the 1968 election and had the opportunity to appoint four new, more conservative members to the Court in his first term. His first and most important appointment was the replacement of Chief Justice Earl Warren by Warren Burger, who had been harshly critical of the criminal rights decisions of the Warren Court. Nixon also had the opportunity to replace three other Warren Court members with more conservative justices: Harry Blackmun for Abe Fortas, Lewis Powell for Hugo Black, and William Rehnquist for John Marshall Harlan.

Did the Supreme Court under Chief Justice Warren Burger engage in a conservative counterrevolution in regard to the guarantees of the criminally accused? The answer to the question is no. The Burger Court was certainly more conservative than the Warren Court. As can be seen in the data in table 3.9 covering all criminal procedure cases, the Warren Court ruled liberally in 58 percent of its cases compared to a 34 percent liberal voting record by the Burger Court. The Burger Court, however, did not overturn the major criminal rights precedents of the Warren Court, even if some of these precedents were modified and limited. As Tinsley Yarbrough has written, "In the field of criminal justice, the Burger Court perhaps came closest to achieving the constitutional counterrevolution Warren Court critics hoped for and its supporters feared. Yet even here the retrenchment was more subtle than profound" (2000, 193).

If the Burger Court failed to achieve a conservative counterrevolution in regard to the guarantees of the criminally accused, then was the Rehnquist Court with its con-

Table 3.9: Liberal/Conservative Voting in Criminal Procedure Cases by the Warren, Burger, and Rehnquist Courts, 1953–1954 to 2004–2005 Terms

Court Era	Liberal Decisions	Conservative Decisions	Total Cases
Warren Court (1953–1968 Terms)	58% (222)	42% (163)	385
Burger Court (1969–1985 Terms)	34% (187)	66% (361)	548
Rehnquist Court (1986–2004 Terms)	36% (167)	64% (294)	461
Total	41% (576)	59% (818)	1,394

Source: Harold J. Spaeth, *United States Supreme Court Judicial Database, 1953–2004 Terms* (Ann Arbor, MI: Inter-University Consortium for Political and Social Research, 2005).

servative appointees by Republican Presidents Ronald Reagan and George H. W. Bush able to achieve this sharp turn to the Right? The answer to this question seems to be no. The Rehnquist Court's decision making in regard to the guarantees of the criminally accused was one of essential continuity with the Burger Court. This can be observed quite clearly in the data in table 3.9, which shows virtually identical voting records by the Burger and Rehnquist Courts in criminal procedure cases; the Burger Court had a 34 percent liberal record, and the Rehnquist Court voted liberally in 36 percent of its criminal decisions. Similarly, the Rehnquist Court adhered to the major criminal justice precedents of the Warren and Burger Courts. Furthermore, the Rehnquist Court created new liberal precedents in the criminal rights area and also overturned some of the precedent cases of the early Rehnquist Court years.

The Fourth Amendment and Unreasonable Searches and Seizures

The prior analysis of all Rehnquist Court decisions involving criminal procedure issues is both useful and necessary, but it is certainly not sufficient in terms of providing a definitive answer to the question of whether the Rehnquist Court engaged in a conservative counterrevolution in this important area of constitutional law. Each amendment dealing with the guarantees of the criminally accused must be studied in some detail to assess what changes, if any, have occurred in the Rehnquist Court's decision making regarding criminal rights. Thus, we examine the specific clauses of the Fourth, Fifth, Sixth, and Eighth Amendments, comparing the decision-making patterns of the Warren, Burger, and Rehnquist Courts in an effort to analyze if the justices of the Rehnquist Court took a radically conservative shift in cases involving the guarantees of the criminally accused.

The Fourth Amendment states: "The rights of the people to be secure in their persons, houses, papers, and effects, against unreasonable searches and seizures, shall not be violated, and no Warrants shall issue, but upon probable cause, supported by Oath or affirmation, and particularly describing the place to be searched, and the persons or things to be seized." The provisions of the Fourth Amendment stemmed from colonial hatred of arbitrary British law enforcement practices of searching citizens and their property without any judicial authorization or with blanket authorization to search anything and everything under a writ of assistance. The Fourth Amendment was thus concerned with providing individuals with the right of privacy from arbitrary law enforcement activities by requiring officials who want to engage in a search or seizure to present evidence to a neutral court official that constitutes sufficient proof—probable cause—for the judicial officer to issue a precise warrant authorizing a search and seizure. This seemingly clear language has given rise to numerous controversies over the years, and we focus on the two most controversial Fourth Amendment issues: warrantless searches and the exclusionary rule.

One topic of great controversy is warrantless searches. The language of the Fourth Amendment seems absolutist in regard to the need for a warrant, but the courts have never held that all searches must be accompanied by a warrant. If a police officer is on patrol and observes a bank robbery in progress, then the officer can act immediately to attempt to apprehend the robbers; no issue would arise about the failure of the officer to have first obtained a warrant. Most cases are not this easy, however, and the Supreme Court over the years has been confronted with many different cases involving the question of when a warrantless search can be conducted without violating the Fourth Amendment.

A second major controversy associated with the Fourth Amendment involves the exclusionary rule. This judicial principle requires that any evidence obtained unconstitutionally should not be used to try a case. Although the exclusionary rule is primarily associated with the Fourth Amendment, it also applies to evidence obtained in violation of other constitutional guarantees. This exclusionary rule is not part of the Constitution but rather was created by the Supreme Court in a 1914 case, *Weeks v. United States*. This rule has been controversial since its creation, with some critics arguing that it is ineffective and harmful. Other critics argue that even if it should not be abolished, it should be modified by various exceptions.

Before turning to a detailed analysis of the Rehnquist Court's handling of the Fourth Amendment topics of warrantless searches and the exclusionary rule, we can first engage in a quantitative analysis of the Rehnquist Court's Fourth Amendment cases. As with our prior analysis of the constitutional guarantees of the First Amendment, quantitative analysis provides important and unique insights into the question of whether the Rehnquist Court engaged in a conservative constitutional counterrevolution.

The data in table 3.10 compare the Warren, Burger, and Rehnquist Courts in all Fourth Amendment cases. The figures show that the Warren Court was moderately liberal in its Fourth Amendment decision making, deciding 58 percent of its cases liberally. The Burger Court had a decidedly more conservative record in this area, voting liberally in only 32 percent of its Fourth Amendment cases. The Rehnquist Court was even more conservative, deciding only 21 percent of its Fourth Amendment cases in a liberal manner. These data thus suggest that in regard to the Fourth Amendment, the biggest shift occurred from the Warren to the Burger Court, with the Rehnquist Court extending somewhat the conservative orientation of the Burger Court.

Table 3.11 enables us to examine the individual voting records of each justice who has served on the Rehnquist Court. Several interesting insights can be gleaned from this table. One important characteristic is the predominance of conservative voting patterns; ten justices had predominantly conservative voting records compared to only

Table 3.10: Liberal/Conservative Voting in Fourth Amendment
Search and Seizure Cases by the Warren, Burger,
and Rehnquist Courts, 1953–1954 to 2004–2005 Terms

Court Era	Liberal Decisions	Conservative Decisions	Total Cases
Warren Court (1953–1968 Terms)	58% (37)	42% (27)	64
Burger Court (1969–1985 Terms)	32% (39)	68% (85)	124
Rehnquist Court (1986–2004 Terms)	21% (15)	79% (56)	71
Total	35% (91)	65% (168)	259

Source: Harold J. Spaeth, *United States Supreme Court Judicial Database, 1953–2004 Terms* (Ann Arbor, MI: Inter-University Consortium for Political and Social Research, 2005).

Table 3.11: Liberal/Conservative Voting Records of the Justices of the Rehnquist
Court in Fourth Amendment Search and Seizure Cases, 1986–1987 Term to
2004–2005 Term (Justices Ranked from Most Conservative to Most Liberal)

Justices	Liberal Decisions	Conservative Decisions	Total Cases
Powell	0% (0)	100% (9)	9
Rehnquist	12% (8)	88% (60)	68
Scalia	17% (12)	83% (58)	70
Thomas	19% (7)	81% (30)	37
White	19% (7)	81% (29)	36
Kennedy	24% (12)	76% (39)	51
O'Connor	24% (17)	76% (53)	70
Breyer	32% (11)	68% (23)	34
Blackmun	39% (14)	61% (22)	36
Souter	43% (18)	57% (24)	42
Ginsburg	56% (19)	44% (15)	34
Stevens	66% (46)	34% (24)	70
Brennan	96% (25)	4% (1)	26
Marshall	97% (32)	3% (1)	33

Source: Harold J. Spaeth, *United States Supreme Court Judicial Database, 1953–2004 Terms* (Ann Arbor, MI: Inter-University Consortium for Political and Social Research, 2005).

four justices with liberal records. Important insights can also be obtained by examining the voting records of the natural court, which served from 1994 to 2005. Five justices, a majority, had strongly conservative voting records, including Rehnquist at 88 percent, Scalia with 83 percent, Thomas at 81 percent, and Kennedy and O'Connor with 76 percent conservative voting. These five justices seemed to constitute a solid voting bloc that could prevail in most cases. Furthermore, unlike many other areas of constitutional law, the conservative majority was not facing a four-person liberal alignment. Only Ginsburg (56 percent liberal) and Stevens (66 percent liberal) voted liberally in a majority of Fourth Amendment cases. Breyer and Souter were predominately conservative in Fourth Amendment cases, with Breyer voting conservatively in 68 percent of his cases and Souter deciding conservatively in 57 percent. Thus, in Fourth Amendment cases, the conservatives on the Rehnquist Court not only had a majority bloc but also could typically count on having six or seven votes in a case.

These data do not provide a clear answer to the question of whether the Rehnquist Court engaged in a conservative counterrevolution in regard to the Fourth Amendment. A five-person conservative coalition existed since Thomas replaced Marshall, and the Rehnquist Court was more conservative than the Burger Court and substantially more conservative than the Warren Court; however, a detailed analysis of leading precedent cases of the Warren, Burger, and Rehnquist Courts is necessary before any firm conclusions can be offered. We begin with the subject of warrantless searches and then discuss exclusionary rule cases.

Warrantless Searches

The Pre–Warren Court Period

The Warren Court inherited a limited but important body of Fourth Amendment cases involving warrantless searches. The number of cases was relatively small because the Fourth Amendment was not nationalized until the decision of *Wolf v. Colorado*, in 1949. In this case, a local sheriff entered the office of Dr. Wolf, who was suspected of illegally performing abortions, and took his appointment book without first obtaining a search warrant. The Supreme Court under Chief Justice Fred Vinson ruled that the Fourth Amendment protection against unreasonable searches and seizures applies to state and local officials as well as to federal officers and also that the seizure of Dr. Wolf's appointment book without a warrant violated his Fourth Amendment rights. Interestingly, however, the Court did not extend the exclusionary rule to the states in this case, and thus the illegally obtained evidence could be used against Dr. Wolf.

Although the pre–Warren Court period did not witness a large number of Fourth Amendment cases involving the issue of valid warrantless searches, several exceptions to the warrant requirement were established. One example involved moving vehicles. In *Carroll v. United States* (1925) the Court recognized the principle that automobiles need to be treated differently than homes because of their mobility. Thus, if probable cause exists, an officer does not need to obtain a search warrant to stop and search a car. Another example of a valid warrantless search established in the pre–Warren Court period involved open fields. In *Hester v. United States* (1924), the Court ruled that if probable cause existed for the search of a home, then it was permissible to engage in a warrantless search of open fields surrounding the house. A final example of valid warrantless search exceptions decided in the pre–Warren Court years involved searches incident to lawful arrest. In two 1947 cases—*Rabinowitz v. United States* and *Harris v. United States*—the Court allowed federal agents to engage in full searches of an office and of a four-room apartment, establishing the principle that a complete warrantless search of a premise is permissible if the search follows a valid arrest of a suspect.

The Warren Court Period

The Warren Court faced many more Fourth Amendment warrantless search cases than had previous Courts because of the nationalization decision in *Wolf*, and the Warren Court did create new exceptions to the warrant requirement. In keeping with its liberal orientation, however, the Warren Court recognized relatively few exceptions to the warrant requirement. The justices of the Warren era also placed tight controls over the extent of these warrantless searches, and the Warren Court introduced new limitations over police activities in regard to prior Court rulings concerning search incident to lawful arrest.

Two important examples of the Warren Court's creation of new exceptions to the warrant requirement involved "stop and frisk" and "hot pursuit." Despite permitting warrantless searches in both situations, however, the Warren Court justices placed strict limitations on the types of activities in which police could engage.

The famous case of *Terry v. Ohio* (1968) created the stop and frisk exception. An experienced police officer in Cleveland observed Terry acting suspiciously as though he might be preparing to rob a store. The officer approached Terry, questioned him briefly, and then patted him down for weapons. The officer found a gun and then arrested Terry. The Warren Court in an 8–1 decision found this warrantless search to be permissible because this was necessary to protect the safety of the officer. However, the Warren Court limited the search just to weapons in a companion case of *Sibron v. New York* (1968), where in similar circumstances an officer pulled a packet of drugs from a pocket of the suspect; in this case, the Court ruled that there was no concern for the officer's safety, and thus the seizure of the drugs violated the Fourth Amendment.

The Warren Court also introduced in *Warden v. Hayden* (1967) the hot pursuit warrantless search exception, but, as with the stop and frisk exception, the justices sharply prescribed the range of activities in which officers could engage. In this case, the Court established the principle that officers do not need to obtain a warrant if probable cause exists that a crime has occurred and a suspect has entered a building to hide. Police can engage in hot pursuit after the individual because of the need for quick action—escape could occur, evidence could be destroyed, and lives could be threatened. The Warren Court emphasized, however, that this type of warrantless search required probable cause, and the search had to focus on the purposes justifying the exception to the warrant requirement.

A final case that illustrates the Warren Court's liberal orientation toward warrantless searches is *Chimel v. California* (1969). The issue in this case was how extensively the police could engage in a warrantless search incident to a lawful arrest. As discussed above, the 1947 precedents of *Rabinowitz* and *Harris* allowed officers to search an entire office or apartment if a valid arrest had occurred. In *Chimel*, however, the Warren Court explicitly overturned these two precedents and established a new principle: warrantless searches incident to lawful arrest can involve only the individual and the area under the suspect's immediate control. The Warren Court majority reasoned that this would allow an officer to protect against harm, escape, or the destruction of evidence. Any broader search, however, required a warrant.

The Burger Court Period

The Burger Court, like the Warren Court, found its agenda to contain numerous Fourth Amendment cases involving the constitutionality of warrantless searches. The justices of the Burger Court were much more sympathetic to law enforcement interests, however. The Burger Court not only created many new exceptions to the warrant requirement but also provided extremely pro-police interpretations to existing warrantless search exceptions. As Yarbrough writes, "The Warren Court required search warrants except under a number of limited, exceptional circumstances, but the Burger Court substantially enlarged upon the scope of permissible warrantless searches" (2000, 197). Despite these decidedly conservative directions, however, the Burger Court cannot be considered to have engaged in a conservative counterrevolution because radical changes in precedent did not occur, and the basic Fourth Amendment principles continued to be observed.

Numerous examples can be cited of new warrantless exceptions recognized by the justices of the Burger Court. For example, in *Schneckloth v. Bustamante* (1973), the Court ruled 6–3 that an officer can seek consent to engage in a warrantless search without informing the person of the Fourth Amendment's warrant requirement.

Another example involved public school children. In *New Jersey v. T.L.O.* (1985), the Burger Court gave school officials wide authority to engage in warrantless searches in a case in which an assistant principal opened the purse of a student suspected of smoking and then, upon finding evidence of possible drug use, thoroughly searched her purse, finding marijuana. The Burger Court justices also approved in a 5–4 vote the warrantless search of a prisoner's cell.

In addition to these and other exceptions to the warrant requirement, the Burger Court provided extremely conservative interpretations to several existing precedents allowing warrantless searches. Two important and illustrative cases are *New York v. Belton* (1981) and *United States v. Ross* (1982).

Belton involved a conservative interpretation of the Warren Court's decision in *Chimel* in which the principle had been established that warrantless searches incident to lawful arrest had to be limited to the suspect and the area under the suspect's immediate control. In the *Belton* case, an officer had stopped and arrested the driver of a car and his passengers on drug charges. The officer searched each person and then went to the car, opened the door, pulled out Bolton's jacket, and searched its pockets, finding additional drugs. The Burger Court majority argued that the jacket was within Belton's immediate control and thus within the guidelines of *Chimel*, but the liberal dissenters found this to be beyond any reasonable interpretation of the *Chimel* guidelines.

Ross was concerned with a long line of cases dating back to *Carroll v. United States* (1925) dealing with warrantless searches of moving vehicles. In the *Ross* case, Washington, D.C., police were informed that a man named Bandit Ross was at a certain location dealing drugs out of the trunk of his car. Police located Ross, who jumped into his car and fled. Police eventually stopped him, found a weapon, and arrested him. They then searched the trunk of his car, opening two separate containers with money and drugs. The issue before the Burger Court involved the question of proper guidelines for police to follow in conducting warrantless searches of automobiles when probable cause exists. The majority answered this question by stating that police officers could conduct a search as extensive as they believe a neutral judge would allow when presented with the evidence about probable cause. The liberal dissenters objected strongly to what they saw as a new interpretation of *Carroll* and its progeny, arguing that the *Ross* principle in effect eliminated the role of a judicial officer in the warrant process.

The Rehnquist Court Period

How did the Rehnquist Court deal with Fourth Amendment warrantless search cases? The Rehnquist Court was even more conservative than the Burger Court but was not radically different and did not engage in a conservative counterrevolution. The justices of the Rehnquist Court recognized additional types of warrantless searches and gave pro-police interpretations to various Burger and Warren Court exceptions to the warrant requirement. The Rehnquist Court did not create new conservative precedents that overturned existing liberal precedents, however, and in many important decisions, the Rehnquist Court ruled various warrantless law enforcement search activities unconstitutional, especially if the activities involved a suspect's home.

Fourth Amendment warrantless search cases constituted the Court's biggest agenda item, and in analyzing the Rehnquist Court's decision making in this area, we therefore need to divide the cases into various categories. This can be done in many ways, but the most prominent and useful categories are drug-testing programs, automobile searches, and searches of homes and apartments.

Drug-testing cases have been an important component of the Rehnquist Court's Fourth Amendment jurisprudence. Government drug testing of employees became rather common in the eighties in response to growing concerns over the usage of illegal drugs in American society. Drug-testing programs took a wide variety of forms, but they tended to raise the same Fourth Amendment issues: no warrants are obtained, no probable cause exists, and typically no suspicion whatsoever exists that a particular person is using illegal drugs. The Rehnquist Court took a conservative position in their drug-testing cases, supporting a wide variety of government programs despite the absence of warrants or any degree of probable cause. The Rehnquist Court justices have, however, drawn lines that have found some types of drug-testing programs to be unconstitutional.

The initial drug-testing cases to come before the Rehnquist Court centered on two federal programs. In *National Treasury Employee Union v. Von Rabb* (1989), personnel in the U.S. Customs Service were required to participate in a random drug-testing program. The companion case of *Skinner v. Railway Labor Executives' Association* (1989) involved a program by the Federal Railroad Administration that required drug and alcohol testing of all railroad employees who were involved in an accident.

The Rehnquist Court gave approval to both programs, although the Federal Railroad Administration program received a 7–2 vote while the Customs Service policy was approved by a 5–4 margin. Justice Kennedy authored both majority opinions. He acknowledged that these were difficult cases because no warrants were obtained, no probable cause existed, and not even reasonable suspicion was established. For Kennedy and the Court majority, however, these considerations were not the critical ones. Rather, the key to interpreting the Fourth Amendment is whether a search or seizure is unreasonable, and this is determined by a careful balancing of the interests of the government versus the intrusion on the privacy rights of the individual. In both of these cases, Kennedy argued, the special needs of the federal government were strong whereas the intrusion on privacy rights was relatively minimal, and thus the Fourth Amendment was not violated.

In two subsequent cases, the Rehnquist Court justices gave approval to random drug testing in public schools. The first of these cases was *Vernonia School District 47J v. Acton*, in 1995. An Oregon school district required that all senior high and junior high athletes had to participate in a urinalysis drug-testing program. A seventh-grade football player and his parents challenged the program, but the Court ruled 6–3 that the program did not violate the Fourth Amendment. The reasoning in Scalia's majority opinion followed the logic of *National Treasury Employee Union* and *Skinner.* He acknowledged that the program involved a warrantless search with no element of individualized suspicion, but he concluded the policy was a reasonable one using a balancing approach under which the intrusion on the individual was relatively minor whereas the special needs of the school district in controlling illegal drug use by students was a compelling one. The second school drug-testing case that the Rehnquist Court decided was *Board of Education of Pottawatomie County v. Earls*, in 2002. In this case a local school board required drug testing for students participating in any extracurricular activity, not just athletics. A majority of the justices found the logic of the *Acton* precedent to control this case, thus upholding the school's drug-testing program.

Despite this line of cases upholding warrantless searches through drug testing, the Rehnquist Court on two occasions ruled unconstitutional certain types of government drug-testing programs. *Chandler v. Miller* (1997) involved a Georgia law that required candidates for political office to pass a urinalysis drug test. Although the Court relied upon the precedents of *National Treasury Employee Union, Skinner,* and *Acton* in this warrantless search case, the justices ruled 8–1 that the program was unconstitutional because the balancing test to assess if the program was reasonable weighed in favor of the individual. The Court identified two specific weaknesses with the Georgia law: (1) no evidence existed of a drug problem among elected officials, and (2) the test could be scheduled by the candidate over a thirty-day period, allowing a candidate using drugs to refrain for a period of time and thus test negatively.

The second drug-testing case in which the Rehnquist Court ruled liberally was *Ferguson v. City of Charleston* (2001). In this case, the Medical University of South Carolina in Charleston developed a policy under which certain pregnant women were tested for cocaine without their consent. If a woman either had received incomplete prenatal care or had a condition where her fetus was in jeopardy, then a urine sample was to be taken. If the first test was positive and the woman either missed a drug-abuse counseling session or tested positive a second time, then the police were to be notified and the woman arrested. Writing for a six-person majority, Stevens argued that the case should be approached from the same conceptual framework as the previous drug-testing cases, but he argued this case had two major differences that made the program unconstitutional. First, the invasion of privacy in this case was substantially greater than in previous cases because the results were given to the police. Second, the special needs of the government in the previous cases had been independent of the state's law enforcement powers. The Charleston program had a central objective related to law enforcement, and law enforcement is not a "special need" of government justifying a warrantless search without any individualized suspicion.

In addition to the drug-testing cases, another major area of warrantless search decisions involves moving vehicles. The Rehnquist Court's approach was similar in both areas. As with drug-testing programs, the Rehnquist Court justices were highly supportive of law enforcement interests in cases involving warrantless searches of cars and other moving vehicles. The Rehnquist Court did not, however, give a green light to officials to engage in any and all searches of moving vehicles; lines have been drawn and limits have been set by the Rehnquist Court regarding warrantless searches of moving vehicles.

The Rehnquist Court ruled conservatively in favor of law enforcement interests in the vast majority of its Fourth Amendment warrantless search cases involving moving vehicles. Several major cases can be cited as evidence to support this proposition.

Michigan v. Sitz (1990) raised the issue of the constitutionality of sobriety checkpoints where law enforcement officers stop all vehicles on a road to check for signs of intoxication. Like the drug-testing cases, this case involved a search of individuals without a warrant and without any degree of individualized suspicion. A six-person majority used the balancing approach to assess whether such a search was unreasonable and thus unconstitutional, finding that the government's interest in dealing with problems of driving under the influence of drugs or alcohol outweighed the relatively minor invasion of individual privacy, a privacy that is much diminished in a car as opposed to one's home.

The 1991 case of *Florida v. Bostick* involved the warrantless search of a passenger aboard a bus, with the Rehnquist Court by a 6–3 vote providing another decision favoring the interests of law enforcement. The case occurred from an encounter at a bus stop in Fort Lauderdale, Florida, where two officers boarded a bus and, without any articulable suspicion, asked Bostick for his ticket and for identification. They then asked for permission to search his luggage and subsequently found illegal narcotics in one of his bags. Writing for the majority, Justices O'Connor argued that no Fourth Amendment violation had occurred because Bostick had not been seized and could refuse to answer questions or to agree to a search.

Two Rehnquist Court decisions dealing with warrantless searches of passengers further illustrate the predominant tendency of the current justices to favor law enforcement interests. *Maryland v. Wilson* (1997) involved an officer pursuing and stopping a speeding car that lacked a regular license plate. The driver got out of the car immediately, but the officer noticed two passengers behaving nervously and suspiciously. After questioning the driver briefly, the officer ordered the front-seat passenger out of the car. As he exited the car, some crack cocaine fell onto the ground, and he was arrested. The Maryland courts ruled that the state trooper lacked sufficient grounds to order the passenger from the vehicle, but a 7–2 Rehnquist Court reversed, finding no Fourth Amendment violation. Once again, the justices used a balancing formula to assess if the warrantless search was unreasonable, and again they came down on the side of law enforcement, emphasizing statistics showing the number of officers killed or assaulted annually during automobile stops.

Wyoming v. Houghton (1999) was a case closely related to *Maryland v. Wilson*. In the *Houghton* case, an officer stopped a car that had a faulty brake light. In searching the male driver, the officer found a hypodermic syringe in his pocket, and the driver then admitted to drug use. The issue in this case stemmed from the next step, when the officer then searched the purse of a female passenger, finding illegal drugs. A 6–3 Rehnquist Court ruled that the warrantless search of the passenger's purse did not violate the Fourth Amendment. Writing for the majority, Scalia argued that probable cause for the search had been established, and, once established, a search can extend to all articles and containers that might contain illegal items.

The Rehnquist Court continued in very recent years to rule in favor of law enforcement interests in cases involving Fourth Amendment warrantless searches of moving vehicles. In the 2003–2004 term, for example, the justices decided three warrantless automobile search cases in favor of law enforcement. The Court ruled unanimously in two cases. In *Maryland v. Pringle* (2004), officers lawfully stopped a vehicle and found five envelopes of cocaine in the backseat of the car. When nobody admitted owning the drugs, all the occupants of the car were searched. The Rehnquist Court reversed the Maryland Supreme Court, arguing that probable cause existed to support the warrantless search. *Illinois v. Lidster* (2004) involved a man who was arrested at a police roadblock for driving under the influence when he nearly hit a police officer. The defendant argued that the police checkpoint was invalid because it was created for the purpose of gaining information about a hit-and-run accident that had occurred a week earlier, but the Court unanimously saw this case as controlled by the *Michigan v. Sitz* (1990) precedent. In yet another Fourth Amendment warrantless search case involving automobiles, *Thorton v. United States* (2004), the justices in a 7–2 decision relied upon the Burger Court precedent of *New York v. Belton* (1981) in upholding the warrantless search of the car of a man who had been arrested on drug and firearm possession.

These cases could certainly leave the impression that the Rehnquist Court was willing to give blanket approval to warrantless searches of moving vehicles, including both the vehicles and its passengers, but the reality is the Rehnquist Court justices on occasion ruled against law enforcement interests. We will examine three of these liberal decisions, one involving the search of an automobile (*Knowles v. Iowa*, 1998), one involving a traffic checkpoint (*Indianapolis v. Edmond*, 2000), and a third case dealing with a search of luggage on a bus (*Bond v. United States*, 2000).

Knowles v. Iowa involved a challenge to an Iowa law authorizing an officer to engage in a warrantless search of an automobile whenever a traffic ticket is issued.

The Rehnquist Court unanimously ruled the law unconstitutional. Using a balancing approach to determine if such a search was unreasonable, the Court found that the individual's privacy interests outweighed the interests of law enforcement, which were minimal in this case.

In the case of *Indianapolis v. Edmond*, the issue again involved the constitutionality of a police checkpoint. Indianapolis police were concerned with the problem of illegal drug sales and usage, stopping each car for about five minutes. In addition to checking for a valid driver's license and registration, a trained dog sniffed around the car for any evidence of drugs. If the dog gave evidence of smelling drugs, then a search of the car was undertaken. O'Connor wrote for a six-person majority finding the program to violate the Fourth Amendment. Unlike the limited focus of the sobriety checkpoint approved in *Michigan v. Sitz* (1990), the Indianapolis approach involved the search for ordinary criminal activity and thus went beyond the narrow circumstances where the Court had approved suspicionless searches.

The Rehnquist Court justices also reached a liberal decision in a warrantless search case involving moving vehicles in *Bond v. United States*, a bus case. Bond was a passenger on a Greyhound bus, and he placed a piece of soft luggage in an overhead rack. A U.S. Border Patrol agent boarded the bus and squeezed the piece of luggage, feeling a bricklike object. Bond admitted to owning the bag and also agreed to the agent searching the bag, which revealed a brick of methamphetamine. Chief Justice Rehnquist wrote for a seven-person majority in finding Bond's Fourth Amendment rights to be violated. Bond had a reasonable expectation of privacy regarding his bag, and the agent lacked any individualized suspicion to examine the bag initially.

In analyzing the topic of warrantless search cases decided by the Rehnquist Court, thus far we have examined the issues of drug testing and moving vehicles. We have found that the Rehnquist Court justices were predominantly conservative in these cases, ruling that warrantless searches do not violate the Fourth Amendment. A somewhat different pattern emerges when we examine the next warrantless search area, involving individuals' dwellings. The Rehnquist Court, following the logic of preceding Courts, viewed Fourth Amendment privacy rights as reaching their height in regard to one's home. Thus, although the Rehnquist Court justices typically ruled in favor of law enforcement interests in cases involving the warrantless searches of homes, the justices were more willing to hold police to higher standards when searches involved the home.

The cases of *Griffin v. Wisconsin* (1987) and *Illinois v. Rodriguez* (1990) illustrate the conservative tendency of the Rehnquist Court in cases involving warrantless searches of dwellings. The *Griffin* case involved the issue of whether persons on probation have lower constitutional rights in regard to warrantless searches of their homes than regular citizens. Specifically, Wisconsin police engaged in a warrantless search of Griffin's home based only on a suspicion that Griffin had contraband in his residence. A five-person Rehnquist Court majority gave approval to this warrantless search, arguing that those on probation have less Fourth Amendment protection than other persons.

The *Illinois v. Rodriguez* case raised the question of who can give permission for police to enter a residence. A woman called Illinois police to report a physical attack on her daughter. The daughter told police that she had been beaten at an apartment in another part of the city. The young woman indicated to police that she shared the apartment with the man, he was presently at the apartment, and she had a key to the apartment and would allow police to enter. Upon unlocking the door, police discovered cocaine in plain view and arrested the defendant, Rodriguez, on drug charges. He sought to have the evidence suppressed because the woman lacked authority to grant consent to have the apartment searched because she did not live at the apartment, paid no rent, and was only an occasional visitor. Justice Scalia, writing for a six-person majority, argued that no Fourth Amendment violation had occurred. Scalia utilized the reasonableness standard and stated that the police officers' actions were reasonable under the circumstances, even if they were erroneous.

Despite cases such as *Griffin* and *Rodriguez*, the Rehnquist Court was more protective of Fourth Amendment rights in cases involving people's homes than in cases involving drug testing or moving vehicles. *Kyllo v. United States* (2001) illustrates the importance the justices gave to privacy rights in one's home. The *Kyllo* case involved the use of high-technology equipment to engage in a warrantless search for evidence of a crime. Kyllo was under suspicion by federal drug agents for growing marijuana in his home, and they set up across the street from his house a device for detecting heat emission. Because the agents did not enter Kyllo's home or property, they thought they did not need to obtain a warrant. The instrument recorded unusually high levels of heat leaving the garage, and they used this evidence to obtain a search warrant, subsequently finding more than 100 marijuana plants. A closely divided Rehnquist Court ruled 5–4 that the use of the thermal imaging device without a warrant violated Kyllo's Fourth Amendment rights because the use of the instrument constituted an invasion of the defendant's reasonable expectation of privacy. The voting division in this case was interesting, with liberal and conservative justices aligning in unusual patterns. Scalia and Thomas were joined in the majority by Breyer, Ginsburg, and Souter in ruling against the federal agents; Stevens joined Rehnquist, O'Connor, and Kennedy in ruling for the government.

Despite the close vote in *Kyllo*, however, both sets of justices agreed upon the general principle about the important emphasis within the Fourth Amendment on the privacy of one's home and the need for law enforcement officials to obtain a warrant before searching a home. Justice Scalia in his majority opinion wrote: "'At the very core of the Fourth Amendment' stands the right of a man to retreat into his own home and there be free from unreasonable government intrusion." Scalia continued: "With few exceptions, the question whether a warrantless search of a home is reasonable and hence constitutional must be answered no" (533 U.S. at 31, citing *Silverman v. United States*, 1961). Justice Stevens's dissenting opinion echoed this general principle, noting that a core ideal of Fourth Amendment jurisprudence is that "searches and seizures inside a home without a warrant are presumptively unreasonable" (533 U.S. at 42, citing *Payton v. New York*, 1980).

Exclusionary Rule

Having examined the controversial Fourth Amendment issue of warrantless searches, we now shift our attention to the other major topic associated with the Fourth—the exclusionary rule. As was stated previously, the exclusionary rule requires the suppression of any evidence obtained unconstitutionally; that is, the evidence cannot be used in the trial by the government. The exclusionary rule is not part of the Constitution but rather was created by the Supreme Court in the 1914 case of *Weeks v. United States*. It has been controversial since its creation, and we trace this controversy through the Warren, Burger, and Rehnquist Courts, seeking to assess if the Rehnquist Court engaged in a conservative counterrevolution in regard to the exclusionary rule.

Lee Epstein and Thomas Walker state that "the exclusionary rule provides yet another example of the Warren Court's revolutionary treatment of the rights of the criminally accused," a view shared widely by Court scholars (2004, 548). To understand the important liberal change introduced by the Warren Court, we need to examine the two major exclusionary rule cases in the pre–Warren Court period, *Weeks v. United States* (1914) and *Wolf v. Colorado* (1949).

The Pre–Warren Court Period

The *Weeks* case involved a man who was arrested for fraudulent use of the mail and subsequently had his house thoroughly searched and papers seized by federal and local officials without a warrant being obtained. In a unanimous decision, the Supreme Court ruled that Week's Fourth Amendment rights had been violated and introduced the exclusionary rule in federal cases, thus prohibiting the federal government from using any of the illegally obtained evidence. This was a dramatic new precedent because prior to *Weeks*, the standard for valid evidence had been whether it was truthful. The Court advanced two major reasons to support the creation of the new exclusionary rule. One argument involved the deterrence rationale, which reasoned that this rule was necessary to deter law enforcement personnel from violating the Fourth Amendment or "to police the police." The second argument was a due process, or fairness, rationale that the government must follow the law and cannot be allowed to gain convictions through its own lawless actions.

Important as the *Weeks* case was, it had limited applicability because it applied only to Fourth Amendment decisions involving the federal government, and most Fourth cases involve the activities of state and local law enforcement personnel. The 1949 case of *Wolf v. Colorado* presented the Court with the opportunity to extend the exclusionary rule to the states, but the Vinson Court declined to do so. The Court majority did nationalize the Fourth Amendment in finding unconstitutional the warrantless search and seizure of Dr. Wolf's office, but Justice Frankfurter, writing for the majority, failed to apply the exclusionary rule to the states because the majority of the states had not yet adopted this rule and other options existed to ensure compliance with the Fourth Amendment.

The Warren Court Period

The Warren Court in the landmark case of *Mapp v. Ohio* (1961) overturned *Wolf* and applied the exclusionary rule to the states. In this case, police unlawfully searched Dolly Mapp's apartment for a criminal suspect, and in the process they seized allegedly obscene materials in her possession. This was a remarkable and controversial decision for several reasons. First, it initially came before the Court as a First Amendment obscenity case, but the Court decided it as a Fourth Amendment exclusionary case even though it had not been briefed or argued on those grounds. Second, the case had a major effect on the activities of state and local police and prosecutors throughout the country, requiring the suppression of evidence obtained in violation of the Fourth Amendment—and subsequently of any other amendments as well.

Writing for a narrow five-person majority, Justice Clark offered several reasons for the application of the exclusionary rule to the states. Most importantly, he reaffirmed the arguments advanced by the *Weeks* Court that the exclusionary rule was needed to deter police misconduct and that principles of fundamental fairness require that individuals should not be tried with evidence obtained unconstitutionally. In regard to the federalism issue, Clark argued that a majority of the states had now adopted the exclusionary rule.

The Burger Court Period

The Warren Court's decision to nationalize the exclusionary rule in *Mapp* was a source of enormous controversy, and a leading critic of the rule was the person who was to become the next U.S. Supreme Court chief justice—Warren Burger. In his writings on both the lower federal courts and the Supreme Court, Burger harshly criticized the exclusionary rule on several grounds. Burger argued that it frequently allowed the guilty to go free or to receive more lenient sentences; it undercut the truth-seeking function of the courts; it created disrespect for the courts, the law, and the Constitution; and it failed to achieve its stated objective of deterring police misconduct. The approach favored by Burger was to abolish the exclusionary rule, reintroduce truthfulness as the test for excluding evidence, and provide civil remedies for those who felt their Fourth Amendment rights had been violated.

Many Court experts thought that Burger would succeed in having the exclusionary rule overturned, but, despite his efforts, the rule remained intact during the Burger Court era. The exclusionary rule was weakened considerably, however, by a series of exceptions created by the Burger Court justices, who operated under the conviction that the rule was simply a judicially created method of deterring police misconduct, thereby allowing the justices to engage in cost-benefit analysis of the rule in individual cases. For example, in *United States v. Calandra* (1974), the Burger Court ruled that the exclusionary rule does not apply to grand jury hearings. A further exception to the exclusionary rule was added by the Burger Court in the 1971 case of *Harris v. New York*, in which the Court ruled that evidence obtained in violation of the *Miranda* warnings could be used at trial to impeach the credibility of the defendant's own testimony. An additional exception was created in the 1976 case of *United States v. Janis* when the Court said the exclusionary rule does not apply in civil proceedings involving a government agency. Two especially important exceptions were established in 1984 near the end of the Burger Court era. In *United States v. Leon*, a six-person majority argued that the exclusionary rule is not applicable for evidence seized by officers relying in "good faith" upon a search warrant even though the warrant is subsequently found to have been issued invalidly. And in *Nix v. Williams*, the Burger Court created the "inevitability of discovery" exception to the exclusionary rule under which evidence obtained illegally can still be used at trial if the evidence would have inevitably been discovered by lawful means.

The Rehnquist Court Period

Having established that the Burger Court left the core of the exclusionary rule intact but weakened through a series of exceptions, we now raise the question of how did the Rehnquist Court deal with the exclusionary rule? In contrast with the Burger Court, the justices of the Rehnquist Court gave relatively little attention to the exclusionary rule, and no conservative constitutional counterrevolution occurred. *Weeks* and *Mapp* remained controlling precedent, and, unlike the Burger Court, the Rehnquist Court created few new exceptions to the exclusionary rule. Two cases from Illinois—*Illinois v. Krull* (1987) and *James v. Illinois* (1990)—illustrate these generalizations.

The *Krull* case is one of the few in which the Rehnquist Court created a new exception to the exclusionary rule, specifically a "good faith" exception to a search executed under a statute that was subsequently ruled unconstitutional. An Illinois law authorized police to engage in warrantless administrative searches of businesses dealing with new and used cars, including wrecking yards, where stolen cars are frequently processed. Operating under this statute, an Illinois police officer entered a wrecking yard and asked to see the licenses and records of recently acquired vehicles. The officer subsequently determined that several cars in the yard had been stolen, and he arrested the operators of the yard. The statute was held to be unconstitutional the next day by an Illinois court, and a series of Illinois courts granted a motion by the defendant to suppress the evidence because it was seized under an invalid statute.

A five-person majority of Justices Blackmun, Rehnquist, Scalia, White, and Powell overturned the Illinois courts, using the balancing test of the *Leon* case to extend the good faith exception to the exclusionary rule to cases in which officers act with objectively reasonable reliance on a statute that is subsequently determined to be unconstitutional. Writing for the majority, Justice Blackmun argued: "As with any remedial device, application of the exclusionary rule properly has been restricted to those situations in which its remedial purpose is effectively advanced. Thus, in various circumstances, the Court has examined whether the rule's deterrent effect will be achieved, and has weighed the likelihood of such deterrence against the costs of withholding reliable information from the truth-seeking process" (480 U.S. at 347). For Blackmun and the majority, the logic was the same as in *Leon;* no deterrent effect was involved in this case, but significant costs would occur in excluding truthful evidence.

If *Krull* illustrates the willingness of the Rehnquist Court to create additional exceptions to the exclusionary rule, the *James* case shows the commitment of the Court to maintaining the rule as an important component of Fourth Amendment jurisprudence. The *James* case raised the question of the scope of the "impeachment exception" to the exclusionary rule. As we saw earlier, the Burger Court in *Harris v. New York* (1971) allowed the prosecution to introduce illegally obtained evidence to impeach the credibility of a defendant's own testimony. The specific issue in *James* was whether this impeachment exception could be extended to the testimony of all defense witnesses. Writing for a five-person majority, Justice Brennan answered this question negatively. Utilizing the balancing approach associated with cases involving exceptions to the exclusionary rule, Brennan argued that creating this new exception would not enhance the truth-seeking function of the courts but would have the negative effect of undermining the deterrence purpose of the exclusionary rule. In concluding his opinion, Brennan argued strongly about the importance of the exclusionary rule: "So long as we are committed to protecting the people from the disregard of their constitutional rights during the course of criminal investigations, inadmissibility of illegally obtained evidence must remain the rule, not the exception" (493 U.S. at 319).

How do we account for the Rehnquist Court's perhaps surprising handling of the exclusionary rule, characterized by the creation of few new exceptions and by the acceptance of the core of *Weeks* and *Mapp?* Any attempt to resolve this question must be speculative because the justices do not provide us with clear answers in their opinions, but two reasons can be suggested. First, the conservative majority on the Rehnquist Court may have thought that the adverse effects of the exclusionary rule had been met sufficiently by the numerous exceptions that have been created, primarily by the Burger Court. Second, the justices may have reasoned that the continued existence of the exclusionary rule could serve useful purposes in terms of deterring police misconduct and ensuring fundamental fairness in the criminal justice process.

To conclude this examination of the Rehnquist Court's Fourth Amendment cases, our analysis shows that the Court did not move sharply to the right. The Rehnquist Court justices were certainly strongly conservative in Fourth Amendment cases, deciding 79 percent of them in favor of the government, and seven justices on the last natural court voted conservatively a majority of the time. But the Rehnquist Court was not significantly more conservative than the Burger Court, which voted conservatively in 68 percent of its Fourth Amendment cases. In regard to warrantless search cases, the Rehnquist Court created new exceptions to the warrant requirement, but the justices of the Rehnquist Court were willing to declare various types of warrantless searches unconstitutional, especially those involving personal residences. And the Rehnquist Court maintained the exclusionary rule, albeit a much weakened rule because of Burger Court decisions.

The Fifth Amendment Guarantees of Protection against Self-Incrimination and Double Jeopardy

Having completed our examination of the Fourth Amendment, we can now shift our attention to the guarantees of the criminally accused found in the Fifth Amendment, focusing again on the central question of whether the Rehnquist Court engaged in radically different decision-making patterns than in prior Court eras. The Fifth Amendment contains a variety of guarantees, including the right to a grand jury, the protection against self-incrimination, the guarantee against double jeopardy, the right to just compensation for the taking of private property, and the Due Process Clause. We focus on self-incrimination and double jeopardy because the grand jury guarantee has never been nationalized, the Just Compensation Clause does not involve criminal cases and is discussed later in this chapter, and the Due Process Clause is broad and general.

In regard to the protection against self-incrimination, the Fifth Amendment states: "No person shall be . . . compelled in any criminal case to be a witness against himself." The origins of the guarantee against self-incrimination date back several centuries to English religious courts, which attempted to force individuals into admitting their views were at odds with those of the church or the king. Over time, such practices were abolished by Parliament, and then the principle against self-incrimination spread to English common law courts and then to courts in the colonies and states. The existence of the guarantee against self-incrimination did not ensure, however, that law enforcement personnel would not use coercive tactics, including torture, to extract confessions from suspects. Concern over police abuses of their power eventually led the Warren Court to nationalize the Self-Incrimination Clause and then to link it to the Sixth Amendment right to counsel in *Miranda v. Arizona* (1966). As we will see, *Miranda* was controversial when it was decided, and it remains controversial today.

The Fifth Amendment guarantee against double jeopardy is written as follows: "No person shall be . . . subject for the same offense to be twice put in jeopardy of life or limb." This guarantee also has deep roots in English and colonial law. It seeks to ensure that the government cannot abuse its power by continually retrying a person for the same crime, thus exhausting the individual's financial resources, subjecting a person to continual harassment, and possibly requiring continuous punishments for one crime. Although the Supreme Court has not decided a large number of double jeopardy cases, the justices have had to struggle with the issue of nationalization of the guarantee as well as its proper meaning in a variety of contexts.

Before turning to a somewhat detailed case study analysis of Rehnquist Court decisions involving these two Fifth Amendment guarantees, we can engage in a quantitative analysis that can help us to answer the question of whether the Rehnquist Court radically altered Supreme Court policy regarding the protections against self-incrimination and double jeopardy. In both areas, the pattern we see is distinctively conservative decision making by the Rehnquist Court, that is, decisions rejecting claims by individuals that their Fifth Amendment rights have been violated. However, the Rehnquist Court was not significantly more conservative than the Burger Court, and, surprisingly perhaps, the Rehnquist Court's voting patterns were not too much more conservative than those of the Warren Court.

Beginning with the protection against self-incrimination, table 3.12 reveals that the Rehnquist Court was distinctively conservative, rejecting individual's claims against the government in 75 percent of its cases. This figure is nearly identical to the 77 percent conservative figure for the Burger Court, and thus it is not possible to argue that the Rehnquist Court became significantly more conservative in its interpretation of the self-incrimination guarantee. Furthermore, the record of the Warren Court in this area was one of only moderate liberalism because they decided only 56 percent of their self-incrimination cases liberally.

Table 3.12: Liberal/Conservative Voting in Fifth Amendment Self-Incrimination Cases by the Warren, Burger, and Rehnquist Courts, 1953–1954 to 2004–2005 Terms

Court Era	Liberal Decisions	Conservative Decisions	Total Cases
Warren Court (1953–1968 Terms)	56% (27)	44% (21)	48
Burger Court (1969–1985 Terms)	23% (14)	77% (46)	60
Rehnquist Court (1986–2004 Terms)	25% (6)	75% (18)	24
Total	36% (47)	64% (85)	132

Source: Harold J. Spaeth, *United States Supreme Court Judicial Database, 1953–2004 Terms* (Ann Arbor, MI: Inter-University Consortium for Political and Social Research, 2005).

The voting records in self-incrimination cases of the fourteen justices who served on the Rehnquist Court are presented in table 3.13. These data show that a conservative majority existed throughout the Rehnquist Court era in regard to self-incrimination cases, with Rehnquist, Thomas, Scalia, O'Connor, and White voting against the individual claimant in virtually every case. In the natural court era since 1994, Kennedy typically joined the conservative bloc to create a five-person majority of Rehnquist, Thomas, Scalia, O'Connor, and Kennedy. The Rehnquist Court's liberal justices—Stevens, Souter, Breyer, and Ginsburg—had widely divergent voting records in self-incrimination cases, ranging from Steven's liberal record of 56 percent to Ginsburg's 91 percent liberal voting record. Thus, although the Rehnquist Court was clearly conservative in its self-incrimination rulings with a five-person coalition controlling the vote, the Rehnquist Court was not any more conservative than its predecessor, the Burger Court.

Turning to the protection against double jeopardy, the data in table 3.14 reveal some surprising results. The Rehnquist Court was decidedly conservative, ruling against the individual in 75 percent of its cases. This is not a significantly different record than those established by the Warren and Burger Courts, however, and it is interesting to observe that the Warren Court, at 67 percent conservative, was more conservative than the Burger Court, at 63 percent conservative in double jeopardy cases.

An analysis of the individual voting records of the fourteen justices of the Rehnquist Court era in double jeopardy case also produces some interesting results. As can be observed in table 3.15, the fourteen justices split evenly between seven liberals and seven conservatives. This close division is also reflected in the 1994–2005 natural

Table 3.13: Liberal/Conservative Voting Records of the Justices of the Rehnquist Court in Fifth Amendment Self-Incrimination Cases, 1986–1987 Term to 2004–2005 Term (Justices Ranked from Most Conservative to Most Liberal)

Justices	Liberal Decisions	Conservative Decisions	Total Cases
Powell	0% (0)	100% (3)	3
Rehnquist	4% (1)	96% (23)	24
Thomas	9% (1)	91% (10)	11
Scalia	12% (3)	88% (21)	24
O'Connor	13% (3)	87% (20)	23
White	15% (2)	85% (11)	13
Kennedy	35% (7)	65% (13)	20
Blackmun	43% (6)	57% (8)	14
Stevens	56% (13)	44% (10)	23
Brennan	67% (8)	33% (4)	12
Souter	73% (8)	27% (3)	11
Breyer	80% (8)	20% (2)	10
Ginsburg	91% (10)	9% (1)	11
Marshall	92% (11)	8% (1)	12

Source: Harold J. Spaeth, *United States Supreme Court Judicial Database, 1953–2004 Terms* (Ann Arbor, MI: Inter-University Consortium for Political and Social Research, 2005).

Table 3.14: Liberal/Conservative Voting in Fifth Amendment Double Jeopardy Cases by the Warren, Burger, and Rehnquist Courts, 1953–1954 to 2004–2005 Terms

Court Era	Liberal Decisions	Conservative Decisions	Total Cases
Warren Court (1953–1968 Terms)	33% (7)	67% (14)	21
Burger Court (1969–1985 Terms)	37% (17)	63% (29)	46
Rehnquist Court (1986–2004 Terms)	25% (5)	75% (15)	20
Total	33% (29)	67% (58)	87

Source: Harold J. Spaeth, *United States Supreme Court Judicial Database, 1953–2004 Terms* (Ann Arbor, MI: Inter-University Consortium for Political and Social Research, 2005).

Table 3.15: Liberal/Conservative Voting Records of the Justices of the Rehnquist Court in Fifth Amendment Double Jeopardy Cases, 1986–1987 Term to 2004–2005 Term (Justices Ranked from Most Conservative to Most Liberal)

Justices	Liberal Decisions	Conservative Decisions	Total Cases
Powell	0% (0)	100% (3)	3
Rehnquist	4% (1)	96% (23)	24
Thomas	9% (1)	91% (10)	11
Scalia	12% (3)	88% (21)	24
O'Connor	13% (3)	87% (20)	23
White	15% (2)	85% (11)	13
Kennedy	35% (7)	65% (13)	20
Stevens	56% (13)	44% (10)	23
Blackmun	57% (8)	43% (6)	14
Brennan	67% (8)	33% (4)	12
Souter	73% (8)	27% (3)	11
Breyer	80% (8)	20% (2)	10
Ginsburg	91% (10)	9% (1)	11
Marshall	100% (8)	0% (0)	8

Source: Harold J. Spaeth, *United States Supreme Court Judicial Database, 1953–2004 Terms* (Ann Arbor, MI: Inter-University Consortium for Political and Social Research, 2005).

court era. Four justices had strongly conservative records: Rehnquist, 96 percent conservative; Thomas, 91 percent conservative; Scalia, 88 percent conservative; and O'Connor, 87 percent conservative. Justice Kennedy also voted predominantly conservative, but his voting record was a more moderate 65 percent conservative. The four-person liberal group that we have frequently observed can also be seen in table 3.15, consisting of Stevens, Souter, Breyer, and Ginsburg. Given these voting data, it is not difficult to understand why the Rehnquist Court has ruled pro-government in 75 percent of the double jeopardy cases.

The Guarantee against Compelled Self-Incrimination

Quantitative analysis is extremely useful in analyzing and comparing the Rehnquist Court with its preceding counterparts, but it is also necessary to engage in the study of major cases to determine if the Rehnquist Court engaged in a conservative counterrevolution regarding the Fifth Amendment guarantees against compelled self-incrimination and double jeopardy. We begin with self-incrimination. The argument we develop is that the Warren Court did engage in revolutionary liberal decision making in this area of constitutional law by nationalizing the protection against compelled self-incrimination and then in *Miranda* requiring law enforcement officers to inform people of this right prior to custodial interrogation. The Burger Court gave numerous conservative interpretations to *Miranda*-related cases and created various exceptions to *Miranda*, but the Burger Court justices upheld the core of the *Miranda* decision. The Rehnquist Court followed the pattern of the Burger Court, reaching conservative decisions in most self-incrimination cases but remaining committed to *Miranda*. Thus, no dramatic shift to the right occurred in the Rehnquist Court era in regard to the Fifth Amendment protection against compelled self-incrimination.

The Pre–Warren Court Period

These generalizations require an analysis of leading cases from the major eras of Supreme Court history, beginning with the pre–Warren Court era. During the many decades prior to Earl Warren becoming chief justice, the Court heard few self-incrimination cases because this guarantee had not been incorporated or applied to the states. This was not because of a lack of opportunity; the Court in *Twining v. New Jersey* (1908) and *Adamson v. California* (1947) explicitly rejected the opportunity to nationalize the protection against compelled self-incrimination.

Because the Fifth Amendment Self-incrimination Clause applied only to the federal government, few cases reached the Supreme Court, and no federal protection existed for those at the state level who believed they were improperly coerced into confessions. And although reliable statistical evidence is not available, abuses were undoubtedly common, especially by white police officers against African Americans. In Mississippi, for example, police would hang suspects from trees by their necks and use leather straps to whip them to obtain confessions. In *Brown v. Mississippi* (1936), the Court found such practices to violate the Constitution, but the ruling was based upon the Fourteenth Amendment due process guarantee rather than the Fifth Amendment protection against compelled self-incrimination.

The Warren Court Period

The Warren Court's decisions regarding self-incrimination can be viewed as their most dramatic in all of the areas of the guarantees of the criminally accused. An especially important case was *Malloy v. Hogan*, in 1964, when the Court nationalized the protection against compelled self-incrimination, thus reversing the prior decisions of

Twining and *Adamson*. But the Warren Court justices were determined to go much further in interpreting the protection against self-incrimination, and in *Escobedo v. Illinois* (1964) and *Miranda v. Arizona* (1966), the justices provided detailed guidelines for law enforcement personnel throughout the nation to follow.

In *Escobedo*, the Warren Court dealt with the question of whether a suspect's rights were violated when police questioned him in a murder case for more than fourteen hours while denying him the chance to talk with his attorney. The Warren Court majority found this to be unconstitutional and recognized a critical linkage between the Fifth Amendment protection against compelled self-incrimination and the Sixth Amendment guarantee of an attorney. The majority opinion stated that a criminal suspect has the right to consult with an attorney when the suspect is in custody and the police are ready to begin an interrogation that could lead to incriminating statements. This is the principle that a person has the right to counsel at the custodial interrogation stage, and it represents the idea that the privilege against compelled self-incrimination can best be ensured if the right to counsel is provided.

The controversial *Miranda* decision extended the logic of the *Escobedo* case. Ernesto Miranda had been arrested and charged with kidnapping and rape. Arizona police interrogated Miranda for several hours and eventually elicited a confession from him. The central issue considered by the Court in this case was whether Miranda should have been informed before questioning began of his constitutional guarantees regarding self-incrimination and counsel. A narrow five-person majority found in favor of Miranda. Chief Justice Warren authored the majority opinion, setting forth the famous *Miranda* warnings that police must tell suspects who are under arrest and are about to undergo interrogation: you have the right to remain silent, anything you say can and will be used against you in a court of law, you have the right to the assistance of legal counsel, and counsel will be provided to you if you cannot afford it. Warren argued that the inherently coercive nature of police interrogation and the documented evidences of police abuses required these warnings to give meaning to the protection against self-incrimination. Anticipating the criticism that these warnings would significantly harm police effectiveness, Warren pointed out that the Federal Bureau of Investigation (FBI) had been warning federal suspects of their rights for several years without compromising their ability to gain convictions.

The four dissenting justices sharply criticized Warren's opinion, and numerous law enforcement authorities, journalists, and political figures joined the attack. Some questioned Warren's emphasis on the prevalence of police abuses. Others argued that the Court was engaged in improper judicial activism by rejecting long-standing police practices that had historically been viewed as constitutional. Great concern was expressed over the effects of this policy, which it was feared would dramatically reduce the ability of police to obtain incriminating evidence, thus harming the ability of the government to prosecute successfully those guilty of crime. In Justice White's words, "In some unknown number of cases the Court's rule will return a killer, a rapist, or other criminal to the streets and to the environment which produced him, to repeat his crime whenever it pleases him" (384 U.S. at 542).

The Burger Court Period

The future of *Miranda* was uncertain as the Warren Court era ended and the Burger Court period began. As we have noted previously, President Richard Nixon had the opportunity in his first term to replace four members of the Warren Court with more conservative appointments: Burger for Warren, Blackmun for Fortas, Powell for Black, and Rehnquist for Harlan. *Miranda* had been supported by only a five-person majority, which included Warren, Fortas, and Black, and thus many Court observers predicted the overturning of *Miranda*. However, this did not happen. The Burger Court typically interpreted *Miranda* and other self-incrimination cases conservatively in favor of law enforcement interests, and this era saw many limitations and exceptions regarding *Miranda;* but the Burger Court refused to overturn *Miranda*, thus providing time for the seedling precedent to establish firm roots in the constitutional soil.

Conservatives applauded and liberals lamented many of the Burger Court's decisions that limited the scope of *Miranda* or created exceptions to it. In *New York v. Quarles* (1984), for example, a 6–3 Court created a public safety exception to *Miranda*, ruling that an arrested suspect could be questioned before the *Miranda* warnings were read if a direct threat to public safety was involved, in this case the location of a gun used in a crime. Another example of a controversial conservative decision came in *Moran v. Burbine* (1986). In this case, a suspect had been arrested by the police initially for burglary and then came under suspicion for murder. A public defender contacted the police regarding the burglary charge and was told they would not question the suspect until morning, and furthermore she was not told the client was a murder suspect. Police then began a series of sessions questioning the suspect, who was read his *Miranda* rights before each session but was not informed of the efforts of his attorney. He eventually confessed to the murder. A six-person Burger Court majority saw no constitutional problems with the police deception in this case.

Despite cases like *Quarles, Burbine,* and others, the Burger Court refused to overturn *Miranda* and did on occasion provide pro-suspect interpretations to *Miranda*. For example, *Brewer v. Williams* (1977) involved a highly emotional case in which Robert Williams was accused of kidnapping and then murdering a ten-year-old girl on Christmas Eve in 1968 in Des Moines, Iowa. He was arrested in eastern Iowa, but the girl's body was not in his car. Williams was in contact with an attorney in Des Moines, and the attorney told him not to say anything and told Des Moines police who

were to pick him up not to question Williams. On the way back to Des Moines, however, the police, playing upon Williams's religious beliefs, talked about the importance
of finding the girl's body so that she could be given a proper Christian burial. Williams
broke down and took the police to the place where he had dumped the body. The issue
before the Burger Court was whether the police statements constituted questioning
within the meaning of *Miranda*, but Iowa and other states in an amicus capacity asked
the Court to overturn *Miranda*. A five-person Burger Court majority not only refused
to overturn *Miranda* but also ruled that Williams's *Miranda* rights had not been violated by the subtle interrogation tactics of the police.

The Rehnquist Court Period

How did the Rehnquist Court deal with the Fifth Amendment protection against compelled self-incrimination and *Miranda?* Our analysis shows that the Rehnquist Court
followed a path remarkably similar to that of the Burger Court. Both Courts ruled in
favor of the government in three-fourths of these cases, and various limitations and
exceptions were created; however, both Courts were willing to draw lines beyond
which law enforcement officials could not go, and both Courts refused explicit
requests to overturn *Miranda*.

Certainly the predominant pattern for the Rehnquist Court was to find that law
enforcement officials had not violated the basic principles underlying *Miranda* and
the guarantee against self-incrimination. Several major example cases can be cited.

In *Duckworth v. Eagan* (2000), a five-person majority gave approval to a form of
the *Miranda* warnings that deviated significantly from the language in the original
opinion and that was generally used by police. In this case, a man was arrested for
attempted murder in the stabbing of a woman. Police informed him of his right to
silence and to an attorney, but they also stated: "We have no way of giving you a
lawyer, but one will be appointed for you, if you wish, if and when you go to court"
(492 U.S. at 198). Writing for the conservative majority, Chief Justice Rehnquist argued
that no exact format was required for the *Miranda* warnings. The critical issue is
whether the suspect is provided a reasonable description of his rights, and in this case
that criterion was met. The dissenting justices—Blackmun, Brennan, Marshall, and
Stevens—angrily accused the majority of "mak[ing] a mockery of [*Miranda*]" (492 U.S.
at 215) and of "disemboweling *Miranda* directly" (492 U.S. at 221).

Another example of the Rehnquist Court providing a narrow interpretation of
Miranda that favored law enforcement interests was in *Illinois v. Perkins* (1990). In
this case, a prison inmate was suspected of having committed a murder in addition to
the crimes for which he had been incarcerated. An undercover law enforcement officer was placed in prison with the suspect. Eventually, the suspect made incriminating

statements to the undercover agent, who did not make any mention of the *Miranda* warnings. The Rehnquist Court ruled that this did not constitute a violation of *Miranda* because these warnings were intended to address the inherently coercive nature of law enforcement interrogation, and no coercion existed in this case.

Pennsylvania v. Muniz (1990) provides a final illustration of the Rehnquist Court's conservative orientation toward *Miranda* and the protection against self-incrimination. Muniz was arrested for drunken driving and was taken to the police station. Without reading him his *Miranda* rights, police videotaped him while asking him a series of questions about his name, address, age, birth date, and other personal information. He was also videotaped doing a series of sobriety tests. Only then was he read his *Miranda* rights. Muniz claimed that he should have been read his *Miranda* warnings before the videotaping began, but the Rehnquist Court disagreed, arguing that the videotaped activities were nontestimonial evidence and thus did not implicate *Miranda*, which only involves testimonial evidence.

Although the dominant pattern of the Rehnquist Court has been to rule against individuals claiming that their *Miranda* rights have been violated, the justices of the Rehnquist Court have on occasion handed down rulings that law enforcement officers have violated *Miranda*. Most importantly, in the 2000 case of *Dickerson v. United States*, a seven-person majority strongly supported the *Miranda* warnings in a case in which they were invited to overturn the landmark 1966 decision.

Arizona v. Roberson (1989) is an example of the Rehnquist Court applying *Miranda* in a liberal manner. Arizona police sought to question Roberson about a crime, and Roberson stated that he would not answer any questions without his attorney present. Police honored this position but then sought to question him again regarding a separate crime. A seven-person majority found that this practice violated *Miranda*, ruling that all questioning must cease when the suspect requests an attorney.

In a closely related decision in *Minnick v. Mississippi* (1990), another seven-person majority provided a pro-defendant interpretation of *Miranda*. Minnick had asserted his right to counsel and had met with his attorney. Following this meeting, law enforcement personnel approached Minnick again, read him the *Miranda* warnings, and sought to question him. The majority found this to violate *Miranda*, arguing that police cannot reinitiate questioning after a suspect asserts his right to counsel and meets with counsel.

Yet another example of a liberal *Miranda* decision by the Rehnquist Court came in *Arizona v. Fulminante* (1991), a case closely related to the conservative *Illinois v. Perkins* (1990) decision we discussed above. In *Perkins*, the majority ruled that incriminating statements made by an inmate to an undercover agent posing as a prisoner were admissible because no coercion was involved. The *Fulminante* case also involved evidence obtained by an undercover agent posing as a prisoner, but the Rehnquist Court ruled law enforcement activities in this case violated *Miranda* because the undercover agent told Fulminante that he would protect him from other inmates if he confessed. For a five-person majority, this constituted the type of coercion that *Miranda* sought to prevent.

The most widely watched and most important Rehnquist Court decision involving *Miranda* occurred in the 2000 case of *Dickerson v. United States*, in which a seven-person majority strongly reaffirmed *Miranda* against a direct challenge to the ruling. The origins of this case dated back to the sixties. In reaction to *Miranda*, Congress passed a law in 1966 that declared that a confession should be admissible in a criminal case if it was given voluntarily. This meant that the *Miranda* warnings did not have to be given as long as convincing evidence existed that the confession was voluntary. This law was not used for decades because the Nixon and subsequent administrations assumed it was unconstitutional.

This dormant law challenging the validity of *Miranda* remained unnoticed until it was invoked by the Fourth Circuit Court of Appeals in 1999. Dickerson was a suspect in a bank robbery in Alexandria, Virginia, and FBI agents questioned him without providing his *Miranda* warnings. Based upon his responses, federal agents obtained a warrant and found incriminating evidence in his apartment. Dickerson sought to have his statements and the evidence suppressed because his *Miranda* warnings were not read, and a trial judge agreed. The Fourth Circuit, however, overturned the trial judge on the basis of the 1966 federal law. In an unusual development, the Clinton Justice Department refused to defend the law and the Fourth Circuit's opinion, resulting in a conservative law professor, Paul Cassell, of the University of Utah, representing the United States in the case before the Supreme Court. Cassell pressed the Rehnquist Court justices to find the law valid and to overturn *Miranda*.

In an opinion authored by Chief Justice Rehnquist, a seven-person majority found the law to be unconstitutional and reaffirmed the validity of *Miranda*. In Rehnquist's words, "We hold that *Miranda*, being a constitutional decision of this Court, may not be in effect overruled by an Act of Congress, and we decline to overrule *Miranda* ourselves. We therefore hold that *Miranda* and its progeny in this Court govern the admissibility of statements made during custodial interrogation in both state and federal courts" (68 USLW at 4566). Scalia wrote a harsh dissent that was joined by Thomas.

We conclude this analysis of the Rehnquist Court's decisions regarding *Miranda* and the guarantee against compelled self-incrimination by stating that the Court did not engage in a conservative constitutional counterrevolution. The Rehnquist Court certainly favored law enforcement interests in this area of criminal rights, ruling conservatively in three-fourths of its decisions and creating a variety of constraints on *Miranda*. The Rehnquist Court, however, maintained the core of *Miranda* and rejected an opportunity to overturn the decision. At least four reasons seem to be relevant to explaining the Rehnquist Court's commitment to *Miranda*. First, as expressed by Rehnquist in *Dickerson*, the principle of *stare decisis* carries great weight, and

Miranda is deeply engrained in not only American legal culture but also American popular culture. A second reason is that some of the more conservative justices may think that Burger and Rehnquist Court decisions have significantly limited *Miranda* so that it maintains a proper balance between the interests of the criminal defendant and the criminal justice system. Third, law enforcement personnel across the country seem to have accepted *Miranda* and do not view it as an unreasonable impediment to their work. Fourth, the justices seem to think that *Miranda* does promote fundamental principles of fairness in America's criminal justice system.

The Guarantee against Double Jeopardy

We have observed a similar pattern of Supreme Court decision making in regard to the Fourth Amendment protection against unreasonable searches and seizures and the Fifth Amendment guarantee against compelled self-incrimination: the Warren Court engaged in a liberal revolution, and the Burger and Rehnquist Courts were distinctively more conservative but did not overturn the major Warren Court precedents. In switching our focus to the Fifth Amendment protection against double jeopardy, however, we find a different pattern. Although the Warren Court did nationalize this guarantee, the predominant pattern of decision making by the Warren Court justices was distinctively conservative, with 67 percent of these cases going against the individual. The decisional pattern of the Burger Court was similar, at 63 percent conservative, and the Rehnquist Court decided 75 percent of its double jeopardy cases in favor of the government. Thus, the Supreme Court has been consistently conservative in this area for fifty years, and the Rehnquist Court did not engage in a conservative counterrevolution.

The pre–Warren Court era gave rise to some important double jeopardy decisions. Perhaps the most important case was *Palko v. Connecticut*, in 1937. The Court refused in an 8–1 decision to nationalize the protection against double jeopardy, arguing that this guarantee was not a fundamental principle of liberty and justice. The *Palko* decision did become the foundation for the eventual nationalization of most of the Bill of Rights guarantees, but this could not have been of much consolation to the defendant who died in the Connecticut electric chair in 1938 on the basis of his first-degree murder conviction in a second trial against him. The other major double jeopardy case decided in the pre–Warren Court era was *Blockberger v. United States*, in 1932. This case created the principle that the guarantee against double jeopardy means that a second trial may not be conducted when two criminal offenses involve the government in proving the same elements of a crime. This "*Blockberger* rule," or "same-elements test," remains a central part of the Court's double jeopardy jurisprudence today.

The most notable double jeopardy decision of the Warren Court was its nationalization decision in *Benton v. Maryland* (1969), reversing the earlier *Palko* decision.

Benton was originally convicted on a burglary charge but was acquitted on a larceny charge. A state appeals court set aside his burglary conviction because of deficiencies in juror oaths, and in a retrial he was convicted on both the burglary and larceny charges. The Warren Court's decision to nationalize the protection against double jeopardy meant that Benton's larceny charge was invalidated.

Despite this important incorporation decision, the Warren Court gave predominantly conservative interpretations in double jeopardy cases, a pattern followed by the Burger Court. *Heath v. Alabama* (1985) was perhaps the most notable double jeopardy decision of the Burger Court era, raising the issue of whether a person can be tried in two separate states for the same crime. Heath hired two men to kill his pregnant wife, and they kidnapped her in Alabama and drove to Georgia, where they killed her. Heath pleaded guilty to murder in Georgia in exchange for a life sentence, and a year later an Alabama jury found him guilty of murder and sentenced him to death. Heath argued before the U.S. Supreme Court that the Alabama trial subjected him to double jeopardy, but a majority of the Burger Court justices disagreed. Establishing a "dual sovereignty doctrine" recognizing the sovereignty of individual states, the Court ruled that different states can prosecute an individual for the same crime.

The Rehnquist Court has been distinctively conservative in double jeopardy cases but not significantly more than the Warren and Burger Courts. The Rehnquist Court has ruled in favor of an individual bringing a double jeopardy claim in only five cases, and the justices overturned their own liberal precedent in one of these four cases. In *Grady v. Corbin* (1990), the Rehnquist Court considered the application of the *Blockberger* rule. A drunken driver had crashed into another car, killing one person and seriously injuring another individual. In a bizarre series of events, an assistant prosecutor began pursuing evidence for a charge of homicide, but he did not make contact with prosecutors in traffic court. The defendant entered a guilty plea in traffic court and was subsequently fined and had his driver's license temporarily revoked by a judge who was unaware that a fatality was involved in the case. Subsequently, a grand jury brought a charge of reckless manslaughter against the defendant, who argued that this grand jury indictment involved double jeopardy. A five-person majority of the Rehnquist Court agreed with the defendant by extending the *Blockberger* rule: "The Double Jeopardy Clause bars subsequent prosecution if, to establish an essential element of an offense charged in that prosecution, the government will prove conduct that constitutes an offense for which the defendant has already been prosecuted" (495 U.S. at 510).

In *United States v. Dixon*, in 1993, however, the Rehnquist Court overturned its own *Grady* precedent. This dramatic reversal can be attributed directly to changes in the Court's personnel. The four dissenters in *Grady*—Rehnquist, Scalia, O'Connor, and Kennedy—were joined by the Court's newest justice, Thomas, who had replaced Marshall.

The Rehnquist Court's most widely publicized double jeopardy cases have been conservative decisions where the double jeopardy issue has involved both criminal and civil law. In *United States v. Ursery* (1996), Guy Ursery was arrested, convicted, and sentenced to five years in prison for the illegal production of marijuana. The federal government also used a property forfeiture law, a civil law, seeking to have the house and land used in the criminal activity forfeited to the government. Ursery argued that bringing both actions against him constituted double jeopardy, and the Sixth Circuit Court of Appeals agreed. The Rehnquist Court reversed in an 8–1 decision written by Chief Justice Rehnquist. He argued that the Fifth Amendment protection against double jeopardy applies only to criminal cases, and the property forfeiture action was civil in nature. Thus, double jeopardy was not involved in this case.

The Rehnquist Court reached a somewhat similar decision in the 1997 case of *Kansas v. Hendricks*. A Kansas law, the Sexually Violent Predator Law, provided that convicted sexual offenders could be kept in custody even after they had served their criminal sentence. Hendricks, who had been sexually molesting children for forty years, was completing his jail sentence, and Kansas used their law to commit Hendricks to a mental institution after a jury found beyond a reasonable doubt that he was a threat to the community. Hendricks challenged the action as violating his protection against double jeopardy, but a five-person Rehnquist Court majority disagreed, ruling that the confinement under the sexual predator law was a civil action and thus did not trigger the double jeopardy guarantee.

Having examined both the protection against compelled self-incrimination and the guarantee against double jeopardy, we can offer some conclusions about the Rehnquist Court's Fifth Amendment jurisprudence. The evidence shows that the Rehnquist Court did not engage in a conservative constitutional counterrevolution. The Warren Court did engage in a liberal revolution in regard to the protection against self-incrimination, and the Burger and Rehnquist Courts have been substantially more conservative in this area of constitutional law, creating various limitations and exceptions to *Miranda*. But *Miranda* remains good law, with the Rehnquist Court committed to its core principles. In regard to the protection against double jeopardy, the Warren, Burger, and Rehnquist Courts have all been predominantly conservative, providing relatively few victories for individuals claiming a violation of this Fifth Amendment guarantee.

The Sixth Amendment Guarantees of Counsel and a Fair Trial

In examining the Constitution's guarantees of individual rights in regard to the criminal justice process, we have thus far analyzed the Fourth and Fifth Amendments, which are primarily concerned with pretrial stages of the criminal system. We now turn to the Sixth Amendment's guarantees, which focus on the trial stage, and our central concern is, once again, whether the Rehnquist Court changed constitutional interpretation in a radically conservative direction.

The Sixth Amendment reads as follows:

> In all criminal prosecutions, the accused shall enjoy the right to a speedy and public trial, by an impartial jury of the State and district wherein the crime shall have been committed, which district shall have been previously ascertained by law, and to be informed of the nature and cause of the accusation; to be confronted with the witnesses against him; to have compulsory process for obtaining witnesses in his favor, and to have the Assistance of Counsel for his defence.

The Sixth Amendment thus contains numerous guarantees for the criminally accused, and at least two important reasons explain this focus on trial rights. First, a great deal is at stake in a criminal trial because the defendant may lose his or her freedom and may even face execution. Second, criminal trials are relatively rare and represent the most difficult and significant cases in the criminal justice system. Less than 5 percent of cases go to trial, with the other 95 percent being dismissed or plea-bargained. The small percentage of cases that do go to trial are typically high-publicity cases, such as murder, and cases in which substantial doubt exists regarding the outcome.

In analyzing these Sixth Amendment rights, we create two categories: the right to counsel and the other guarantees of a fair trial. A consensus exists that the right to counsel is the most important of the Sixth Amendment guarantees, and it is the most litigated of the rights in the Sixth Amendment. Significant as the other Sixth Amendment rights are, they have not been the source of a large number of Supreme Court cases, and hence we can analyze them together. Following the pattern established in this book, we begin with a quantitative analysis that not only compares the Rehnquist Court with the Warren and Burger Courts but also analyzes the individual voting records of the fourteen justices who served on the Rehnquist Court. Once we have completed the quantitative analysis, then we engage in a qualitative examination of major Supreme Court Sixth Amendment cases throughout history to determine if the Rehnquist Court radically altered prior Court precedent regarding the trial rights of the criminally accused.

Tables 3.16 and 3.17 contain data relevant to the Sixth Amendment right to counsel. In table 3.16, we see the voting records of the Warren, Burger, and Rehnquist Courts. The differences are large and significant. The Warren Court was extremely liberal, deciding 86 percent of its right to counsel cases in favor of the individual claiming an abridgement of this right. The Burger Court, in contrast, was much more moderate, ruling liberally in nearly half—44 percent—of its counsel cases. The Rehnquist Court was highly conservative, handing down liberal decisions in only 24 percent of its

Table 3.16: Liberal/Conservative Voting in Sixth Amendment
Right to Counsel Cases by the Warren, Burger, and
Rehnquist Courts, 1953–1954 to 2004–2005 Terms

Court Era	Liberal Decisions	Conservative Decisions	Total Cases
Warren Court (1953–1968 Terms)	86% (18)	14% (3)	21
Burger Court (1969–1985 Terms)	44% (14)	56% (18)	32
Rehnquist Court (1986–2004 Terms)	24% (5)	76% (16)	21
Total	50% (37)	50% (37)	74

Source: Harold J. Spaeth, *United States Supreme Court Judicial Database, 1953–2004 Terms* (Ann Arbor, MI: Inter-University Consortium for Political and Social Research, 2005).

Table 3.17: Liberal/Conservative Voting Records of the Justices of the
Rehnquist Court in Sixth Amendment Right to Counsel Cases, 1986–1987 Term to
2004–2005 Term (Justices Ranked from Most Conservative to Most Liberal)

Justices	Liberal Decisions	Conservative Decisions	Total Cases
White	10% (1)	90% (9)	10
Scalia	14% (3)	86% (18)	21
Kennedy	16% (3)	84% (16)	19
Thomas	17% (2)	83% (10)	12
Rehnquist	20% (4)	80% (16)	20
O'Connor	24% (5)	76% (16)	21
Souter	54% (7)	46% (6)	13
Breyer	60% (6)	40% (4)	10
Ginsburg	73% (8)	27% (3)	11
Stevens	76% (16)	24% (5)	21
Powell	100% (1)	0% (0)	1
Brennan	100% (8)	0% (0)	8
Marshall	100% (9)	0% (0)	9
Blackmun	100% (11)	0% (0)	11

Source: Harold J. Spaeth, *United States Supreme Court Judicial Database, 1953–2004 Terms* (Ann Arbor, MI: Inter-University Consortium for Political and Social Research, 2005).

right to counsel cases. These are dramatic shifts, larger than we have seen thus far in any of the constitutional areas we have examined. The numbers certainly support the possibility that the Rehnquist Court engaged in a conservative constitutional counter-revolution in regard to the guarantee of counsel, but any final conclusion must await our qualitative analysis of the Rehnquist Court's right to counsel cases.

Table 3.17 provides additional insight into the decision making of the Rehnquist Court in this area of criminal rights. The justices have been sharply split in regard to right to counsel cases. Focusing upon the nine justices on the natural court from 1994 to 2005, we can observe a solid, five-person conservative coalition composed of Justices Scalia (86 percent conservative), Kennedy (84 percent conservative), Thomas (83 percent conservative), Rehnquist (80 percent conservative), and O'Connor (76 percent conservative). The four liberal justices—Souter, Breyer, Stevens, and Ginsburg—show less cohesion than the conservative majority, with liberal scores varying from Souter's 54 percent to Stevens's 76 percent liberal. Individuals claiming violations of their Sixth Amendment right to counsel have thus found it very difficult to prevail throughout the era of the Rehnquist Court.

Quite different results emerge when we shift our analysis to the other Sixth Amendment fair trial guarantees. As can be observed in table 3.18, the Warren Court's strongly liberal voting record of 87 percent was nearly identical to its 86 percent liberal mark in right to counsel cases. The Burger Court's voting record in fair trial cases was significantly more conservative, as they decided only 24 percent of their cases in favor of the individual claiming a Sixth Amendment fair trial violation. Perhaps some-

Table 3.18: Liberal/Conservative Voting in Sixth Amendment Fair Trial Cases by the Warren, Burger, and Rehnquist Courts, 1953–1954 to 2004–2005 Terms

Court Era	Liberal Decisions	Conservative Decisions	Total Cases
Warren Court (1953–1968 Terms)	87% (20)	13% (3)	23
Burger Court (1969–1985 Terms)	24% (15)	76% (48)	63
Rehnquist Court (1986–2004 Terms)	43% (13)	57% (17)	30
Total	41% (48)	59% (68)	116

Source: Harold J. Spaeth, *United States Supreme Court Judicial Database, 1953–2004 Terms* (Ann Arbor, MI: Inter-University Consortium for Political and Social Research, 2005).

what surprisingly, the Rehnquist Court has been substantially more liberal than the Burger Court, ruling liberally in 43 percent of its cases involving fair trial issues.

This moderate voting pattern cannot be easily explained by examining the individual voting records of the justices of the Rehnquist Court that are contained in table 3.19. These data reveal that ten of the Rehnquist Court justices have voted conservatively in a majority of the cases, and only four justices have voted liberally a majority of the time. On the natural court from 1994 to 2005, seven of the justices have conservative records. This includes not only the familiar five-person conservative coalition of Rehnquist, Scalia, Thomas, Kennedy, and O'Connor but also Breyer and Souter, who are typically moderate liberals. These individual voting records suggest that the Rehnquist Court should have been more conservative than its 57 percent conservative record in fair trial cases. The most reasonable explanation for the moderate conservatism of the Rehnquist Court justices in Sixth Amendment fair trial cases seems to be the occurrence of a substantial number of cases in which somewhat unusual coalitions of justices came together to reach liberal decisions. We examine these cases shortly.

Table 3.19: Liberal/Conservative Voting Records of the Justices of the Rehnquist Court in Sixth Amendment Fair Trial Cases, 1986–1987 Term to 2004–2005 Term (Justices Ranked from Most Conservative to Most Liberal)

Justices	Liberal Decisions	Conservative Decisions	Total Cases
Thomas	23% (3)	77% (10)	13
Rehnquist	23% (7)	77% (23)	30
O'Connor	27% (8)	73% (22)	30
Kennedy	27% (6)	73% (16)	22
White	29% (6)	71% (15)	21
Breyer	33% (3)	67% (6)	9
Scalia	33% (10)	67% (20)	30
Souter	40% (6)	60% (9)	15
Powell	40% (2)	60% (3)	5
Blackmun	43% (9)	57% (12)	21
Ginsburg	56% (5)	44% (4)	9
Stevens	73% (22)	27% (8)	30
Brennan	93% (14)	7% (1)	15
Marshall	94% (15)	6% (1)	16

Source: Harold J. Spaeth, *United States Supreme Court Judicial Database, 1953–2004 Terms* (Ann Arbor, MI: Inter-University Consortium for Political and Social Research, 2005).

Right to Counsel

We have already encountered the right to counsel in our analysis of *Miranda* and its progeny, where we saw that the Court viewed the presence of counsel as critical to ensuring the protection against compelled self-incrimination. In this section we focus on right to counsel cases independent of *Miranda*. The argument is made that the Warren Court engaged in a liberal revolution in this important area of criminal rights. The Burger Court was moderately conservative in regard to the right to counsel, extending the Warren Court precedents at times and limiting them on other occasions, but the Burger Court supported the major precedents of the Warren Court. The Rehnquist Court was distinctively more conservative in right to counsel cases than either the Warren or Burger Courts, but the Rehnquist Court did not decide many major right to counsel cases, and the Rehnquist Court justices did not overturn leading precedents of the earlier Court periods. Thus, we cannot conclude that the Rehnquist Court engaged in a conservative counterrevolution in regard to the Sixth Amendment right to counsel.

The Pre–Warren Court Period

Although the right of counsel has been viewed as a critical element in the American criminal justice process since the Warren Court era, earlier Supreme Court justices took a more limited view of the importance of the right of counsel. Following the precedent of *Barron v. Baltimore* (1833), the Court for more than a century did not view the guarantee of an attorney as applicable to the states, where the vast majority of criminal cases occurred. In the thirties, the Court did, however, expand the applicability of the Sixth Amendment right to counsel in two important cases: *Powell v. Alabama* (1932) and *Johnson v. Zerbst* (1938). *Powell v. Alabama* involved the "Scottsboro boys," nine African American youths who were arrested for the alleged rape of two white girls. The young men received only the most minimal representation by counsel and were quickly tried in a racially charged atmosphere and sentenced to death. The Supreme Court ruled 7–2 that they had been denied their constitutional right to receive effective aid from legal counsel. However, the Court did not view this as a Sixth Amendment case because the guarantee had not been nationalized and instead argued that it involved the Fourteenth Amendment's guarantee of due process. *Johnson v. Zerbst* expanded the applicability of the right to counsel guarantee further when the Court in 1938 ruled that indigent federal criminal defendants must have an attorney appointed to represent them if they faced imprisonment.

Despite expanding the right of counsel to state defendants in capital cases and to indigent federal defendants facing imprisonment, the Court refused in *Betts v. Brady* (1942) to nationalize the right. In this case, the defendant was arrested and convicted for robbery. He could not afford an attorney and requested one, but Maryland law only provided counsel to indigents faced with rape or murder charges. In a 6–3 decision, the majority argued against incorporation of the right to counsel because it was not critical to achieving fairness and justice. In dissent, Justice Hugo Black argued that denying an indigent defendant the right to counsel "seems to me to defeat the promise of our democratic society to provide equal justice under law" (316 U.S. at 477).

The Warren Court Period

Justice Black's position was to triumph during the Warren Court era in the case of *Gideon v. Wainwright* (1963), in which the Court did make the right of counsel applicable to the states when a defendant could be imprisoned. Clarence Earl Gideon was arrested in Florida for breaking and entering as well as theft, and he requested that the trial judge appoint an attorney to represent him. The judge rejected Gideon's appeal because the federal Constitution did not require it under *Betts* and because Florida law provided for a court-appointed attorney only in capital cases. Gideon was convicted and sentenced to five years in prison, and while in prison he wrote a petition in pencil to the U.S. Supreme Court asking it to review his case. The justices agreed to hear Gideon's appeal and appointed one of Washington's most prominent attorneys—Abe Fortes, a future Supreme Court justice—to represent Gideon. Justice Black authored the opinion for a unanimous Court, explicitly overturning *Betts v. Brady*. The more liberal justices of the Warren Court now viewed the right to counsel as fundamental and essential to a fair trial for indigent defendants facing imprisonment for serious crimes. Unlike the Warren Court's unpopular criminal rights decisions involving the exclusionary rule and the *Miranda* warnings, the *Gideon* decision met with widespread approval because by this time most states already provided free counsel for indigent defendants facing serious charges.

Gideon was certainly not the Warren Court's only significant right to counsel case. As we saw in table 3.16, the justices of this era ruled liberally in eighteen of twenty-one right to counsel cases, and these do not include *Miranda* and its progeny. In *Douglas v. California* (1963), for example, the Warren Court ruled that states must appoint counsel for indigent defenders making their initial postconviction appeal. The Warren Court thus can be accurately portrayed as engaging in a liberal constitutional revolution regarding the Sixth Amendment right to counsel.

The Burger Court Period

Given the popularity of the *Gideon* decision and the widespread consensus regarding the importance of the right of counsel, it is not surprising that the Burger Court did not engage in a radical conservative reaction to the Warren Court's right of counsel jurisprudence. As we observed in table 3.16, the Burger Court's overall record in this area was one of moderation, deciding 44 percent of thirty-two decisions liberally. The Burger Court did not overturn any of the Warren Court's precedents, and on occasion the Burger Court justices gave liberal expansions to Warren Court decisions; however, the Burger Court also drew some conservative lines that likely would have been drawn differently by the Warren Court.

Argersinger v. Hamilton (1972) is an important Burger Court case in which the justices expanded upon the logic of the *Gideon* case. The *Gideon* decision focused on serious offenses, those that could lead to six months or more in prison. What about less-serious offenses that could still result in a jail term? In *Argersinger*, a Burger Court majority ruled that indigent defendants were entitled to assistance of counsel if they faced the possibility of incarceration.

The Burger Court justices also handed down a notable liberal decision in *Strickland v. Washington*, in 1984, ruling that a criminal defendant had received such inadequate assistance from his attorney that his Sixth Amendment right of counsel was violated. Despite the liberal outcome, however, the Burger Court emphasized that a reviewing authority should be highly deferential to an attorney being reviewed. Thus, a criminal defendant must prove under the two-part *Strickland* test not only that counsel was deficient because of serious errors but also that these errors deprived the defendant of a fair trial because the result was unreliable.

The Burger Court was also willing to limit the Sixth Amendment right of counsel. In *Ross v. Moffitt* (1974), for example, the justices limited the 1963 *Douglas* decision by ruling that the guarantee of assistance of counsel does not extend beyond the first appeal. *Scott v. Illinois* (1979) provides another important example of the Burger Court's willingness to limit the range of the right to counsel. In *Scott*, the state sought only a fine rather than imprisonment against a defendant charged with shoplifting. Because no imprisonment was involved, the defendant was denied his request for an appointed lawyer. Writing for a five-person majority, Justice Rehnquist agreed with the state, refusing to extend the *Argersinger* rule to cases not involving imprisonment.

The Rehnquist Court Period

How do we characterize the Rehnquist Court's treatment of the Sixth Amendment's right of counsel? As we observed in tables 3.16 and 3.17, the Rehnquist Court was decidedly conservative in these cases, ruling liberally only 24 percent of the time. The Court under Chief Justice Rehnquist, however, handed down few right to counsel decisions that are considered to be of major importance, and the Rehnquist Court justices have not disturbed the liberal right to counsel precedents of the Warren and Burger Court eras. Thus, despite the dominance of five- and six-person conservative coalitions throughout the Rehnquist Court era in right to counsel cases, we cannot conclude that the Rehnquist Court engaged in a conservative constitutional counter-revolution.

Numerous examples can be cited of the Rehnquist Court's conservative inclinations in Sixth Amendment right of counsel cases. We will discuss three of these. A decision that raised considerable controversy was the 1989 case of *United States v. Monsanto*. The case involved a challenge to a federal government practice of freezing assets of a defendant accused of illicit drug dealing to prevent the suspect from hiring defense counsel. The defendant argued that this practice violated his Sixth Amendment right to counsel, but the Rehnquist Court ruled 5–4 in favor of the government practice. Another example of the Rehnquist Court's conservative orientation in right to counsel cases can be found in *Perry v. Leake* (1989), where a six-person majority found no constitutional violation in the action of a trial judge who barred a defendant from talking with his attorney during a brief break from the trial. As a final example, in *Martinez v. Court of Appeals of California* (2000), the Rehnquist Court unanimously ruled against a convicted defendant who was asserting a constitutional right to represent himself at an appellate hearing.

Despite these and many other conservative decisions by the Rehnquist Court in right of counsel cases, the Rehnquist Court justices on occasion ruled in favor of individuals claiming a violation of their constitutional guarantee of counsel. *Williams v. Taylor* (2001) and *Alabama v. Shelton* (2002) are good examples. *Williams* involved the issue of the effectiveness of legal counsel. Williams claimed that he received ineffective assistance of counsel in violation of his Sixth Amendment right because his attorney in a murder trial failed to present important mitigating evidence at the sentencing stage of the trial and shortly after the trial was disbarred because of problems relating to mental illness. A six-person Rehnquist Court majority applied the conservative two-pronged *Strickland* test established by the Burger Court, finding not only that serious error was associated with failure to present key mitigating evidence but also that the result would likely have been different.

The 2002 *Shelton* case also illustrates that the Rehnquist Court was willing to support criminal defendants claiming their right of counsel has been violated. This case involved the important Burger Court precedents of *Argersinger* and *Scott*. Shelton was convicted without assistance of counsel to thirty days in jail, but the judge suspended the sentence and placed Shelton on two years' probation. He argued that he should have received appointed counsel because of the possibility of a jail sentence, and a five-person majority of the Rehnquist Court agreed that the logic of *Argersinger* and *Scott* required the appointment of counsel in a case like this.

Fair Trial Guarantees of the Sixth Amendment

Having examined the Rehnquist Court's decision making in Sixth Amendment right of counsel cases, we now shift our attention to the fair trial guarantees of the Sixth Amendment. These constitutional rights include a speedy, public trial by an impartial jury; the right to be informed of the charges against you; the right to confront witnesses against you; and the right to obtain witnesses in your favor. Our central focus remains the same—did the Rehnquist Court engage in a conservative constitutional counterrevolution in this area of the guarantees of the criminally accused? In analyzing statistical data in tables 3.18 and 3.19, we discovered a surprising finding: the Rehnquist Court was substantially more liberal in regard to the trial rights of the Sixth Amendment than the Burger Court. By examining leading Supreme Court fair trial cases, we find that this qualitative analysis parallels the quantitative analysis, supporting the conclusion that the Rehnquist Court did not engage in a conservative shift in interpreting the Sixth Amendment fair trial guarantees.

The Warren Court Period

The Warren Court had relatively little precedent upon which to draw in this area. Only two Sixth Amendment rights had been nationalized prior to the Warren Court era: the right to a public trial, in *In re Oliver* (1948), and the right to be informed of the charges being brought against you, in *Cole v. Arkansas* (1948). Thus, most Sixth Amendment trial rights applied only to the federal government before the Warren Court era, and federal criminal trials are only a small portion of the criminal trials in the United States.

As is the case in so many other areas of constitutional law, Court experts agree that the Warren Court engaged in a liberal constitutional revolution in regard to the jury trial rights of the Sixth Amendment. The most significant decisions were those that nationalized the vast majority of the jury trial rights. We have already given substantial attention to *Gideon v. Wainwright* (1963), the landmark case in which the Warren Court unanimously incorporated the right to counsel in felony cases. In addition, the Warren Court justices nationalized the Confrontation Clause in *Pointer v. Texas* (1965), the right to a speedy trial in *Klopfer v. North Carolina* (1967), the Compulsory Process Clause in *Washington v. Texas* (1967), and the right to a jury trial in *Duncan v. Louisiana* (1968). The Warren Court also ruled consistently liberal in other

Sixth Amendment fair trial cases, with 87 percent of its twenty-three cases favoring the claim of the individual that a Sixth Amendment right had been violated.

The Burger Court Period

The Burger Court was dramatically more busy and more conservative than the Warren Court in deciding Sixth Amendment fair trial cases. Because of the nationalization decisions of the Warren Court, the Burger Court decided sixty-three fair trial cases compared to twenty-three by the Warren Court. Furthermore, the Burger Court was far less sympathetic to criminal defendants, ruling liberally in only 24 percent of its cases compared to the 87 percent liberal voting record of the Warren Court.

Several examples of major conservative decisions can be cited involving the Burger Court's fair trial rights jurisprudence. Cases involving the size and voting requirements of juries are especially noteworthy. Long-standing federal practice required twelve-person juries who had to reach unanimous decisions in criminal cases, but the Burger Court altered these traditions in state cases. Emphasizing principles of state judicial federalism, the Burger Court held in *Williams v. Florida* (1970) that six-person juries were permissible in criminal cases, and in *Apodaca v. Oregon*, in 1972, the Burger Court justices found constitutional Oregon's system that allowed ten or eleven jurors to convict a defendant. The Burger Court provided further jury guidelines later in the seventies when ruling in *Ballew v. Georgia* (1978) that juries must have a minimum of six members and in *Burch v. Louisiana* (1979) that a jury of only six persons must reach a unanimous decision.

The Burger Court did, however, hand down important pro-defendant decisions in one area of trial rights cases—the jury selection process. In *Taylor v. Louisiana* (1975), for example, the Burger Court ruled unconstitutional a Louisiana law that required women to submit a written request to be considered for jury duty; absent such a declaration, a woman would not be considered. The Court ruled that the Sixth Amendment requires a genuine cross section of the community, and this law interfered with this requirement. In addition to being concerned with fair jury representation for women, the Burger Court justices also gave attention to the racial composition of juries. In *Batson v. Kentucky* (1986), the Court dealt with peremptory challenges, which allow attorneys to exclude potential jury members without providing any reasons for the exclusion. This was a long-standing practice even though it involved evidence of racial bias. In *Batson*, however, the Burger Court ruled that the use of peremptory challenges by prosecutors in a systematic way to exclude potential jurors from a specific racial group violated the Fourteenth Amendment Equal Protection Clause.

The Rehnquist Court Period

How do we most accurately characterize the decision making of the Rehnquist Court in regard to jury trial rights? We have already discussed in examining table 3.18 the surprising and unusual voting pattern in which the Rehnquist Court was distinctively more liberal (43 percent) than the Burger Court (24 percent). An analysis of the most important Sixth Amendment trial rights cases of the Rehnquist Court lends further support to a conclusion about the surprising liberalism of the Rehnquist Court in this area of constitutional law. In three major Sixth Amendment areas—obtaining impartial juries, the right to confront your accusers, and the ability of juries to determine sentences—the Rehnquist Court justices issued important new liberal decisions, and thus they certainly did not engage in a conservative constitutional counterrevolution in regard to the fair trial rights of the Sixth Amendment.

Turning first to the topic of selecting an impartial jury, the Rehnquist Court expanded in significant ways on the *Batson* decision of the Burger Court, discussed earlier. In *Powers v. Ohio* (1991), the justices ruled that a white defendant can contest the exclusion of African Americans through peremptory challenges. Also in 1991, the Rehnquist Court ruled in *Edmondson v. Leesville Concrete Co.* that the *Batson* rule against the racially biased use of peremptory challenges in criminal cases also applies to civil cases. Then, in *Georgia v. McCullum*, in 1992, the Rehnquist Court further extended the logic of *Batson; Batson* applied to prosecutors, and in *McCullum*, the justices ruled that defense attorneys cannot use peremptory challenges in a racially biased manner. Finally, in *J.E.B. v. Alabama ex rel. T.B.* (1994), a Rehnquist Court majority used the precedents of *Batson* and *McCullum* to prohibit the use of peremptory challenges that involved intentional gender discrimination. All of these Rehnquist Court decisions were based upon the Fourteenth Amendment Equal Protection Clause, but they have clear and direct relevance for the principles underlying the Sixth Amendment fair trial rights.

The Rehnquist Court has also handed down an important line of liberal decisions in regard to the Confrontation Clause of the Sixth Amendment. A particularly significant issue has involved the question of whether criminal defendants have the right to a face-to-face confrontation with children who have allegedly been sexually abused. In the 1988 case of *Coy v. Iowa*, Iowa used a screen to separate a defendant from two young girls who testified that he had sexually abused them. A six-person majority of the Rehnquist Court ruled that this practice violated the Sixth Amendment requirement of face-to-face confrontation. A related pro-defendant decision occurred in the 1990 case of *Idaho v. Wright*, in which a five-person majority ruled against the use of testimony by a pediatrician who reported what a child had said regarding sexual abuse by the defendant. The Rehnquist Court did rule against the defendant, however, in *Maryland v. Craig* (1990), approving the use of closed-circuit television for the testimony of a child who was the victim of child abuse. The majority in *Craig* distinguished the case from *Coy* because no determination had been made in *Coy* about the need for special protection for the young witnesses, but in *Craig*, special circumstances had been established justifying the use of closed-circuit television rather than face-to-face confrontation.

The Rehnquist Court's most important Confrontation Clause decision came in the 2004 case of *Crawford v. Washington*, involving the use of hearsay evidence in criminal trials. As a general principle, hearsay evidence is inadmissible in a criminal trial because it is based upon what a witness heard others say rather than the personal knowledge of the witness. In *Ohio v. Roberts* (1980), however, the Burger Court created a major exception to the hearsay rule by allowing testimonial hearsay to be admissible if the circumstances clearly showed that the statements were reliable. In *Crawford*, the Rehnquist Court overturned *Roberts* and rejected its underlying logic. In this unanimous liberal decision, the Court reversed the conviction of a Washington State man on charges of assault and attempted murder. In this case, the prosecution was allowed to introduce a recorded statement by Crawford's wife that was made during police interrogation; she did not testify at trial under the state of Washington's law regarding marital privilege, and Crawford's attorneys argued that his right to confront witnesses was being denied. Justice Scalia's majority opinion stated that "dispensing with confrontation because testimony is obviously reliable is akin to dispensing with jury trial because the defendant is obviously guilty. This is not what the Sixth Amendment prescribes" (72 USLW at 4237). One noted scholar writes that "the impact of *Crawford* on the criminal justice system will be monumental" because the decision "calls into question the continued vitality of virtually all the exceptions to the hearsay rule that have become part of the legal landscape over several decades" (Mickenberg 2004, S8).

A final area of fair trial rights in which the Rehnquist Court issued important pro-defendant decisions involved the right to a trial by a jury, specifically the authority of juries rather than judges to determine sentences. Four cases are especially noteworthy: *Apprendi v. New Jersey* (2000), *Ring v. Arizona* (2002), *Blakely v. Washington* (2004), and *Booker v. United States* (2005). These cases concern a development over the past few decades that provides for significant discretionary power by judges in determining criminal sentences. These laws have been enacted at both the state and federal levels. Under these sentencing laws, juries can find a person guilty, and a maximum imprisonment term is specified; however, a judge is permitted to engage in independent fact-finding and to impose a sentence exceeding the maximum if he or she finds certain legislatively stipulated facts. These laws have been challenged in numerous jurisdictions, and the Rehnquist Court found in *Apprendi*, *Ring*, *Blakely*, and *Booker* that such laws violate a criminal defendant's right to a trial by jury, with rather unusual voting coalitions emerging in these cases.

Charles Apprendi Jr. was arrested and convicted for firing shots into the house of an African American family because he did not want them living in the neighborhood. He pleaded guilty and faced a prison term of five to ten years. The state then filed a motion to enhance his sentence on the grounds that the crime was racially motivated. Under the applicable New Jersey hate crime statute, the trial judge was authorized to determine by a preponderance of the evidence if the crime was motivated by racial hatred. The judge made such a determination and increased the sentence to twelve years. An unusual five-person coalition of Justices Stevens, Ginsburg, Souter, Scalia, and Thomas ruled that New Jersey's law violated Apprendi's Sixth Amendment right to a trial by jury. Specifically, the majority argued that except for the fact of a prior prison conviction, a jury must determine beyond a reasonable doubt any fact that could increase a prison term beyond the prescribed statutory maximum.

The Rehnquist Court went farther in the 2002 case of *Ring v. Arizona*, explicitly overturning its own conservative precedent of *Walton v. Arizona* (1990). *Ring* was a capital case involving an Arizona law that allowed judges, not juries, to make critical factual determinations in murder cases. Specifically, the statute stipulated that a judge and not a jury must determine the existence of at least one statutorily defined aggravating factor to sentence a defendant to death. Justice Ginsburg wrote the majority opinion, joined by Stevens, Souter, Kennedy, Scalia, and Thomas. Although the Court had approved Arizona's sentencing scheme in *Walton*, Ginsburg found *Apprendi*'s ruling to be irreconcilable with the *Walton* decision and overruled *Walton:* "Capital defendants, no less than non-capital defendants, . . . are entitled to a jury determination of any fact on which the legislature conditions an increase in their maximum punishment" (70 USLW at 4667).

The Court extended *Apprendi* and *Ring* even farther in the 2004 *Blakely* case. Ralph Blakely was convicted of kidnapping his estranged wife and received the maximum sentence of fifty-three months in prison. The state of Washington's sentencing guidelines provided, however, that a trial judge could impose an additional thirty-seven months if he or she made an independent finding that the crime was committed with deliberate cruelty. This occurred in Blakely's case, resulting in a ninety-month sentence. Blakely's attorney argued that the logic of *Apprendi* and *Ring* applied to this case, and an unusual five-person majority of Justices Scalia, Thomas, Stevens, Ginsburg, and Souter agreed. This was, not surprisingly, the same majority coalition as in *Apprendi*, and their logic was the same: "Other than the fact of a prior conviction, any fact that increases the penalty for a crime beyond the prescribed statutory maximum must be submitted to a jury, and proved beyond a reasonable doubt" (72 USLW at 4547, citing *Apprendi*).

The *Blakely* decision raised immediate questions about the validity of federal sentencing guidelines, and the first oral argument heard by the Rehnquist Court in its

2004–2005 term challenged federal guidelines. In *Booker v. United States* (2005), the Court used the logic of *Blakely* to rule unconstitutional existing congressional guidelines, but the Court was deeply divided over the issues in the case. Justice Stevens wrote for a five-person majority that existing federal sentencing guidelines violated the Sixth Amendment right to a jury trial because judges, not juries, were empowered to find facts that can allow the alteration of sentences beyond what was decided by a jury. In regard to a solution to this issue, a starkly different majority ruled that the guidelines should now be made advisory rather than mandatory.

The *Booker* case is likely to have long and profound effects. A major political question is what will be the reaction of Congress, which has sought to constrain the discretionary power of the federal courts in regard to sentencing. Among the numerous questions confronting the federal court system are who should be entitled to a new sentencing hearing, should the decision be applied retroactively, and what are the standards that constitute a reasonable sentence.

Having reviewed both the Sixth Amendment guarantee of the right of counsel as well as the other fair trial rights of the Sixth Amendment, the evidence indicates that the Rehnquist Court did not engage in a conservative constitutional counterrevolution in regard to the Sixth Amendment. The Rehnquist Court justices were strongly conservative in right to counsel cases; however, they did not overturn major Warren and Burger Court right to counsel cases, and they handed down some significant decisions favoring the criminally accused. In addition, the Rehnquist Court provided support for the right to counsel through some of its *Miranda* decisions. In regard to the fair trial rights of the Sixth Amendment, the Rehnquist Court was far less conservative than might have been expected. In the era under Chief Justice Rehnquist's leadership, the Court was substantially more liberal than was the Burger Court and handed down liberal decisions in important cases involving impartial juries; the right of confrontation; and sentencing by juries, not judges, and these cases even involved the creation of new liberal precedents.

The Eighth Amendment Guarantee against Cruel and Unusual Punishments

Having analyzed the guarantees of the criminally accused found in the Fourth, Fifth, and Sixth Amendments, we now turn to the final amendment dealing with criminal rights, the Eighth Amendment, which states: "Excessive bail shall not be required, nor excessive fines imposed, nor cruel and unusual punishments imposed." We will focus our attention on the Cruel and Unusual Punishments Clause because the Supreme Court has not nationalized either the Excessive Bail Clause or the Excessive Fines Clause and therefore has decided very few cases involving either clause.

The Court has, however, given a great deal of attention to the guarantee against cruel and unusual punishments. The vast majority of these cases have involved capital punishment, putting to death a person convicted of a crime. A majority of the Court has never viewed capital punishment per se as violating the Constitution but instead has focused its attention on the conditions under which the government may execute someone without violating the constitutional prohibition on cruel and unusual punishments. Despite the predominance of capital punishment cases, however, the Court has also decided a substantial number of cases dealing with noncapital punishment, including conditions in prisons.

In analyzing both capital and noncapital cases, we again have as our central concern the issue of whether the Rehnquist Court engaged in a conservative constitutional counterrevolution. Both quantitative and qualitative methods of analysis are employed, and some of the results we discovered may be rather surprising.

Quantitative Analysis

Turning first to quantitative methods of analysis, we initially compare the voting records of the Warren, Burger, and Rehnquist Courts in regard to both capital and non-capital cases, and then we analyze the voting records of the individual justices of the Rehnquist Court. Table 3.20 compares the voting records of the three Courts in capital punishment cases, with a liberal decision being one in which the Court rules in favor of an individual claiming an Eighth Amendment violation and a conservative decision involving a ruling in favor of the government that no constitutional violation has occurred. Table 3.20 has several interesting results.

Looking first at the Warren Court, it is perhaps surprising to see that only three capital punishment cases were decided in this period, with one liberal and two conservative results. The explanation for this is related to the social movement to abolish the death penalty, led by the ACLU and the Legal Defense Fund of the National Association for the Advancement of Colored People (NAACP). This abolitionist movement became active in the sixties in association with the civil rights movement because of the strong belief that the death penalty was racially biased, with African Americans being disproportionately executed, especially when they were convicted of murdering a white person. These cases took time to work their way through the lower courts, and they did not reach the Supreme Court until the Warren Court had been replaced by the Burger Court. Thus, unlike other areas of the guarantees of the criminally accused, the Warren Court did not engage in a liberal constitutional revolution in regard to Eighth Amendment capital punishment cases because only three minor cases were decided.

The Burger Court, in contrast, was extremely busy with Eighth Amendment capital punishment cases, deciding thirty-two cases nearly evenly in terms of liberal (47 percent) and conservative (53 percent) outcomes. The Burger Court accepted the principle that the Cruel and Unusual Punishments Clause permitted capital punishment, but the Burger Court justices established detailed guidelines for the government to follow in carrying out capital punishment. The Burger Court was continuously confronted with challenges and questions regarding these guidelines, and the Court decided these cases nearly equally in terms of liberal and conservative outcomes. Based upon these quantitative data, we certainly cannot suggest that the Burger Court engaged in a conservative constitutional counterrevolution.

The data in table 3.20 also support the view that the Rehnquist Court did not engage in a dramatic conservative shift in regard to capital punishment cases. Like the Burger Court, the Rehnquist Court had Eighth Amendment capital cases as a significant part of its workload, deciding thirty-nine cases. Also like the Burger Court, the Rehnquist Court's overall voting record has been a moderate one, with 41 percent liberal and 59 percent conservative.

Table 3.21 provides comparative data across the Warren, Burger, and Rehnquist Court eras regarding noncapital punishment cases that also suggest strongly that the justices of the Rehnquist Court have not engaged in a conservative counterrevolution in this area of constitutional law. As in capital punishment decisions, the Warren Court decided only two cases, splitting evenly between liberal and conservative outcomes. The Burger Court was substantially conservative, deciding 83 percent of the six cases in favor of the government. In sharp contrast, the Rehnquist Court ruled liberally in one-half of its eight noncapital punishment cases. The three courts together have thus

Table 3.20: Liberal/Conservative Voting in Eighth Amendment Capital Punishment Cases by the Warren, Burger, and Rehnquist Courts, 1953–1954 to 2004–2005 Terms

Court Era	Liberal Decisions	Conservative Decisions	Total Cases
Warren Court (1953–1968 Terms)	33% (1)	67% (2)	3
Burger Court (1969–1985 Terms)	47% (15)	53% (17)	32
Rehnquist Court (1986–2004 Terms)	41% (16)	59% (23)	39
Total	46% (32)	54% (42)	74

Source: Harold J. Spaeth, *United States Supreme Court Judicial Database, 1953–2004 Terms* (Ann Arbor, MI: Inter-University Consortium for Political and Social Research, 2005).

Table 3.21: Liberal/Conservative Voting in Eighth Amendment
Noncapital Punishment Cases by the Warren, Burger, and
Rehnquist Courts, 1953–1954 to 2004–2005 Terms

Court Era	Liberal Decisions	Conservative Decisions	Total Cases
Warren Court (1953–1968 Terms)	50% (1)	50% (1)	2
Burger Court (1969–1985 Terms)	17% (1)	83% (5)	6
Rehnquist Court (1986–2004 Terms)	50% (4)	50% (4)	8
Total	38% (6)	62% (10)	16

Source: Harold J. Spaeth, *United States Supreme Court Judicial Database, 1953–2004 Terms* (Ann Arbor, MI: Inter-University Consortium for Political and Social Research, 2005).

only decided a total of sixteen noncapital cases, making generalizations tenuous. Clearly, however, the data do not support an argument that the Rehnquist Court shifted constitutional law in a radically conservative direction in regard to Eighth Amendment noncapital punishment cases.

In addition to comparing voting patterns for the three eras of the Supreme Court, we can also examine the voting records of the individual justices of the Rehnquist Court, focusing on capital punishment cases. Table 3.22 reveals that the Rehnquist Court justices have divided sharply in death penalty cases, with a five- or six-person conservative coalition typically being dominant. Once Kennedy replaced Powell, a five-person pro-government coalition existed with Scalia, Rehnquist, White, Kennedy, and O'Connor. This conservative coalition was vigorously opposed by four liberal justices who voted for the individual in virtually every death penalty case; Blackmun's overall liberal record was 94 percent, Stevens was at 95 percent liberal, and both Brennan and Marshall voted liberally in 100 percent of the capital cases. Marshall's replacement by Thomas increased the conservative coalition to six members, while Ginsburg replacing White reduced the conservative alignment back to a majority of five, where it remained for more than a decade. Thomas, Scalia, and Rehnquist consistently voted for the government in capital cases, Thomas at 93 percent conservative, Scalia at 90 percent, and Rehnquist at 90 percent. They were typically, but not always, joined by Kennedy (72 percent conservative) and O'Connor (69 percent conservative.) The four liberal justices show much greater variation; Souter voted liberally 56 percent, Ginsburg is at 64 percent liberal, Breyer voted liberally in 75 percent of the cases, and Stevens, at 95 percent, voted conservatively only twice in thirty-nine cases.

Table 3.22: Liberal/Conservative Voting Records of the Justices of the Rehnquist Court in Eighth Amendment Capital Punishment Cases, 1986–1987 Term to 2004–2005 Term (Justices Ranked from Most Conservative to Most Liberal)

Justices	Liberal Decisions	Conservative Decisions	Total Cases
Thomas	7% (1)	93% (14)	15
Scalia	10% (4)	90% (35)	39
Rehnquist	10% (4)	90% (35)	39
White	25% (7)	75% (21)	28
Kennedy	28% (9)	72% (23)	32
O'Connor	31% (12)	69% (27)	39
Souter	56% (10)	44% (8)	18
Powell	60% (3)	40% (2)	5
Ginsburg	64% (7)	36% (4)	11
Breyer	75% (6)	25% (2)	8
Blackmun	94% (29)	6% (2)	31
Stevens	95% (37)	5% (2)	39
Brennan	100% (21)	0% (0)	21
Marshall	100% (24)	0% (0)	24

Source: Harold J. Spaeth, *United States Supreme Court Judicial Database, 1953–2004 Terms* (Ann Arbor, MI: Inter-University Consortium for Political and Social Research, 2005).

These data suggest the Rehnquist Court justices could have moved Eighth Amendment capital punishment jurisprudence in a radically conservative direction but only if the strongly conservative justices could gain the support of O'Connor and Kennedy. To see if this happened, we need to turn to a qualitative analysis of leading death penalty cases. As we have done in previous sections, we will examine the pre–Warren Court era, the Warren Court period, and the Burger Court years to establish the proper perspective for analyzing the Rehnquist Court.

Eighth Amendment Capital Punishment Cases

The argument advanced is that the Rehnquist Court has not engaged in a conservative constitutional counterrevolution concerning Eighth Amendment capital punishment cases. The Warren Court decided almost no capital punishment cases and thus did not create a liberal revolution in this area of criminal rights jurisprudence. The Burger Court heard numerous death penalty cases, but its overall record is best characterized as one of moderation, allowing the state and federal governments to use capital punishment but establishing detailed guidelines that sought to provide fairness in the process. In the initial years of the Rehnquist Court, it appeared that a conservative majority was going to give government a wide range of discretion in regard to the death penalty, but the radical conservatism of the early Rehnquist Court years seems to have given way to a far more moderate approach to the death penalty in the later years of the Rehnquist Court era.

The Pre–Warren Court and Warren Court Periods

Capital punishment cases were rare during both the long period of Supreme Court history before the Warren Court as well as the decade and one-half of the Warren Court era. The death penalty was accepted by both society and the Supreme Court, with the Court ruling that the death penalty was neither cruel nor unusual in the 1947 case of *Louisiana ex rel. Frances v. Resweber*. As we saw earlier in this chapter, the Court did insist in *Powell v. Alabama* (1932) on the provision of effective counsel in state capital punishment cases. In the 1968 case of *Witherspoon v. Illinois*, the Warren Court ruled that jurors could not be excluded from a trial if they merely questioned the validity of the death penalty; they could only be excused if they could not return a guilty verdict because of opposition to capital punishment. The Warren Court thus provided little guidance to future courts regarding the Cruel and Unusual Punishments Clause and the death penalty. As Tinsley Yarbrough has written, "In the death penalty field, the Burger Court did not enlarge upon or narrow the reach of Warren Court decisions but moved instead through a virtually uncharted course" (2000, 206).

The Burger Court Period

The Burger Court had no real choice about hearing death penalty cases because of the activity of abolitionist attorneys in initiating and appealing capital punishment cases. In its initial decisions—for example, *McGautha v. California* (1971) and *Crampton v. Ohio* (1971)—the Burger Court gave states substantial leeway in regard to capital punishment, but in *Furman v. Georgia* (1972) and companion cases, a five-person majority ruled unconstitutional all existing death penalty laws. Justices Brennan, Marshall, Douglas, Stewart, and White could only agree, however, that the death penalty in the cases under review would violate the Eighth Amendment prohibition against cruel and unusual punishments. Brennan and Marshall took the most extreme position, that the death penalty per se was unconstitutional; Douglas, Stewart, and White, in separate opinions, presented different reasons why current death sentence laws were arbitrary and unfair, including the issue of racial bias.

State legislators immediately went to work to rewrite statutes that would meet the objections raised by the Burger Court. One approach was to use mandatory sentencing that would eliminate a great deal of judicial discretion and thus presumably the arbitrary nature of the death penalty, but the Court rejected this approach in *Woodson v. North Carolina* (1976). A second approach using a two-stage model was approved, however, by the Burger Court in *Gregg v. Georgia* (1976). Under this system, an initial trial is conducted to determine if a defendant is guilty of a crime for which capital punishment can be imposed. If the defendant is found guilty, then a second trial is held to determine if the death penalty should be imposed. At this sentencing stage, the defense introduces mitigating evidence as to why the death penalty should not be imposed, and the prosecution introduces aggravating evidence in support of the death penalty, with at least one element of the aggravating evidence required to be based upon statutory guidelines. If the jury decides in favor of the death penalty, the defendant is guaranteed an appeal. Interestingly, although seven members of the Burger Court agreed that the Georgia law was constitutional, a majority could not agree on a common opinion. Brennan and Marshall were in dissent, arguing that all death penalty laws violated the Eighth Amendment.

The Burger Court continued to be confronted with capital punishment cases in the aftermath of *Gregg* and *Woodson*. The Court divided rather evenly between pro-government and pro-criminal defendant outcomes, but several of the most noted cases were decided liberally. In *Coker v. Georgia* (1977), the Court ruled that capital punishment could not be imposed for the crime of rape. *Lockett v. Ohio* (1978) concerned mitigating evidence, with the Burger Court justices ruling that a jury cannot "be precluded from considering, as a mitigating factor, any aspect of a defendant's character or record and any of the circumstances of the offense that the defendant proffers as a basis for a sentence less than death" (438 U.S. at 605). In *Eddings v. Oklahoma* (1982), the Burger Court issued another liberal decision in ruling that a trial judge must allow a jury to hear mitigating evidence regarding a defendant's age, a difficult childhood, and mental problems. As a final example, in the 1986 case of *Ford v. Wainwright*, the Burger Court ruled that insane prisoners could not be given the death penalty.

The Rehnquist Court Period

The Rehnquist Court established a record in Eighth Amendment death penalty cases that paralleled that of the Burger Court, and thus we cannot conclude that the Rehnquist Court engaged in a conservative constitutional counterrevolution in regard to death penalty jurisprudence. This was certainly a busy area for the Rehnquist Court, which decided thirty-nine cases. Two primary factors characterize the essential moderation of the Court: a commitment to the two-stage process set forth in *Gregg v.*

Georgia (1976) and the close division between conservative (59 percent) and liberal (41 percent) outcomes. Interestingly, however, it appeared initially that the Rehnquist Court was going to take a radically conservative approach to death penalty cases, but several more recent decisions have been pro-defendant and have included the overturning of two of the Rehnquist Court's major conservative decisions.

During the first two terms of the Rehnquist Court, before Kennedy replaced Powell, the Court was extremely busy with death penalty cases, hearing eleven cases and deciding seven of them liberally. Despite this strongly pro-defendant orientation, however, the Court's most important and controversial decision was a conservative one. *McCleskey v. Kemp* (1987) was a case championed by the ACLU and the Legal Defense Fund of the NAACP. McCleskey was an African American who was found guilty of murder and was sentenced to death for killing a white police officer during the robbery of a furniture store in Atlanta, Georgia. Attorneys for the ACLU and the Legal Defense Fund had been convinced for decades of the strong racial bias in death penalty cases, and in the *McCleskey* case, they relied heavily on a recent study of Georgia's murder cases from 1973 to 1979 that revealed a strong racial bias in capital sentencing, specifically a far higher likelihood of the death sentence being imposed when blacks were found guilty of murdering whites. In a narrow 5–4 decision, Powell wrote the majority opinion that rejected the applicability of the study to this case. The study was viewed as merely showing a correlation between race and the death sentence; the study provided no evidence that racial bias had influenced McCleskey's case.

The *McCleskey* case was a watershed case because opponents of the death penalty believed that it presented them with their best chance to win a major victory and to undermine the entire death penalty system because of the pervasive influence of racial bias. The result of *McCleskey* was quite the opposite, however, because it marked the beginning of a series of major conservative decisions in death penalty cases by the Rehnquist Court. This development was heightened by Powell's resignation from the Court after the 1986–1987 term and his eventual replacement by the more conservative Kennedy.

When Kennedy joined the Court, in 1988, a solid conservative majority existed that seemed willing to allow state governments to impose the death penalty with few limitations. This conservative coalition was led by Scalia and Rehnquist, but White, O'Connor, and Kennedy were also predictable votes in favor of the government. This five-person conservative coalition was strengthened substantially when Marshall resigned in 1991 and was replaced by the far more conservative Thomas, thus creating a six-person conservative coalition. In a series of major decisions in the late eighties and early nineties, the Court's conservative justices approved of the death penalty for minors aged sixteen and seventeen, found no prohibition on executing the mentally retarded, overturned existing precedent in allowing victim impact statements to be used at the sentencing stage of capital cases, and sharply limited habeas corpus petitions by those sentenced to death.

Stanford v. Kentucky (1989) involved the issue of whether it was cruel and unusual punishment to execute minors, specifically persons aged sixteen and seventeen. The Rehnquist Court had previously ruled in *Thompson v. Oklahoma*, in 1988, that it was unconstitutional to execute a person younger than sixteen, but this was decided before Kennedy joined the Court. Kennedy joined Rehnquist, Scalia, White, and O'Connor to rule in *Stanford* that no convincing evidence existed of a national consensus opposing the death penalty for sixteen- and seventeen-year-olds, and thus the Eighth Amendment principle of measuring cruel and unusual punishments by the "evolving standards of decency that mark the progress of a maturing society" was not violated by executing minors.

The Court heard an equally emotion-charged death penalty case in the 1988–1989 term involving the execution of the mentally retarded in *Penry v. Lynaugh* (1989). The defendant in this case had the mental age of a six- to seven-year-old. The impact of Kennedy's appointment to the Court was apparent once again, because he joined the same conservative coalition that decided *Stanford* in finding that the Cruel and Unusual Punishments Clause does not prohibit the execution of the mentally retarded.

Payne v. Tennessee (1991) was yet another major conservative decision in the early Rehnquist Court years. This case involved victim impact statements, which are testimonies given by friends and relatives of a victim of a capital offense at the sentencing stage of a murder case. The Rehnquist Court had ruled in *Booth v. Maryland* (1987) and *South Carolina v. Gathers* (1989) that victim impact statements were impermissible because they could introduce such emotionally biased factors as the wealth, power, influence, and race of the murder victim rather than focusing the jury's attention on the crime and the accused. The Court's composition had changed again by 1991 with Souter replacing Brennan, and Souter joined Rehnquist, Scalia, White, and Kennedy to form a five-person majority that overturned *Booth* and *Gathers* in permitting victim impact statements.

A final example of the conservative decision making of the Rehnquist Court in the late eighties and early nineties can be found in *McCleskey v. Zant*, in 1991. The petitioner in this case was Warren McCleskey, who was also the petitioner in the *McCleskey v. Kemp* (1987) case we examined earlier. In the 1991 case, McCleskey was seeking a writ of habeas corpus from the federal courts because an informant had been placed in his cell and the prosecution withheld important information from McCleskey's attorney. The Rehnquist Court in a 6–3 ruling refused to grant the writ; the Court ruled that prisoners must present all of their habeas claims in a single petition, and McCleskey had exhausted his opportunity when he filed in his 1987 case. This ended McCleskey's appeal avenues, and he was executed a few months later in Georgia.

By the 1991–1992 term, it appeared that the Rehnquist Court would rarely if ever rule in favor of a criminal defendant in an Eighth Amendment death penalty case. By this time, the five-person conservative alignment of Rehnquist, Scalia, White, Kennedy, and O'Connor had been dramatically strengthened by the additions of Souter and Thomas, who had replaced the Court's two leading liberals, Brennan and Marshall, respectively. And the two Clinton appointees were not expected to have a huge impact; Ginsburg's replacement of White did reduce the size of the conservative coalition, but Breyer's assumption of Blackmun's position had relatively little impact.

In the long natural court period after Breyer joined the Court, however, the death penalty jurisprudence of the Rehnquist Court surprised many observers. The justices not only handed down some major liberal decisions but also overturned two leading conservative precedents of the earlier Rehnquist Court era. Rehnquist, Scalia, and Thomas were the only consistently conservative justices regarding the death penalty. Stevens was the most liberal, but Breyer, Ginsburg, and Souter were frequent liberal allies with Stevens. Kennedy and O'Connor were thus the two critical votes in the death penalty cases of the last natural court era, and they frequently supported the claims of criminal defendants. We turn, then, to an examination of some of the surprising liberal death penalty cases of the Rehnquist Court in recent years.

Two cases decided liberally in 2001 dealt with the adequacy of jury instructions in death penalty cases. In *Shafer v. South Carolina*, the issue involved a trial judge's refusal to comply with the defense counsel's request that the sentencing jury be informed that the life sentence alternative to the death penalty meant that the defendant could never be released on parole. Furthermore, when the jury asked the judge about the defendant's eligibility for parole if he received a life sentence, the judge refused to provide the information, stating that the matter of parole eligibility was not relevant to the jury's deliberations. With only Scalia and Thomas in dissent, the Court ruled that the judge had violated the defendant's rights because information regarding parole is important information for a jury at the sentencing stage of a capital case. *Penry v. Johnson* (2001) also involved jury instructions, specifically in cases involving the mentally retarded. In this case, the Court ruled 6–3 that a trial judge in his instructions to the jury at the sentencing state of a capital case had not given adequate opportunity for the jurors to consider mitigating evidence regarding the defendant's mental retardation and severe abuse as a child.

One of the most important and most controversial recent liberal death penalty decisions was *Atkins v. Virginia* (2002). The case involved Daryl Atkins, a man with an IQ estimated at fifty-nine, who was found guilty and sentenced to death by a Virginia jury for the brutal murder of a man whom he shot eight times. The issue before the Supreme Court was whether the Eighth Amendment Cruel and Unusual Punishments Clause prohibits the execution of the mentally retarded. The Rehnquist Court had answered this question negatively in the 1989 case of *Penry v. Lynaugh*, but in

Atkins, a 6–3 majority consisting of Justices Stevens, Ginsburg, Breyer, Souter, O'Connor, and Kennedy overturned *Penry* in ruling that the Eighth Amendment does prohibit the execution of the mentally retarded.

Writing for the majority, Stevens drew upon all of the major doctrinal standards in the Court's jurisprudence dealing with the Cruel and Unusual Punishments Clause. Stevens argued that the Eighth Amendment requires that punishment must be proportionate to the nature of the crime, and proportionality review requires the Court to consider the evolving standards of decency that characterize a maturing society. The most objective way of determining this according to Stevens's analysis was the actions of the country's legislatures. He argued that only two state legislatures prohibited executing the mentally retarded when *Penry* was decided in 1989, but since then sixteen additional legislatures had passed laws banning execution of the mentally retarded. Stevens also used the Eighth Amendment standards of whether the purposes of punishment— retribution and deterrence—are being served, and he argued they were not in regard to the death penalty for the mentally retarded. In addition, Stevens argued that the Court's own judgment should enter into the decision making, and he argued that "our independent evaluation of the issue reveals no reason to disagree with the judgment of the 'legislatures that have recently addressed the matter' and concluded that death is not a suitable punishment for a mentally retarded criminal" (536 U.S. at 321).

Scalia and Rehnquist both wrote impassioned dissents, with Thomas joining them. Scalia attacked every major point in Stevens's majority opinion, arguing that neither the text of the Eighth Amendment nor its history nor current legislative practices supported the Court's holdings, with a majority of the states that use the death penalty permitting it for the mentally retarded. Accusing the majority of writing their own opinions into the law, Scalia stated, "Seldom has an opinion of this Court rested so obviously upon nothing but the personal views of its Members" (536 U.S. at 338). Rehnquist's dissent attacked the majority for what the dissenters saw as an inappropriate reliance on opinion polls, the arguments of professional and religious organizations, and foreign laws. The chief justice argued that the Court's precedents did not support the use of these sources and that they undermined principles of federalism.

Paralleling the *Atkins* decision, the Rehnquist Court in the 2005 case of *Roper v. Simmons* explicitly overturned its own precedent of *Stanford v. Kentucky* (1989) in ruling that it is unconstitutional to execute a person who was sixteen or seventeen years of age at the time of the crime. In this close and bitter 5–4 decision, Justice Kennedy wrote the majority opinion, joined by the Court's four liberals: Stevens, Ginsburg, Souter, and Breyer. Kennedy advanced numerous arguments in his majority opinion, while Scalia in dissent challenged each and every argument. Kennedy argued that a new national consensus against the death penalty for minors had emerged since 1989 because the number of states supporting this position had grown from eighteen to thirty; Kennedy emphasized eighteen as the widely accepted age in American society for adult activities and responsibilities; he cited social science evidence regarding the differences of youth and adults; and he recognized the overwhelming weight of international opinion against the death penalty for minors.

Two additional capital punishment decisions decided liberally by the Rehnquist Court can also be mentioned, although these are primarily Sixth Amendment cases. In *Ring v. Arizona* (2002), the Court considered an Arizona statute that required a judge and not a jury to determine beyond a reasonable doubt at least one aggravating factor at the sentencing state of a capital case. The Court ruled that this violated the defendant's Sixth Amendment jury trial rights, which require this determination to be made by a jury not a judge. *Ring* overturned a prior Rehnquist Court precedent, *Walton v. Arizona* (1990), which had upheld Arizona's law requiring judges to determine aggravating factors. This issue of effective counsel and the Sixth Amendment was involved in *Wiggins v. Smith* (2003). A seven-person majority ruled that the defendant's right to effective counsel had been violated because his attorneys had failed to undertake an adequate examination regarding an abusive childhood.

Eighth Amendment Noncapital Punishment Cases

Having examined in some detail the history of the Court's Eighth Amendment capital punishment jurisprudence and having concluded that the Rehnquist Court certainly did not engage in a conservative constitutional counterrevolution in this area of constitutional law, we can now give attention to noncapital punishment cases involving the Eighth Amendment. As we saw in table 3.21, this has not been a busy area for the Court; the Warren Court decided only two cases, the Burger Court ruled in six cases, and the Rehnquist Court made decisions in eight of these cases. The Burger Court was decidedly conservative, ruling against the criminal defendant in all but one case—83 percent conservative. In contrast, the Rehnquist Court decided 50 percent of its noncapital punishment cases liberally. Thus, as with the capital punishment cases, the Rehnquist Court certainly did not engage in a conservative revolution regarding noncapital punishment Eighth Amendment cases, as the following summary of leading cases will show.

The Rehnquist Court's liberal decisions in noncapital cases have included the topics of physical abuse of prisoners and conditions in prison cells. In *Hudson v. McMillan* (1992), Hudson, a prisoner, was placed in handcuffs and beaten by two corrections officers, suffering bruises, bleeding, and damage to his teeth. A circuit court of appeals ruled against Hudson's claim that his Eighth Amendment protection against cruel and unusual punishments was violated because Hudson suffered only minor injuries rather than significant injuries. Justice O'Connor in a 7–2 decision rejected this distinction, relying instead on the question of whether the physical force was to serve legitimate penological purposes or to cause harm for malicious and sadistic reasons. *Helling v. McKinney* (1998) involved prison cell conditions, specifically a complaint by a prisoner whose cell mate smoked five packs of cigarettes a day. Writing for a seven-person majority, Justice White argued that a prisoner's Eighth Amendment rights are violated if incarceration officials are deliberately indifferent to a prisoner's health and safety. Justices Scalia and Thomas dissented in both cases.

The Rehnquist Court has also issued pro-government decisions in important noncapital Eighth Amendment cases. *Wilson v. Seiter* (1991) involved a claim by an Ohio inmate that prison conditions were seriously inhumane. A five-person majority led by Justice Scalia rejected his claim, arguing that Eighth Amendment challenges to jail conditions should not be judged by the conditions inside a prison but rather by proving deliberate indifference by the responsible prison officials.

The issue of severe sentencing arose in the important case of *Harmelin v. Michigan*, in 2001, in which Harmelin was sentenced to a mandatory term of life imprisonment without the possibility of parole for the possession of more than 650 grams of cocaine. Harmelin claimed that his Eighth Amendment protection against cruel and unusual punishments was violated because the sentence was disproportionate to the crime, but a 5–4 majority disagreed, although no majority opinion could be reached. Scalia wrote the plurality opinion. One of his arguments was that proportionality review should not be used in noncapital cases, but only Rehnquist supported this idea. Scalia's primary argument was that the Eighth Amendment prohibits cruel and unusual punishments, with an emphasis on *and*. Because severe, mandatory sentences have been used throughout the nation's history, Scalia argued, they cannot be considered unusual. The four dissenting justices—Blackmun, Marshall, Stevens, and White—took strong opposition to Scalia's rejection of the proportionality principle and argued that Harmelin's mandatory life imprisonment was unconstitutionally disproportionate to the crime, violating his Eighth Amendment protection against cruel and unusual punishments.

The recent case of *Ewing v. California* (2003) also raised the question of sentencing that was disproportionate to the crime. California voters in 1994 approved a "three strikes and you're out" law under which a person convicted of three felonies would be sentenced to a term of twenty-five years to life. Gary Ewing had already been convicted of two felony charges when he was arrested for stealing three golf clubs from a Los Angeles store. Prosecutors had the choice of charging him with either a felony or misdemeanor, and they chose a felony. He was found guilty and sentenced to a term of twenty-five years to life. Ewing appealed his sentence as violating the Eighth Amendment prohibition against cruel and unusual punishments because it was grossly disproportionate, California courts ruled against him, and the Supreme Court agreed to hear his case. A five-person majority ruled against Ewing, but the Court was unable to achieve a majority opinion. O'Connor, Kennedy, and Rehnquist in the plurality opinion used proportionality analysis and found that Ewing's sentence was not grossly dispro-portionate based upon his long criminal record and society's interest in removing recidivist felons from society. Scalia and Thomas agreed with the Court's judgment but rejected the use of proportionality analysis. The four dissenting justices—Stevens, Ginsburg, Souter, and Breyer—applied the proportionality principle and found Ewing's rights to be violated.

Conclusion

This analysis of the Eighth Amendment capital and noncapital cases has revealed that the Rehnquist Court did not engage in a conservative constitutional counterrevolution in this area of the law. In capital punishment cases, the Rehnquist Court justices estab-lished a moderate voting record (59 percent conservative), a record similar to the Burger Court (53 percent conservative). The Rehnquist Court supported the key precedent of *Gregg v. Georgia* (1976), which established the two-stage approach to death penalty cases. Very importantly, in two recent cases, the Rehnquist Court not only ruled liberally but also overturned its own earlier, conservative precedents. *Atkins v. Virginia* (2002) saw the Court rule 6–3 that the Eighth Amendment Cruel and Unusual Punishments Clause forbids the execution of the mentally retarded, over-turning the Rehnquist Court's previous decision, in 1989, of *Penry v. Lynaugh.* In *Roper v. Simmons* (2005), a 5–4 majority overturned the 1989 case of *Stanford v. Ken-tucky,* ruling that it is unconstitutional to execute a person who was sixteen or seven-teen years of age at the time of the crime. The Rehnquist Court was also moderate in noncapital cases involving the Eighth Amendment, deciding 50 percent of these cases in favor of the criminal defendant.

The Terrorism Cases of 2004

A final topic needs to be examined regarding the Rehnquist Court's decisions involv-ing the guarantees of the criminally accused—the three terrorism-related cases decided in 2004. These cases involved challenges to the Bush administration's position that persons arrested or captured in regard to the U.S. War on Terror did not have access to the federal courts to challenge their detentions. These cases basically involved the question of habeas corpus rights, the constitutional guarantee of a person to seek an order requiring an incarcerating official to show why a person is being detained. The cases do not fit neatly into the criminal rights categories we have exam-ined thus far, which have involved the Fourth, Fifth, Sixth, and Eighth Amendments, because the habeas corpus guarantee is found in the main body of the Constitution, not the amendments. The cases must be examined, however, because they are among the most important ones in the history of the Rehnquist Court.

These cases had their origins in the attacks of September 11, 2001, on the World Trade Center buildings in New York City and the Pentagon in Washington, D.C., by members of the al Qaeda terrorist organization. These terrorist attacks resulted in the loss of the lives of about 3,000 American citizens and hundreds of millions of dollars in property. Responding to these attacks, the U.S. Congress authorized President George W. Bush to use all necessary and appropriate force against individuals and groups that were involved in the terrorist attacks. The primary activity undertaken immediately by the Bush administration was to send American troops into Afghanistan against al Qaeda and the Taliban regime of Afghanistan that had provided support for al Qaeda. American soldiers were successful in defeating the Taliban and disrupting al Qaeda, although Osama Bin Laden, the al Qaeda leader, escaped. As a direct result of the armed conflict, more than 600 foreign citizens were captured and eventually incarcerated at the U.S. Naval Base at Guantanamo Bay, Cuba. In addition to the Guantanamo Bay prisoners, numerous other foreign nationals and U.S. citizens were arrested for their suspected involvement in the terrorism activities on September 11.

The Supreme Court agreed to hear three separate cases arising from these events. *Rasul v. Bush* (2004) involved two Australian citizens and twelve Kuwaiti citizens captured abroad and being incarcerated at Guantanamo Bay. They sought habeas corpus relief in the federal courts, arguing that they were not enemy combatants or terrorists, they had not been formally charged, they had not been permitted to talk to an attorney, and they had been given no access to any court. *Hamdi v. Rumsfeld* (2004) was a narrower case involving Yaser Esam Hamdi. Hamdi was captured on a battlefield in Afghanistan, but it was later discovered that he was an American citizen. He challenged his incarceration at a naval brig in Charleston, South Carolina, seeking a writ of habeas corpus. The third case, *Rumsfeld v. Padilla* (2004), involved an American citizen, Jose Padilla, who was arrested in Chicago, initially incarcerated in New York, and then transferred to the Charleston naval brig. Like the other detainees in these cases, Padilla had been held indefinitely with no formal charges and no assistance of counsel, and he sought a writ of habeas corpus.

An enormous amount of speculation surrounded these cases, and many experts thought that the Rehnquist Court would rule in favor of the Bush administration. One important factor supporting this view was the Court's history of deferring to executive authority in time of war. For example, during and after World War I, the Court ruled conservatively in a series of freedom of expression cases in which laws criminalizing criticism of the government were upheld; during World War II, the Court gave approval to the relocation of Japanese Americans from the West Coast to detention camps in the Midwest; during the Korean War, the Court upheld arrests of American Communists for discussing the revolutionary ideas of Karl Marx; and the Court was hesitant to hear any cases involving the Vietnam War but did uphold the conviction of a protestor who burned his draft card in protest of the war.

It appeared to many observers that history could repeat itself. The U.S. War on Terror had by now expanded into armed conflict in Iraq, and the American public was deeply concerned with both war abroad and the threat of terrorism at home. Given these circumstances, it seemed probable that the Court would favor the government's position.

This view was strengthened by the decisions of the lower courts in all three cases. In *Rasul*, both courts rejected the detainees' arguments and ruled for the Bush administration. The district court and the court of appeals agreed that the controlling precedent in the case was *Johnson v. Eisentrager* (1950). In the *Eisentrager* case, German nationals were captured in hostilities in China in World War II, convicted in a military court, and then held in a prison in Germany. They sought a writ of habeas corpus, but the Supreme Court denied this appeal, holding that foreign military prisoners held outside the sovereign territory of the United States had no access to American courts. Similarly in the *Rasul* case, the district and appeals courts ruled that Guantanamo Bay, Cuba, was not within the sovereign territory of the United States, and thus the detainees had no access to American courts.

The *Hamdi* and *Padilla* cases presented somewhat different issues because both detainees were U.S. citizens. In the *Hamdi* case, the circuit court of appeals ruled in favor of the government, arguing that the Bush administration had acted legally under congressional authorization and the war powers of the political branches. The circuit court thus dismissed Hamdi's habeas petition. The lower courts did disagree in the *Padilla* case. The district court agreed with the Bush administration that the executive branch had authority to detain American citizens determined to be enemy combatants at a time of war and captured on American soil. The appeals court reversed, however, ruling that the Bush administration lacked authority to detain Padilla.

In June 2004, the Rehnquist Court surprised many observers by ruling liberally in both *Rasul* and *Hamdi* in favor of the detainees and by issuing a ruling in *Padilla* that required him to refile his case in a different jurisdiction. In the *Rasul* case, a 6–3 majority reversed the decision of the lower federal courts, finding that the Guantanamo Bay detainees did have access to the federal courts to challenge their incarcerations. Stevens wrote the majority opinion, joined by Breyer, Souter, Ginsburg, and O'Connor. Stevens argued that the *Eisentrager* precedent relied upon by the Bush administration had been subsequently modified, and "the Federal courts have jurisdiction to determine the legality of the Executive's potentially indefinite detention of individuals who claim to be wholly innocent of wrongdoing" (72 USLW at 4601). Kennedy wrote a concurring opinion, while Rehnquist, Scalia, and Thomas were in dissent.

The Court decided *Hamdi* even more decisively, by an 8–1 vote, although the justices could not achieve a majority opinion. Writing the plurality opinion joined by

Rehnquist, Breyer, and Kennedy, O'Connor concluded that "due process demands that a citizen held in the United States as an enemy combatant be given a meaningful opportunity to contest the factual basis for that detention before a neutral decision maker" (72 USLW at 4608). And in what may well be the most famous and most quoted statement of her long tenure on the Court, O'Connor wrote: "We have long since made clear that a state of war is not a blank check for the President when it comes to the rights of the Nation's citizens" (72 USLW at 4616). Thomas was the only justice to side with the Bush administration.

The *Padilla* case was decided 5–4 on jurisdictional grounds rather than on the merits. Chief Justice Rehnquist—joined by Scalia, Thomas, O'Connor, and Kennedy— argued that the suit should not have been filed in the Southern District Court of New York because Padilla was being incarcerated in South Carolina; thus, Padilla needed to bring his habeas petition to the South Carolina District Court. Justice Stevens wrote a dissenting opinion joined by Souter, Ginsburg, and Breyer in which he argued that the New York court had jurisdiction, and Stevens also made clear his view on the merits of the case: "Unconstrained Executive detention for the purpose of investigating and pre- venting subversive activity is the hallmark of the Star Chamber" (72 USLW at 4595).

The terrorism cases of 2004 are certainly major decisions in the history of the Rehnquist Court and perhaps in all of Supreme Court history as a powerful statement not only for constitutional liberties even during wartime but also for the power of the judiciary to check the authority of the executive branch. One commentator, Michael Greenberger, writing in *The National Law Journal*, suggested that these cases con- stituted a third Magna Carta, occupying a position of importance similar to the Magna Carta and the Constitution (2004). This argument seems too extreme at this point in time because it remains unclear exactly how these cases will eventually be resolved given the lack of specific guidance in the Court's opinions. In addition, the Court is likely eventually to hear other cases associated with the war on terror, including pro- visions of the USA Patriot Act passed by Congress soon after the September 11 attacks. We can safely conclude, however, that the 2004 terrorism cases add important weight to the argument that the Rehnquist Court did not engage in a conservative con- stitutional counterrevolution in regard to the guarantees of the criminally accused.

The Takings Clause

We have now completed an examination of the Constitution's criminal justice guaran- tees, but one more topic—the Takings Clause—needs to be evaluated before we can turn to an analysis of the various topics not associated directly with the Bill of Rights guarantees: racial equality, gender equality, affirmative action, other equal protection issues, privacy and abortion, and government powers. The Fifth Amendment to the

Constitution contains a provision called the "Takings Clause," and it reads as follows: "nor shall private property be taken for public use, without just compensation." This guarantee was considered by supporters of the Bill of Rights to be an important constraint upon the power of the federal government. The importance of property can be seen clearly in the words of the Due Process Clause, which states: "No person . . . shall be deprived of life, liberty, or *property* without due process of law" (emphasis added). The Takings Clause allows the government to exercise its power of eminent domain to assume ownership of private property, but it limits this power by requiring that the government must make public use of the property and that the property owner must be paid a fair price. What has been the Rehnquist Court's record in regard to the Takings Clause? We once again use both quantitative data and qualitative case analysis to answer this question.

We begin with the quantitative analysis. Before examining the data, however, it is necessary to explain two unusual features of the data. First, the terms *liberal* and *conservative* have a different meaning than in most topics we have examined. In the context of the Takings Clause, the liberal decision is considered to be in favor of the government, which is using the power of eminent domain, while a conservative decision is one that favors the individual challenging the government action. Second, the data being utilized involve cases that not only involve the Fifth Amendment Takings Clause but also statutory cases decided by the Supreme Court regarding the seizing of private property for public use.

With these preliminaries out of the way, we can turn our attention to table 3.23, which compares the Warren, Burger, and Rehnquist Courts. The data reveal that the

Table 3.23: Liberal/Conservative Voting in Takings Clause Cases by the Warren, Burger, and Rehnquist Courts, 1953–1954 to 2004–2005 Terms

Court Era	Liberal Decisions	Conservative Decisions	Total Cases
Warren Court (1953–1968 Terms)	88% (15)	12% (2)	17
Burger Court (1969–1985 Terms)	73% (22)	27% (8)	30
Rehnquist Court (1986–2004 Terms)	52% (12)	48% (11)	23
Total	70% (49)	30% (21)	70

Source: Harold J. Spaeth, *United States Supreme Court Judicial Database, 1953–2004 Terms* (Ann Arbor, MI: Inter-University Consortium for Political and Social Research, 2005).

Warren Court was extremely liberal, deciding 88 percent of these cases in favor of the government. The Burger Court was also strongly liberal, supporting the government in 73 percent of its cases. The Rehnquist Court has been evenly balanced in its takings cases, deciding a bare majority of its cases liberally, specifically 52 percent liberal. Thus, while the Rehnquist Court has been significantly less liberal in Takings Clause cases than either the Warren or Burger Courts, the Rehnquist Court has ruled liberally in a majority of its cases and thus does not appear to have engaged in a conservative counterrevolution.

Table 3.24 gives us a look at the voting records of the fourteen justices who have sat on the Supreme Court during the Rehnquist Court era, and the data suggest a divided Court with no dominant coalition that could radically change Takings Clause jurisprudence. Focusing upon the justices during the last natural court period, from the 1994 term to the 2004 term, three somewhat familiar groups can be identified. Justices Rehnquist, Scalia, and Thomas constituted a conservative wing, although Thomas's record (83 percent conservative) was substantially more conservative than either Scalia (65 percent conservative) or Rehnquist (61 percent conservative). At the other

Table 3.24: Liberal/Conservative Voting Records of the Justices of the Rehnquist Court in Takings Clause Cases, 1986–1987 Term to 2004–2005 Term (Justices Ranked from Most Conservative to Most Liberal)

Justices	Liberal Decisions	Conservative Decisions	Total Cases
Thomas	17% (2)	83% (10)	12
Scalia	35% (8)	65% (15)	23
Rehnquist	39% (9)	61% (14)	23
Powell	43% (3)	57% (4)	7
Kennedy	47% (7)	53% (8)	15
O'Connor	48% (11)	52% (12)	23
White	69% (9)	31% (4)	13
Ginsburg	70% (7)	30% (3)	10
Breyer	78% (7)	22% (2)	9
Souter	82% (9)	18% (2)	11
Marshall	82%(9)	18% (2)	11
Brennan	82% (9)	18% (2)	11
Stevens	91% (21)	9% (2)	23
Blackmun	92% (12)	8% (1)	13

Source: Harold J. Spaeth, *United States Supreme Court Judicial Database, 1953–2004 Terms* (Ann Arbor, MI: Inter-University Consortium for Political and Social Research, 2005).

end of the spectrum, Stevens had an extremely liberal voting record at 91 percent liberal, and he had strong support from Souter (82 percent liberal), Breyer (78 percent liberal), and Ginsburg (70 percent liberal). As we have observed on several occasions, Justices O'Connor and Kennedy were moderates who exerted substantial power over the outcomes of these cases. The three conservatives typically needed both O'Connor (52 percent conservative) and Kennedy (53 percent conservative) if they were to prevail, but this was not an easy task given the closely divided records of both O'Connor and Kennedy.

As we are well aware, valuable as voting data can be, it is also necessary to engage in qualitative case analysis that can provide important insights into the utilization of particular tests or doctrines as well as the Court's treatment of precedent. And once again, we examine briefly the various Court eras before the Rehnquist Court to provide the necessary historical foundation by which to analyze the Rehnquist Court.

The Pre–Warren Court Period

We can begin with a brief examination of two nineteenth-century cases involving the issue of incorporation, making the Bill of Rights applicable to the states. In the famous case of *Barron v. Baltimore*, in 1833, Chief Justice John Marshall, writing for a unanimous Court, ruled that the Bill of Rights guarantees limit only the federal government and not the states. In the 1897 case of *Chicago, Burlington, and Quincy Railroad Company v. Chicago*, however, the Court ruled that the Fifth Amendment Takings Clause applies not only to the federal government but also to state and local governments.

The Warren Court Period

The nationalization of the Takings Clause created the opportunity for the Supreme Court to establish a substantial body of case law, and the general pattern in the various Court eras before the Rehnquist Court was to defer to governmental authority. This is seen quite clearly in the voting patterns of the Warren Court; as we saw in table 3.23, the Warren Court justices decided 88 percent of its takings cases in a liberal manner, supporting the government. The deference of the Warren Court to government takings can be seen in the 1954 case of *Berman v. Parker*.

The *Berman* case involved the constitutionality of the 1945 District of Columbia Redevelopment Act, which provided not only for the extensive utilization of the power of eminent domain for the purpose of redeveloping slum areas but also for the sale or lease of the condemned properties to private individuals and groups. The issue in this case was whether the act involved the "public use" of the condemned land when private interests were involved. Drawing upon a substantial body of precedent, the Court ruled that the Redevelopment Act did not violate the Takings Clause. Importantly, the Warren Court utilized the rational basis or minimal scrutiny test as the appropriate standard in Takings Clause cases. Thus, the Warren Court in *Berman* strongly reaffirmed the authority of the government in Takings Clause cases, requiring the government only to establish that its purpose is legitimate and that the means chosen are rationally related to this legitimate purpose.

The Burger Court Period

The Burger Court ruled liberally in 73 percent of its Takings Clause cases, thus following closely the liberal pattern of the Warren Court. Several Burger Court cases need to be discussed because of their relevance to subsequent Takings Clause cases decided by the Rehnquist Court. These include *Penn Central Transportation Company v. City of New York* (1978), *Agins v. City of Tiburon* (1980), and *Hawaii Housing Authority v. Midkiff* (1984).

The *Penn Central* case involved the issue of what constitutes a taking, specifically whether extensive government regulation of property constitutes a taking within the meaning of the Fifth Amendment Takings Clause. The *Penn Central* case involved New York City's 1965 Landmark Preservation Law to protect historic districts and buildings. The Penn Central Transportation Company owned the Grand Central Terminal, which had been designated a historical landmark in 1967. Penn Central wanted to build a fifty-story addition above the terminal, but the commission administering the Landmarks Preservation Law rejected Penn Central's proposal. In response, Penn Central filed suit claiming that this action constituted a violation of the Takings Clause because it involved a taking of their property without just compensation. By a 6–3 vote, the Burger Court rejected Penn Central's arguments. Writing for the majority, Justice Brennan recognized that the Court had not been able to establish clear criteria for what constitutes a taking under the Fifth Amendment. Based upon existing precedent and the facts of the case, however, Brennan argued that the application of the law had not created a taking of Penn Central's property because the law was substantially related to the promotion of the general welfare and allowed Penn Central sufficient opportunities to enhance their site.

Agins v. City of Tiburon (1980) also raised the important issue of what constitutes a takings under the Fifth Amendment. This case involved the question of whether a general zoning law applied to a particular property constitutes a taking. In ruling unanimously for the city, the Burger Court set forth a "substantially advances" formula, which states that applying a general zoning law to a particular property constitutes a taking if the ordnance does not substantially advance legitimate state interests. In this case, the city did meet the standard.

A third Burger Court Takings Clause precedent that is especially relevant for subsequent Rehnquist Court decisions is *Hawaii Housing Authority v. Midkiff* (1984). Unlike the previous *Penn Central* and *Agins* cases, which raised the question of what constitutes a taking, *Midkiff* dealt with the matter of what constitutes "public use" within the meaning of the Takings Clause. The specific issue in the case was the constitutionality of Hawaii's 1967 Land Reform Act. This act was directed at the concentration of land ownership in Hawaii, where the federal government owned 49 percent of the land and only seventy-two private persons owned another 47 percent of the land, a system dating back to a feudal period. In an effort to reduce the concentration of land ownership, which was viewed as harmful to Hawaii's economy and overall welfare, the Hawaiian legislature passed the Land Reform Act, which allowed the state to condemn residential property, seize the property, compensate the owner, and then sell the land to private persons who had previously rented the land. A unanimous Burger Court ruled that this practice did not violate the "public use" provision of the Takings Clause. Embracing the rational basis or minimal scrutiny test of *Berman*, Justice O'Connor wrote: "When the legislature's purpose is legitimate and its means are not irrational, our cases make clear that empirical debates over the wisdom of takings— no less than debates over the wisdom of other kinds of socioeconomic legislation— are not to be carried out in federal courts" (467 U.S. at 243).

The Rehnquist Court Period

The Rehnquist Court thus inherited a strongly liberal line of precedents from earlier Courts regarding the Takings Clause. Although private property owners had occasionally prevailed before the Supreme Court, the government typically emerged victorious. The previous Courts had applied a rather narrow interpretation of what constitutes a taking and a rather broad interpretation of what is a public use.

The Rehnquist Court's Takings Clause cases have been a surprise to many Court observers. As the Court's membership changed, the Rehnquist Court justices seemed increasingly willing to revisit past Takings Clause rulings and to rule in favor of property owners challenging the government. Recently, however, especially in three 2005 cases, the Rehnquist Court justices provided pro-government interpretations of the Takings Clause.

The first major Takings Clause case decided by the Rehnquist Court came in the 1987 case of *Nollan v. California Coastal Commission*. The Nollans wanted to replace their small beach cottage in Ventura County, California, with a larger home, but they needed the approval of the California Costal Commission. The commission granted their request but stipulated that the Nollans had to grant the public an easement across their property to allow people to walk between public beaches on either side of the Nollans' property. The Nollans filed suit, arguing that the easement constituted a taking under the Fifth Amendment, for which they should be compensated. Writing for a five-person majority, Justice Scalia agreed with the Nollans. Although Scalia did not introduce a new doctrinal standard in this case, his opinion seemed to suggest a tougher standard than the minimal scrutiny test.

The next major Rehnquist Court Takings Clause case, *Lucas v. South Carolina Coastal Council*, in 1992, saw six justices—Rehnquist, Scalia, Thomas, O'Connor, Kennedy, and White—give another conservative interpretation regarding what constitutes a taking. The case centered on David Lucas, who had purchased in 1986 two vacant lots along the ocean in South Carolina, hoping to build single-family homes similar to existing homes along the oceanfront. In 1987, however, South Carolina passed the Beachfront Management Act, which gave the South Carolina Coastal Council substantial authority to protect the environment of the coastline, and it refused Lucas's request to build the new houses because of environmental concerns. Lucas brought suit that he was entitled to just compensation under the Takings Clause because South Carolina's decision was a takings within the meaning of the Fifth Amendment. Writing for the majority, Justice Scalia argued that this case involved a government taking because the decision deprived Lucas of any economically beneficial use of the properties. Scalia also used a "total taking" inquiry, under which governmental authorities had to take into account a wide variety of variables to support their decision. Although Scalia did not reject explicitly the rational basis test, the future of the test was now in some doubt.

The undercutting of past liberal precedents continued in *Dolan v. City of Tigard*, in 1994. This case involved Florence Dolan, the owner of a small store, who wanted to increase the size of her store and put pavement over her parking lot. Municipal officers of Tigard, Oregon, made their acceptance of her request dependent on satisfying two conditions: (1) that she devote part of her land to public green space and (2) that she allow a pedestrian-bicycle path to cross her property. A 5–4 Rehnquist Court sided with Dolan, requiring the government to provide evidence of a relationship between the imposed regulations and the conditions that gave rise to them.

Thus, by 1994, the Rehnquist Court seemed to be charting a new course in regard to the Takings Clause. Citizens bringing takings claims were increasingly successful, and the Court's deference to the government under the rational basis test seemed to be ending. A series of recent cases, however, produced liberal outcomes and suggests that a five-person majority of Stevens, Kennedy, Souter, Ginsburg, and Breyer supports the liberal rational basis test, which favors the government, in Takings Clause cases.

The 2002 case of *Tahoe-Sierra Preservation Council v. Tahoe Regional Planning Agency* is an important recent case upholding the government. California and Nevada both have portions of the Lake Tahoe Basin, and they formed the Tahoe Regional Planning Agency to oversee the development of this area. The agency imposed two moratoria on residential development of the area while a comprehensive land-use plan was being developed. When the moratoria reached eighty-two months, an association of persons who owned land in the area brought suit that this lengthy delay constituted a violation of the Takings Clause because their property was taken without just compensation. Justices O'Connor and Kennedy joined the liberal group of Stevens, Ginsburg, Souter, and Breyer in rejecting the home-owners' claim. Writing for the majority, Justice Stevens rejected the *Lucas* case as the best precedent to follow, and he argued instead that *Penn Central* provided the best standard with inquiry into all the relevant circumstances surrounding the case. Using this standard, the Court majority found that a taking had not occurred.

The 2004–2005 term of the Court produced three Takings Clause cases, and, perhaps surprisingly, all three were decided liberally, in favor of the government. The most widely watched case was *Kelo v. City of New London* (2005). In 2000, New London, Connecticut, an economically depressed city, adopted a development plan that hoped to create more than 1,000 new jobs, increase the tax base, and revitalize the downtown and waterfront areas. The plan required the city to purchase a substantial amount of property, and most property owners willingly sold their properties to the city. Several owners refused, however, and this required the city to use its power of eminent domain to acquire the remaining property for just compensation. Susette Kelo and other property owners filed suit, claiming among other things that using eminent domain would violate the "public use" stipulation of the Takings Clause because some of the property would be acquired by private interests.

Justice Stevens wrote the majority opinion in favor of the city, and he was joined by Justices Kennedy, Souter, Ginsburg, and Breyer. Relying heavily upon the Warren Court's *Berman v. Parker* (1954) and the Burger Court's *Hawaii Housing Authority v. Midkiff* (1984), Stevens argued that the Court's precedents provide for an interpretation of "public use" as "public purpose." The city of New London, Stevens reasoned, had clearly shown in its extensive development plan that the project would serve a public purpose. Further, Stevens explicitly invoked the rational basis test to support New London.

O'Connor wrote a strong dissenting opinion, joined by Rehnquist, Scalia, and Thomas. She argued that the Court's precedents required the Court to find that this case did not qualify as an instance of public use under the Takings Clause. Furthermore, O'Connor argued, the majority's decision meant that under the label of economic development, all private property was now susceptible to government taking.

The Court decided two additional takings cases in 2005, *Lingle v. Chevron* and *San Remo Hotel v. City and County of San Francisco*. The *Lingle* case involved legislation passed by the Hawaii legislature that placed limits on the rent that could be charged to dealers who lease company-owned service stations. Chevron filed suit, claiming this legislation was an unconstitutional taking of property in violation of the Fifth Amendment. Both the district court and the circuit court ruled in favor of Chevron, relying upon *Agins v. City of Tiburon* (1980), in which the Burger Court ruled that government regulation of private property involves a taking if the regulation does not "substantially advance" legitimate governmental interests. Writing for a unanimous Court, Justice O'Connor argued that the "substantially advance" formula of *Agins* was not the appropriate standard in a case like this involving whether a regulation constitutes a Fifth Amendment takings; however, O'Connor presented a lengthy argument that the Court was not overturning *Agins* or any other Takings Clause cases. The proper test, O'Connor argued, was set forth in the 1978 Burger Court decision of *Penn Central Transportation Company v. City of New York*, which involved two primary considerations: the economic magnitude of a regulation and the extent of the interference with legitimate property interests. Chevron did not raise this argument, however, relying only on the *Agins* case with its "substantially advance" test, and thus the Court reversed and remanded the case.

The third Takings Clause case of the 2004–2005 term was *San Remo Hotel v. City and County of San Francisco*, and once again the Rehnquist Court issued a unanimous decision, with Justice Stevens writing the majority opinion. The case stemmed from a San Francisco ordinance that required the San Remo Hotel to pay a $567,000 fee because they were converting residential rooms to tourist rooms. In a complex lawsuit, the hotel sought to use both state and federal courts to press its claim that this action constituted an unconstitutional taking. The narrow issue before the Rehnquist Court was whether to create an exception to the federal law that provides for full faith and credit, requiring that parties cannot relitigate issues that have already been resolved by appropriate courts. In his majority opinion, Stevens rejected the hotel's argument, refusing to grant an exception to the full faith and credit statute. Thus, because the state court had resolved the constitutional issue, the federal courts would not be involved.

To conclude this section, it seems that the Rehnquist Court did not engage in a conservative revolution regarding the Takings Clause of the Fifth Amendment. The Supreme Court has traditionally been supportive of government taking activities challenged by citizens, and the Rehnquist Court generally followed this pattern. They ruled in favor of the government in a majority of cases—52 percent—and they did not overturn any major liberal precedents. Court observers did wonder if radical conservative change was on the horizon when the Court decided *Nollan*, *Lucas*, and *Dolan* in the early years of the Rehnquist Court, but more recent decisions show that the Court adhered to past precedents and tests that made it difficult for citizens to prevail in Takings Clause cases.

Equal Protection and Race

Thus far in this chapter the focus has been upon the Rehnquist Court's decisions involving individual liberties found in the Bill of Rights guarantees. We have now completed this analysis through our examination of the religious guarantees of the First Amendment; the freedom of expression rights of the First Amendment; the guarantees of the criminally accused found in the Fourth, Fifth, Sixth, and Eighth Amendments; and the topics of the 2004 terrorism cases and the Takings Clause. This brings us to the next major category of Rehnquist Court decisions, those concerned with the principle of equality.

The concept of equality cannot be found in the Bill of Rights, the first ten amendments to the Constitution, because the writers of the Constitution could not achieve agreement on the issue of slavery. Indeed, if slavery would have been prohibited, then the Constitution would have never been approved. The Constitution actually contains various references to the institution of slavery, thus legitimizing it. In Article I, Section 2, slaves are counted as three-fifths of a person for purposes of determining representatives. Section 9 of Article I also prohibited Congress from regulating the slave trade until at least 1808. The Founding Fathers did have a progressive view of equality for the time period in which they lived, but the language of the Declaration of Independence proclaiming that "all men are created equal" was initially limited to all white men who held some property. African Americans, Native Americans, women, and many other groups were not included.

In many ways, American history can be viewed as the struggle for equality in the United States. Slavery was an enormously contentious issue throughout the first half of the nineteenth century, with the Civil War ultimately deciding the issue. The great struggle between the North and the South resulted in the ratification of the three Civil War amendments. The Thirteenth Amendment abolished slavery; the Fourteenth Amendment sought to protect the newly freed slaves by establishing their citizenship and guaranteeing them due process of the law, equal protection of the laws, and the privileges or immunities of U.S. citizens. Finally, the Fifteenth Amendment guaranteed that no citizen could be denied the right to vote on account of race. The ratification of these amendments did not suddenly transform American society, however, and the struggle for equality continues to this day. We study important, major areas of equality in the next sections of this chapter. These topics include racial equality, sexual equality, affirmative action, and the struggle for equality by other groups, including homosexuals. Throughout these analyses, our central focus will remain the same as it has been earlier—did the Rehnquist Court engage in a conservative constitutional counterrevolution?

Equal Protection Doctrinal Framework

Before we can turn to the initial topic of racial equality, however, it is necessary to present a discussion of the equal protection doctrinal framework that has been utilized by the Rehnquist Court and to which we will frequently refer. This framework is not unique to the Rehnquist Court but rather was already in place when Rehnquist was appointed chief justice. The Rehnquist Court justices have made small modifications in the legal framework, but they have not altered its basic structure or logic.

The equal protection doctrinal framework is presented in table 3.25. As the table shows, four different tests can be used by the Court in equal protection cases, depending upon the type of case before the Court. The tests provide various levels of protection to individuals bringing equal protection claims to the Court, varying from minimal scrutiny through intermediate scrutiny to strict scrutiny, the Court's toughest standard. These tests are mutually exclusive and exhaustive; that is, only one test can be applied in any equal protection case, and all equal protection cases involve one of these tests.

The first test presented in table 3.25 is the rational basis test. This test is the general one that the Court will typically apply unless one of the exceptional types of cases occurs, which triggers a different test with a higher level of scrutiny. The rational basis test recognizes that governmental laws will almost inevitably treat people unequally; for example, people pay different levels of taxes depending upon their income. Such laws do not violate the Equal Protection Clause of the Fourteenth Amendment as long as (1) the government is pursuing a legitimate purpose and (2) the means used are rationally related to this legitimate interest. This is an easy test for the government to meet. It essentially requires only that the government is not acting in an arbitrary, capricious, or unreasonable manner.

At the other end of the spectrum is the suspect classification test, which uses the strict scrutiny approach associated with a high level of proof on the government to show that it is pursuing a compelling government interest by means that are narrowly tailored to avoid any interference with constitutional rights. The suspect classification test has historically been used in cases involving race and alienage discrimination and affirmative action. Three interrelated reasons have been advanced to justify this high level of Court scrutiny of such claims. First, racial and ethnic minorities have suffered a long history of discrimination in American society, and thus any claim of such discrimination triggers the suspicion that it may be occurring again. Second, personal

Table 3.25: The Supreme Court's Equal Protection Doctrinal Framework

Test	Type of Case	Level of Security	Questions Posed
Rational Legitimate Basis Test	General—Most Social and Economic Programs	Minimal	1. Is there a government purpose? 2. Are the means rationally related?
Important Government Objective Test	Gender and Illegitimacy	Intermediate	1. Is there an important government objective? 2. Are the means substantially related?
Fundamental Rights Test	Marriage and Procreation, Interstate Travel Voting, Access to Justice	Strict	1. Is there a compelling government interest? 2. Are the means narrowly tailored?
Suspect Classification Test	Race, Alienage	Strict	1. Is there a compelling government interest? 2. Are the means narrowly tailored?

attributes such as race and ethnicity are immutable characteristics unrelated to ability; because these are qualities over which a person has no control, alleged discrimination related to these characteristics should be closely examined by the courts. Third, racial and ethnic minority groups typically lack the political and economic resources needed to utilize effectively the elected branches of government—the executive and legislative branches—and thus the courts have a special obligation to ensure that their rights are not being violated. It is important to note that all three of these conditions must be present to trigger the suspect classification test.

A third equal protection case is the important government objective test. This is a relatively recent test created in a 1976 case, *Craig v. Boren*, that involved gender discrimination. As we will discuss in much greater detail in the next section of this chapter, the justices of the Burger Court were deeply divided in the early seventies over the proper test to apply in cases involving gender discrimination. On the one hand, the suspect classification test did not seem appropriate to a majority of the justices. Women had suffered a long history of discrimination, and gender was an immutable characteristic unrelated to ability; but women had the potential to be represented effectively in the popularly elected branches of government. On the other hand, the rational basis test seemed to provide too little protection in an area where discrimination had been rampant. What emerged in the *Craig v. Boren* case was a new, intermediate scrutiny standard for gender discrimination and illegitimacy cases that required the government to show that it was pursuing an important government objective through means that were substantially related to the important objective.

The fourth equal protection test is not utilized much and is rather complex, but it does need to be mentioned. This test arises in cases in which a person is claiming that he or she is being treated unequally because a fundamental but implicit constitutional right is being violated. The Court has recognized four such fundamental, implicit rights: marriage and procreation, interstate travel, voting, and access to justice. These are implicit rights because they are not explicitly stated in the Constitution, but the Court has recognized these as being clearly implied and deserving of the same level of protection as those rights that are stated explicitly in the Constitution. Thus, these cases trigger strict scrutiny, requiring the government to show it is pursuing a compelling government interest through narrowly tailored means.

Quantitative Analysis

Having discussed the Rehnquist Court's equal protection doctrinal framework, we can now begin our analysis of the subject of racial discrimination by engaging in a quantitative analysis that not only compares the Warren, Burger, and Rehnquist Courts but also presents the voting patterns of the individual justices of the Rehnquist Court. Table 3.26 compares the voting records of the Warren, Burger, and Rehnquist Courts in racial discrimination cases, those defined in the Spaeth data as involving desegregation issues both in school settings and in other settings as well. The data reveal important differences in the three Court eras. Race cases were a major agenda item for the Warren Court, with sixty-nine cases being decided. The Warren Court was extremely liberal; they decided 94 percent of the time in favor of the individual claiming racial discrimination by the government. Table 3.26 also shows that race discrimination cases were a major concern of the Burger Court, which also had a strongly liberal orientation, deciding 67 percent of its forty-nine cases liberally.

We see a different pattern with the Rehnquist Court, however. Two major features can be identified. First, the Rehnquist Court was more moderate than either the Warren or Burger Courts, deciding 57 percent of its cases liberally. Second, the Rehnquist Court heard only fourteen racial discrimination cases through the 2004–2005 term, about one-fourth of the number heard by the Warren and Burger Courts. Furthermore, most of these cases were heard early in the Rehnquist Court era; only five race cases were heard in the natural court era since Breyer joined the Court in 1994. In light of the control that the Court has over its agenda, it is not accidental that the

Table 3.26: Liberal/Conservative Voting in Racial Discrimination Cases by the Warren, Burger, and Rehnquist Courts, 1953–1954 to 2004–2005 Terms

Court Era	Liberal Decisions	Conservative Decisions	Total Cases
Warren Court (1953–1968 Terms)	94% (65)	6% (4)	69
Burger Court (1969–1985 Terms)	67% (33)	33% (16)	49
Rehnquist Court (1986–2004 Terms)	57% (8)	43% (6)	14
Total	80% (106)	20% (26)	132

Source: Harold J. Spaeth, *United States Supreme Court Judicial Database, 1953–2004 Terms* (Ann Arbor, MI: Inter-University Consortium for Political and Social Research, 2005).

Rehnquist Court dramatically reduced its caseload regarding racial discrimination cases. Rather, as is subsequently argued in more detail, the Rehnquist Court appears to have decided consciously to withdraw from playing a role in most race cases, allowing the legislative and executive branches to deal with the most pressing issues of racial discrimination in American society.

Table 3.27 provides us with a look at the voting records of the individual justices who served on the Rehnquist Court. Only four justices—Scalia, Rehnquist, O'Connor, and Thomas—had distinctively conservative voting patterns. Three justices can be classified as moderates: Kennedy, Ginsburg, and Breyer. Six justices had predominately liberal records—Souter, White, Stevens, Blackmun, Brennan, and Marshall. It is difficult to draw generalizations about the natural court since 1994 because only five cases were decided, but the limited data show a balanced Court with four conservatives (Scalia, Rehnquist, O'Connor, Thomas), three moderates (Kennedy, Ginsburg, Breyer), and two liberals (Souter, Stevens).

What, if anything, can we conclude thus far regarding the central question of whether the Rehnquist Court engaged in a conservative constitutional counterrevolution regarding the subject of race discrimination? In regard to the doctrinal framework we have examined, the argument was made that the Rehnquist Court inherited and largely maintained the four tests used in equal protection cases, and this certainly suggests continuity rather than change in regard to the issue of race. The quantitative data are difficult to interpret because the Rehnquist Court heard far fewer cases than the Warren and Burger Courts, especially in the last decade. The overall voting records as well as the individual records suggest, however, a pattern of moderation rather than radical conservatism.

Table 3.27: Liberal/Conservative Voting Records of the Justices of the Rehnquist Court in Racial Discrimination Cases, 1986–1987 Term to 2004–2005 Term (Justices Ranked from Most Conservative to Most Liberal)

Justices	Liberal Decisions	Conservative Decisions	Total Cases
Scalia	0% (0)	100% (14)	14
Rehnquist	31% (4)	69% (9)	13
O'Connor	36% (5)	64% (9)	14
Thomas	38% (3)	62% (5)	8
Kennedy	50% (7)	50% (7)	14
Ginsburg	60% (3)	40% (2)	5
Breyer	60% (3)	40% (2)	5
Souter	67% (8)	33% (4)	12
White	67% (6)	33% (3)	9
Stevens	79% (11)	21% (3)	14
Blackmun	89% (8)	11% (1)	9
Brennan	100% (1)	0% (0)	1
Marshall	100% (5)	0% (0)	5
Powell	0% (0)	0% (0)	0

Source: Harold J. Spaeth, *United States Supreme Court Judicial Database, 1953–2004 Terms* (Ann Arbor, MI: Inter-University Consortium for Political and Social Research, 2005).

We certainly need to engage in detailed analysis of leading cases to develop a clearer answer to this question. Following our earlier pattern, we will examine the pre–Warren Court era, the Warren Court period, and the Burger Court to provide the foundation for our analysis of the Rehnquist Court's racial discrimination cases.

The Pre–Warren Court Period

The long period of American history from the development of the Constitution to the beginning of the Warren Court era in the early fifties was one of intense racism not only by private individuals and groups but also by governments, and the Supreme Court frequently gave its approval to these racist policies. As we noted previously, the Constitution recognized the institution of slavery. As the Civil War approached, the Supreme Court in *Dred Scott v. Sandford* (1857) gave support to slavery by treating slaves not as persons but as property to be bought and sold at the owner's will. The three Civil War amendments were intended to change American race relations dramatically, but racism was a deeply engrained cultural value that would take many decades to change. In the aftermath of the Northern withdrawal from the South after the Civil War, for example, a system of laws requiring strict racial segregation arose in the South, the Jim Crow laws. In *Plessy v. Ferguson* (1896), the Court by a 7–1 vote gave approval to this racist legal system based upon the doctrine of "separate but equal," which argued that the Equal Protection Clause of the Fourteenth Amendment allowed the segregation of people by race as long as separate facilities were provided that were of equal quality, which they rarely were. Racial conditions had not improved much fifty years later as seen in the 1944 decision of *Korematsu v. United States*, in which the Supreme Court approved the removal of Japanese Americans from the West Coast and their internment in camps in the Midwest. Although this was the case in which the Court introduced the suspect classification or strict scrutiny test, the Court found that the federal government met both prongs of the test.

The pre–Warren Court era did have some liberal decisions in regard to racial segregation, however, particularly in regard to higher education. In *Gaines v. Canada* (1938), the Court ruled that the state of Missouri could not deny African American students admission to the University of Missouri's law school and pay for them to attend law school in an adjacent state. And in two 1950 cases, the Vinson Court also ruled against segregationist practices in higher education. In *Sweatt v. Painter*, the Court ruled that a separate law school that Texas had established for African Americans was clearly not equal to the white law school at the University of Texas, and in *McLaurin v. Oklahoma State Regents for Higher Education*, a unanimous Court ruled that the equal protection guarantee is violated if a state admits an African American to a graduate program but submits the student to segregationist practices such as sitting in a classroom behind a sign marked "For Coloreds Only."

The Warren Court Period

The Warren Court is probably best known for its groundbreaking decisions in regard to racial equality and especially the *Brown v. Board of Education* case of 1954. Although substantial debate exists regarding the direct effect of *Brown* on school integration in the South (e.g., Rosenberg 1991), *Brown* can be viewed as the single most important event that began America's equality revolution that is still unfolding today, and a widespread consensus exists that the Warren Court engaged in a liberal constitutional revolution regarding racial equality.

Brown was a case of enormous magnitude. It was actually five separate cases involving southern and border states as well as the District of Columbia. In each case, racial segregation was either required or permitted by law. The cases had been carefully selected by the NAACP; the schools for black children were substantially equal to the all-white schools, and thus the justices would have to decide if separation per se created unconstitutional conditions. If the justices chose to overturn the separate but equal doctrine, then all public schools of the South would have to become racially integrated.

Chief Justice Earl Warren was the driving force behind the Court's unanimous 9–0 decision that overturned *Plessey v. Ferguson* and the principle of separate but equal. Warren worked extremely hard to achieve a unanimous decision because he knew how strong the opposition would be to this decision, which challenged the entire social system of the southern United States. In his opinion for the Court, Warren avoided the strict scrutiny test because he did not want to accuse the states of racism, and instead he relied upon social psychology data to support the Court's opinion, arguing that the effects of racial segregation were to create feelings of racial inferiority on the part of African American children and feelings of racial superiority in white children.

Warren did not address the important question of how the tremendous challenge of racial integration was to be achieved, but instead he asked both sides to prepare briefs and oral arguments regarding the implementation process. Thurgood Marshall, lead attorney for the NAACP Legal Defense Fund, argued that the Constitution had been violated for almost 100 years, and racial integration should be achieved immediately. Attorneys for the southern and border states told the Court in nice legal language that they would never comply with what they viewed as an outrageous decision. Against these two extreme positions, the Warren Court produced a three-part compromise. First, a prompt and reasonable start to achieving racial integration needed to occur. Second, given the difficulty and magnitude of the task, the process should then proceed with "all deliberate speed." Third, the process was to be overseen by the respective federal district judges who were most familiar with the varying local situations.

The white power structures in the southern states initially prevented any real progress from being made for almost a decade. Social patterns of centuries were not going to change easily. By the midsixties, however, important changes began to occur in American society. The civil rights movement had an enormous impact on American attitudes and behaviors. Following John F. Kennedy's death, the new president, Lyndon Johnson, was a Texan who could speak to southerners more effectively than his predecessor. Congress passed a variety of civil rights acts, including the withholding of federal funds for districts that refused to comply with *Brown*. All of these dramatic changes produced an environment in which significant changes began to occur in the racial integration of the southern schools. Thus, in 1954, only .001 percent of black students attended schools with whites, but by 1968 this figure had risen to 32 percent, and it increased to 91.3 percent by 1972 (Epstein and Walker 2004, 676).

Although the Warren Court was dependent on the other branches for enforcing its decisions, the justices ruled consistently in favor of achieving racially integrated schools. In their final major decision, *Green v. School Board of New Kent County* (1968), the Court reacted strongly against the refusal of white school board members to integrate and set forth specific guidelines that had to be achieved. Writing for a unanimous Court, Justice Brennan stated: "The burden on a school board today is to come forward with a plan that promises realistically to work, and promises realistically to work *now*" (391 U.S. at 439, emphasis in original). Further, Brennan identified six specific areas in which integration had to be achieved: student body composition, faculty, staff, transportation, extracurricular activities, and facilities.

The Warren Court is best known for its *Brown* line of decisions, but the liberal justices of this Court era also handed down major decisions in other areas. Two especially important cases were *Heart of Atlanta Motel v. United States* (1964) and *Loving v. Virginia* (1967).

Heart of Atlanta Motel dealt with the important issue of discrimination in public accommodations. African Americans had historically been denied service in restaurants, hotels, and other places generally available to the public. This type of discriminatory action was defended as being constitutional because it involved actions by private owners rather than any type of state action, and the Fourteenth Amendment prohibited only discriminatory action by the government. In response to this situation, Congress passed Title II of the 1964 Civil Rights Act that prohibited racial discrimination in places of public accommodation involved in interstate commerce. The Warren Court ruled unanimously in favor of Title II in *Heart of Atlanta Motel* and a companion case of *Katzenbach v. McClung* (1964), deciding the case not upon the Equal Protection Clause but rather upon Congress's power to regulate interstate commerce. These cases are illustrative of the willingness of the Warren Court to find various forms of discriminatory activities by private individuals to have a sufficient link to governmental activities to transform private action into state action that must conform to constitutional standards of equality.

Loving was another major decision of the Warren Court involving race. This case involved a Virginia law that banned interracial marriage. In a unanimous decision, the Warren Court applied the strict scrutiny test to rule the law unconstitutional.

The Burger Court Period

The Warren Court had clearly engaged in a liberal constitutional revolution regarding racial equality in America. In the aftermath of the 1968 presidential election, however, the Court's membership changed dramatically, as we have noted earlier, with Republican President Richard Nixon naming Warren Burger to replace Earl Warren as chief justice and then appointing three additional justices during his first term: Harry Blackmun, Lewis Powell, and William Rehnquist. Would the new Burger Court follow in the path of the Warren Court regarding *Brown* and race issues more generally, or would this new Court move in a more conservative direction?

The initial answer by the Burger Court to this question was a strong statement supporting *Brown* in *Alexander v. Holmes Board of Education* (1969). In this case, a federal appeals court had given permission to thirty-three school districts in Mississippi to postpone indefinitely the desegregation of their schools. In a brief *per curiam* opinion, the Court under Chief Justice Burger reversed this decision, stated that the "all deliberate speed" guidelines were no longer valid, and demanded the immediate achievement of integrated schools.

The Burger Court continued to hand down major liberal decisions in school desegregation cases. In the case of *Swann v. Charlotte–Mecklenburg County Board of Education* (1971), the Court ruled unanimously that if school officials continuously refused to integrate public schools, then a wide variety of remedies could be imposed by the federal courts to achieve desegregation, including the use of the controversial approach of busing. Two years later, the Burger Court handed down another major and controversial decision in *Keyes v. School District No. 1, Denver* (1973). This was an important case because it raised the issue of applying *Brown* to the North. *Brown* had only applied to the southern and border states because these were the only states to have laws on the books that required or permitted racially segregated schools. Many northern states had high levels of racial segregation in their public schools, but it was argued that these segregated schools were not unconstitutional because they were the result of *de facto* segregation created by private choices, not *de jure* segregation created by governmental laws. In *Keyes*, however, the Court ruled 7–1 that *de jure* segregation involved both governmental laws and governmental actions that created or maintained racially segregated schools; thus, decisions by school boards involving such things as where to build schools and where to draw attendance lines could violate the Equal Protection Clause of the Fourteenth Amendment. *Keyes* thus had the effect of expanding *Brown* from the South to the entire United States.

In *Alexander*, *Swann*, and *Keyes*, the Burger Court had gone far beyond the decisions of the Warren Court, but the Burger Court justices drew a conservative line in the controversial 1974 decision of *Milliken v. Bradley*. This case challenged the decision of a federal district judge who had found both the city of Detroit and the state of Michigan guilty of contributing to racially segregated schools in the Detroit system, and as a remedy he ordered large-scale busing between Detroit and its surrounding white suburbs. A narrow five-person majority ruled that the district judge had gone too far in this case. Operating under the principle that the remedy must be tailored to the scope of the violation, the Burger Court ruled that the suburban school districts had not engaged in any unconstitutional activity and therefore could not be included in the busing plan.

Marshall authored a strong dissent, arguing that the suburbs could be included in the busing because state officials had contributed to creating and maintaining the racially segregated school systems. In addition, Marshall lamented that this decision would make it impossible to fulfill the promise of *Brown* because whites would move increasingly to the suburbs, making inner cities even more segregated.

The Burger Court also decided several important cases involving racial discrimination in areas other than school integration. As with the post-*Brown* decisions, the Burger Court was less willing than the Warren Court to rule against government actors accused of race discrimination. One of the most important cases was *San Antonio Independent School District v. Rodriguez* (1973), a case that was not about race but had major implications for racial equality in America's schools. *Rodriguez* involved a challenge to the manner in which the state of Texas and the school district of San Antonio funded public schools. This system, utilized in most states, involved the state providing a certain minimum level for all schools and then individual school districts raising their own support from local property taxes. This typically results in different school districts throughout the state having vastly different levels of funding, depending upon the wealth of the school district and the willingness of the district's citizens to be taxed. In *Rodriguez*, a 5–4 majority ruled that the system did not violate the Equal Protection Clause of the Fourteenth Amendment. Applying the lenient rational basis test, the Court ruled that the government had a legitimate purpose of promoting local control of the public school system and that the means were rationally related to this objective. This landmark decision has meant that challenges to unequal public school funding have had to occur in each of the state courts, but these efforts have generally not been successful.

The Burger Court also ruled conservatively in two major public accommodation cases. In *Palmer v. Thompson* (1971), city officials in Jackson, Mississippi, decided to close all public swimming pools rather than operate them on an integrated basis, arguing that financial problems and safety concerns made this the best course of action. A 5–4 Burger Court majority found no violation of the Equal Protection Clause because all persons were being treated the same. *Moose Lodge v. Irvis* (1972) involved a suit filed by an African American who was a guest at a Harrisburg, Pennsylvania, Moose Lodge and who was refused service because of his race. In a 6–3 decision, Rehnquist argued for the majority that the Moose Lodge was a private organization whose activities were not within the scope of state action required by the Equal Protection Clause.

One important area in which the Burger Court did rule liberally regarding racial discrimination involved jury selection. As we discussed earlier in this chapter when analyzing the Sixth Amendment, the Burger Court in *Batson v. Kentucky* (1986) ruled that prosecutors in state criminal cases cannot use peremptory challenges to exclude potential jurors based upon their race.

The Rehnquist Court Period

The Rehnquist Court inherited a complex set of precedents from the Warren and Burger Courts in regard to racial equality. The Warren Court established broad, sweeping principles embracing the achievement of racial equality. The Burger Court extended these principles in some areas but in other areas limited sharply the role of the courts in the struggle for racial integration and equality. What has been the record of the Rehnquist Court in this important area of constitutional law? This is not an easy question to answer because the Rehnquist Court justices were strongly committed to principles of racial equality in some areas but were more cautious in other areas. The Rehnquist Court largely abandoned the legacy of *Brown* in regard to achieving racially integrated public schools. The Rehnquist Court strongly supported principles of racial equality in regard to jury selection issues, but the Court was less supportive of racial equality concerns in voting rights and affirmative action cases.

The Rehnquist Court heard only a small number of cases involving school desegregation, and these were generally decided in a conservative fashion, limiting the authority of federal district judges to promote racially integrated schools. The Rehnquist Court certainly did not repudiate the basic principles of *Brown*, but the Court adopted a stance that saw a rather limited role for the federal courts in the effort to integrate America's public schools.

The first major school desegregation case decided by the Rehnquist Court, *Missouri v. Jenkins* (1989), supported extensive powers by a federal district judge. The Kansas City, Missouri, school system had developed a magnet school plan to create strong schools in the district that would attract white students from the suburbs. The costs of these magnet schools were high, and state and local tax monies were inadequate. The federal district judge therefore ordered the local school board to increase property taxes above the limits set by the state. This was challenged, but a five-person Rehnquist Court majority composed of Marshall, Brennan, Blackmun, Stevens, and White ruled that this was an appropriate exercise of judicial power to obtain racially integrated schools.

The 1989 *Missouri v. Jenkins* case suggested that the Rehnquist Court was going to support strongly the implementation of *Brown*. This was not to be the situation, however, as this was the only liberal decision of the Rehnquist Court in regard to integration of the nation's public schools. This is explained in part by changes in the Court's membership. The Court's three most liberal justices in racial discrimination cases—Marshall, Brennan, and Blackmun—were on the Court in 1990, but they all resigned in the next few years, leaving only Justice Stevens to argue in favor of an aggressive role for the federal courts in integrating public schools.

The Rehnquist Court justices began their more conservative interpretation of *Brown* and its progeny the next year in *Board of Education of Oklahoma City Public*

Schools v. Dowell (1991). This case involved the question of when court-ordered busing could be eliminated. In a majority opinion for a 5–3 Court, Chief Justice Rehnquist argued that busing could be ended if a district's desegregation plans had successfully eliminated all aspects of *de jure* segregation. This had been accomplished by the Oklahoma City School District, and thus busing could be terminated and neighborhood schools reestablished even though this would mean the emergence of racially segregated schools.

In the 1992 case of *Freeman v. Pitts*, the Rehnquist Court handed down another conservative decision reducing the power of federal judges over the desegregation process. This case from DeKalb County in Georgia raised the issue of the duration and extent of federal court control over school systems found guilty of *de jure* segregation. DeKalb County had been under federal court control since 1969. In 1986, the district argued that they had achieved integrated status in regard to four of the six *Green* factors: student assignments, extracurricular activities, transportation, and physical facilities. Therefore, the district argued, they should be given full control over these areas, with the federal court retaining authority only over the two areas where compliance had not yet been reached. An 8–0 Court agreed with the school board, but the Court did not speak with one voice. Scalia argued for an immediate termination of judicial overview if a district no longer engaged in *de jure* segregation; Kennedy wrote that the courts have no authority to deal with racial segregation caused by demographic factors; and Blackmun, Stevens, and O'Connor urged district courts to engage in a thorough analysis of all *Green* factors before ending their authority over a district's desegregation plans.

The Rehnquist Court's more conservative orientation toward school desegregation cases became quite clear when *Missouri v. Jenkins* returned to the Court in 1995. In this case, the federal judge had ordered the Kansas City, Missouri, School Board to provide salary increases for teachers and to fund remedial programs intended to raise student achievement scores to the national level. Unlike the 1990 decision upholding the federal judge's authority, the Rehnquist Court this time ruled that the judge had exceeded his authority. Relying on the precedents of *Milliken v. Bradley* (1974) and *Freeman v. Pitts* (1992), Chief Justice Rehnquist argued that the remedy went beyond the scope of the violation.

The Rehnquist Court also decided one major race case involving higher education. *United States v. Fordice* (1992) involved Mississippi's college and university system, which was created with five white schools and three black schools. Mississippi modified its system after *Brown* by adopting a "freedom of choice" program, but the schools remained highly segregated. An 8–1 Court found that Mississippi's plan was an inadequate response to past *de jure* segregation practices and continued to perpetuate racially segregated institutions. Writing for the majority, Justice White stated: "Surely the state may not leave in place policies rooted in its prior officially segregated system that serve to maintain the racial identifiability of its universities if those poli-cies can practically be eliminated without eroding sound educational policies" (112 S. Ct. at 2743).

The Rehnquist Court certainly gave conservative interpretations to *Brown* and its progeny, but did the Rehnquist Court engage in a conservative constitutional coun-terrevolution in this important area of constitutional law? The answer seems to be no. Critics of the Rehnquist Court do have an argument with some validity that the prom-ise of *Brown* to end separate but equal has failed and that America's urban public schools are becoming increasingly separate and unequal. Even if this is true, it does not mean that the Rehnquist Court dramatically changed constitutional law. The Rehn-quist Court was consistently firm in its opposition to all forms of *de jure* segregation; the Rehnquist Court did not overturn any school desegregation cases of either the Warren or Burger Courts; and the justices of the Rehnquist Court provided reasonable, if controversial, interpretations of such key precedents as *Green* and *Milliken*.

The Rehnquist Court's record in other areas of race discrimination was rather mixed. One area in which the Rehnquist Court justices established a strong liberal record was jury selection cases. As we discussed earlier in this chapter, under Sixth Amendment rights, the Rehnquist Court expanded dramatically upon the Burger Court's *Batson v. Kentucky* (1986) decision, which used the Equal Protection Clause to restrict dramatically the use of peremptory challenges by prosecutors who excluded African Americans from juries in cases involving African Americans as defendants. In *Powers v. Ohio* (1991), the Rehnquist Court expanded *Batson* by allowing criminal defendants to challenge race-based peremptory challenges regardless of whether the defendant and excluded juror were of the same race. Also in 1991, the Rehnquist Court extended the *Batson* precedent to civil cases in ruling that peremptory challenges to jurors cannot be used in a racially discriminatory manner. Finally, in the 1992 case of *Georgia v. McCullum* (1992), the Rehnquist Court further expanded the logic of *Batson* in ruling that the prosecution in a criminal case can object to the defense using its peremptory challenges in a racially biased manner.

The Rehnquist Court has been far more resistant to efforts to promote minority rights in redistricting cases. These cases arose in the aftermath of the reappointment and redistricting efforts that occurred after the 1990 census. In many southern states the effort was made to create "majority-minority" congressional districts, that is, dis-tricts in which citizens of minority groups would constitute the majority within the dis-trict, thus increasing the probability of electing minority representatives to Congress. These majority-minority districts were frequently challenged in the courts, and the Rehnquist Court granted certiorari to consider the constitutionality of some of these proposals. The initial case of *Shaw v. Reno* (1993) involved a challenge by white vot-ers to two strangely shaped districts in North Carolina. The Rehnquist Court did not decide this case on the merits but rather sent it back to the lower courts with the requirement that the strict scrutiny test must be utilized. Next came *Miller v. Johnson* (1995), a case involving redistricting in Georgia to create a majority-minority district. Writing for a five-person majority that included O'Connor, Rehnquist, Scalia, and Thomas, Justice Kennedy argued that race was the overriding consideration in drawing the district, this triggered the strict scrutiny standard, and Georgia could not meet the demanding requirements of the test. The five-person conservative coalition of Justices Kennedy, O'Connor, Rehnquist, Scalia, and Thomas also prevailed in subsequent cases involving successful challenges to majority-minority districts: *Shaw v. Hunt* (1996) and *Bush v. Vera* (1996).

Conclusion

Although the record is mixed, the Rehnquist Court did not engage in a dramatic conservative shift in regard to racial equality in American society. The Rehnquist Court certainly did not champion the cause of racial equality in the manner of the Warren Court; rather, the Rehnquist Court justices followed the path of the Burger Court, generally favoring claims of racial discrimination but limiting somewhat the role of the courts in the struggle for racial equality. In terms of its liberal orientation, the Rehnquist Court remained committed to the suspect classification or strict scrutiny test for cases involving claims of racial discrimination, the Rehnquist Court justices decided a majority of their race discrimination cases liberally, and they handed down a series of decisions prohibiting the use of peremptory jury challenges based upon race. The Rehnquist Court's more conservative orientation is seen in its school desegregation and redistricting cases. The justices applied precedents stemming from *Brown* in a conservative manner; furthermore, they heard relatively few school desegregation cases; and in the last decade, they did not rule in any such cases, leaving the continuing issue of school desegregation to the legislative and executive branches. The Rehnquist Court also rejected various efforts by states to create majority-minority districts based upon racial considerations. Finally, we see shortly that the Rehnquist Court's affirmative action cases provide further evidence of the mixed and ambiguous record of the Rehnquist Court on matters of racial equality, but our analysis of these cases will not be undertaken until we examine the topic of sexual equality.

Equal Protection and Gender

Race discrimination is certainly not the only form of discrimination with which the Supreme Court has dealt. Another important issue that has confronted the Court throughout history has involved equal protection claims regarding gender bias. Just as

American history has been characterized by a long and unfortunate pattern of race discrimination, so too has sex discrimination been a pervasive feature of U.S. history. Women were denied the right to vote when the Constitution was ratified, and it was not until the Nineteenth Amendment was passed, in 1920, that women could not be denied the right to vote. Sex discrimination went far beyond the right to vote, however, extending into virtually every area of American life. It was not until the women's movement of the sixties and seventies that truly dramatic change began to occur in regard to the struggle for sexual equality. The Supreme Court played a role in this struggle and continues to do so today, although the Court's role is arguably less central and important than the role it played in regard to the movement for racial equality.

In this section of chapter 3, we explore in regard to sexual discrimination the familiar theme of whether the Rehnquist Court engaged in a conservative constitutional counterrevolution, and we use both quantitative and qualitative methods of analysis. Our results are somewhat surprising because we see that the Rehnquist Court has been more liberal than either the Warren or Burger Courts.

Quantitative Analysis

The data in table 3.28 compare the liberal and conservative voting patterns of the Warren, Burger, and Rehnquist Courts, with a liberal vote being in favor of an individual claiming some type of sexual discrimination by the government and a conservative vote favoring the government and denying illegal sexual discrimination. The results

Table 3.28: Liberal/Conservative Voting in Sex Discrimination Cases by the Warren, Burger, and Rehnquist Courts, 1953–1954 to 2004–2005 Terms

Court Era	Liberal Decisions	Conservative Decisions	Total Cases
Warren Court (1953–1968 Terms)	0% (0)	100% (1)	1
Burger Court (1969–1985 Terms)	64% (30)	36% (17)	47
Rehnquist Court (1986–2004 Terms)	75% (18)	25% (6)	24
Total	67% (48)	33% (24)	72

Source: Harold J. Spaeth, *United States Supreme Court Judicial Database, 1953–2004 Terms* (Ann Arbor, MI: Inter-University Consortium for Political and Social Research, 2005).

are surprising, especially in light of the voting patterns we have previously observed. The Warren Court heard only one sex discrimination case and decided it conservatively. In sharp contrast, the Burger Court decided forty-seven cases involving claims of gender discrimination, ruling liberally in 64 percent of these cases. The Rehnquist Court was less active than the Burger Court in this area, deciding twenty-four cases, but the Rehnquist Court justices were even more liberal than the Burger Court members in deciding 75 percent of the cases liberally.

How do we explain these surprising results, which run counter to the data in every area we have thus far examined? The answer involves the rapid development of the women's movement in the sixties. Although strong advocates of women's rights had long been present in American society, the modern women's movement emerged as a major social force in the sixties, fueled by the momentum of the civil rights movement, the sexual revolution, and the accumulated pressures of centuries of gender discrimination against women. Congress and the state legislatures responded with legislation to seek sexual equality, providing the basis for lawsuits based upon statutory law in addition to cases based upon constitutional law. By the time these cases had worked their way through the lower courts, however, the Warren Court era had ended, and the Burger Court faced the tidal wave of lawsuits stemming from the women's movement. In regard to the liberal voting patterns of both the Burger and Rehnquist Courts, they are probably best explained by the nature of the cases that were decided; the vast majority of these cases involved such clear violations of principles of sexual equality that the strongly liberal voting patterns should come as no surprise.

An examination of the voting patterns of the justices of the Rehnquist Court in table 3.29 provides support for this argument. As the data reveal, the Rehnquist Court has not had a strongly conservative voice. Justice Powell is the only one of the fourteen persons who have served on the Rehnquist Court who has had a distinctively conservative voting record, and he participated in only three cases. The Rehnquist Court's three most conservative members—Thomas, Scalia, and Rehnquist—present an interesting picture; unlike any other area, the three justices can be considered moderates in regard to gender discrimination cases, with Thomas at 40 percent liberal, Scalia at 46 percent liberal, and Rehnquist with a 58 percent liberal record. The other ten members of the Rehnquist Court were distinctively liberal, ranging from White's 62 percent liberal voting record to Blackmun's 100 percent. In terms of the natural court in place since Breyer's appointment, in 1994, an overwhelming liberal coalition existed, including Souter (94 percent liberal), Ginsburg (94 percent liberal), Breyer (93 percent liberal), Stevens (88 percent liberal), O'Connor (77 percent liberal), and Kennedy (67 percent liberal). Ginsburg and O'Connor, the Court's only female justices, do not stand out noticeably in their voting behavior from their male colleagues. Ginsburg has voted more liberally then O'Connor, however, and we observe in our qualitative analysis that

Table 3.29: Liberal/Conservative Voting Records of the Justices of the Rehnquist Court in Sex Discrimination Cases, 1986–1987 Term to 2004–2005 Term (Justices Ranked from Most Conservative to Most Liberal)

Justices	Liberal Decisions	Conservative Decisions	Total Cases
Powell	33% (1)	67% (2)	3
Thomas	40% (6)	60% (9)	15
Scalia	46% (11)	54% (13)	24
Rehnquist	58% (14)	42% (10)	24
White	62% (5)	38% (3)	8
Kennedy	67% (14)	33% (7)	21
O'Connor	77% (17)	23% (5)	22
Brennan	83% (5)	17% (1)	6
Marshall	86% (6)	14% (1)	7
Stevens	88% (21)	12% (3)	24
Breyer	93% (13)	7% (1)	14
Ginsburg	94% (15)	6% (1)	16
Souter	94% (17)	6% (1)	18
Blackmun	100% (8)	0% (0)	8

Source: Harold J. Spaeth, *United States Supreme Court Judicial Database, 1953–2004 Terms* (Ann Arbor, MI: Inter-University Consortium for Political and Social Research, 2005).

Ginsburg has been a leading advocate of doctrinal changes that would move gender discrimination from intermediate to strict scrutiny.

The Pre–Warren Court Period

In the pre–Warren Court era, the Supreme Court heard relatively few cases involving sex discrimination, and the precedents that were created did little to promote the cause of sexual equality. The Court typically ruled against women bringing claims of gender discrimination, basing these decisions on a chauvinistic view of the natural and proper dominance of men in society and a limited, domestic role for women. The Court did on occasion uphold legislation that favored women, but the underlying attitude in such cases was the paternalistic view that women were weak creatures who needed to be protected.

Two cases arising soon after the ratification of the Fourteenth Amendment, in 1868, illustrate the pervasiveness of male chauvinism on the Court. In *Bradwell v.*

Illinois (1873), the state of Illinois had passed a law preventing women from practicing law. When the Illinois courts upheld the law, Bradwell brought the case to the U.S. Supreme Court under the newly ratified Fourteenth Amendment. The Court ruled 8–1 against Bradwell, with Justice Bradley expressing the following view in a concurring opinion:

> . . . the civil law, as well as nature herself, has always recognized a wide difference in the respective spheres and destinies of man and women. Man is, or should be, woman's protector and defender. The natural and proper timidity and delicacy which belongs to the female sex evidently unfits it for many of the occupations of civil life. The constitution of the family organization, which is founded in the divine ordnance, as well as in the nature of things, indicates the domestic sphere as that which properly belongs to the domain and functions of womanhood (83 U.S. at 446).

The Court's acceptance of blatant discrimination against women can also be seen in the 1875 case of *Minor v. Happersett*, in which the Court unanimously upheld Missouri's prohibition on women voting.

The Court in the pre–Warren Court era did give constitutional approval to some laws that favored women, but the underlying rationale of these laws and Court decisions was that women were weak creatures who needed to be protected by men. In *Muller v. Oregon* (1908), for example, the Court upheld Progressive Era legislation that established the maximum hours of work for women at ten hours a day. Nearly three decades later, the Court in *West Coast Hotel v. Parrish* (1937) upheld a Washington State law that established minimum wages for children and women. Writing for the Court majority, Chief Justice Hughes stated: "What can be closer to the public interest than the health of women and their protection from unscrupulous and over-reaching employers?" (300 U.S. at 398).

The Warren Court Period

As we observed earlier, the Warren Court heard only one case involving sexual discrimination claims, deciding this case conservatively. *Hoyt v. Florida* (1961) involved a Florida law that automatically excluded women from jury duty unless they requested to be included, while men were automatically included on the jury list unless they sought an exemption. Gwendolyn Hoyt was convicted of second-degree murder of her husband by an all-male jury, and she claimed that she was denied equal protection of the law. The Warren Court unanimously rejected her claim, however, using the rational basis test and embracing the stereotyped role of women in society, stating that "woman is still regarded as the center of home and family life. We cannot say it is constitutionally impermissible for a state, acting in pursuit of the general welfare, to conclude that a woman should be relived from the civic duty of jury service unless she herself determines that such service is consistent with her own special responsibilities" (368 U.S. at 62).

It is impossible to know if the Warren Court would have taken a different approach to sex discrimination cases in the seventies. We can safely conclude, however, that the record is clear that the Warren Court did not engage in a liberal constitutional revolution regarding gender discrimination. That task would be left to the Burger Court.

The Burger Court Period

The Warren Court era was the quiet before the storm of the Burger Court era in regard to gender discrimination cases. As we saw earlier, in table 3.25, the Burger Court justices decided forty-seven cases compared to only one by the Warren Court. This explosion of cases resulted from the powerful momentum of the women's rights movement; effective legal advocacy, with future Supreme Court Justice Ruth Bader Ginsburg playing a leading role as head of the Women's Project of the ACLU; and the passage of several major pieces of legislation that provided the foundation for lawsuits alleging illegal sexual discrimination. Among the most important congressional enactments were the Equal Pay Act of 1963; Title VII of the 1964 Civil Rights Act, which prohibited employers from refusing to hire a person based upon his or her sex; Title IX of the 1972 educational amendments, which prohibited sexual discrimination in educational programs receiving federal funding; and the Pregnancy Discrimination Act of 1978.

The Burger Court's initial challenge was to establish a proper standard of review for gender discrimination cases. Three cases are of major significance: *Reed v. Reed* (1971), *Frontiero v. Richardson* (1973), and *Craig v. Boren* (1976).

The *Reed* case is important because it was the first time the Supreme Court had ever ruled a law unconstitutional based upon sex discrimination. The case involved an Idaho law that made the father the preferred executor of an estate involving a child who died without a will. Mrs. Reed, who was divorced from Mr. Reed, challenged this on Fourteenth Amendment equal protection grounds, and a 7–0 majority agreed with her. Although this was a landmark decision, leaders of the women's movement were disappointed because the Court used the minimal scrutiny or rational basis test, finding that Idaho's argument about administrative efficiency was an "arbitrary legislative choice" prohibited by the Equal Protection Clause. The serious problem for women's rights advocates was that the government could be expected to prevail in most cases using the rational basis test.

Ginsburg led an assault on the rational basis standard in the next major case, *Frontiero v. Richardson*. The case involved a U.S. Air Force policy that provided automatic benefits for the spouse of a male officer but required a female officer to prove her spouse was financially dependent on her. Sharon Frontiero's attorneys, with Ginsburg playing a prominent role, argued that the appropriate test was not minimal scrutiny under the rational basis test but rather strict scrutiny under the suspect classification standard because sexual discrimination had the same three characteristics as racial discrimination: (1) a long and pervasive history of discrimination existed, (2) gender was an immutable characteristic unrelated to ability, and (3) women lacked the political power to address these grievances through the elected branches. The Court ruled 8–1 in favor of Frontiero, and Justice Brennan's controlling opinion accepted the strict scrutiny standard; however, only three other justices joined Brennan's plurality opinion, with the other justices using the minimal scrutiny standard to rule in favor of Frontiero. Thus, the rational basis test remained the controlling standard in gender discrimination cases.

The struggle to find an appropriate standard culminated in the 1976 case of *Craig v. Boren*, in which Justice Brennan led a six-person majority in establishing a new test for gender discrimination cases—the important government objective or intermediate scrutiny test. The case interestingly involved a male, Curtis Craig, claiming gender discrimination under an Oklahoma law that prohibited young men from purchasing beer until they were twenty-one but allowing women to purchase beer at age eighteen. Applying the new test, Brennan argued that the state did have an important objective, keeping the highways safe. However, Brennan argued, the means chosen were not substantially related to this important objective because the law did not prohibit the consumption of beer by eighteen-, nineteen-, and twenty-year-old males.

The important government objective, or intermediate scrutiny, standard has been the controlling test in equal protection gender discrimination cases since 1976. The individual claiming illegal sexual bias usually wins under this standard, but the government can prevail on occasion. Two Burger Court cases of the early eighties illustrate these varying outcomes.

Rostker v. Goldberg (1981) involved a challenge to the Military Selective Service Act, which required males but not females to register for the draft. Males challenged this as violating the constitutional guarantee of equal protection of the laws, but a 6–3 Burger Court upheld the law under the intermediate scrutiny standard. The government was pursuing an important objective of preparing a draft of combat troops, and the means were substantially related to this objective because women could not serve in combat under existing policy of each branch of the military.

In contrast, the Burger Court found unconstitutional under the intermediate scrutiny standard the policy of preventing males from being admitted to the Mississippi University for Women. In *Mississippi University for Women v. Hogan* (1982),

Joe Hogan sought admission to pursue a degree in nursing but was denied on account of his sex. Writing for a five-person majority, O'Connor argued that Mississippi failed both prongs of the intermediate scrutiny test.

A final, important observation about the Burger Court's sexual discrimination cases is that many of them involved statutory rather than constitutional cases. This should not be surprising in light of the numerous national and state legislative enactments concerned with achieving sexual equality. An especially important statutory case that was a key precedent in subsequent Rehnquist Court cases was *Meritor Savings Bank v. Vinson*, a 1986 case involving sexual harassment. This was the Supreme Court's first full consideration of this important topic, and the Burger Court resolved some issues but left others open for further adjudication. The Court ruled that sexual harassment does constitute gender discrimination within Title VII of the 1964 Civil Rights Act. The Court furthermore ruled that sexual harassment includes not only "quid pro quo" activity involving sexual favors for employment and advancement but also sexual misconduct that creates a hostile work environment. The Burger Court could not, however, reach agreement on the question of the extent to which employers were liable for supervisory personnel who engaged in sexual harassment.

We can conclude that the Burger Court engaged in a liberal constitutional revolution in regard to sexual discrimination. During the Burger Court era, the area of equal protection and gender was a major topic of the Court's agenda, with forty-seven cases being decided, compared to only one in the Warren Court era. The vast majority of these cases—64 percent—were decided liberally in favor of the individual claiming illegal sexual discrimination. The underlying values of male chauvinism and paternalism disappeared from Court opinions during the Burger Court era. The Burger Court, for the first time in Supreme Court history, ruled government laws unconstitutional based upon sexual discrimination. Finally, the Burger Court justices created a new, liberal doctrinal standard—the intermediate scrutiny or important government objective test—that provided considerably stronger protection than the rational basis test for persons claiming sexual discrimination.

The Rehnquist Court Period

We can now turn our attention to the gender discrimination cases of the Rehnquist Court, focusing on the question of whether the Rehnquist Court justices engaged in a conservative counterrevolution in this area of the law. We already have strong evidence regarding this question because we saw in table 3.28 that the Rehnquist Court was even more liberal than the Burger Court, deciding 75 percent of its twenty-four sexual discrimination cases liberally. Furthermore, as is argued below, the Rehnquist Court maintained the intermediate scrutiny standard in gender discrimination cases, and in some areas of sexual discrimination, such as sexual harassment, the Rehnquist Court gave important liberal interpretations to Burger Court precedents. Thus, the Rehnquist Court certainly did not engage in a conservative counterrevolution regarding sexual discrimination but instead expanded the liberal orientation of the Burger Court.

The Rehnquist Court consistently utilized the intermediate scrutiny or important government objective test in its decisions involving gender discrimination and the Fourteenth Amendment Equal Protection Clause. Despite the consistent use of this test, however, this area of constitutional law is not necessarily settled. Justice Ginsburg argued in the seventies that strict scrutiny should be the appropriate test in gender discrimination cases, and she has apparently not abandoned this view. In the 1993 case of *Harris v. Forklift Systems, Inc.*, for example, she wrote in a footnote of her concurring opinion: "Indeed, even under the Court's equal protection jurisprudence, which requires an exceedingly persuasive justification for a gender-based classification, it remains an open question whether classifications based on gender are inherently suspect" (510 U.S. at 25).

Ginsburg also advocated the exceedingly persuasive justification criterion in her majority opinion in *United States v. Virginia* (1996), creating ambiguity as to whether this criterion is simply part of the intermediate scrutiny test or whether it is part of an effort to undermine intermediate scrutiny and support strict scrutiny. Ginsburg's language did not go unnoticed by the Court's more conservative justices. In a dissenting opinion, Justice Scalia sharply criticized Ginsburg's language: "As to precedent: It drastically revises our established standards for reviewing sex-based classification" (518 U.S. at 566). Scalia stated that he would have no problem with the term "exceedingly persuasive justification" if it meant that the government must have an important objective it is pursuing by means that are substantially related to this objective. He argued, however, that "the Court proceeds to interpret 'exceedingly persuasive justification' in a fashion that contradicts the reasoning of . . . our . . . precedents" (518 U.S. at 572).

The future of the proper test for gender discrimination cases is uncertain. Ginsburg is not alone in her views. In *United States v. Virginia* (1996), for example, the Justice Department of the Clinton administration argued that the Court should abandon the intermediate scrutiny test and replace it with the strict scrutiny test in gender discrimination cases. The Court does not easily overturn long-established precedent, however, and new membership on the Court—even female membership—does not ensure change, especially if the new appointments hold more conservative attitudes.

In applying the intermediate scrutiny test to gender discrimination cases, the Rehnquist Court usually reached a liberal outcome. Two cases, *J.E.B. v. Alabama ex rel. T.B.* (1994) and *United States v. Virginia* (1996), are leading examples in which the Court found governmental practices unconstitutional. On occasion, however, the Court has found that the government can meet the tough standards of the intermediate scrutiny test; *Nguyen v. Immigration and Naturalization Service* (2001) is discussed as an example of a case decided conservatively in favor of the government.

We briefly referenced *J.E.B.* when we discussed Sixth Amendment rights and peremptory jury challenges. The Burger Court, in *Batson v. Kentucky* (1986), had begun a process of prohibiting prosecuting attorneys from using preemptory challenges to exclude persons from jury duty based upon racial considerations. *J.E.B.* raised the issue of whether the Equal Protection Clause was violated by the use of preemptory challenges to exclude potential jurors based upon their gender. The Rehnquist Court's answer was that the Fourteenth Amendment was violated. Writing for the majority, Justice Blackmun argued: "Today we reaffirm what, by now, should be axiomatic: Intentional discrimination on the basis of gender by state actors violates the Equal Protection Clause, particularly where, as here, the discrimination serves to ratify and perpetuate invidious, archaic, and overbroad stereotypes about the relative abilities of men and women" (511 U.S. at 130–131).

United States v. Virginia (1996) was probably the Rehnquist Court's most publicized gender discrimination case. The case involved a challenge to the constitutionality of the male-only admission policy of the Virginia Military Institute (VMI). The case pitted the U.S. government, representing young women who had been denied admission because of their gender, against the state of Virginia and VMI. When Virginia and VMI lost their case at the federal court of appeals, Virginia established a parallel school for women, the Virginia Women's Institute for Leadership (VWIL). The Rehnquist Court agreed to hear the case to decide two issues: (1) does Virginia's policy of excluding women from attending VMI violate the Equal Protection Clause of the Fourteenth Amendment? And (2) if it does, what remedy is required? Justice Ginsburg wrote the 7–1 majority opinion; Scalia was in dissent, and Thomas did not participate because his son was attending VMI. As we noted earlier, Ginsburg argued that the intermediate scrutiny test required the government to show that it had an exceedingly persuasive justification for its actions, and Ginsburg rejected Virginia's two arguments in support of their exclusionary policy: (1) it offered unique educational benefits that contribute to educational diversity, and (2) VMI's unique adversative approach would have to be changed if women were admitted. Ginsburg strongly rejected these arguments: "However 'liberally' this plan serves the State's sons, it makes no provision whatsoever for her daughters. That is not *equal* protection" (518 U.S. at 540, emphasis in original). Turning to the second question, Ginsburg argued that VWIL was a weak imitation of VMI, and the only remedy that would satisfy the Equal Protection Clause was to admit women to VMI.

J.E.B. and the VMI case illustrate that the intermediate scrutiny standard is a difficult one for governments to meet, but this test can be satisfied when the gender-based distinctions are not based upon stereotypes, chauvinism, or paternalism. Very real differences of course do exist between men and women, and laws that are based upon these differences may be found constitutional. *Nguyen v. Immigration and Naturalization Service* (2001) is an example of this. Tuan Anh Nguyen was born in Vietnam to an American citizen, Joseph Boulais, and a Vietnamese woman. Nguyen came to the United States at the age of six and lived with his father. Under federal law, children are citizens at birth if they are born in a foreign county to a citizen mother and alien father, but children born to an alien mother and citizen father must show proof of paternity by the age of eighteen to become a citizen. Boulais never established proof of paternity for Nguyen, and when Nguyen was twenty-two, he committed sexual assault on a child, leading to deportation proceedings because he was not an American citizen. Nguyen and his father challenged the policy as violating the guarantee against equal protection of the laws, but a 5–4 Court found the policy to be constitutional under the intermediate scrutiny test. Justice Kennedy for the majority argued that two important government objectives existed: to ensure the presence of a biological father-son relationship and to ensure the opportunity of a meaningful parent-child relationship. Furthermore, the means chosen bore a substantial relationship to these objectives.

In addition to deciding sexual discrimination cases on constitutional grounds, the Rehnquist Court, like the Burger Court, has also decided numerous gender-based cases on statutory grounds. As with its constitutionally based decisions, the Rehnquist Court has overwhelmingly decided these statutory cases liberally in favor of the individual bringing the complaint, but on occasion the Court has rejected statutorily based claims of gender discrimination.

Two statutory cases decided in 1987 provided clear indications that the Rehnquist Court was sympathetic to claims of gender discrimination based on statutory grounds. *California Federal Savings and Loan Association v. Guerra* (1987) was a major sexual discrimination case that involved the 1978 Pregnancy Discrimination Act. Lillian Garland was a receptionist for California Federal Savings and Loan who took a maternity leave. When she attempted to return to her job, the bank refused to rehire her, arguing that this was its policy regarding all employees who took a leave of absence. The Court ruled 6–3 in favor of Garland based upon the legislative history and intent of the Pregnancy Discrimination Act.

Another major gender discrimination case decided in 1987 was *Board of Directors of Rotary International v. Rotary Club of Duarte*, a case involving a California law, the Unruh Civil Rights Act. The act prohibited discrimination on the basis of sex and many other characteristics by California business establishments. The Rotary Club, a private organization, excluded women from membership, but a local chapter—the Duarte Club—admitted women to membership. This resulted in the Duarte chapter being expelled from the international organization. The Duarte Club filed suit claiming that the Unruh Civil Rights Act was being violated by Rotary International.

The parent organization responded that they were not a business and hence not under the Unruh Act, and they also claimed that they had a First Amendment freedom of association right to choose whether to admit women to membership. By a unanimous 7–0 vote, the Rehnquist Court rejected the arguments of Rotary International, thus opening the doors for women to participate in Rotary.

The next major case involving sexual discrimination under statutory law was *Price Waterhouse v. Hopkins*, in 1989, a Title VII case. Ann Hopkins was a senior manager at Price Waterhouse when she was denied promotion to full partner in the firm. She brought suit, claiming that this decision was based at least in part on sexual discrimination because some evaluations criticized her as being too masculine—aggressive, macho, and so forth—and suggested she should be more feminine in appearance and action. Price Waterhouse maintained that their decision was based solely on her interpersonal skills, not gender-based considerations. A 6–3 Court ruled in favor of Hopkins, but the justices were unable to agree upon a standard for determining if improper gender considerations affected a decision.

The Rehnquist Court decided another major case involving Title VII of the Civil Rights Act of 1964 in *International Union, UAW v. Johnson Controls, Inc.* (1991). At issue was a fetal protection policy of Johnson Controls, a company that manufactured batteries. Because of concerns about dangers to a developing fetus from toxic substances like lead in battery production, the company excluded women of childbearing ability from jobs where they would be exposed to such materials. Several persons directly affected by this policy filed suit that the policy violated Title VII of the 1964 Civil Rights Act. A unanimous 9–0 Rehnquist Court agreed with the employees, invoking both Title VII and the 1978 Pregnancy Discrimination Act. Writing for a five-person majority, Justice Blackmun stated: "The bias in Johnson Controls' policy is obvious. Fertile men, but not fertile women, are given a choice as to whether they wish to risk their reproductive health for a particular job" (499 U.S. at 197).

The substantive topic within the area of sexual discrimination that was given the most attention by the Rehnquist Court was sexual harassment. As we discussed previously, the Burger Court provided the major precedent of *Meritor Savings Bank v. Vinson Bank* (1986), which established the important principles that sexual harassment was a form of sexual discrimination under Title VII and that sexual harassment involves not only "quid pro quo" activities but also sexual conduct that creates a hostile work environment. Building upon *Meritor*, the Rehnquist Court decided several major statutory cases that have sought to answer questions left unresolved by *Meritor*.

The 1993 case of *Harris v. Forklift Systems, Inc.* raised the question of whether a person claiming sexual harassment in the workplace needs to establish psychological injury to win monetary damages. A unanimous Court ruled this was not necessary. Invoking a lenient rational person standard, Justice O'Connor wrote: "So long as the environment would reasonably be perceived, and is perceived, as hostile and abusive, there is no need for it also to be psychologically injurious" (510 U.S. at 22).

The issue of whether same-sex harassment comes under Title VII arose in the 1998 case of *Oncale v. Sundowner Offshore Services*. The Rehnquist Court unanimously answered this question affirmatively. Writing for the Court, Justice Scalia stated that the key concern is not the gender of the parties involved but rather if the behavior creates an "objectively hostile or abusive work environment" (523 U.S. at 81).

Two additional major sexual harassment cases also decided in 1998 involved the question of whether employers are liable when sexual harassment occurs by supervisory employees. In the case of *Burlington Industries v. Ellerth* (1998), the issue was whether employer liability existed in a quid pro quo case where the employee did not have adverse job consequences. *Faragher v. City of Boca Raton* (1998) involved the question of employer liability when a supervisor engages in conduct that creates a hostile work environment. Voting 7–2 in both cases, the Rehnquist Court ruled that companies can be found liable for sexual harassment by their supervising personnel, regardless of job consequences. Employers could, however, avoid liability according to the Court majority if reasonable measures were taken promptly to prevent and correct sexual harassment and if the employee failed to utilize preventive or corrective activities provided by the employer. Thus, an affirmative defense for an employer would be to develop and communicate a clear sexual harassment policy with a reasonable grievance procedure.

The Rehnquist Court has on occasion rejected claims of sexual harassment. In yet another 1998 case, *Gebseret v. Lago Vista Independent School District*, an issue arose under Title IX as to whether a school district could be held financially liable for the sexual harassment of a student by a teacher if the school's administrators were unaware of the situation. A five-person majority consisting of Justices O'Connor, Kennedy, Rehnquist, Scalia, and Thomas ruled that a district could not be found liable under such circumstances. O'Connor's majority opinion established that a school district could be liable only if a school authority has been notified about a teacher's misconduct and has been deliberately indifferent to the situation. The four liberal dissenters—Stevens, Ginsburg, Breyer, and Souter—argued that this standard would make it extraordinarily difficult for students ever to prevail in sexual harassment complaints against teachers.

The Court reverted to its liberal orientation a year later in another Title IX suit in *Davis v. Monroe County* (1999). This case involved the issue of whether school districts could be sued under Title IX if they failed to respond effectively to protect students who have been subjected to severe and continuous sexual harassment by other students. In this 5–4 decision, O'Connor wrote the majority opinion for Stevens, Souter, Breyer, and Ginsburg, arguing that schools are liable for damages if they are aware of such harassment and fail to respond to end the activity.

Conclusion

The topic of equal protection and gender presents a dramatically different situation than we have thus far observed regarding the Rehnquist Court. The Warren Court did not engage in a liberal revolution in this area of the law, hearing only one case and deciding it conservatively based upon stereotypical views of men and women. The Burger Court, in contrast, did engage in a liberal revolution, hearing almost fifty cases, deciding two-thirds of them liberally, and creating a new heightened standard of scrutiny for gender discrimination cases. The Rehnquist Court in turn continued and expanded the liberal pattern of the Burger Court. The justices of the Rehnquist Court remained committed to the intermediate scrutiny test for sexual discrimination cases, and Justice Ginsburg seems committed to the goal of making strict scrutiny the appropriate test in gender cases. Furthermore, sexual discrimination cases were an important agenda item for the Rehnquist Court, which decided twenty-four such cases, and these cases were overwhelmingly decided in favor of the individual claiming sexual discrimination. Clearly, then, the Rehnquist Court did not engage in a conservative counterrevolution in regard to the topic of gender discrimination but rather established a strongly liberal record exceeding that of both the Warren and Burger Courts.

Affirmative Action

Affirmative action is an area of the law that is closely related to both racial discrimination and gender discrimination. Affirmative action programs involve a wide variety of activities that seek to address the effects of past discrimination. These programs can range from relatively uncontroversial activities such as making certain that underrepresented groups are made aware of opportunities to much more controversial programs that set aside a certain number of positions for members of underrepresented groups.

Affirmative action programs began in the late sixties out of concern that antidiscrimination laws were not sufficient to deal with the centuries-long effects of discrimination in American society. The runners' analogy was sometimes used to explain the need for affirmative action programs. If you have two persons in a race, it is clearly an unfair situation if one has had good training conditions and the other has been in chains. Fairness certainly requires removing the chains of the disadvantaged runner, but the runner is still not able to compete because this person is still suffering the effects of being in the chains. Thus, the argument goes, some type of affirmative response is necessary to create a truly equal situation or level playing field. Based upon these types of considerations, the federal government, state and local governments, and private groups adopted a wide variety of affirmative action programs in the late sixties and early seventies to respond to the effects of past discrimination.

These programs created strong controversy, however. Among the criticisms of affirmative action programs were the arguments that they constituted reverse discrimination, penalizing white males who had not been guilty of any discriminatory actions. Critics of affirmative action programs also argued that such programs could unfairly reward members of underrepresented groups that were middle and upper class. In addition, such programs were criticized by some as stigmatizing minority group members, implying they lacked the ability to make it on their own.

Affirmative action cases presented an especially difficult problem for the Supreme Court in regard to which equal protection doctrinal test to utilize. The rational basis or minimal scrutiny test did not seem appropriate because a government program would rarely if ever be found unconstitutional under this lenient standard; the government could easily defend any affirmative action program by establishing that it had a legitimate purpose it was pursuing—addressing the effects of past discrimination—and that the means chosen bore some rational relationship to this objective. At the other end of the equal protection doctrinal framework, the suspect classification or strict scrutiny test did not seem appropriate either. The logic of the suspect classification test has been that racial and ethnic minorities had been subjected to centuries of discrimination, that race and ethnicity were immutable characteristics unrelated to ability, and that these groups lacked the political and economic power to pursue their interests successfully in the majoritarian branches of government. Affirmative action cases are typically brought by white males, and they have certainly not suffered centuries of discrimination nor do they lack political power. The only other available equal protection test is intermediate scrutiny or the important government objective test, but that test had been limited to gender discrimination cases and was based upon a logic not unlike that used for suspect classification.

This section of chapter 3 focuses on how the Rehnquist Court dealt with the controversial subject of affirmative action, specifically our central question of whether the justices of the Rehnquist Court engaged in a conservative constitutional counterrevolution. We compare the Rehnquist Court with the preceding Warren and Burger Courts, and we again use both quantitative methods of analysis as well as the qualitative examination of leading affirmative action cases, especially those that addressed directly the question of what equal protection test should be applied in affirmative action cases.

Quantitative Analysis

Table 3.30 compares the voting records of the Warren, Burger, and Rehnquist Courts in affirmative action cases. Before we look at the data in this table, it is important to be clear about the meaning of the terms *liberal* and *conservative*. Unlike other areas that we have examined, a liberal decision in an affirmative action case means a vote in favor of a government program that seeks to address the effects of past discrimination. In contrast, a conservative affirmative action decision is one that finds a government program illegal or unconstitutional.

The data in table 3.30 reveal several interesting results. The Warren Court did not hear a single affirmative action case. This is similar to what we saw in the last section when we discussed gender discrimination. Affirmative action programs began in the late sixties; by the time the legal challenges to such programs reached the Supreme Court, the Warren Court era had ended and the Burger Court period was under way. The data reveal that the Burger Court heard a significant number of affirmative action cases—sixteen—and decided the majority of them—62 percent—liberally. The Rehnquist Court decided eleven affirmative action cases and was somewhat more conservative than the Burger Court, deciding 46 percent of its cases liberally, but these results do not suggest a radical change by the Rehnquist Court.

Important insights into the voting behavior of the Rehnquist Court can be obtained by examining the individual voting records of the justices of the Rehnquist Court, which are presented in table 3.31. The data in this table reveal a division among the justices that is more pronounced than in any other area we have studied.

Table 3.30: Liberal/Conservative Voting in Affirmative Action Cases by the Warren, Burger, and Rehnquist Courts, 1953–1954 to 2004–2005 Terms

Court Era	Liberal Decisions	Conservative Decisions	Total Cases
Warren Court (1953–1968 Terms)	0% (0)	0% (0)	0
Burger Court (1969–1985 Terms)	62% (10)	38% (6)	16
Rehnquist Court (1986–2004 Terms)	46% (5)	54% (6)	11
Total	56% (15)	44% (12)	27

Source: Harold J. Spaeth, *United States Supreme Court Judicial Database, 1953–2004 Terms* (Ann Arbor, MI: Inter-University Consortium for Political and Social Research, 2005).

Six justices were strongly conservative, while eight justices were strongly liberal; four justices voted conservatively 100 percent of the time, while six justices voted liberally in 100 percent of the cases. Membership change had a profound effect on the Rehnquist Court, especially the replacement of Powell with Kennedy and of Marshall with Thomas. If we focus on the most recent natural court, we see a narrow but strongly committed group of conservative justices composed of Rehnquist, Scalia, Kennedy, Thomas, and O'Connor. All but O'Connor voted conservatively in every affirmative action case, and O'Connor had a strong conservative record of 82 percent. In contrast, the Rehnquist Court of the last decade had four strongly liberal justices: Souter and Ginsburg at 100 percent liberal, Stevens at 91 percent liberal, and Breyer at 67 percent liberal. The data in table 3.31 thus suggest that the Rehnquist Court was sharply divided throughout its existence over affirmative action and that a strongly conservative majority existed that could have changed the Court's interpretation of affirmative action. We now turn to an examination of the Court's major affirmative action cases to see if this has occurred.

Table 3.31: Liberal/Conservative Voting Records of the Justices of the Rehnquist Court in Affirmative Action Cases, 1986–1987 Term to 2004–2005 Term (Justices Ranked from Most Conservative to Most Liberal)

Justices	Liberal Decisions	Conservative Decisions	Total Cases
Rehnquist	0% (0)	100% (11)	11
Scalia	0% (0)	100% (11)	11
Kennedy	0% (0)	100% (9)	9
Thomas	0% (0)	100% (3)	3
O'Connor	18% (2)	82% (9)	11
White	25% (2)	75% (6)	8
Breyer	67% (2)	33% (1)	3
Stevens	91% (10)	9% (1)	11
Ginsburg	100% (3)	0% (0)	3
Souter	100% (3)	0% (0)	3
Blackmun	100% (8)	0% (0)	8
Brennan	100% (8)	0% (0)	8
Marshall	100% (8)	0% (0)	8
Powell	100% (2)	0% (0)	2

Source: Harold J. Spaeth, *United States Supreme Court Judicial Database, 1953–2004 Terms* (Ann Arbor, MI: Inter-University Consortium for Political and Social Research, 2005).

The Pre–Burger Court Period

Although no affirmative action cases were heard by the Supreme Court before the Burger Court era, the foundation for these cases occurred in the sixties, when affirmative action programs were initiated throughout the country. The first major initiative is generally considered to be Executive Order 11246, by President Lyndon Johnson, in 1965. This policy was directed toward the Department of Labor and sought to ensure that businesses holding contracts with the Labor Department were not involved in discriminatory practices, leading to the significant recruitment and hiring of minority workers. This Executive Order was monitored by the Office of Federal Contract Compliances, which was created in 1966. Affirmative action programs then spread into other federal agencies, state governments began to initiate a variety of affirmative action policies, colleges and universities followed suit, and the private sector began to participate as well.

Legal challenges soon arose to these programs, usually taking one of two forms. One approach was to challenge affirmative action programs as being unconstitutional under the Fourteenth Amendment Equal Protection Clause for state programs or the Fifth Amendment Due Process Clause for federal programs. The other approach was to challenge affirmative action programs on statutory grounds, especially Title VII of the 1964 Civil Rights Act, which prohibits employment discrimination based upon race, color, gender, national origin, or religion.

Thus, America's courts were being asked the intriguing and important question of whether the nation's constitutional and statutory provisions that were created to protect minorities and women could also be used to address the affirmative action concern of white males. Ultimately, answers to this question would have to come from the U.S. Supreme Court; and by the time these cases worked their way through the lower courts, the Warren Court era was over and the Burger Court era was well under way.

The Burger Court Period

Affirmative action cases were certainly among the most important and controversial ones decided by the Burger Court. In general, the justices of the Burger Court were supportive of affirmative action programs as long as no person was specifically harmed by such programs; if, however, a person would suffer direct harm such as the loss of a job, then the Burger Court justices would rule against the program. The Burger Court justices were not successful, however, in determining the proper equal protection test to apply to affirmative action cases.

The Burger Court's initial and most famous affirmative action case was *Regents of the University of California v. Bakke* (1978). Alan Bakke was a white male seeking admission to medical school at the University of California at Davis. He was rejected and brought suit challenging the legality of Davis's affirmative action program, which guaranteed 16 of 100 admission spots to minority students, with all of the admitted minority students having lower MCAT scores and grade point averages than Bakke.

The Court's first affirmative action decision revealed a deeply divided Court that gave cautious approval to affirmative action. Four justices—Burger, Rehnquist, Stewart, and Stevens—took the position that the Davis affirmative action program was in violation of Title VII of the 1964 Civil Rights Act, which prohibits race discrimination in any programs that receive federal financial aid. Four other members of the Court—Brennan, Marshall, Blackmun, and White—argued that the program was constitutional under the Equal Protection Clause of the Fourteenth Amendment using intermediate scrutiny or the important government objective test. Justice Powell was the critical voice on the Court in this case. He argued that the Davis program was impermissible because it involved a rigid quota system, but he argued that race could be among the considerations for university admissions. The case was complicated further by Powell's position that the strict scrutiny test should apply in affirmative action programs, with Powell arguing that diversity was a compelling government interest.

Not surprisingly, the Burger Court continued to struggle with affirmative action programs in the aftermath of *Bakke*. Although the Burger Court justices were generally supportive of most affirmative action plans, they did draw a line against programs that resulted in whites losing jobs.

The Burger Court gave approval to affirmative action programs that promoted employment opportunities for minorities, and the Burger Court justices were also highly deferential to federal affirmative action programs. Two good examples of the Court's support for affirmative action programs dealing with employment are *United Steelworkers of America v. Weber* (1979) and *Fullilove v. Klutznick* (1980).

Weber involved a voluntary program developed by Kaiser Aluminum and Chemical Company and the United Steelworkers Union to set up training programs to create more opportunities for African Americans, with one-half of the positions reserved for blacks and admission to the programs based on seniority within each group. Brian Weber was not admitted to the white pool based on seniority, but he had more seniority than some African Americans who were admitted. Weber argued that this violated Title VII of the 1964 Civil Rights Act prohibiting discrimination in employment, but a 5–2 Court gave a liberal interpretation to the act in upholding the program.

The *Fullilove* case centered on a federal employment case involving "set asides." In this specific case, Congress created the 1977 Public Works Employment Act, under which state and local governments contracting with the federal government had to set aside, or ensure, that 10 percent of the contract had to go to minority business enterprises. The Court found this program to be permissible, but the justices could not agree on a majority opinion.

Despite their general support for affirmative action programs, the Burger Court justices rejected plans that resulted in whites losing their jobs. In *Firefighters Local Union No. 1784 v. Statts* (1984), for example, a conflict arose between an affirmative action program and a seniority policy. The city of Memphis, Tennessee, had entered into a consent decree to increase the number of minority firefighters, but a financial crisis requiring firings meant that more senior white firefighters would have to be discharged to maintain the affirmative action program. A 6–3 Burger Court ruled that under Title VII seniority programs must be honored even if they compromise affirmative action programs. Similarly, in the 1986 case of *Wygant v. Jackson Board of Education*, the Burger Court in a 5–4 decision rejected a collective bargaining agreement provision related to layoffs that required minority teachers to be retained over white teachers with more seniority.

The Burger Court thus struggled mightily with affirmative action. They had no precedent from the Warren Court to provide guidance, and strong arguments existed on both sides regarding not only the legal issues associated with affirmative action but also the public policy issues. In general, the Burger Court was supportive of affirmative action programs. The Court approved the consideration of race as a factor in university admissions policies and endorsed various employment programs to increase minority participation. The Burger Court seemed especially deferential to federal affirmative action programs. But the Burger Court justices rejected strict quota systems as well as programs that resulted in job losses for white workers. Affirmative action cases typically involved sharp disagreements among the justices, and the Burger Court justices were never able to reach a majority consensus on the proper equal protection test to apply in affirmative action cases. Yarbrough summarizes nicely the Burger Court's treatment of affirmative action cases by calling them "the most troublesome equal protection issues confronting the justices during Burger's tenure" (2000, 218).

The Rehnquist Court Period

The subject of affirmative action proved to be equally troublesome for the justices of the Rehnquist Court, and changes in the Court's membership had important effects on the Court's decisions. In the initial years of the Rehnquist Court, a narrow majority of the justices supported affirmative action programs. When Kennedy replaced Powell, in 1988, however, the opponents of affirmative action now controlled the Court, and gradually a conservative majority was able to establish strict scrutiny as the controlling test in affirmative action cases. This development seemed to mean that the Court would approve few if any affirmative action programs. The Rehnquist Court surprised Court observers, however, in two cases in 2003 involving the University of Michigan by resurrecting Powell's opinion in *Bakke* that prohibited any type of rigid quota system but that allowed race to be considered as one factor in the admissions decision. Thus, although it is a close call, the Rehnquist Court did not engage in a conservative counterrevolution in the area of affirmative action. A detailed examination of leading affirmative action decisions of the Rehnquist Court is now necessary to support these generalizations.

In the early Rehnquist Court era, when Rehnquist became chief justice and Scalia was named to Rehnquist's associate justice seat, a narrow five-person majority supported most affirmative action programs. This coalition consisted of Justices Brennan, Marshall, Blackmun, Stevens, and Powell. This group approved two controversial affirmative action programs in the 1987 cases of *United States v. Paradise* and *Johnson v. Transportation Agency of Santa Clara County, California.*

Paradise involved the discriminatory hiring and promotion policies of the Alabama Department of Public Safety. In 1972, a federal district court ruled their hiring practices were discriminatory because they had never hired an African American trooper in the thirty-seven years of their existence. The district court ordered the department to end its discriminatory hiring and promotion practices. Twelve years later, however, only four African Americans had been promoted to the rank of corporal, and none had been promoted to higher ranks. The court then created a temporary plan requiring the promotion of one African American for every white promotion until blacks constituted 25 percent of the officers. The Reagan administration was strongly opposed to affirmative action programs and urged the Court to overturn it, but a 5–4 majority of Brennan, Marshall, Blackmun, Powell, and Stevens upheld the plan as consistent with the Equal Protection Clause. Like the Burger Court, however, a majority could not agree about the proper equal protection test to apply.

In the same term, the Rehnquist Court in the *Johnson* case faced for the first time the issue of the applicability of affirmative action programs to women. Diane Joyce and Paul Johnson both applied for a promotion to road dispatcher with the Santa Clara County (California) Transportation Agency. Both were rated well qualified, but Johnson had a slightly higher point total without affirmative action being taken into account. The agency, however, had developed an affirmative action program to deal with past discriminatory practices against women and minorities, and a finding revealed that no woman had ever been chosen in the 238 previous appointments in this classification. Based upon this affirmative action policy, Joyce was appointed to the position, and Johnson filed suit that this plan violated Title VII. The Rehnquist Court ruled 6–3 that the policy did not violate Title VII, with O'Connor joining the Court's typical five-person liberal coalition of Brennan, Marshall, Blackmun, Stevens, and Powell. Brennan authored the majority opinion and relied heavily on the Burger Court's 1979 *Weber* decision. Brennan argued that the plan was consistent with the spirit of Title VII because it avoided any rigid quotas, it allowed gender to be considered as one factor, and the plan was temporary.

The delicate balance in affirmative action cases shifted with Justice Powell's resignation at the end of the 1986–1987 term and Justice Kennedy finally joining the Court during the 1987–1988 term after the long and difficult struggle to find Powell's replacement. With Powell's departure from the Court, the liberal coalition was reduced to four justices, and Kennedy's opposition to affirmative action programs created a conservative majority of Rehnquist, Scalia, White, O'Connor, and Kennedy, although O'Connor and White would occasionally support affirmative action programs.

The impact of Kennedy's replacement of Powell became apparent in the 1989 case of *City of Richmond v. J. A. Croson Co.*, in which the Court rejected a set-aside program by the city of Richmond, Virginia, and for the first time found majority agreement to apply strict scrutiny to affirmative action cases. Responding to evidence that minority contractors in Richmond had received less than 1 percent of the city's prime contracts, the city in 1983 adopted a set-aside program under which prime contractors who were awarded city contracts had to subcontract at least 30 percent of the total contract to minority business enterprises, although a waiver could be granted if no qualified company could be found. When the J. A. Croson Company's application for a waiver was denied, the company filed suit, claiming that the Richmond affirmative action program was unconstitutional. Richmond defended its plan largely on the basis of *Fullilove*, in which the Court approved a federal set-aside program.

O'Connor authored the majority opinion in this precedent-setting case. She began by distinguishing this case from *Fullilove* on the basis that Congress has much broader powers under the Constitution to enforce the Equal Protection Clause of the Fourteenth Amendment. Then O'Connor turned to the appropriate equal protection test, arguing that the suspect classification or strict scrutiny test should apply. She disregarded the standard justifications for strict scrutiny, arguing that "the standard of review under the Equal Protection Clause is not dependent on the race of those burdened or benefited by a particular classification" (488 U.S. at 494). The reason for this, O'Connor argued, is that "classifications based on race carry a danger of stigmatic harm. Unless they are strictly reserved for remedial settings, they may in fact promote notions of racial inferiority and lead to a politics of racial hostility" (488 U.S. at 493).

In applying the strict scrutiny test, O'Connor argued that Richmond failed both prongs. To have a compelling government interest, Richmond would have to establish specifically identified discrimination in the construction industry, but the city only provided evidence that past discrimination may have existed based upon generalized statistical patterns. In addition, O'Connor argued for the majority that the program was not narrowly tailored because no clear justification was offered for the 30 percent target.

Marshall wrote a strong dissent joined by Brennan and Blackmun. Marshall argued that the appropriate doctrinal test in affirmative action programs was intermediate scrutiny and that the city of Richmond easily met these standards because it was pursuing an important government objective through means that were substantially related to this important objective. Marshall's most impassioned words were directed toward the majority's adoption of the strict scrutiny test: "Today, for the first time, a majority of this Court has adopted strict scrutiny as its standard of Equal Protection Clause review of race-conscious remedial measures" (488 U.S. at 551). He continued, "In concluding that remedial classifications warrant no different standard of review under the Constitution than the most brutal and repugnant forms of state-sponsored racism, a majority of this Court signals that it regards racial discrimination as largely a phenomenon of the past, and that government bodies need no longer preoccupy themselves with rectifying racial injustice" (488 U.S. at 552).

Croson was clearly a landmark case, but it left open many questions regarding affirmative action. A major issue was whether the strict scrutiny standard would apply not only to state cases but also to federal cases. The 1990 case of *Metro Broadcasting, Inc. v. FCC* provided an answer to that question.

Metro Broadcasting involved two affirmative action programs developed by the Federal Communications Commission regarding the awarding of broadcast licenses for television and radio stations. One policy involved "minority enhancement," under which minority-owned companies received additional credit in the bidding competition for a license. A second policy was a "distress sale," under which minority-owned businesses could be granted a license before hearings were completed on the qualifications of a station owner.

Brennan wrote the majority opinion in the 5–4 decision, with White supplying the key vote by joining Blackmun, Marshall, and Stevens. Drawing upon the Court's emphasis on the power of Congress to legislate under the Fourteenth Amendment and citing *Fullilove* and *Croson*, Brennan argued that for federal affirmative action programs, the appropriate test was intermediate scrutiny. Applying this test to the FCC policies, Brennan reasoned that the policies served the important government objective of achieving broadcast diversity and that the means chosen were substantially related to that objective.

O'Connor authored a strongly worded dissent joined by Rehnquist, Scalia, and Kennedy. She rejected the logic of Brennan's majority opinion in every manner. O'Connor argued that the proper test in all affirmative action cases was strict scrutiny and that the FCC's policies failed both prongs. She also maintained that the policies would fail both prongs of the intermediate scrutiny standard. In concluding her argument, O'Connor wrote: "The Court has determined, in essence, that Congress and all federal agencies are exempted, to some ill-defined but significant degree, from the Constitution's equal protection requirements. This break with our precedents greatly undermines equal protection guarantees, and permits distinctions among citizens based on race and ethnicity which the Constitution clearly forbids" (497 U.S. at 631).

O'Connor's position eventually triumphed in the 1995 case of *Adarand Constructors, Inc. v. Pena*, which explicitly overturned *Metro Broadcasting*. Membership change played a critical role in this major reversal of precedent, specifically Thomas's replacement of Marshall. As shown in table 3.31, the Court now was composed of five justices opposed to affirmative action programs—O'Connor, Rehnquist, Scalia, Kennedy, and Thomas—and they would prevail in *Adarand Constructors*.

The *Adarand* case arose when Adarand Constructors, a company owned and operated by a white male, did not get awarded a subcontracting bid to do guardrail work on a federal highway construction project in Colorado. The Adarand company submitted the lowest bid, but the prime contractor—Mountain Gravel and Construction Company—awarded the subcontract to Gonzales Construction, a minority-owned business. Mountain Gravel made this decision because it received a $10,000 bonus under a federal affirmative action program that provided financial bonuses to prime contractors if they awarded at least 10 percent of the overall contract to disadvantaged business enterprises owned and operated by African Americans, Hispanics, and other minority groups. Adarand filed suit charging that this policy violated the equal protection guarantee of the Due Process Clause of the Fifth Amendment. The lower federal courts ruled against Adarand, holding that *Metro Broadcasting* gave the federal government greater latitude in regard to affirmative action programs than the states had under *Croson*.

O'Connor wrote the majority opinion in *Adarand* and was joined by Rehnquist, Scalia, Thomas, and Kennedy in overturning *Metro* and establishing strict scrutiny as the appropriate test in all affirmative action cases, both state and federal. O'Connor argued that the Court's affirmative action decisions through *Croson* had established the principle that "any person, of whatever race, has the right to demand that any governmental actor subject to the Constitution justify any racial classification subjecting that person to unequal treatment under the strictest judicial scrutiny" (515 U.S. at 224). Because *Metro Broadcasting* departed from that principle, it had to be overruled. The conservative majority did not apply the strict scrutiny test to this case, however, but rather returned it to the lower courts for further consideration based upon the Court's new doctrinal standards.

The conservative majority did not speak with one voice in *Adarand*, however. Scalia authored a concurring opinion in which he argued that affirmative action programs can never be found constitutional under strict scrutiny because the "government can never have a 'compelling interest' in discriminating on the basis of race in order to 'make up' for past racial discrimination in the opposite direction" (515 U.S. at 239). In a concurring opinion, Thomas was especially critical of affirmative action programs, arguing that "there can be no doubt that racial paternalism and its unintended consequences can be as poisonous and pernicious as any other form of discrimination" (515 U.S. at 241).

Adarand seemed to many Court observers to signal the Court's opposition to all affirmative action programs. The strict scrutiny test was now the standard for all affirmative action programs, and it would not be easy for any governmental entity to show that it was pursuing a compelling interest through narrowly tailored means, especially if the Court would recognize a compelling interest to exist only if the government was addressing proven discrimination against specific individuals. However, the Court did not state in *Adarand* exactly what could constitute a compelling government interest, and only Scalia in *Adarand* stated that the government can never have a compelling enough interest to justify an affirmative action program.

The Rehnquist Court was quiet regarding affirmative action for nearly a decade after *Adarand*, but two major cases were decided in 2003 regarding the University of Michigan that answered some important questions left unanswered by *Adarand*. *Grutter v. Bollinger* (2003) involved a challenge to the constitutionality of the admissions standards of the University of Michigan Law School, which took race into account as one of many factors to achieve a diversified student body with a critical mass of African American, Hispanic, and Native American students. *Gratz v. Bollinger* (2003) raised the issue of the constitutionality of the undergraduate admissions policy of the University of Michigan; this system provided a maximum of 150 points, with 100 points being required for admission and 20 points being awarded to students who were African American, Hispanic, or Native American.

Drawing heavily from Justice Powell's opinion in *Bakke*, the Court approved the admissions policy of the law school but rejected as unconstitutional the undergraduate point system. O'Connor proved to be the key justice, joining the four liberals—Stevens, Ginsburg, Breyer, and Souter—and writing the majority opinion in *Grutter* that upheld the affirmative action program of Michigan's law school. However, O'Connor joined the four conservatives—Rehnquist, Scalia, Thomas, and Kennedy—in rejecting the undergraduate affirmative action policy, which Breyer also opposed, to create a 6–3 vote.

O'Connor's majority opinion in *Grutter* drew heavily from Powell's opinion in *Bakke*. Utilizing the strict scrutiny approach endorsed by Powell in the *Bakke* case and subsequently accepted by Court majorities in *Croson* and *Adarand*, O'Connor wrote: "Today we endorse Justice Powell's view that student body diversity is a compelling state interest that can justify the use of race in university admissions" (156 L. Ed. 2d at 330). O'Connor acknowledged the numerous benefits the law school identified as stemming from a diverse student body, and she also recognized the arguments supporting the law school in friends of the court briefs filed by business and military leaders. Turning to the second prong of the strict scrutiny test, O'Connor argued that the means utilized were narrowly tailored to achieve the compelling interest of a diversified student body. The admissions program did not operate as a quota system according to O'Connor; rather, "the Law School engages in a highly individualized, holistic review of each applicant's file, giving serious consideration to all the ways an applicant might contribute to a diverse educational environment" (156 L. Ed. 2d at 338). Rehnquist, Scalia, Thomas, and Kennedy all wrote dissenting opinions, accepting strict scrutiny as the appropriate test but arguing that the law school's admission standards failed the test.

Although the conservatives lost in *Grutter*, they prevailed in the companion case of *Gratz* in finding the Michigan undergraduate admissions program to be unconstitutional. O'Connor joined Rehnquist's majority opinion along with Scalia, Thomas, and Kennedy. The chief justice used the strict scrutiny test to analyze the case and argued that "the University's use of race in its current freshman admissions policy is not narrowly tailored to achieve respondents' asserted compelling interest in diversity" (156 L. Ed. 2d at 284). For Rehnquist and his fellow conservatives, the awarding of the automatic twenty points to all members of underrepresented minority groups did not provide the individualized consideration that was required and instead made race the decisive factor, allowing admission "for virtually every minimally qualified underrepresented minority applicant" (156 L. Ed. 2d at 284).

Conclusion

Did the Rehnquist Court engage in a conservative counterrevolution in the area of affirmative action? This is not an easy question to answer because the Warren Court made no decisions regarding this issue, and the Burger Court, while generally supportive of affirmative action programs, failed to develop a doctrinal standard for evaluating affirmative action cases. Thus, it is difficult to argue that a liberal revolution ever occurred in regard to affirmative action. The record of the Rehnquist Court does support the conclusion, however, that this era witnessed a conservative shift because of the *Croson* and *Adarand* decisions, which firmly established the strict scrutiny test as the appropriate standard of analysis in affirmative action cases.

The recent decisions of *Grutter* and *Gratz* seem to indicate, however, that affirmative action programs can be constitutional, thus undercutting the argument that the Rehnquist Court turned sharply to the right in affirmative action cases. A Court majority agreed that obtaining a diversified student body is a compelling government interest and that a holistic, individualized review of student applicants that includes the consideration of race is a narrowly tailored means to achieve this interest. Quotas and rigid point systems are not valid, however.

Many questions remain, however, and the Court will continue to be confronted with difficult affirmative action cases. It is not clear what types of programs beyond college admissions can be justified as involving compelling government issues. For example, is diversity in the workplace as compelling as diversity on a college campus? The second prong of the strict scrutiny test also involves numerous uncertainties. Although quotas and numeric point systems are not permissible, considerable ambiguity surrounds the question of how race can be taken into account in affirmative action programs. These considerations are made even more difficult by the membership changes that inevitably occur on the Court. We have observed the effect of membership change on the Rehnquist Court's past affirmative action cases; and given the Court's current close divisions on affirmative action, new appointees could have major effects on Court policy.

Other Equal Protection Cases

Although the Supreme Court's most famous and controversial equal protection cases have primarily involved issues of racial discrimination, gender discrimination, and affirmative action, the Court has also heard a wide variety of other cases involving claims of the denial of equal protection of the law. Numerous groups have sought to convince the Court not only that they have been treated unequally but also that they deserve to be included in the intermediate or suspect classification categories where the Court places much more difficult standards for the government to meet. In this section of chapter 3, we examine the Rehnquist Court's decision making in regard to these other areas of equal protection jurisprudence, analyzing the Court's approach to cases brought by such diverse groups as the poor, the aged, the mentally ill, illegitimate children, and gays and lesbians. We also include in this section two additional, major equal protection cases decided recently involving physician-assisted suicide laws and the 2000 presidential election between George W. Bush and Al Gore. Because the Rehnquist Court decided relatively few cases in this area, we do not engage in quantitative analysis.

The Rehnquist Court generally followed the lead of the Warren and Burger Courts in regard to which groups should be placed into the higher levels of the equal protection doctrinal framework. As seen in table 3.25, only gender and illegitimacy cases can be considered under intermediate scrutiny and only cases violating fundamental rights or cases involving race or alienage discrimination and affirmative action trigger strict scrutiny. We examine three areas—economic status, age, and mental illness—in which the Rehnquist Court has refused to expand the types of cases where heightened scrutiny can apply.

The issue of economics status was central to the 1973 Burger Court case of *San Antonio Independent School District v. Rodriguez*. The case involved a challenge to the constitutionality of Texas's system of public education, which relied heavily on local property taxes and resulted in vastly different funding among school districts. Attorneys for Demetrio Rodriguez argued that discrimination based upon economic status should be considered under suspect classification. Writing for a five-person majority, Justice Powell rejected this claim and instead applied the rational basis or minimal scrutiny test, and he argued that Texas's system met both prongs of the test because it involved methods that were reasonably related to the promotion of local control of education. Any changes to the system, Powell argued, must come from the legislatures, not the federal courts.

The Rehnquist Court upheld the view that economic status must be treated under the minimal scrutiny test in *Kadrmas v. Dickinson Public Schools*, in 1988. This case arose in North Dakota, where the state legislature passed a law allowing local school districts to impose a charge for riding on school buses. A 5–4 majority argued that the appropriate standard was the rational basis test and that the state met both prongs of the test.

In addition to resisting attempts to have economics status considered under heightened scrutiny, the Rehnquist Court has also followed the precedent of previous Courts in rejecting age as a basis for increased scrutiny beyond the rational basis test. An important case is *Gregory v. Ashcroft* (1991), which involved a provision of the Missouri Constitution that required most state judges to retire when they reached the age of seventy. Ellis Gregory and several other judges challenged this as a violation of the Equal Protection Clause. Relying heavily on the Burger Court precedent of *Massachusetts Board of Retirement v. Murgia* (1976), Justice O'Connor for the 7–2 Court argued that the rational basis test was the well-established approach: "Petitioners are correct to assert their challenge at the level of rational basis. This Court has said repeatedly that age is not a suspect classification under the Equal Protection Clause" (501 U.S. at 470). Acknowledging the deference to the government under the rational basis test, O'Connor argued that requiring retirement at age seventy was rationally related to the state's legitimate interest in having a judiciary capable of meeting the high level of demands that exists.

A final example of the unwillingness of the Rehnquist Court to add new groups to either the intermediate or strict scrutiny categories involves the mentally retarded. In *Heller v. Doe* (1993), the Court considered a Kentucky law that required "clear and convincing evidence" to commit a mentally retarded individual but required a more stringent standard of "proof beyond a reasonable doubt" to commit a mentally ill person. The case was brought on behalf of a group of mentally retarded individuals whose attorneys argued that heightened scrutiny should be used. A 5–4 Rehnquist Court, however, applied the rational basis test to rule in favor of Kentucky. Justice Kennedy authored the majority opinion, arguing that the distinction in standards was a reasonable means to achieve the state's legitimate objective of committing the mentally retarded because it is much more difficult to diagnose the mentally ill.

Just as the Rehnquist Court generally followed closely the Warren and Burger Courts' precedents in regard to the types of cases to be considered under the rational basis test, so too the Rehnquist Court followed precedent in regard to the appropriate cases to consider under intermediate and strict scrutiny. We have already discussed the Rehnquist Court's commitment to intermediate scrutiny for gender cases and to strict scrutiny for race and alienage cases and affirmative action, and the justices of the Rehnquist Court have also followed the Burger Court precedents of using intermediate scrutiny in cases involving illegitimate children. *Clark v. Jeter* (1988) is a good example of this point.

Cherlyn Clark was unmarried when she gave birth in 1973 to her daughter, Tiffany. Ten years later, Cherlyn filed a court complaint in Pennsylvania naming Gene Jeter as Tiffany's father and demanding child support. Tests indicated that Jeter was probably Tiffany's father, but Jeter's attorneys argued that the case should be dismissed because Pennsylvania had a six-year statute of limitations regarding paternity actions. The Pennsylvania courts ruled in favor of Jeter, and Clark appealed to the Supreme Court on equal protection grounds, specifically that the statute of limitation law for illegitimate children was unconstitutional because a legitimate child could seek support from a delinquent parent until the age of eighteen. The Rehnquist Court agreed unanimously with Clark in finding the law unconstitutional. Writing for the Court, Justice O'Connor argued that the Court's past precedents such as *Mills v. Habluetzel* (1982) and *Pickett v. Brown* (1983) established that the appropriate test in cases involving illegitimate children is intermediate scrutiny, and Pennsylvania failed the test. The six-year statute of limitations "is not substantially related to Pennsylvania's interest in avoiding the litigation of stale or fraudulent claims. In a number of circumstances, Pennsylvania permits the issue of paternity to be litigated more than six years after the birth of an illegitimate child" (486 U.S. at 464).

Thus far in our examination of "other" equal protection areas, we have noted that the Rehnquist Court has adhered closely to past precedent and has usually reached conservative results. The Rehnquist Court justices have, however, produced a major, new liberal ruling in one important equal protection area—sexual orientation. The Warren and Burger Courts never heard a case involving an equal protection claim based upon sexual orientation. The Rehnquist Court did, however, in the 1996 case of *Romer v. Evans*, ruling 6–3 that an amendment to the Colorado Constitution violated the equal protection rights of homosexuals. This landmark case was thus the first time the Supreme Court had ever ruled a government action unconstitutional based upon denying equal protection of the law based upon sexual orientation.

Romer arose from a 1991 constitutional amendment—Amendment 2—approved by Colorado citizens that prohibited local governments and the state from enacting or enforcing laws prohibiting discrimination based upon sexual orientation. Amendment 2 arose out of reaction to liberal policies passed by several Colorado communities, including Boulder and Aspen, that banned discrimination based upon sexual orientation. Both the state trial court and the Colorado Supreme Court found in favor of those challenging Amendment 2.

Justice Kennedy wrote the majority opinion and was joined by Justices O'Connor, Stevens, Ginsburg, Breyer, and Souter. Kennedy argued that the rational basis test applied in this case because it did not involve a fundamental right or a suspect class, but he reasoned that the amendment failed to pass even minimal scrutiny.

> Amendment 2 fails, indeed defies, even this conventional inquiry. First, the Amendment has the peculiar property of imposing a broad and undifferentiated disability on a single named group, an exceptional and, as we explain, invalid form of legislation. Second, its sheer breadth is so discontinuous with the reasons offered for it that the amendment seems inexplicable by anything but animus toward the class it affects; it lacks a rational relationship to legitimate state interests (517 U.S. at 865).

Justice Scalia wrote a vigorous dissent, joined by Rehnquist and Thomas. Scalia characterized the majority opinion as "so long on emotional utterance and so short on relevant legal citation" (517 U.S. at 639), and he argued that the Court's decision was " an act, not of judicial judgment, but of political will" (517 U.S. at 653). Scalia argued that the clear controlling precedent was *Bowers v. Hardwick*, a 1986 case in which the Court held constitutional a Georgia law criminalizing homosexual conduct. Scalia did agree that the rational basis test should apply, but he argued that the amendment was a legitimate means of achieving a legitimate government interest, "to prevent piecemeal deterioration of the sexual morality favored by a majority of Coloradans" (517 U.S. at 653).

Romer was a great victory for advocates of gay rights, but it was not a complete victory because the Court used minimal scrutiny. The Court ruled in favor of homosexual rights in this case, but the rational basis test provides a low level of protection for those claiming constitutional violations. Gay rights attorneys argue that homosexuality should be placed under suspect classification because of the long history of discrimination based on sexual orientation, the lack of political power by the gay rights community, and the argument that sexual orientation is an immutable characteristic unrelated to ability. It remains to be seen if the Supreme Court will ever accept this line of reasoning.

Two additional cases decided by the Rehnquist Court under the Equal Protection Clause also need to be discussed because they dealt with important public policy issues. *Vacco, Attorney General of New York, v. Quill* (1997) involved a New York law that prohibited physician-assisted suicide. *Bush v. Gore* (2000) was the famous Rehnquist Court decision that settled the 2000 presidential election in favor of George W. Bush.

In *Vacco*, the New York law criminalized physician-assisted suicide but did allow patients to refuse to receive lifesaving medical treatment. Several physicians and seriously ill patients brought suit that the Equal Protection Clause was violated by the distinction between the ban on physician-assisted suicide and the permission to allow patients to refuse lifesaving medical treatment. The Rehnquist Court ruled 9–0 to uphold the law, with Rehnquist authoring the majority opinion. The chief justice began by reasoning that the strict scrutiny test does not apply because the law neither burdens a fundamental right nor affects a suspect class. Therefore, the appropriate test was the rational basis test, and Rehnquist argued that New York easily met the test: "By permitting everyone to refuse unwanted medical treatment while prohibiting anyone from assisting a suicide, New York law follows a longstanding and rational distinction" (521 U.S. at 808). In a companion case to *Vacco—Washington v. Glucksberg* (1997)—the Court also unanimously ruled in favor of a Washington State law that criminalized physician-assisted suicide, but in *Glucksberg* the issue was whether this law violated the Due Process Clause of the Fourteenth Amendment, which the Court said it did not because a person does not have a right under the liberty guarantee of the Fourteenth Amendment to commit physician-assisted suicide.

The final case to be considered under the category of other equal protection cases is *Bush v. Gore* (2000). If the Rehnquist Court will be remembered for any single case, then it will surely be this case, not because of its importance to constitutional law but instead because it decided the outcome of the 2000 presidential race. The 2000 presidential election was the closest in modern history, and Florida was the pivotal state. By the day after the election, it was clear that Democrat Al Gore had won the popular vote, but the Electoral College vote, and thus the presidency, depended on whether Bush or Gore won the Sunshine State. Bush had a slight edge over Gore in the initial balloting, but the vote was so close that a recount had to occur, and the late-arriving absentee ballots had to be counted. Bush still had a slight lead after the required machine recount occurred and the absentee ballots were counted, and this led Gore to seek a manual recount in heavily Democratic counties.

After an intense political and legal struggle, the Florida Supreme Court handed down a ruling supporting the argument of Gore and the Democrats that a manual recount had to occur in select Florida counties. Bush appealed the Florida Supreme Court's decision to the U.S. Supreme Court, and the Court agreed to hear the case. An anxious nation awaited the Court's decision, which was delivered on December 12, 2000. Justices Kennedy and O'Connor joined the Court's three most conservative members—Rehnquist, Scalia, and Thomas—in a *per curiam* opinion that stated that the manual recount ordered by the Florida Supreme Court would violate the Equal Protection Clause of the Fourteenth Amendment because of the lack of uniform standards by which to recount the ballots. Furthermore, because adequate time did not exist to develop such standards, no recount could occur. The effect of the decision was to give the presidential election to Bush. Justices Souter and Breyer also agreed in separate opinions that there were constitutional problems with the recount ordered by the Florida Supreme Court, but they would have allowed the Florida high court to fashion an appropriate remedy. In contrast, Justices Ginsburg and Stevens argued that the Equal Protection Clause was not violated and that the recount could go forward.

Bush v. Gore has been analyzed in numerous published studies. The decision has been strongly supported (e.g., Huffman 2001) and harshly condemned (e.g., Dershowitz 2001), and other books have attempted to present more balanced assessments (e.g., Sunstein and Epstein 2001).

Alan M. Dershowitz has presented the strongest attack on the Court's decision in his book *Supreme Injustice: How the High Court Hijacked Election 2000*. Dershowitz writes: "This book is about the culpability of those justices who hijacked Election 2000 by distorting the law, violating their own expressed principles, and using their robes to bring about a partisan result" (2001, 12).

Numerous other critics stop short of Dershowitz's extreme position but do present harsh criticisms of the majority's decision making. One argument is that the more conservative justices have long argued for a modest, nonpolitical role for the Court, but in this case they thrust themselves into the middle of the country's most intense political controversy. Yet another criticism of the conservative majority is that they have championed states' rights federalism, but in this case they asserted federal supremacy over the Florida election. Critics of the Court's opinion also argue that it was poorly reasoned equal protection analysis, with little or no convincing use of equal protection doctrine and precedent. Finally, opponents of the decision argue that the Court had seriously damaged its reputation and legitimacy.

Despite the strength of the criticism of *Bush v. Gore*, numerous arguments have been advanced to support the Court's decision. An especially strong point is that two of the Court's liberal justices—Breyer and Souter—concurred with the five-person majority that the decision of the Florida Supreme Court created serious equal protection problems. In addition to the fundamental argument that the Court's decision was correct, supporters of the decision have argued that it was a well-reasoned opinion given the incredible time constraints that existed. Yet another argument is that the Court saved the nation a period of long agony that would have resulted in the same outcome, the election of Bush. Finally, supporters of the decision argue that critics are simply wrong that the Court has damaged its reputation and legitimacy in the eyes of the American people.

In closing this section of chapter 3, what conclusions can we offer regarding the central theme of the book—did the Rehnquist Court engage in a constitutional counterrevolution? In regard to the area of "Other Equal Protection Cases," the answer clearly seems to be no. The Rehnquist Court did not create any new conservative precedents in this field of constitutional law. Indeed, the justices of the Rehnquist

Court established a major, new liberal precedent in *Romer v. Evans* (1996) when they ruled for the first time that a government policy violated the equal protection rights of homosexuals. In addition, the Rehnquist Court adhered closely to the equal protection doctrinal framework developed by the Warren and Burger Courts. *Bush v. Gore* (2000) was certainly a controversial decision, but it cannot be considered to be a major, new conservative precedent. Thus, the Rehnquist Court's "other" equal protection decisions followed precedent closely or were a dramatic departure in the liberal direction.

Privacy and Abortion

As contentious as affirmative action is in American society and on the Supreme Court, the closely related subjects of privacy and abortion have generated even greater controversy. Privacy involves the right to be left alone from arbitrary government interference in one's personal life. Important as this right may be, it is not mentioned anywhere in the Constitution. As we will see, the Supreme Court has agreed that a constitutional right of privacy does exist, but the justices have not been able to achieve consensus on the constitutional basis for this right.

Even if one accepts the argument that a right to privacy does exist, it is quite a different matter to argue that this right extends to the decision to terminate a pregnancy. Those who argue that the abortion decision is not an implicit constitutional right argue that nothing in the text of the Constitution justifies this position, nothing in terms of either original intent or original understanding of the Constitution supports this, American society has historically criminalized abortion, and it is morally wrong to end the life of an unborn child. Despite these strong arguments, the Supreme Court has disagreed with them and has recognized the abortion decision as an aspect of the broader right of privacy in the 1973 case of *Roe v. Wade*. This decision has generated a storm of controversy both within the Court and outside the Court that continues today.

In this section of chapter 3, we continue to explore the central question of the book: did the Rehnquist Court engage in a conservative constitutional counterrevolution in regard to the area of privacy and abortion? We begin with a quantitative analysis of the Court's abortion decisions, but the other privacy cases are not subjected to quantitative analysis because so few have been decided. Turning to the qualitative analysis, we begin with a brief historical discussion of the background and development of the right to privacy that provided the foundation for *Roe*. Then we discuss in some detail the major abortion decisions of the Burger and Rehnquist Courts, focusing on the issue of whether the Rehnquist Court has fundamentally changed the jurisprudence of the Burger Court. Finally, we analyze the other major privacy cases of the Rehnquist Court, specifically the areas of the privacy of homosexuals and the right to die.

Quantitative Analysis

Table 3.32 provides a comparison of the abortion decisions of the Warren, Burger, and Rehnquist Courts. The Warren Court did not decide any cases involving the subject of abortion, although they did create the precedent recognizing the right of privacy upon which *Roe* was built. The Burger Court was extremely busy with abortion cases, deciding *Roe* and twenty-three other abortion-related cases. The Burger Court justices were deeply divided over the issues surrounding abortion, deciding half of the decisions conservatively and half of them liberally. The Rehnquist Court has also heard a substantial number of abortion-related decisions—fifteen—and like the Burger Court has been closely divided in these cases, deciding 53 percent of them liberally. Thus, this aspect of the quantitative analysis suggests that the Rehnquist Court has been involved with continuity rather than change in regard to the abortion controversy.

Additional insight into the decision making of the Rehnquist Court in regard to abortion can be gained from looking at the individual voting records of the justices who have served during the Rehnquist Court era. Table 3.33 reveals a deeply divided Court, and membership change has had an impact. Looking at the overall table, the

Table 3.32: Liberal/Conservative Voting in Abortion Cases by the Warren, Burger, and Rehnquist Courts, 1953–1954 to 2004–2005 Terms

Court Era	Liberal Decisions	Conservative Decisions	Total Cases
Warren Court (1953–1968 Terms)	0% (0)	0% (0)	0
Burger Court (1969–1985 Terms)	50% (12)	50% (12)	24
Rehnquist Court (1986–2004 Terms)	53% (8)	47% (7)	15
Total	51% (20)	49% (19)	39

Source: Harold J. Spaeth, *United States Supreme Court Judicial Database, 1953–2004 Terms* (Ann Arbor, MI: Inter-University Consortium for Political and Social Research, 2005).

Table 3.33: Liberal/Conservative Voting Records of the Justices of the
Rehnquist Court in Abortion Cases, 1986–1987 Term to 2004–2005 Term
(Justices Ranked from Most Conservative to Most Liberal)

Justices	Liberal Decisions	Conservative Decisions	Total Cases
White	0% (0)	100% (8)	8
Scalia	7% (1)	93% (14)	15
Thomas	11% (1)	89% (8)	9
Kennedy	20% (3)	80% (12)	15
Rehnquist	27% (4)	73% (11)	15
Breyer	60% (3)	40% (2)	5
Souter	64% (7)	36% (4)	11
O'Connor	67% (10)	33% (5)	15
Ginsburg	71% (5)	29% (2)	7
Stevens	93% (14)	7% (1)	15
Brennan	100% (4)	0% (0)	4
Marshall	100% (6)	0% (0)	6
Blackmun	100% (10)	0% (0)	10

Note: Powell is omitted because he did not participate in any abortion decisions.

Source: Harold J. Spaeth, *United States Supreme Court Judicial Database, 1953–2004 Terms*
(Ann Arbor, MI: Inter-University Consortium for Political and Social Research, 2005).

Court was rather sharply divided. Five justices—White, Scalia, Thomas, Kennedy, and Rehnquist—were strongly conservative. Four justices were moderately liberal: Breyer, Souter, O'Connor, and Ginsburg. Finally, Stevens, Brennan, Marshall, and Blackmun have been consistently liberal. (Powell did not participate in any decisions on abortion.)

The importance of membership change can be seen by a close examination of the data. When the Rehnquist Court era began, in 1986, three justices—White, Rehnquist, and Scalia—were opposed to *Roe*. When Kennedy replaced Powell in 1988, this number grew to four, and then Thomas's replacement of Marshall, in 1991, seemed to give the opponents of *Roe* a deciding fifth vote. However, White's retirement and replacement by Ginsburg, in 1993, shifted the five-person majority back to the liberal side, which was composed in the last natural court period of Breyer, Souter, Ginsburg, O'Connor, and Stevens.

These statistics provide important insights into the Rehnquist Court's abortion jurisprudence, but they certainly do not tell the whole story. Thus, we need to turn to a qualitative analysis of the Court's major decisions involving privacy and abortion to obtain greater insight into the abortion policies of the Rehnquist Court.

Development of the Right to Privacy

The key case in which the Supreme Court formally recognized the right to privacy was *Griswold v. Connecticut* (1965), but the Court had given consideration to this concept in previous cases. The most widely cited reference to privacy before *Griswold* came in a dissent written by Justice Louis Brandeis in the 1928 case of *Olmstead v. United States* In this case, the Court majority approved of the federal government's use of wiretapping to obtain evidence for a conviction. In his dissent, Brandeis argued: "The makers of our Constitution . . . conferred as against the government the right to be let alone—the most comprehensive of rights and the right most valued by civilized men. To protect that right, every unjustifiable intrusion by the government upon the privacy of the individual, whatever the means employed, must be deemed a violation of the Fourth Amendment" (277 U.S. at 478).

Although successive Courts made decisions implicitly relating to the right to privacy, it was not until the 1965 case of *Griswold v. Connecticut* that the Court explicitly recognized this right. Estelle Griswold was the executive director of Planned Parenthood in Connecticut, and she was arrested and convicted in 1961 for violating an 1879 state law that criminalized the sale, possession, or use of contraceptive devices as well as the counseling of anyone regarding the use of contraceptives.

The Warren Court ruled 7–2 that the law was unconstitutional because it violated the right of privacy, but the justices could not agree on where this right was to be found in the Constitution. Justices Douglas and Clark argued that the privacy guarantee was implicit in the guarantees of the First, Third, Fourth, Fifth, and Ninth Amendments. Authoring the controlling opinion, Douglas asserted: "Specific guarantees in the Bill of Rights have penumbras, formed by emanations from those guarantees that help give them life and substance. Various guarantees create zones of privacy" (381 U.S. at 484). Justices Goldberg, Brennan, and Warren took a somewhat different approach, emphasizing the importance of the Ninth Amendment, which states: "The enumeration in the Constitution, of certain rights, shall not be construed to deny or disparage others retained by the people." Finally, two justices—Harlan and White—argued that the right of privacy was properly found in the liberty guarantee of the Due Process Clause of the Fourteenth Amendment. Regardless of these diverging views on where the right of privacy was to be found in the Constitution, the justices agreed that it was a fundamental right triggering strict scrutiny and that the Connecticut law failed to meet the requirements of this test.

The Burger Court Period

Although the Warren Court established the right of privacy as a fundamental constitutional right, the Warren Court justices did not consider the issue of whether the right of privacy extended to a woman's decision about whether to have an abortion. This was the challenge presented to the Burger Court in the 1973 landmark case of *Roe v. Wade*. Writing for a seven-person majority, Justice Blackmun ruled unconstitutional a Texas law that prohibited abortions except to save the life of the pregnant woman. Blackmun was joined by Justices Marshall, Brennan, Douglas, Powell, Stewart, and Black. Justices Rehnquist and White filed vigorous dissents.

After beginning his opinion with recognition of the difficult and controversial nature of the issue, Blackmun focused on the central question of whether the abortion decision is a constitutionally protected fundamental right. He argued that the right of privacy was well established in the Court's precedents and that the abortion decision was closely related to other privacy issues relating to procreation, marriage, and family. Blackmun recognized but rejected the major arguments of Texas, including its position that human life begins at conception and that the historical record supports the criminalizing of abortion.

Having established that the abortion decision is a fundamental right, Blackmun then argued that Texas must justify any interference with this decision by the strict scrutiny test, requiring the presence of a compelling government interest achieved by narrowly tailored means. Blackmun argued that Texas asserted two interests: protecting the woman's health and protecting the unborn fetus. Given the evolving status of a nine-month pregnancy, Blackmun reasoned that these interests had to be considered in terms of the three distinct stages, or trimesters, of pregnancy. In the first trimester, Blackmun argued, the state had no compelling interest in regulating the abortion decision. Abortion is less risky to the woman's health than giving birth. In regard to the critical, central issue of protecting the fetus, Blackmun argued that the state had no compelling interest because no consensus existed on when human life begins, and the law has never recognized the unborn as having legal rights. In the second trimester, the state's interests in the woman's health increase because of medical considerations, and thus the state may pass regulations narrowly focused on the woman's health but may not prohibit abortion. Finally, Blackmun concluded, in the third trimester, the state's interests are even stronger in regard to protecting the woman, and at this point the state's interest in the fetus becomes compelling because the fetus has achieved viability, the ability to live outside the woman's body. Thus, the state has the authority to prohibit abortions during the third trimester of pregnancy.

White and Rehnquist authored sharp dissents to Blackmun's opinion, rejecting virtually every argument in the majority opinion. White, joined by Rehnquist, wrote:

I find nothing in the language or history of the Constitution to support the Court's judgment. The Court simply fashions and announces a new constitutional right for pregnant women and, with scarcely any reason or authority for its actions, invests that right with sufficient substance to override most existing state abortion statutes. As an exercise of raw judicial power, the Court perhaps has authority to do what it does today; but in my view its judgment is an improvident and extravagant exercise of the power of judicial review that the Constitution extends to this Court (410 U.S. at 221–222).

The *Roe* decision set off a firestorm in American society, with opponents of the decision committing themselves to undermining and eventually overturning the decision. The Burger Court was thus confronted with numerous abortion cases following *Roe*, but a majority of the Court remained firmly committed to the core principles of the decision. However, the Burger Court justices did not reject all attempts to regulate the abortion process, especially when the regulations involved government funding.

Two of the most significant abortion decisions by the Burger Court upholding *Roe* were *Planned Parenthood of Central Missouri v. Danforth* (1976) and *Akron v. Akron Center for Reproductive Health* (1983). *Danforth* involved a challenge to a broad legislative enactment by Missouri involving regulation of the abortion process. Justice Blackmun wrote the majority opinion for a 6–3 Court that found several provisions of the law to be unconstitutional under *Roe*. These included requirements that a woman receive spousal consent, that physicians use the same standard of care for an abortion procedure as for a live birth, that parental consent be required for unmarried women under eighteen, and that a procedure involving saline amniocentesis could not be used after the first trimester.

The Burger Court similarly ruled unconstitutional key parts of a broad Akron, Ohio, law regulating the abortion procedure in *Akron v. Akron Center for Reproductive Health*. Writing for a 6–3 Court, Justice Powell rejected five specific requirements of the Akron law: (1) hospitalization for all first-trimester abortions, (2) parental consent for minors who are unmarried and younger than age fifteen, (3) an "informed consent" requirement that included having physicians inform abortion patients that a fetus is a human life from the moment of conception, (4) a twenty-four-hour waiting period, and (5) a requirement that the remains of an abortion procedure be disposed of in a sanitary and humane manner.

The *Akron* case is important not only because the Burger Court rejected these efforts to regulate the abortion decision but also because Justice O'Connor in her first abortion case joined Rehnquist and White in finding the regulations to be constitutionally permissible. In her dissent O'Connor advanced a novel argument that was eventually to become the controlling interpretation of the Rehnquist Court. Criticizing the trimester formula as unworkable, she argued that the Court should begin its analysis in abortion cases by asking if a regulation creates an undue burden on a woman. If it does, then the Court would use the strict scrutiny approach. If it does not, then the appropriate test would be the rational basis standard. For O'Connor, none of the Akron regulations created an undue burden, and they all met the lenient standards of the rational basis test.

Although the Burger Court upheld the basic principles of *Roe*, the Court did give constitutional approval to various states and federal laws that prohibited government funding of abortions. In *Beal v. Doe* (1977), for example, the Burger Court justices approved a Pennsylvania law that allowed Medicaid funding only for those abortions determined to be medically necessary by a physician. At the federal level, the so-called "Hyde Amendment," named after its sponsor, Republican Henry Hyde, was part of several pieces of legislation prohibiting federal funds for abortion unless the life of the woman was endangered. The Hyde Amendment was determined not to conflict with *Roe* in the 1980 case of *Harris v. McCrae*. In *Harris* a Court majority used the rational basis test to conclude that the Hyde Amendment was rationally related to the legitimate government objective of protecting potential human life.

This brief analysis of the activities of the Warren and Burger Courts in regard to privacy and abortion reveals that the two Courts did engage in a liberal constitutional revolution in this controversial area. The Warren Court's contribution was creating the right of privacy in *Griswold*, and the Burger Court dramatically extended this right to the abortion decision in *Roe*.

The Rehnquist Court Period

Did the Rehnquist Court engage in a conservative counterrevolution in regard to abortion jurisprudence? The answer in a close call is no, but *Roe* was nearly overturned as new members joined the Court and *Roe* was modified significantly. The future of *Roe* thus remains uncertain.

Membership change was an important factor in the Rehnquist Court's abortion decisions. When Rehnquist became chief justice, replacing Burger, and Scalia took Rehnquist's seat, the number of justices on record as opposing *Roe* had grown from the original two—Rehnquist and White—to perhaps four; Scalia was certainly critical of *Roe*, and O'Connor had expressed her serious doubts about *Roe* in the 1983 *Akron* case. When Kennedy replaced Powell, in 1988, it appeared that a five-person majority now existed to overturn *Roe*.

The first major abortion decision decided by the newly constituted Rehnquist Court came in the 1989 case of *Webster v. Reproductive Health Services*. Four provisions of the 1986 Missouri law were being challenged: a preamble declaring that life begins at conception, a prohibition on using public employees or facilities in abortions, a prohibition on the use of public funds for abortion counseling, and a regulation for physicians to undertake viability testing before performing an abortion. The specifics of the law were less important than the larger question of the future of *Roe*. Opponents of *Roe* sensed that the new membership composition was ready to overturn *Roe*, and the Bush administration filed an amicus brief explicitly inviting the rejection of *Roe*.

When *Webster* was announced, both sides could claim a partial victory. The Rehnquist Court voted 5–4 to uphold two provisions of the law—viability testing and the prohibition on using public facilities or employees for abortions—but did not rule on the other two provisions. Most importantly, *Roe* was not overturned. Chief Justice Rehnquist wrote a plurality opinion joined by White and Kennedy—the Court's newest member—in which he was highly critical of *Roe*. Rehnquist argued that the principle of *stare decisis* does not prevent the Court from reconsidering precedents that have proven to be "unsound in principle and unworkable in practice," which was the situation with *Roe*.

> In the first place, the rigid *Roe* framework is hardly consistent with the notion of a Constitution cast in general terms, as ours is, and usually speaking in general principles, as ours does. The key elements of the *Roe* framework—trimesters and viability—are not found in the text of the Constitution or in any place else one would expect to find a constitutional principle.
>
> In the second place, we do not see why the state's interest in protecting potential human life should come into existence only at the point of viability, and that there should therefore be a rigid line allowing state regulation after viability but prohibiting it before viability (492 U.S. at 518–519).

Despite this harsh criticism of *Roe*, Rehnquist did not argue for its explicit overturn because the law had been found constitutional under *Roe*.

O'Connor and Scalia agreed with the judgment of the plurality but offered different reasoning. Scalia called for the explicit overturning of *Roe*. O'Connor remained committed to her use of an undue burden threshold question to determine the proper level of scrutiny.

The future of *Roe* became even more precarious when Justice Brennan resigned, in 1990, followed by Marshall, in 1991. David Souter, Brennan's replacement, was an unknown in regard to the abortion controversy, but all evidence indicated that Clarence Thomas, Marshall's replacement, would vote to overturn *Roe*. Thus, when the Rehnquist Court heard its next major abortion case, *Planned Parenthood of Southeastern Pennsylvania v. Casey*, in 1992, Court observers counted at least five justices—Rehnquist, White, Scalia, Kennedy, and Thomas—opposing *Roe*, and Souter could possibly make it six. O'Connor was also critical of *Roe*, but her vote to overturn *Roe* might not be needed.

The *Casey* decision involved a Pennsylvania law that regulated the abortion decision in a variety of ways: informed consent by the woman, a twenty-four-hour waiting period, notice of one's spouse, parental consent for minors, and various reporting and record-keeping requirements. The underlying issue in the case, however, was the future of *Roe*. Interestingly, both sides asked the Court to rule directly on *Roe*'s status by ruling either to affirm it or overturn it.

Based upon recent publications, the initial vote in conference was 5–4 to overturn *Roe* and approve the provisions of the Pennsylvania law. This five-person majority consisted of Rehnquist, Scalia, White, Thomas, and Kennedy. Kennedy developed second thoughts about this, however, and after much agonizing, he decided to join a plurality opinion jointly authored with O'Connor and Souter. In this opinion, the three justices reaffirmed the Court's commitment to the key principles of *Roe*, but they also modified *Roe* significantly by adopting O'Connor's undue burden approach instead of the trimester formulation.

Kennedy, O'Connor, and Souter made clear at the outset of their opinion that *Roe* remained the controlling precedent. "After considering the fundamental constitutional questions resolved by *Roe*, principles of institutional integrity, and the rule of stare decisis, we are led to conclude this: the essential holding of *Roe v. Wade* should be retained and once again reaffirmed" (505 U.S. at 845–846). The three justices then stated explicitly what they viewed as the three parts of *Roe*'s essential holding. First, a woman has the right free of undue state interference to choose to have an abortion before viability. Second, the state does have the authority to prohibit abortions beyond viability if the law makes adequate provision for the health and life of the woman. Third, the state does have legitimate interests throughout pregnancy in regard to the woman's health and the life of the fetus.

Kennedy, O'Connor, and Souter did not, however, view the trimester formula as an essential part of the *Roe* decision and instead supported the undue burden standard originally articulated by O'Connor in the 1983 *Akron* case. Thus, a court's initial inquiry in an abortion case is whether the regulation creates an undue burden on a women's right to obtain an abortion, and "an undue burden exists . . . if its purpose or effect is to place a substantial obstacle in the path of a woman seeking an abortion before the fetus attains viability" (505 U.S. at 878). If an undue burden does not exist, then the lenient rational basis test would apply, but if an undue burden does exist, then the much more stringent strict scrutiny test must be used. In applying this new undue burden standard to the Pennsylvania law, the three justices found all the provisions except spousal notification to be constitutional.

Blackmun and Stevens would have gone farther in finding the law unconstitutional. Blackmun was clearly relieved that *Roe* had not been overturned, and he praised O'Connor, Kennedy, and Souter for their "act of personal courage and consti-tutional principle" (505 U.S. at 923). Blackmun, however, argued that all of the regula-tions were unconstitutional. Stevens maintained that all of the provisions should be struck down except the informed consent and the public reporting and disclosure requirements.

In dissent, Justices Rehnquist, Scalia, Thomas, and White argued not only that all of the Pennsylvania provisions were constitutional but also that *Roe* should be over-turned. Writing for the dissenters, Rehnquist argued: "We believe that *Roe* was wrongly decided, and that it can and should be overruled consistently with our traditional approach to stare decisis in constitutional cases" (505 U.S. at 944).

The *Casey* decision thus maintained at least the "essential holding" of *Roe*, but it left many questions open. One critical issue was the close vote, with four justices favoring the rejection of *Roe*. One more vote could mark the end of *Roe*, and thus the resignation of one or more justices might have a profound effect on the Court's abor-tion jurisprudence. A second major question involved the new "undue burden" stan-dard because of the ambiguity associated with the concept. What would constitute a "substantial obstacle" to a woman's attempt to obtain an abortion? Both of these ques-tions have been at least partially answered.

In regard to changes in Supreme Court membership since *Casey*, developments have favored the pro-choice movement, but this may change with the two most recent additions to the Court. Two justices resigned shortly after *Casey;* White, a longtime opponent of *Roe*, stepped down in 1993, and Blackmun, the author of *Roe*, retired in 1994. Democrat William Clinton was president during both of these retire-ments, and he nominated moderate liberals to the bench, with Ruth Bader Ginsburg replacing White and Stephen Breyer assuming Blackmun's seat. Both Ginsburg and Breyer have been supportive of *Roe*. The replacement of White by Ginsburg was especially critical because this reduced the bloc advocating the rejection of *Roe* from four to three justices—Rehnquist, Scalia, and Thomas. In regard to more recent developments, the replacement of Chief Justice Rehnquist by John Roberts will not affect the level of opposition to *Roe* even if Roberts holds conservative views on this issue like Rehnquist. The retirement of O'Connor may be more important because her replacement, Samuel Alito, could be willing to overturn *Roe*, shifting the align-ment in abortion-related decisions from 6–3 to 5–4, but a majority still will not exist to overturn *Roe*.

Regarding the question of how the Rehnquist Court would use the new undue burden standard, we turn to the Court's most important decision since *Casey*—*Sten-berg v. Carhart* (2000). This case involved the controversial abortion procedure com-monly referred to as "partial birth abortion." Although the procedure can take various forms, it is defined in the challenged Nebraska law as involving a second-term preg-nancy in which a physician "deliberately and intentionally [delivers] into the vagina a living unborn child, or substantial portion thereof, for the purpose of performing a procedure that the person performing such procedure knows will kill the unborn child and does kill the unborn child" (530 U.S. at 922). A majority of the states had similar laws to Nebraska's, which provided for a prison term up to twenty years, a fine of up to $25,000, and automatic revocation of the physician's license.

Justice Breyer authored a majority opinion for himself and four other justices—Stevens, Ginsburg, Souter, and O'Connor—that invalidated the Nebraska law. Breyer began by acknowledging the irreconcilable nature of the abortion controversy. He then argued that the Court over the course of a generation had established basic principles in *Roe* and *Casey* to decide abortion cases, and for two reasons the law failed these principles. The first problem was that the law did not make any provision for the health of the woman. The second shortcoming of the law was that it did create an undue burden for a woman seeking an abortion.

Rehnquist, Scalia, Thomas, and, interestingly, Kennedy were in dissent. Scalia continued to argue that *Casey* and *Roe* should be overturned. Rehnquist, Thomas, and Kennedy acknowledged that *Casey* was the controlling precedent in this case, but they argued that the Nebraska law easily met the Court's undue burden standard. In Kennedy's words, "The law denies no woman the right to choose an abortion and places no undue burden upon the right. The legislation is well within the State's competence to enact" (530 U.S. at 957).

What conclusions can we offer regarding the Rehnquist Court's abortion jurisprudence? *Roe* remains good law in regard to its essential principles, although the strict scrutiny approach of the trimester formula has been modified by the more flexible undue burden standard set forth in *Casey*. The Rehnquist Court thus engaged in a conservative modification of abortion law but certainly has not engaged in a conservative counterrevolution. This will remain a controversial and volatile area of constitutional law, however, and proponents on both sides will be deeply concerned with the nomination and appointment processes when new vacancies occur on the Court.

Other Privacy Issues

Abortion is not the only controversial issue associated with the right of privacy. Two additional topics of great importance that have been confronted by the Rehnquist Court involve the privacy rights of homosexuals and the right to die. We will examine each of these in turn.

In regard to the right of privacy relating to homosexuality, the Rehnquist Court created a major, new liberal precedent in the 2003 case of *Lawrence v. Texas*, which explicitly overturned the 1986 case of *Bowers v. Hardwick*. *Bowers* was the first case in which the Court confronted the issue of whether homosexual activity between consenting partners was constitutionally protected under the right of privacy. *Bowers* arose when police were trying to serve an arrest warrant on Michael Hardwick for his failure to meet a court date, and they observed him engaged in sodomy with another man. The police arrested Hardwick under a Georgia law that prohibited oral and anal sex. Hardwick and the ACLU took his case to the Supreme Court, arguing that the law violated his right to privacy as established in the landmark *Griswold* case of 1965. In a narrow 5–4 decision, the Burger Court rejected Hardwick's argument. Writing for the majority, Justice White rejected the argument that the Constitution provides a fundamental right to engage in homosexual activity. To be a fundamental right qualified for strict scrutiny protection, the liberty must be "implicit in the concept of ordered liberty" and "deeply rooted in the Nation's history and tradition" (478 U.S. at 191–192). White argued strongly that neither criterion was met in this case: "It is obvious to us that neither of these formulations would extend a fundamental right to homosexuals to engage in acts of consensual sodomy" (478 U.S. at 192).

The Rehnquist Court dramatically reversed *Bowers* in the 2003 case of *Lawrence v. Texas. Lawrence* involved factual circumstances remarkably similar to *Bowers*. Police had lawfully entered John Lawrence's apartment and found him engaging in homosexual conduct with another man. Lawrence and his companion were arrested and convicted under a Texas law criminalizing sodomy by people of the same sex. Texas courts, relying on *Bowers*, rejected their appeals, and the Rehnquist Court agreed to hear the case.

Justice Kennedy's majority opinion was joined by Stevens, Ginsburg, Souter, and Breyer, and O'Connor concurred in the judgment to create a 6–3 decision. Kennedy harshly criticized White's majority opinion in *Bowers*, arguing that the historical analysis was seriously flawed and that the clear pattern in both the fifty states and in European countries was against criminalizing homosexual conduct. Kennedy also argued that the logic of the major, recent precedents of *Casey* and *Romer* strongly undermined *Bowers*. Kennedy's opinion was also notably more supportive of homosexuality than White's argument in *Bowers:* "[*Bower's*] continuance as precedent demeans the lives of homosexual persons" (156 L.Ed.2d at 523). Thus, Kennedy concluded, "*Bowers* was not correct when it was decided, and it is not correct today. It ought not to remain binding precedent. *Bowers v. Hardwick* should be and now is overruled" (156 L.Ed.2d. at 541). Lawrence's homosexuality activity was therefore protected under the liberty guarantee of the Due Process Clause of the Fourteenth Amendment, and the Texas law was ruled unconstitutional.

Scalia authored a lengthy dissenting opinion, joined by Rehnquist and Thomas. Scalia harshly criticized the entire logic of Kennedy's opinion, and he argued that the Court had essentially accepted the homosexual agenda: "It is clear from this that the Court has taken sides in the culture war, departing from its role assuring, as neutral observer, that the democratic rules of engagement are observed" (156 L.Ed.2d. at 541).

The Rehnquist Court has also confronted another major privacy issue, the right to die. Unlike the area of homosexuality, the Rehnquist Court had little direct precedent to guide its decision making. This opportunity arose in the 1990 case of *Cruzan v. Director, Missouri Department of Health*. Nancy Cruzan was a victim of a car accident in 1983 that left her in a condition where she had motor reflexes but no cognitive functions. Eventually, her parents asked her doctors to remove the feeding tubes that were keeping her alive, based upon a statement she had made that she would not want to stay alive if she could not live a halfway normal life. Her doctors refused, and the Missouri Supreme Court ruled against Cruzan's parents because they could not present "clear and convincing evidence" regarding her wishes. The Rehnquist Court agreed to hear the case.

In an opinion authored by Chief Justice Rehnquist, the Court ruled 5–4 against Cruzan's parents and for the state of Missouri. Rehnquist did acknowledge "that the United States Constitution would grant a competent person a constitutionally protected right to refuse lifesaving hydration and nutrition" (497 U.S. at 279). In regard to an incompetent person, however, the state can impose a stringent "clear and convincing evidence" standard, and the information presented to the courts regarding Nancy Cruzan's wishes did not meet this standard.

Cruzan's parents subsequently went back to state court, where testimony was presented by three friends that she had said she did not want to live in a vegetative state. The state judge found the accumulated evidence to be "clear and convincing," and her feeding tubes were removed. Tragic as it was, Cruzan's case did give strong impetus to the living-will movement, through which a person provides specific instructions for medical care if in an incompetent state.

One final privacy case needs to be mentioned—*Washington v. Glucksberg* (1997)—involving physician-assisted suicide. We have already discussed under our equal protection analysis the companion case of *Vacco v. Quill* (1997), in which the Court found a New York law prohibiting assisted suicide to be constitutional on equal protection grounds. *Glucksberg* involved a challenge based on a due process argument to the state of Washington's law criminalizing physician-assisted suicide. As with *Vacco*, the Rehnquist Court unanimously upheld the law, arguing that the liberty guarantee of the Fourteenth Amendment does not extend to a right of physician-assisted suicide. Writing for the Court, Chief Justice Rehnquist reasoned that although this is not a fundamental right requiring strict scrutiny, Washington did have to meet the standards of the rational basis test. Washington easily met this test according to Rehnquist because it was pursing several legitimate interests, including preserving human life, guarding the medical profession's integrity and ethics, and protecting potentially vulnerable groups like the elderly and disabled from neglect, abuse, and mistakes.

Conclusion

What are we to conclude about the Rehnquist Court's jurisprudence regarding privacy and abortion? The evidence we have examined shows that the Rehnquist Court did not engage in a conservative constitutional counterrevolution in this important area of constitutional law. The Rehnquist Court justices not only continued the Warren and Burger Court records of recognizing the right of privacy but also extended it to include the right of homosexuals to engage in consensual sexual activity. The Rehnquist Court also acknowledged the right of a competent person to reject life-sustaining medical treatments, although they required a higher standard for those who are not competent to make this judgment. In regard to the subject of abortion, the Burger and Rehnquist Courts were virtually identical in their voting records in abortion cases, with both Courts deciding half of the cases liberally and half conservatively. *Roe v. Wade* still remains the controlling precedent, but the trimester formula based upon strict scrutiny has been replaced by the undue burden standard, which triggers strict scrutiny only when a regulation places an undue burden on a woman's decision to have an abortion. The Court did not have much occasion to apply this test, but the *Stenberg* case shows that the Court was willing to strike down abortion laws under this test. Thus, in comparing the Burger and Rehnquist Courts in regard to privacy and abortion, we see far more continuity than change, and a significant part of the change has been in a liberal direction in regard to the privacy rights of homosexuals.

Federalism

Thus far in chapter 3 we have focused upon the civil rights and liberties decisions of the Rehnquist Court. The constitutional foundations for these cases have been the Bill of Rights guarantees of the first nine amendments as well as the Fourteenth Amendment. The Rehnquist Court has also handed down several important decisions regarding the original Constitution that need to be examined. We will first look at the area of federalism and then turn to other cases involving the structure and operation of our national political institutions.

Federalism involves the relationship between the federal, or national, government and the fifty state governments. The appropriate division of power between the federal government and the states has been a subject of controversy since the Articles of Confederation, and the controversy continues to this day. Although federalism is a most complex topic, we can usefully identify two basic approaches that have been taken toward federalism throughout U.S. history: dual federalism and cooperative federalism.

Dual federalism places great emphasis upon the independence and sovereignty of the state governments, limiting the federal government to those matters expressly delegated to the national government in the Constitution. Dual federalist advocates emphasize the importance of the Tenth Amendment: "The powers not delegated to the United States by the Constitution, nor prohibited by it to the states, are reserved to the states respectively, or to the people." Supporters of dual federalism emphasize that state and local governments are closer to the people, are more responsive to their needs and values, and are more efficient. Supporters further argue that dual federalism is a major factor in preventing the national government from becoming too powerful and infringing basic rights and liberties. Dual federalist supporters also stress the importance of the Eleventh Amendment, ratified in 1795, that prohibits states from being sued in U.S. courts by citizens of another state or citizens of a foreign government.

In contrast, advocates of cooperative federalism argue that the national government and state governments should work closely together but that the national government is supreme with far-reaching power over the states. Supporters of cooperative federalism point to several constitutional provisions to bolster their argument. One important component is the Supremacy Clause of Article VI, which reads: "This Constitution, and the Laws of the United States which shall be made in Pursuance thereof . . . shall be the supreme Law of the Land." Another important constitutional provision cited by cooperative federalists is the "Necessary and Proper Clause" of Article I, Section 8, of the Constitution. Section 8 specifies the wide range of powers available to Congress and then gives Congress the power "to make all Laws which shall be necessary and proper for carrying into Execution the Foregoing Powers, and all other Powers vested by this Constitution in the Government of the United States, or in any Department or Officer thereof."

Advocates of cooperative federalism also cite the Commerce Clause and Section 5 of the Fourteenth Amendment as constitutional sources of authority for the federal government. The Commerce Clause (Article I, Section 8, Clause 3) gives Congress the power "to regulate Commerce . . . among the several states," while Section 5 of the Fourteenth Amendment gives Congress the power to enforce the equal protection and due process provisions of that amendment.

In this section of chapter 3 we examine American history to determine how dual federalism and cooperative federalism have been predominant in various eras and how the Supreme Court has adjusted its federalism jurisprudence to meet the changing values of American society. Our central concern will remain on the Rehnquist Court and whether it engaged in a conservative constitutional counterrevolution in this area of the law.

Quantitative Analysis

We can begin with an examination of the voting patterns of the Warren, Burger, and Rehnquist Courts in federalism cases. Table 3.34 reveals that federalism cases have been an important component of all three Court eras, with approximately 100 cases decided in each period. The Warren Court was the most liberal (66 percent), with the liberal position being defined as favoring the national government over the states. The Burger and Rehnquist Courts have also decided a majority of their federalism cases liberally, with the Burger Court voting liberally 60 percent of the time and the Rehnquist Court recording a 54 percent liberal record. These data thus suggest consistency rather than dramatic change across Court eras.

The voting records of the individual justices of the Rehnquist Court in federalism cases are presented in table 3.35. The results are somewhat surprising. Unlike most other areas we have examined, distinct liberal and conservative groupings do not appear to be present in the federalism cases. Thomas has the strongest conservative voting record, but his conservatism score is only 61 percent. Conversely, White has the highest liberalism mark, but he voted liberally in only 70 percent of his cases. These data thus suggest that the differences among the justices in federalism cases are relatively modest, but this is somewhat misleading because we will see that profound differences emerged among the Rehnquist Court justices in regard to federalism.

Table 3.34: Liberal/Conservative Voting in Federalism Cases by the Warren, Burger, and Rehnquist Courts, 1953–1954 to 2004–2005 Terms

Court Era	Liberal Decisions	Conservative Decisions	Total Cases
Warren Court (1953–1968 Terms)	66% (61)	34% (31)	92
Burger Court (1969–1985 Terms)	60% (61)	40% (41)	102
Rehnquist Court (1986–2004 Terms)	54% (70)	46% (59)	129
Total	60% (192)	40% (131)	323

Source: Harold J. Spaeth, *United States Supreme Court Judicial Database, 1953–2004 Terms* (Ann Arbor, MI: Inter-University Consortium for Political and Social Research, 2005).

Table 3.35: Liberal/Conservative Voting Records of the Justices of the
Rehnquist Court in Federalism Cases, 1986–1987 Term to 2004–2005 Term
(Justices Ranked from Most Conservative to Most Liberal)

Justices	Liberal Decisions	Conservative Decisions	Total Cases
Thomas	39% (33)	61% (52)	85
Rehnquist	46% (59)	54% (70)	129
O'Connor	47% (58)	53% (65)	123
Scalia	49% (62)	51% (65)	127
Kennedy	50% (57)	50% (57)	114
Stevens	59% (76)	41% (52)	128
Souter	59% (52)	41% (36)	88
Ginsburg	60% (42)	40% (28)	70
Blackmun	60% (38)	40% (25)	63
Brennan	63% (24)	37% (14)	38
Breyer	66% (42)	34% (22)	64
Marshall	66% (27)	34% (14)	41
Powell	67% (8)	33% (4)	12
White	70% (41)	30% (18)	59

Source: Harold J. Spaeth, *United States Supreme Court Judicial Database, 1953–2004 Terms* (Ann Arbor, MI: Inter-University Consortium for Political and Social Research, 2005).

Major Eras of American Federalism Prior to the Rehnquist Court Period

Unlike civil rights and liberties cases, which are largely products of the last half of the twentieth century, federalism cases reach far back in U.S. history to the very beginning of the republic. An understanding of this history is necessary to place the Rehnquist Court's federalism decisions into proper context. This history reveals an interesting ebb and flow in which dual federalism is dominant in one era and cooperative federalism dominates another era.

The formative era of the United States can be identified as the period from the creation of the Constitution through the Civil War (1789–1865). Throughout most of this period, the Supreme Court was a strong proponent of a powerful and expansive national government. Chief Justice John Marshall, who led the Court from 1801 to 1835, was a great champion of cooperative federalism, and his opinion for a unanimous Court in the landmark case of *McCulloch v. Maryland* (1819) established a major precedent favoring federal power over the states. The case involved an attempt by the state of Maryland to tax a branch of the U.S. Bank that had been established in Maryland. The federal government argued that the tax was unconstitutional, and Maryland maintained that the U.S. Bank violated the Constitution. Marshall eloquently argued all of the major points favoring national supremacy over the states. He stated that the Constitution was a compact between the federal government and the people, not the states; he argued that the Supremacy Clause meant that states could not interfere with the laws of Congress; he maintained that Congress was not limited to its enumerated powers but could pass laws implied by its enumerated powers under the Necessary and Proper Clause; and he placed a limiting interpretation on the powers of the states under the Tenth Amendment. These arguments led Marshall to conclude that the Maryland law was unconstitutional.

The Court's approach to federalism shifted somewhat toward dual federalism when Marshall left the Court and Roger Taney became chief justice, in 1836, serving until 1864. Court decisions were less consequential, however, than the challenge created by the Civil War from 1861 to 1865. Although the Civil War was certainly a battle over slavery and economic interests, it was also a struggle over federalism. The Northern forces representing the federal government prevailed ultimately, and the three Civil War amendments—the Thirteenth, Fourteenth, and Fifteenth—dramatically extended national control over the states, especially the Southern states.

Although cooperative federalism dominated during the post–Civil War Reconstruction era, dual federalism was predominant during the era of laissez-faire capitalism that began with the Industrial Revolution of the late nineteenth century and extended to the Great Depression, which began in 1929. The laissez-faire era was characterized by vast urban and industrial growth, a strong commitment to capitalism in which business should not be encumbered by government regulations, and a belief in Social Darwinism allowing for harsh competition and survival of the fittest.

The Supreme Court during this period was composed of justices supportive of the cultural values of laissez-faire capitalism, and this frequently took the form of decisions supporting dual federalism because the power of Congress to regulate business was strictly limited. *Hammer v. Dagenhart* (1918) provides an excellent example. Laissez-faire capitalism allowed owners to abuse workers in many ways, including low pay, long hours, and unhealthy working conditions. One of the worst abuses was child labor, and in response to this social issue, Congress passed in 1916 the Child Labor Act, which banned interstate commerce of products produced by children under fourteen years of age and by fourteen- to sixteen-year-olds who worked more than eight hours per day. The Supreme Court supported the challenge to the constitutionality of the law by business interests. In a 5–4 opinion, Justice William Day presented classical dual federalist arguments. He asserted that Congress had far exceeded its authority under the Commerce Clause. Rather, the Tenth Amendment reserved to the states the power to regulate child labor. This law was thus unconstitutional, because finding it constitutional would, according to Day, end freedom of commerce and indeed practically destroy the U.S. system of government.

Although the Court in this era of laissez-faire capitalism was more concerned with protecting business from government regulation than in protecting states' rights, the effect was the same. Congress and the federal government were severely limited in regard to regulating businesses, with the Commerce Clause being interpreted radically different than in the previous century under Marshall.

The Great Depression, triggered by the stock market crash of 1929, was the catalyst for a dramatic shift away from dual federalism and back to cooperative federalism. This shift did not come easily, however. When Democratic Party leader Franklin Delano Roosevelt was first elected president, in 1932, he and a Democratic Congress introduced the New Deal, an attempt to create a variety of national programs to meet the pressing needs of American citizens and to pull the country out of the Depression. The Supreme Court, however, heard challenges to many of these programs and, using a dual federalism philosophy, rejected many New Deal programs as unconstitutional. This created a constitutional crisis in which Roosevelt sought to expand the membership of the Court up to fifteen justices so that he could appoint New Deal supporters. This proved unnecessary, however, because the Court in 1937 began to support New Deal legislation and its underlying theme of cooperative federalism.

The new dominance of the national government in America's federal system is seen clearly in the 1941 case of *United States v. Darby Lumber*. This case involved a constitutional challenge to the 1938 Fair Labor Standards Act, which required all employers involved in interstate commerce to pay a minimum wage of twenty-five cents per hour and also to pay time and a half for more than forty-four hours of work per week. Fred Darby, the owner of a lumberyard, challenged this law on the basis of the logic of *Hammer*, but a unanimous Court rejected firmly the logic of *Hammer* and overturned it. Justice Stone emphasized the broad power of Congress under the Commerce Clause and minimized the scope of the Tenth Amendment as placing few limitations on the national government.

The concept of cooperative federalism was dominant through the decades of the forties, the fifties, and the sixties. The scope and power of the national government grew dramatically during this period, and the Supreme Court was supportive of this development. In *Maryland v. Wirtz* (1968), for example, the Warren Court approved a law of Congress that extended federal wage and hour benefits to the employees of state and local governments, arguing that a long line of precedents supported this statute.

The political winds began to shift somewhat with Republican Richard Nixon's election to the presidency, in 1968. Nixon called for a "New Federalism" that would shift far greater authority from the national government to the state and local governments. This idea has been repeated by successive Republican presidents, including

Ronald Reagan in the eighties, George H. W. Bush in the nineties, and George W. Bush since his election in 2000. A common theme has been that the federal government has become too big, too bloated, too inefficient, and too wasteful. Therefore, authority should flow back to the states, which are closer to the people, more responsive to their needs, and both more efficient and more effective. How did the Burger Court respond to these ideas, and, more importantly for our purposes, what has been the Rehnquist Court's jurisprudence on federalism?

The Burger Court was closely and deeply divided over federalism issues. This division is best seen in two closely related Commerce Clause decisions involving the Federal Labor Standards Act (FLSA), the same law challenged and upheld in *Darby*.

In *National League of Cities v. Usery* (1976), the issue involved the constitutionality of a 1974 congressional action that extended provisions of the FLSA to state public employees, who had not been included in the original legislation. Although the Warren Court precedent of *Wirtz* seemed to control this case, the four Nixon appointments—Rehnquist, Powell, Blackmun, and Burger—joined with Stewart to rule the federal regulations unconstitutional. Rehnquist wrote the majority opinion, overturning the *Wirtz* precedent and asserting the validity of the dual federalism concept embodied in such cases as *Darby*.

Usery experienced a short life as controlling precedent. Brennan's dissent in *Usery* harshly criticized the Burger Court majority for departing from decades of established Commerce Clause jurisprudence, many legal experts were critical of the decision, and the nation's lower courts were unclear how to interpret *Usery*. All of this led to the Court sharply shifting direction once again in its federalism jurisprudence. In the 1985 decision of *Garcia v. San Antonio Metropolitan Transit Authority*, a 5–4 majority upheld amendments to the FLSA, explicitly overturned *Usery*, and reasserted principles of cooperative federalism.

The Rehnquist Court Period

The Rehnquist Court thus inherited a most ambiguous legacy of federalism jurisprudence. Two distinctive approaches—dual federalism and cooperative federalism—had been in conflict throughout American history, and both had been in ascendance at different periods. The Burger Court had been especially divided, initially accepting a dual federalism approach but then returning to cooperative federalism.

The Rehnquist Court, like the Burger Court, shifted ground dramatically, but in a different direction; recent federalism cases, however, make it difficult to characterize the clear direction of the Rehnquist Court's federalism jurisprudence. The Rehnquist Court justices initially embraced the principle of cooperative federalism but in subsequent cases came to embrace the idea of dual federalism; however, it is unclear how closely the Rehnquist Court embraced dual federalism in light of recent, major decisions that have favored the national government over the states.

The Rehnquist Court's early decisions did not indicate a new approach to federalism that would emphasize state sovereignty. The Court's first major opportunity to strike a blow for state power was *South Dakota v. Dole*, in 1987. In this case, South Dakota claimed that a new federal law designed to withhold federal highway funds to states refusing to raise their minimum drinking age to twenty-one was an illegal intrusion into the rights of states. The Rehnquist Court, however, ruled 7–2 that Congress had the power under its spending authority to set conditions on its aid to states.

The shift of the Rehnquist Court from a cooperative federalism approach to dual federalism can be traced to membership change on the Court after *Dole*, specifically Thomas's replacement of Marshall. At the end of the Burger Court era, four justices supported the concept of dual federalism: Rehnquist, O'Connor, Burger, and Powell. This number did not change when Burger and Powell resigned because their replacements—Scalia (taking Rehnquist's associate seat) and Kennedy (replacing Powell)—also were advocates of dual federalism. The critical fifth vote that the conservatives needed came when Marshall was replaced by Thomas, in 1991. Interestingly, the other personnel changes on the Rehnquist Court—Souter for Brennan, Ginsburg for White, and Breyer for Blackmun—did not have a major impact on the Court's federalism decisions because all of these justices supported cooperative federalism.

With a fifth vote now secured, the majority favoring dual federalism had the potential to alter constitutional law in profound ways. Although federalism cases are especially complex and are not easily categorized, we can usefully examine three major constitutional provisions: the Commerce Clause, the Tenth Amendment, and the Eleventh Amendment.

The first type of doctrinal change in federalism cases involved the Commerce Clause. *United States v. Lopez* (1995) represented the Rehnquist Court's first major effort to limit the scope of the Commerce Clause. By a 5–4 vote, Justices Rehnquist, Scalia, Thomas, O'Connor, and Kennedy overturned the Federal Gun-Free School Zones Act because school safety was not viewed as an issue involving interstate commerce. Prior to *Lopez*, the Court used the cumulative effects test in such interstate commerce cases, asking whether all instances of an activity taken together have an impact on interstate commerce. In *Lopez*, a new test was introduced; in order for the national government to regulate an activity under the Commerce Clause, it must involve either (1) a channel of interstate commerce, (2) an instrumentality of interstate commerce, or (3) a substantial relationship between the law and interstate commerce.

The Rehnquist Court further extended the logic of *Lopez* in the 2000 case of *United States v. Morrison* to assert that even congressional findings of substantial effect were not enough if the case involved an activity traditionally within the scope of state authority. *Morrison* was a case in which a female student at Virginia Tech University charged two athletes with rape. Arguing that the athletes' punishment was inadequate, she sued under the civil remedies provision (Section 13981) of the Violence against Women Act (VAWA). Rehnquist, Scalia, Thomas, O'Connor, and Kennedy ruled 5–4 that Congress did not have the authority under the Commerce Clause to create this legal remedy. In passing VAWA, Congress claimed that violence against women kept women from taking a full part in economic activity and cost the economy billions of dollars every year. This sounded too much like the cumulative effects test, according to Chief Justice Rehnquist, who found no "jurisdictional element" for Congress to enact a law under the Commerce Clause. An additional necessary element of *Morrison* was the Court's determination that Section 5 of the Fourteenth Amendment only empowers Congress to enforce preexisting equal protection and due process rights and not extend additional rights. The Court held that the civil remedies provision was not designed to enforce an existing right against state-sponsored bias. Instead, it was aimed at individuals who could be punished under state remedies.

In another important Commerce Clause case, the Rehnquist Court also ruled unconstitutional the Migratory Bird Rule that was implemented by the Army Corps of Engineers pursuant to the Clean Water Act in *Solid Waste Agency of Northern Cook County v. Army Corps of Engineers* (2001). This case arose out of an effort by Chicago-area cities to create a solid waste facility on a 500-acre site that had been a sand-and-gravel-pit operation. The Army Corps of Engineers challenged this action, arguing that federal approval was needed because the area was used by migratory birds that crossed state lines. Once again, the five-person majority of Rehnquist, Scalia, Thomas, O'Connor, and Kennedy viewed this as an impermissible extension of the federal government's power under the Commerce Clause and an infringement on the traditional powers of state and local governments.

In addition to giving a dual federalism interpretation to the Commerce Clause, the Rehnquist Court also used the dual federalism approach to cases involving the Tenth Amendment. One important example is *New York v. United States*, in 1992. This case involved the Low-Level Radioactive Waste Policy Act of 1980. This law dealt with the disposal of radioactive waste. It provided a variety of incentives for states to participate, but it also had a provision in which states that failed to participate had to "take title," that is, to be responsible for radioactive waste generated within the state. This was challenged by New York, and a 6–3 majority ruled unconstitutional the "take title" provision of the federal law, with the "federalism five" joined by Justice Souter. Writing for the majority, Justice O'Connor argued that the federal government could certainly encourage state participation by offering incentives; it could not, however, require the states to dispose of their radioactive waste in their own states. Drawing upon the Tenth Amendment, O'Connor wrote: "The Constitution . . . 'leaves to the several States a residual and inviolable sovereignty. . . .' Whatever the outer limits of that sovereignty may be, one thing is clear: The Federal Government may not compel the States to enact or administer a federal regulatory program" (505 U.S. at 188).

The decision in *New York* and the Rehnquist Court's commitment to dual federalism were reinforced in the 1997 case of *Printz v. United States*. This case arose out of the attempted assassination of President Ronald Reagan in which James Brady, Reagan's press secretary, was seriously wounded by the gunman. In response, Congress passed the 1993 Brady Handgun Violence Prevention Act. One provision of the act required the U.S. attorney general to establish by 1998 a national system for doing background checks on those wishing to purchase handguns. In the interim period, however, these background checks were to be performed by the chief law enforcement officer (CLEO) of local jurisdictions. This provision was challenged by CLEOs from Arizona and Montana on federalism grounds.

Justice Scalia authored the majority opinion for the "federalism five." He began his opinion by arguing that the issue could be addressed through three sources: history, constitutional structure, and precedent. Scalia argued that the historical record did not provide a clear answer, but answers could be found by examining the structure of the Constitution and Court precedent. In his constitutional analysis, Scalia emphasized the principle of dual sovereignty inherent in the Tenth Amendment: "It is incontestable that the Constitution established a system of 'dual sovereignty.' Although the States surrendered many of their powers to the new Federal Government, they retained 'a residual and inviolable sovereignty'" (521 U.S. at 919). The source of this sovereignty, Scalia argued, was the Tenth Amendment, with the Necessary and Proper Clause of Article I being de-emphasized. Finally, in regard to controlling precedent, Scalia emphasized the 1992 decision of *New York v. United States*.

Justices Stevens, Ginsburg, Souter, and Breyer disagreed profoundly with the majority. Writing for the dissenters, Stevens championed the concept of cooperative federalism. He argued that Congress had ample authority for this legislation under the Commerce Clause, the Necessary and Proper Clause, and the Supremacy Clause. Stevens also dismissed the importance of the Tenth Amendment in this case, arguing that "the [Tenth] Amendment provides no support for a rule that immunizes local officials from obligations that might be imposed on ordinary citizens" (521 U.S. at 942).

In addition to using a dual federalism philosophy to interpret the Commerce Clause and the Tenth Amendment, the Rehnquist Court also interpreted the Eleventh Amendment in a manner consistent with the ideas of dual federalism. The Eleventh Amendment focus on state sovereign immunity from suit has led to the greatest number of recent controversial federalism cases. Some debate exists as to which of these cases is most significant. For those looking for an early example of state immunity from suit, *Seminole Tribe of Florida v. Florida* (1996) is important, because it asserted that the Eleventh Amendment substantially protects the states from being sued in federal court. In *Seminole Tribe*, the Court determined that an Indian tribe could not sue Florida for refusing to negotiate in good faith over the regulation of gaming. This decision overturned the 1989 precedent of *Pennsylvania v. Union Gas Company*, in which the Court upheld the constitutionality of a federal environmental law that allowed suits to be brought into federal courts against states for monetary damages.

Other Court experts cite *Alden v. Maine* (1999) as the more significant case because of Justice Kennedy's espousal of sovereign immunity as the reason that residents of a state could not sue their own state in federal court. In *Alden*, a group of probation officers sued in federal court because the state of Maine was violating the Fair Labor Standards Act by not paying overtime, but the Court by a 5–4 decision found that Maine had not consented to sue. Rejecting the Eleventh Amendment as a bound of sovereign immunity, Justice Kennedy wrote: "[The Constitution] reserves to [states] a substantial portion of the Nation's primary sovereignty, together with the dignity and essential attributes inhering in that status" (527 U.S. at 714).

Seminole Tribe and *Alden* have been reinforced in subsequent Eleventh Amendment cases decided by Justices Rehnquist, Scalia, Thomas, O'Connor, and Kennedy. In *Kimel v. Florida Board of Regents* (2000), for example, Congress amended the 1967 Age Discrimination in Employment Act to remove state immunity from private lawsuits based upon alleged age discrimination in hiring and firing decisions, but the Rehnquist Court ruled that Congress had exceeded its authority in this action.

Despite all of the evidence supporting the argument that the Rehnquist Court engaged in a conservative counterrevolution regarding federalism, evidence does exist that the Rehnquist Court was not deeply committed to the principles of dual sovereignty. Even during the height of the Court's decisions supporting dual federalism, the Rehnquist Court justices frequently ruled in favor of the power of the federal government. Among the important decisions going against state governments were *U.S. Term Limits v. Thorton* (1994), *Reno v. Condon* (2000), and *Nevada Department of Human Resources v. Hibbs* (2003). In *Term Limits*, Kennedy joined Stevens, Ginsburg, Souter, and Breyer in rejecting an amendment to the Arkansas Constitution that placed term limits on members of the U.S. House of Representatives (three terms) and the U.S. Senate (two terms). The Court in *Reno* found that states could be barred from selling information obtained on license registrations. And in *Hibbs*, the Court ruled that individuals could sue states under the Family and Medical Leave Act because Congress expressly abrogated sovereign immunity within the act.

Questions about the extent of the Rehnquist Court's federalism revolution have been heightened by decisions in the two final terms. In the 2003–2004 term, the Court in *Tennessee v. Lane* (2004) decided that states could be sued under the Americans with Disabilities Act by individuals in wheelchairs who were prevented from gaining access to courthouses. In the 2004–2005 term, the Rehnquist Court handed down two more major federalism decisions that favored the federal government over the states. In *Gonzales v. Raich* (2005), the issue was whether California could allow for the production and use of marijuana for medical purposes. A 6–3 majority that included Justices Kennedy and Scalia ruled against California, arguing that Congress's power under the Commerce Clause extended to the prohibition of the possession and use of marijuana even if allowed by state law. Finally, in the case of *Granholm v. Heald* (2005), the Court used the Commerce Clause to rule 5–4 against states that had a policy of prohibiting out-of-state wine producers from sending orders directly to customers but allowed in-state producers to make direct shipments to consumers. The five-person majority involved a most unusual coalition: Kennedy, Souter, Ginsburg, Breyer, and Scalia.

Conclusion

The U.S. Supreme Court has throughout history changed dramatically its interpretation of American federalism, alternatively emphasizing either the predominance of the federal government under cooperative federalism or the importance of state sovereignty under dual federalism. Cooperative federalism had dominated twentieth-century Supreme Court jurisprudence during the decades of the forties, fifties, sixties, seventies, and eighties, covering the Supreme Court chief justiceships of Stone, Vinson, Warren, and Burger. The Rehnquist Court, however, reinvigorated the theory of dual federalism, but recent decisions raise serious questions about the Rehnquist Court's federalism jurisprudence.

Quantitative data do not provide much insight into this development. The numbers in table 3.34 show that the Rehnquist Court ruled liberally, that is, in favor of the national government, in a majority of its federalism cases, and the liberalism records of the Warren and Burger Court eras have not been substantially more liberal than the Rehnquist Court. Furthermore, an examination in table 3.35 of the individual voting records of the justices who have served on the Rehnquist Court reveals relatively moderate voting by all members of the Court in federalism cases.

The real key to understanding if dramatic change has occurred in the Rehnquist Court's federalism jurisprudence, however, involves an analysis of their major decisions regarding the Commerce Clause, the Tenth Amendment, and the Eleventh Amendment. For decades prior to the Rehnquist Court, successive Courts had given Congress virtually unchecked power over the states regarding the Commerce Clause, but in such landmark decisions as *Lopez*, *Morrison*, and *Solid Waste*, the "federalism five"—Justices Rehnquist, Scalia, Thomas, Kennedy, and O'Connor—found that Congress had exceeded its proper authority over the states in regard to the regulation of interstate commerce. Similarly, for decades preceding the Rehnquist Court, the Tenth Amendment had been neglected by the Supreme Court as a truism that had little effect on American federalism; however, the Rehnquist Court's five conservatives reasserted the importance of the Tenth Amendment as a significant check on the power of the federal government in such cases as *New York* and *Printz.* Finally, the Rehnquist Court's five-person coalition of Rehnquist, Scalia, Thomas, Kennedy, and O'Connor injected new life into the previously neglected Eleventh Amendment to provide strong support for the principle of state sovereign immunity in cases such as *Seminole Tribe* and *Alden.*

Despite the impressive set of cases in which the Rehnquist Court supported dual federalism, the Court's most recent federalism cases—for example, *Lane, Gonzales,* and *Granholm*—raise serious uncertainties regarding the abandonment of the principles of cooperative federalism. We therefore cannot conclude that the Rehnquist Court engaged in a conservative counterrevolution in regard to the area of federalism.

Government Powers

The final topic to be discussed in this chapter is government powers, which deals with the structure, operation, and interrelationships among the three branches of the federal government: Congress, the executive branch, and the federal judiciary. These three branches are discussed in the Constitution in Articles I, II, and III. Although the Court hears relatively few government powers cases each term, the Rehnquist Court decided a significant number of interesting and important cases in this area of constitutional law. The familiar liberal-conservative distinction that we have been employing in this chapter is not utilized in this analysis because these concepts are not easily applicable in government powers cases.

Congress

The most important case that the Rehnquist Court decided involving Congress is *U.S. Term Limits v. Thornton* (1994), a case we examined briefly in the previous section on federalism. The term limits movement has been an attempt to limit the number of terms elected representatives may serve. Most term limit efforts have focused on the state legislatures, but Arkansas passed an amendment to their state constitution that provided a maximum of three terms for any member of the U.S. House of Representatives and two terms for the U.S. Senate. This amendment was challenged by

Arkansas representative Ray Thornton and others on the basis that it violated Article I of the Constitution. A 5–4 Rehnquist Court agreed that the amendment violated the U.S. Constitution. Writing for the majority, Justice Stevens argued that Article I of the Constitution states explicitly the qualification for office regarding Congress, and these qualifications are limited to age, residency, and citizenship requirements. Because the Arkansas amendment added another qualification, it was unconstitutional. Term limits for member of the U.S. Congress could only be achieved through amending the U.S. Constitution.

Executive Branch

The Rehnquist Court justices handed down several important decisions involving the presidency and executive branch. These cases involved a variety of topics: executive-judicial relations, the veto power, presidential immunity, and foreign affairs.

The Rehnquist Court issued two significant rulings regarding executive-judicial relations. *Morrison v. Olson* (1988) involved the position of special prosecutor, which was created by Congress in the aftermath of Watergate to investigate and prosecute ranking executive officials engaged in violating federal criminal laws. Because a special prosecutor was to investigate people in the executive branch, Congress placed the power to appoint a special prosecutor in the hands of a panel of three federal judges. This law was challenged as unconstitutional on the grounds that a special prosecutor was a "principal officer" who could only be appointed by the president.

Chief Justice Rehnquist wrote an opinion for a 7–1 Court that the law was constitutional. The case centered on the Appointments Clause of Article II that provides for the president to appoint principal officers such as ambassadors and Supreme Court justices but allows the Congress to oversee the appointment of "inferior" officers. Although Rehnquist acknowledged that this case was not an easy call, he argued that the position of special prosecutor was an inferior office, and hence Congress was within its constitutional prerogative to act as it did. Rehnquist also argued that the position did not create any problems regarding the Constitution's separation of powers principle.

Another important case involving executive-judicial relations was *Mistretta v. United States*, in 1989. This case arose from the 1984 Sentencing Reform Act that was passed because of concern about the wide differences existing in the sentences imposed by federal judges. The act established the U.S. Sentencing Commission, which was to be an independent body within the judicial branch. The commission was to be a seven-person group, nominated by the president and confirmed by the Senate. At least three members were to be federal judges. After the commission was created and developed sentencing guidelines, the act was challenged as violating the delegation of powers principle of the Constitution because it gave excessive legislative authority to the commission. Writing for an 8–1 majority, Justice Blackmun ruled that the law was constitutional. Blackmun recognized the importance of the separation of powers doctrine and the principle of nondelegation inherent in the provision that all legislative powers rested with Congress; in this case, however, Blackmun argued that these principles were not violated because of the constraints and guidance provided by Congress to the U.S. Sentencing Commission.

Another important Rehnquist Court case involving the executive branch was the 1998 case of *Clinton v. City of New York*, involving the constitutionality of the "line item veto." Because of large budget deficits during the late eighties and the early nineties, Congress passed a law in 1996—the Line Item Veto Act—giving the president the authority to block portions of federal appropriation bills without rejecting the entire act. This line item veto, similar to the veto authority of some state governors, was designed to allow presidents to cut excess spending or pork barrel legislation that was not in the best interests of the country as a whole. Once President William Clinton used this power, the line item veto was immediately challenged on the basis that the Constitution only grants the president veto power over entire pieces of legislation.

Writing for a 6–3 Court, Justice Stevens argued that the law was unconstitutional. Stevens recognized that the Constitution does not specifically address the issue of the line item veto. However, he reasoned that the historical record was clear that the president's veto power had to be exercised in regard to an entire bill and not just parts of it. The line item veto could be established by a constitutional amendment, but its legislative creation violated the Constitution.

President Clinton was involved in another major case over executive power, but the case of *Clinton v. Jones* (1997) did not involve any presidential activities but rather his much publicized sexual activities. Paula Corbin Jones, an employee of the state of Arkansas while Clinton was governor of the state, filed suit in 1994 against Clinton, accusing him of sexual harassment and civil rights violations stemming from an alleged lewd and undesired advance by Clinton while they were alone in a hotel room in 1991. Clinton attempted to squash the suit based upon the principle that the president is immune from personal suit during his time in office. A circuit court of appeals rejected Clinton's claim and ordered the trial to go forward, and Clinton appealed to the Supreme Court.

The Court ruled unanimously against Clinton, establishing the important principle involving presidential immunity that presidents may be sued while in office for conduct unrelated to the job of being president. Justice Stevens wrote the majority opinion, rejecting all of Clinton's major arguments. Stevens drew a sharp distinction between official and unofficial acts, noting that protecting a president from suits over his conduct of public policy is far different than protecting him in his personal affairs. Stevens also rejected Clinton's position that the suit would take too much time from his conduct of his duties. Finally, the Rehnquist Court justices rejected the argument that being held to a court's judgment while president violated the separation of powers principle.

The *Jones* case gave rise to further legal problems for Clinton. He eventually settled with Jones out of court for $850,000, but he made no admission of guilt nor issued an apology. The resolution of this case was just the beginning of Clinton's problems, however, because Jones's attorneys had become aware of Clinton's sexual relationship with a White House intern named Monica Lewinsky. When Clinton initially denied the sexual relationship, a process was set in motion that eventually led to the House of Representatives passing two impeachment charges, one on a perjury charge and one on obstructing justice. Chief Justice Rehnquist presided over the historic Senate impeachment trial, with the Senate failing to have the necessary two-thirds votes on either count necessary to remove Clinton from office.

A final and very important area involving the executive branch involves foreign affairs. The president has unique powers under the Constitution in regard to international relations, but executive branch authority does have limitations. The Rehnquist Court handed down several decisions that have helped to define the limits of that authority.

We have already examined two important cases dealing with presidential power in foreign affairs—the 2004 terrorism cases—and we have seen that the Rehnquist Court justices rejected the claims of the Bush administration in dealing with persons captured in the U.S. War on Terror that such persons had no access to U.S. federal courts. In both *Rasul v. Bush* (2004) and *Hamdi v. Rumsfeld* (2004), the Rehnquist Court surprised many observers by rejecting the administration's arguments that the prisoners were enemy combatants who had no legal right to appear in American courts. As O'Connor argued, although the power of the president is extraordinary in regard to waging war, "we have long . . . made clear that a state of war is not a blank check for the President when it comes to the rights of the Nation's citizens" (72 USLW at 4608).

The Rehnquist Court justices also ruled against the executive branch in *Zadvydas v. Davis*, in 2001. The case involved a German citizen named Zadvydas who was a resident alien in the United States. He was ordered back to Germany because of criminal activity, but Germany would not accept him. This resulted in Zadvydas being held indefinitely in American custody, which he claimed violated his Fifth Amendment rights. Writing for a Court majority, Justice Breyer acknowledged the primacy of the executive branch in such a case, but he nonetheless argued that the courts could review the case.

In a final foreign affairs case involving the executive branch, the Rehnquist Court did defer to executive authority. *Demore v. Kim* (2003) involved the constitutionality of the deportation of a man who was a lawful resident alien living permanently in the United States. In upholding executive authority in this case, the Rehnquist Court distinguished the case from *Zadvydas* and emphasized the substantial authority of the executive branch in matters involving foreign affairs.

Judiciary

The Rehnquist Court also handed down several important decisions regarding Article III of the Constitution, which focuses on the judiciary. These cases have involved the issue of judicial review, questions of standing to file federal suits, and the issue of the courts and political questions.

The case of *City of Boerne v. P. F. Flores* (1997) is an important one in regard to the issue of judicial review, the power of the courts to declare legislative enactments and executive actions unconstitutional. *Boerne* occurred against the background of *Oregon v. Smith*, the controversial 1990 free exercise of religion case in which the Court rejected strict scrutiny and the compelling government interest standard and instead substituted the minimal scrutiny of the rational basis test. As we discussed earlier in this chapter, Congress responded to the *Smith* decision by passing the Religious Freedom Restoration Act (RFRA), which reasserted the validity of this strict scrutiny standard.

The *Boerne* case arose when a Roman Catholic Church in the small Texas town of Boerne sought permission to expand to facilitate attendance by its increasing number of parishioners. The city of Boerne, however, refused to grant a building permit because the church was on the national historical register, and the renovation plan would alter the facade. The bishop of San Antonio, who had jurisdiction over the church, filed suit, arguing that the RFRA controlled this case and that the city lacked a compelling interest in preventing the renovation.

Speaking with unanimity, the Court overturned the RFRA and strongly reaffirmed its power of judicial review. Writing for the Court, Justice Kennedy argued that in passing the RFRA, Congress had exceeded its power under Section 5 of the Fourteenth Amendment. Kennedy granted that Congress has substantial authority to determine the legislation necessary to secure the guarantees of the Fourteenth Amendment. However, Kennedy argued, "Congress' discretion is not unlimited . . . and the courts retain the power, as they have since *Marbury v. Madison*, to determine if Congress has exceeded its authority under the Constitution. Broad as the power of Congress is under the Enforcement Clause of the Fourteenth Amendment, RFRA contradicts vital principles necessary to maintain separation of powers and the federal balance" (521 U.S. at 536).

The Rehnquist Court's willingness to confront Congress regarding the power of judicial review was also seen in another case discussed earlier in this chapter— *Dickerson v. United States* (2000). This case involved a congressional enactment in reaction to the 1966 *Miranda* decision. It provided that the key element in determining the admissibility of witness testimony was whether a confession was voluntary, not whether *Miranda* had been read. Chief Justice Rehnquist authored the majority opinion for a seven-person majority, arguing strongly that *Miranda* involved a constitutional principle. Congress cannot override by legislation a constitutional rule, and the law was therefore unconstitutional.

The Rehnquist Court also decided important cases involving the judiciary and the issue of proper standing to sue, the right of a person to initiate a lawsuit because of direct injury in a matter that a court can address effectively. The Rehnquist Court decided several cases that seemed to raise the bar for those who hope to use the courts as a venue for public policy debate. A major case in this area is *Alexander v. Sandoval* (2001). In this case the Court determined that individuals could only sue states or other government actors under the Civil Rights Act if they showed intent on the part of the actor to discriminate. This reversed a long-standing practice of allowing suits in cases where the effect of a practice was discriminatory. Similarly, the Rehnquist Court was skeptical of standing in instances where plaintiffs cannot show an imminent threat of harm or actual harm. In *Lujan v. Defenders of Wildlife* (1992), an environmental group sought to use the Endangered Species Act to bar the government from sending development funds to other countries because it would harm species in those countries; the Court ruled, however, that the environmentalists lacked standing to bring suit because they could only show an interest in these species and were not directly affected.

A final topic involving Article III and the judiciary is the political questions doctrine. This concept is used by the Court to avoid unnecessary clashes with the legislative and executive branches of government. Thus, by declaring an issue to be a political question, the Court can refuse to hear a case and avoid an unwanted confrontation with Congress or the president.

Nixon v. United States (1993) is the most significant political questions case decided by the Rehnquist Court. Walter Nixon was a federal judge who was sentenced to prison for making false statements before a federal grand jury. The House of Representatives adopted three articles of impeachment against Nixon and presented them to the Senate. The Senate then appointed a committee to hear evidence and testimony. Eventually, the case went before the full Senate for consideration, resulting in the necessary two-thirds vote to convict Nixon, who was removed from office. Nixon then filed suit on the basis that the Constitution requires the full Senate to try all aspects of the impeachment rather than creating a committee to do part of the process. Chief Justice Rehnquist authored a majority opinion rejecting Nixon's argument because it was a political question. Rehnquist argued that the case was a nonjusticiable political question because the Constitution clearly specifies the Senate as having the sole power to conduct impeachment hearings, and the judiciary lacks any discoverable and manageable standards for resolving the issue.

Conclusion

What conclusions can we reach regarding the Rehnquist Court's government powers cases? Despite the variation among the cases we have discussed, the most important theme seems to be the willingness of the Rehnquist Court to assert and preserve its power within the federal political system. The Court was quite willing to confront Congress when the legislative branch tried to override constitutional law decisions of the Court. Thus, in both *Boerne* and *Dickerson,* the Rehnquist Court justices strongly rebuked congressional efforts to override the Court's decisions in *Smith* and *Miranda,* respectively. The Rehnquist Court was also willing to use its authority vis-à-vis the executive branch. A good example of this can be seen in the 2004 terrorism cases, where the Rehnquist Court strongly rejected the Bush administration's position on the legal rights of war prisoners. Another example of the Rehnquist Court rebuking the president can be seen in *Clinton v. Jones,* in which the justices ruled that Clinton was not immune from being sued while in the office for private conduct.

This concludes the analysis of the major public law decisions of the Rehnquist Court. Chapter 4 summarizes the results of this chapter in regard to the central question of whether the Rehnquist Court engaged in a constitutional counterrevolution. Then, using this information, we speculate on the likely legacy of the Rehnquist Court.

Notes

1. For a more complete discussion of quantitative techniques of analysis, see Thomas R. Hensley, Christopher E. Smith, and Joyce A. Baugh, *The Changing Supreme Court: Constitutional Rights and Liberties* (Minneapolis/St. Paul: West/Wadsworth, 1997), 866–870.

2. For a more complete discussion of these limitations of quantitative analysis, see Hensley, Smith, and Baugh, *The Changing Supreme Court,* 866–870.

References

Dershowitz, Alan M. *Supreme Injustice: How the High Court Hijacked Election 2000.* New York: Oxford Univ. Press, 2001.

Epstein, Lee, and Thomas Walker. *Constitutional Law for a Changing America: Rights, Liberties, and Justice.* 5th ed. Washington, D.C.: Congressional Quarterly Press, 2004.

Greenberger, Michael. "Terrorism Cases: A Third Magna Carta." *The National Law Journal,* August 2, 2004, S7, S11.

Huffman, James L. "Court Ruling Was Correct." *The National Law Journal,* August 6, 2001, A23.

Mickenberg, Ira. "'Blakely' and 'Crawford.'" *The National Law Journal,* August 2, 2004, S8, S11.

Rosenberg, Gerald N. *The Hollow Hope.* Chicago: Univ. of Chicago Press, 1991.

Spaeth, Harold J. *United States Supreme Court Judicial Database, 1953–2004 Terms.* Ann Arbor, MI: Inter-University Consortium for Political and Social Research, 2005.

Sunstein, Cass, and Richard A. Epstein, eds. *The Vote: Bush, Gore, and the Supreme Court.* Chicago: Univ. of Chicago Press, 2001.

Yarbrough, Tinsley. *The Burger Court: Justices, Rulings, Legacy.* Denver, CO: ABC-CLIO, 2000.

4

Legacy and Impact

This chapter has two purposes. First, the findings of chapter 3 will be summarized in terms of the central question of this book—did the Rehnquist Court engage in a conservative constitutional counterrevolution? Second, attention will be given to the issue of the legacy of the Rehnquist Court in terms of the future development of American constitutional law.

Some cautions need to be mentioned in regard to this second purpose of speculating on how the Supreme Court of the future will treat the body of case law that was created by the Rehnquist Court. Numerous unpredictable developments have influenced and will continue to influence this process. Obviously, a critical development involves which justices retire and when. Chief Justice Rehnquist's death in September 2005 obviously meant the end of the Rehnquist Court, and it is difficult to predict the effect new Chief Justice John Roberts will have on the Court. Predicting how the Court will evolve is made even more difficult with the replacement of Justice O'Connor by Samuel Alito. Given the advanced age of many of the current justices, changes—perhaps numerous—will likely occur sooner rather than later. Closely related to the issue of the retirement of the justices is the question of political control of the presidency and the Senate. Although the Republican Party currently controls both, that could change in upcoming elections. Supreme Court decision making in the future will undoubtedly be affected by numerous other developments that are impossible to predict. New technology is likely to create issues that the Court will be asked to decide. At the end of the Burger Court era, for example, who would have predicted the impact of the Internet on the Court's freedom of expression agenda? Wars have been a regular part of the American political landscape, but predicting the type of war and its implications for constitutional law is most difficult. Certainly the possibility of terrorism in the United States cannot be discounted, and domestic terrorism could have profound effects on the country's approach to issues of civil rights and liberties. Finally, as was discussed in chapter 1, the battle of the cultural war shows no signs of easing, and it is speculative at best to predict how public opinion will evolve regarding these contentious issues.

If we lack any effective means of predicting the significant developments that could affect the decision making of the Supreme Court in the future, then it becomes necessary to look to the past for insight regarding what the future may hold. The Supreme Court throughout history has been characterized by continuity rather than change. Although we know that membership change can lead to policy change, numerous forces limit the extent to which the Court can suddenly shift direction. The principle of *stare decisis*, or following precedent, is an important constraint on the Court, an unelected branch of a democratic society. In addition, the influence of the other branches of government on the Court can be substantial if the Court moves in dramatically different directions from previous periods.

Thus, in discussing the legacy of the Rehnquist Court in terms of the lasting effect of its doctrinal policies, we need to focus upon each major area of constitutional law to assess how the Rehnquist Court has treated the precedents of earlier Court eras. If the Rehnquist Court largely followed the jurisprudence of the Warren and Burger Courts, then we could predict with some degree of certainty that the Supreme Court of the future is likely to maintain the continuity of previous eras. If, however, the Rehnquist Court created new precedent, either liberal or conservative, then the task of predicting the legacy of the Rehnquist Court becomes more difficult. Among the considerations that need to be taken into account are the quality of the arguments supporting the new precedents as well as the likely directions that public opinion may be taking.

First Amendment: The Establishment Clause

Did the Rehnquist Court engage in a conservative constitutional counterrevolution in regard to the Establishment Clause? The answer seems to be no, but the Rehnquist Court certainly moved Establishment Clause jurisprudence in more conservative directions. The Rehnquist Court justices voted considerably more conservatively in this area than either the Warren or Burger Courts. The Rehnquist Court also overturned previous Establishment Clause precedents. In *Agostini v. Felton* (1997), the Court rejected *Aguilar v. Felton* (1985), and in *Mitchell v. Helms* (2000), the Burger Court decisions of *Meek v. Pittenger* (1975) and *Wolman v. Waters* (1977) were overturned. Both *Agostini* and *Mitchell* were relatively narrow decisions, however, that did not necessarily implicate broader Establishment Clause principles.

The primary reason why the Rehnquist Court cannot be considered to have engaged in a conservative counterrevolution is because no new conservative doctrinal guidelines have been agreed upon by a majority of the justices. The important concept of neutrality is widely utilized, but no clear definition of this concept has been accepted by a Court majority. The *Lemon* test has disappeared and then reemerged, and it has not been embraced by a consistent Court majority.

What is the likely legacy of the Rehnquist Court in regard to interpretation of the Establishment Clause? Two possibilities can be suggested. The most extreme development would be that the Rehnquist Court has laid the foundation for an eventual constitutional counterrevolution in Establishment Clause jurisprudence. With the new appointments to the Court, a conservative majority could emerge that would embrace an accommodationist approach to Establishment Clause cases and could perhaps interpret a modified *Lemon* test in a manner that allows substantial church-state involvement. Even with this development, however, the Court would likely uphold at least the basic school prayer decisions.

A second possibility, and the most likely one, is that the legacy of the Rehnquist Court will be one of ambiguity. The history of the Supreme Court's Establishment Clause decision making has been one of uncertainty, confusion, and conflict, with the Rehnquist Court being no more successful than the Vinson, Warren, or Burger Courts in achieving clarity on the meaning of this First Amendment clause. We have no reason to think that future Supreme Court justices will achieve any major breakthroughs in interpreting the Establishment Clause that can consistently command a Court majority. Thus, it seems likely that Justice Thomas's 1995 characterization will remain true: "Our Establishment Clause jurisprudence is in hopeless disarray" (*Rosenberger v. Rector and Visitors of the University of Virginia*, 515 U.S. at 861, 1995). Even if the legacy of the Rehnquist Court is one of doctrinal ambiguity, however, it does seem that the Rehnquist Court's Establishment Clause decisions have moved in a distinctly more conservative direction, allowing significantly greater involvement between church and state than in previous Court periods, and this legacy seems likely to continue.

First Amendment: The Free Exercise of Religion

Unlike the Establishment Clause, the evidence regarding the Free Exercise of Religion Clause seems clear enough to conclude that the Rehnquist Court engaged in a conservative constitutional counterrevolution. Quantitative data do not support this conclusion even though the Rehnquist Court had a more conservative voting record than the Warren and Burger Courts. The basis for concluding that a dramatic change occurred regarding free exercise jurisprudence is the Rehnquist Court's rejection of the strict scrutiny test of *Sherbert v. Verner* (1963) and its replacement with the minimal scrutiny doctrine of *Oregon v. Smith* (1990).

The *Sherbert* strict scrutiny test provided an extraordinary level of protection to individuals bringing a claim that their religious freedom had been violated by the government. If the Court established that the governmental activity placed an undue burden on a person, then the government had to prove that it was pursuing a compelling interest through narrowly tailored means. This was a difficult test for the government to meet, although the standard was met at times, for example, requiring the Amish to pay Social Security taxes.

The *Smith* test drew a much harder line regarding individuals claiming government interference with their free exercise rights. Criticizing the *Sherbert* test as one that invites anarchy because it puts the individual above the law, a five-person majority argued that both logic and precedent required that the Court must rule against individuals challenging neutral, secular laws that apply equally to all people. Thus, no exceptions can be allowed for those claiming that government laws and actions interfere with their religious practices, unless a government activity targets a religious group. This did occur in the 1993 *Hialeah* case, and strict scrutiny was triggered.

If the Rehnquist Court fundamentally changed free exercise jurisprudence, what seems to be the likely legacy of the Rehnquist Court in this important area of First Amendment law? Two possibilities can be discussed. One is that the *Smith* test will continue to remain controlling precedent, thus marking a distinctive contribution of the Rehnquist Court to American constitutional law. The second possibility is that the Supreme Court in the post–Rehnquist Court years could overturn *Smith* and return to the strict scrutiny approach associated with *Sherbert*.

The most probable pattern of the post–Rehnquist Court era is an adherence to the minimal scrutiny approach of *Smith*. *Smith* has now been controlling precedent for fifteen years, and the principle of *stare decisis* places powerful constraints on overturning the decision. Furthermore, the Rehnquist Court has withstood the strong attacks on its *Smith* decision, and the criticism of *Smith* has become more muted. In addition, the *Hialeah* decision shows that individuals can win claims of government encroachment upon their religious freedom under the *Smith* test. For all of these reasons, then, the legacy of the Rehnquist Court is most likely to be one of moving free exercise jurisprudence in a far more conservative direction than under the Warren and Burger Courts.

It is possible, however, that the *Smith* decision will be overturned, thus limiting sharply the legacy of the Rehnquist Court. At least four arguments suggest that *Smith* might be reversed by a future Court. First, *Smith* has been widely criticized on numerous grounds by scholars, religious leaders, and elected officials. *Smith* has few supporters, and its rejection would likely generate substantial approval and support. Second, Scalia's majority opinion in *Smith* contains numerous weaknesses. For example, he argues that *Minersville School District v. Gobitis* is an important precedent when the Court explicitly overturned *Gobitis* in the *Barnette* case; he presents a questionable argument when he classifies several free exercise precedents as "hybrid" cases involving other rights; and he grossly overstates his argument that the *Sherbert* approach invites anarchy. Third, valid concerns exist that the effect of the *Smith* decision will be one of harming the rights of those who belong to religious minorities. Fourth, a good argument can be made that the strict scrutiny approach worked well in the past, not only providing a high level of protection to members of religious minorities but also allowing the government to prevail when it could establish that it was pursuing a compelling interest through narrowly tailored means.

First Amendment: Freedom of Expression

We had little trouble concluding in chapter 3 that the Rehnquist Court did not engage in a sharp turn to the right in the area of freedom of expression. Indeed, our analysis revealed quite the contrary. The Rehnquist Court established a strong liberal record in regard to freedom of speech and the press. This conclusion is supported by comparing the voting records of the Warren, Burger, and Rehnquist Courts. The Rehnquist Court voted liberally in 62 percent of its freedom of expression cases, exceeding the Burger Court's 48 percent liberal record but trailing the 74 percent liberal record of the Warren Court. Furthermore, the Rehnquist Court has not created any major new conservative precedents in regard to freedom of expression.

An examination of the Rehnquist Court's most famous and controversial expression cases also show a distinctive liberal pattern of outcomes. In *Hustler Magazine v. Falwell* (1988), the Court unanimously supported the First Amendment's protection for *Hustler*'s crude parody of Falwell. Disregarding strong public opinion against burning the American flag in political protest, the Rehnquist Court justices found the practice to come within the protection of the First Amendment in *Texas v. Johnson* (1989), and then a majority issued a similar ruling one year later in *United States v. Eichman* (1990) in response to an effort by Congress to criminalize flag burning. *R.A.V. v. City of St. Paul, Minnesota* (1992) found the Court providing constitutional protection for hate speech, and in *Reno v. American Civil Liberties Union* (1997) the Rehnquist Court ruled unconstitutional two provisions of the 1996 Communications Decency Act and, very importantly, applied the strict scrutiny standard to the Internet.

Turning to an examination of the legacy of the Rehnquist Court in the area of freedom of expression, continuity seems to be the most reasonable expectation. The Warren Court established an extensive foundation of liberal precedents that have been continued by both the Burger and the Rehnquist Courts, and we can expect this tradition to continue in the next Court era. This pattern is not guaranteed, of course. The Supreme Court throughout the nineteenth century and early part of the twentieth century was not a champion of freedom of expression rights, and the Court's record of defending freedom of speech and press during periods of war has not been a strong one. Nonetheless, the distinctive trend of the past century by the Supreme Court has been one of expanding individual protection against government interference with freedom of expression. The Rehnquist Court was an important component of this process, adding major precedents to a substantial body of jurisprudence supporting freedom of speech, press, and other forms of communication.

The legacy of the Rehnquist Court may be especially strong in two areas of freedom of expression. One area is commercial speech. Until the Burger Court era, commercial speech received no constitutional protection. The Burger Court changed this dramatically, initially providing minimal scrutiny and then elevating it to intermediate scrutiny. The Rehnquist Court followed precedent, applying intermediate scrutiny in commercial speech cases. Evidence can be found in the 1996 case of *44 Liquormart v. Rhode Island* that some members of the Rehnquist Court thought that commercial speech should be analyzed under strict scrutiny, and this may occur in the post–Rehnquist Court era. The second area where the legacy of the Rehnquist Court may be especially strong involves the Internet. Although it is difficult to predict the exact types of cases that will emerge, it seems clear that freedom of expression cases involving the Internet will be a prominent feature of the agenda of the next Supreme Court. The important legacy of the Rehnquist Court will have been to establish the strict scrutiny test as the appropriate standard for evaluating Internet cases.

A final important legacy of the Rehnquist Court in regard to freedom of expression involves the doctrinal framework discussed in chapter 3. Although this has its origins in earlier Court eras and this framework is not viewed by the Rehnquist Court justices as a definitive and clear guideline to their First Amendment decision making, this analytical approach recognizes the wide varieties of freedom of expression in American society and provides for differing levels of protection based upon the importance of each form of expression for American democracy. The Rehnquist Court justices deserve significant credit for furthering the development of this framework, and it seems likely that future Courts will both utilize and develop further this logical and principled approach to freedom of expression jurisprudence.

Obscenity

The evidence reveals that the Rehnquist Court did not move sharply to the right in regard to obscenity and sexual expression. Although the Rehnquist-era justices were distinctively more conservative than the Warren Court, the Rehnquist Court followed closely the decision-making patterns of the Burger Court. In regard to voting patterns, the Warren Court decided 73 percent of its obscenity decisions in a liberal manner; the Burger Court sharply changed this pattern by deciding only 30 percent of its obscenity cases liberally; and the Rehnquist Court established a voting record nearly identical to that of the Burger Court by deciding liberally in 33 percent of its cases. The Rehnquist Court also adhered closely to the major precedents of the Warren and Burger Courts, especially the *Roth/Miller* test for determining if a work is obscene.

And like its predecessors, the Rehnquist Court found it difficult to arrive at majority opinions in its sexual expression cases.

Despite the similarities of the Burger and Rehnquist Courts in the area of obscenity, important differences do exist. The Rehnquist Court's decisions rarely dealt with obscene materials but rather focused on the limits of government regulation of sexual expression that comes within the protection of the First Amendment. Another important difference between the two Courts is that the Rehnquist Court was increasingly called upon to deal with new technologies, especially cable television and the Internet.

Shifting the focus to the legacy of the Rehnquist Court in regard to obscenity and sexual expression, it seems probable that the next Supreme Court era will see substantial continuity with the Rehnquist Court just as the Rehnquist Court was involved with continuity with the Burger Court. The limits of sexual expression will undoubtedly confront the future Supreme Court. Following the pattern of the past fifty years, the amount and the explicitness of sexual expression will increase significantly, and the Court will be called upon to draw the lines between the constitutionally permissible and impermissible. The *Roth/Miller* test seems likely to remain the controlling precedent, not because it is such a useful test but because no better alternative has been advanced.

Other patterns established by the Rehnquist Court seem likely to continue. The future Supreme Court is more likely to be involved with sexual expression cases within the protection of the First Amendment rather than obscenity cases per se. Issues involving government regulations concerning children and sexual expression will probably confront the Court frequently. Another trend that seems clear is the growth in cases involving the Internet. The Rehnquist Court's confusion as evidenced by the few majority opinions in this area is also likely to continue.

The legacy of the Rehnquist Court in regard to obscenity thus seems not to be one of innovation but rather of continuity with the Burger Court. The future Supreme Court will likely follow in this pattern. Most decisions will be decided conservatively, but the Court will nonetheless be willing to draw the line in some cases where government regulations exceed the requirements of the First Amendment.

The Fourth Amendment and Unreasonable Searches and Seizures

Having completed our examination of First Amendment jurisprudence, we now shift our attention to the guarantees of the criminally accused found in the Fourth, Fifth, Sixth, and Eighth Amendments. In looking initially at all of the criminal rights cases of the Warren, Burger, and Rehnquist Courts, no evidence was found of a conservative constitutional revolution by the Rehnquist Court. The Warren Court had a moderately liberal voting record of 58 percent, the Burger Court was considerably more conservative with a 34 percent liberal record, and the Rehnquist Court, at 36 percent liberal, had a record nearly identical to that of the Burger Court. Thus, the Rehnquist Court was in essential continuity with the Burger Court rather than moving sharply in a more conservative direction. We also suggested that the Rehnquist Court did not engage in the overturning of existing liberal precedents of the previous courts. Finally, we recognized that substantial variation could exist in Rehnquist Court decision making among the four criminal rights amendments, and thus each amendment has to be studied in detail.

Quantitative analysis of Fourth Amendment search and seizure cases revealed the possibility of a conservative counterrevolution by the Rehnquist Court. The Warren Court's voting record in Fourth Amendment cases was 58 percent liberal, and this decreased sharply to 32 percent liberal for the Burger Court and 21 percent liberal for the Rehnquist Court. Furthermore, the last natural court had a strong five-person conservative majority of Justices Rehnquist, Scalia, Thomas, Kennedy, and O'Connor; in addition, both Souter and Breyer voted conservatively in a majority of Fourth Amendment cases. Despite these quantitative data, a qualitative analysis of the leading Fourth Amendment cases involving warrantless searches and the exclusionary rule did not support the argument that the Rehnquist Court engaged in a dramatic rethinking of Fourth Amendment jurisprudence.

Looking initially at warrantless search cases, some evidence does exist that the Rehnquist Court justices fundamentally altered past Court jurisprudence. Paralleling the quantitative data, the qualitative analysis revealed that the Rehnquist Court was even more conservative than the Burger Court, not only creating additional exceptions to the warrant requirement but also providing conservative interpretations to existing warrantless exceptions. The Rehnquist Court also introduced a somewhat novel reasonableness test for the Fourth Amendment that states that the key to interpreting Fourth Amendment cases is not whether a warrant based upon probable cause existed but rather whether a warrantless search was reasonable based upon a weighing of law enforcement's interests against the privacy rights of the individual.

Despite the evidence in support of the occurrence of a constitutional revolution by the Rehnquist Court regarding warrantless searches, other factors weigh more heavily and lead to a rejection of this conclusion. Very importantly, the Rehnquist Court did not create new conservative precedents that have overturned existing liberal precedents. In addition, the justices of the Rehnquist Court recognized Fourth Amendment limitations on warrantless searches by law enforcement personnel, especially in regard to a person's private dwelling. Thus, although it is a close call, the evidence supports the conclusion that the Rehnquist Court did not engage in a conservative counterrevolution regarding Fourth Amendment warrantless searches.

The Rehnquist Court also did not engage in radically conservative changes in regard to the exclusionary rule. The key precedents of *Weeks* (1914) and *Mapp* (1961) remain controlling law. Furthermore, unlike the Burger Court, the Rehnquist Court did not create major new exceptions to the exclusionary rule. The Rehnquist Court justices may have concluded that the Burger Court sufficiently limited the exclusionary rule and that the rule may have some utility in deterring police misconduct.

Speculating on the Rehnquist Court's Fourth Amendment legacy is an especially difficult task. Developments external to the Court could profoundly influence the Fourth Amendment jurisprudence of the future Supreme Court. For example, a dramatic increase in the crime rate could lead to increasingly conservative Court policies. Perhaps even more ominous would be the occurrence of terrorism on American soil. Bush administration officials are already seeking broad new powers regarding searches and seizures, and this would be difficult to resist under greatly heightened terrorism concerns.

Assuming that no major developments occur, the legacy of the Rehnquist Court seems likely to be one of continued conservative decision making without major new precedents being created. With a majority of the current justices voting conservatively in a majority of the Fourth Amendment cases, it seems most unlikely that we will see dramatic changes in a liberal direction by the future Supreme Court, and it is doubtful that a conservative majority will push too much further in promoting the interests of law enforcement officials.

In the area of warrantless searches, the pattern established by the Rehnquist Court seems likely to be emulated by a future Supreme Court. The pattern of distinctively conservative decision making is likely to continue, and it is probable that additional exceptions to the warrant requirement could emerge. Perhaps the most important legacy of the Rehnquist Court in this area is the emphasis on reasonableness as the key concept in interpreting the Fourth Amendment, and under this test it will be extremely difficult for the individual to prevail over the interests of law enforcement.

The legacy of the Rehnquist Court in regard to the exclusionary rule will probably be minimal. The Rehnquist Court heard few cases and did not issue any major new rulings, and this pattern seems likely to hold with a future Supreme Court. Thus, the Warren and Burger Courts dealt with the major exclusionary rule cases, and the Rehnquist Court's legacy will be limited.

The Fifth Amendment

In analyzing the Fifth Amendment, the focus was upon the guarantees against self-incrimination and double jeopardy. The conclusion was offered that although the Rehnquist Court was strongly conservative in both areas, this conservatism did not reach the level that constituted a counterrevolution. Both the quantitative analyses and the analysis of major cases supported the view that the Rehnquist Court's Fifth Amendment decision making was substantially similar to that of the Burger Court.

In regard to the protection against self-incrimination, the voting records of the Burger and Rehnquist Courts were nearly identical; the Burger Court voted liberally in 23 percent of its decisions, and the Rehnquist Court had a 25 percent liberal voting record. This compares to a 56 percent liberal record established by the Warren Court. Justices Rehnquist, Scalia, Thomas, O'Connor, and Kennedy formed a cohesive five-person conservative majority in self-incrimination cases, but they did not create major new conservative precedents in this area of criminal law. Like the Burger Court, the Rehnquist Court majority certainly gave conservative interpretations to existing precedents and on occasion created exceptions to the *Miranda* (1966) warnings. However, the Rehnquist Court remained committed to the core of the *Miranda* decision as seen in the major case of *Dickerson v. United States* (2000), when a 7–2 Court led by Chief Justice Rehnquist rejected the call to overturn *Miranda*.

An analysis of the double jeopardy cases found some surprising results, but the evidence led to the conclusion that the Rehnquist Court did not shift constitutional law in a substantially conservative direction compared to the Warren and Burger Courts. Quantitative data revealed the surprising result that the Warren Court was decidedly conservative in regard to double jeopardy cases, deciding only 33 percent in a liberal direction. The Burger Court was more liberal, at 37 percent, than the Warren Court, and the Rehnquist Court was the most conservative, at 25 percent liberal. Despite this lower support for individuals claiming a double jeopardy violation, however, the Rehnquist Court's voting record is not substantially different than those of the Warren and Burger Courts. The examination of major double jeopardy cases confirmed the view that the Rehnquist Court established a pattern of continuity with the earlier courts rather than a marked change in decision making.

The legacy of the Rehnquist Court's Fifth Amendment jurisprudence seems likely to be modest because the Rehnquist Court justices largely followed the leads of the Warren and Burger Courts, and the future Supreme Court will probably continue this pattern of decision making. In regard to the guarantee against self-incrimination, the Warren Court had a moderate voting record at 56 percent liberal, while both the Burger and Rehnquist Courts were strongly conservative, with the Burger Court voting liberally in only 23 percent of the cases and the Rehnquist Court at 25 percent liberal. This decades-long pattern seems likely to continue. *Miranda* is the critical precedent, and it seems to be on firm ground. It would be remarkable indeed if the next era of Supreme Court history saw an overturning of *Miranda*. The Rehnquist Court's strong reaffirmation of *Miranda* in the 2000 *Dickerson* case is a powerful precedent, *Miranda* has already been limited by the Burger and Rehnquist Courts, law enforcement personnel have accepted the *Miranda* guidelines, and *Miranda* does support important principles of fairness in the criminal justice system.

The decision making of the next Supreme Court era in the area of double jeopardy also seems likely to follow closely the patterns of the past, including the Rehnquist Court. This is a unique area where the Warren, Burger, and Rehnquist Courts have all been decidedly conservative, with the Warren Court at 33 percent liberal, the Burger Court at 37 percent liberal, and the Rehnquist Court at 21 percent liberal. Given these historical patterns and current alignments, the future Supreme Court seems most likely to follow past patterns of consistently ruling against those who bring claims alleging double jeopardy.

The Sixth Amendment Jury Trial Guarantees

Our analysis of the Sixth Amendment jury trial guarantees was broken into two components: the right to counsel and the other guarantees of the Sixth Amendment. The conclusion was offered that the Rehnquist Court did not engage in a conservative constitutional counterrevolution in regard to either component, but the results were somewhat surprising because the Rehnquist Court was distinctively more conservative than the Warren and Burger Courts regarding the right to counsel but was remarkably moderate and even liberal in regard to the other guarantees of the Sixth Amendment.

Turning first to the right to counsel cases, dramatic differences were found among the three Court eras in terms of liberal and conservative voting. The Warren Court voted liberally in 86 percent of its right to counsel cases, the Burger Court established a moderate record of 44 percent liberal voting, and the Rehnquist Court supported the individual contending a denial of the right to counsel in only 24 percent of the cases. For the last natural court, the five most conservative justices—Rehnquist, Scalia, Thomas, Kennedy, and O'Connor—formed a cohesive group that voted conservatively from 76 to 86 percent of the time. Despite this strong statistical evidence of a major shift in the conservative direction in right to counsel cases, it was argued that the Rehnquist Court did not engage in a conservative revolution in this area of constitutional law because the Rehnquist Court heard relatively few major right to counsel cases and did not overturn any leading liberal precedents from earlier Court eras.

Although we might have expected to see somewhat similar results regarding the other Sixth Amendment rights cases, this did not occur because the Rehnquist Court established a moderately conservative voting record characterized by several major liberal decisions. In regard to the comparative voting records, the Warren Court decided 87 percent of these cases liberally, but the Burger Court took a dramatically different approach, deciding only 24 percent of these Sixth Amendment cases conservatively. Perhaps surprisingly in terms of the patterns we have observed thus far, the Rehnquist Court was substantially more liberal than the Burger Court in deciding 43 percent liberally in the jury rights cases. A qualitative analysis of leading Sixth Amendment cases revealed several major liberal Sixth Amendment decisions by the Rehnquist Court in three major areas. First, although they were largely decided on equal protection grounds, the Rehnquist Court greatly expanded the Burger Court's *Batson v. Kentucky* (1986) case in regard to limiting attorneys' ability to dismiss potential jurors from a case. Second, the Rehnquist Court justices strengthened the right of defendants to confront their accusers. *Crawford v. Washington* (2004) is an especially notable case because this was a major new liberal precedent that overturned the 1980 Burger Court decision of *Ohio v. Roberts*, which allowed hearsay evidence to be used in court if it was clearly reliable; under *Crawford*, the accused now has the right to confront the accuser. Third, the Court issued a series of major liberal decisions in *Apprendi v. New Jersey* (2000), *Ring v. Arizona* (2002), *Blakely v. Washington* (2004), and *Booker v. United States* (2005) that have limited the ability of judges rather than juries to make sentencing determinations. Thus, in regard to the other Sixth Amendment rights, the Rehnquist Court certainly did not engage in any sharp conservative movement but instead established a surprisingly strong liberal record.

Turning to a consideration of the possible legacy of the Rehnquist Court in regard to the guarantees of the Sixth Amendment, the impact of the Rehnquist Court justices seems likely to be minimal in regard to right to counsel cases but to be potentially enormous regarding some of the other Sixth Amendment guarantees. Although the Rehnquist Court was strongly conservative in right to counsel cases, the justices heard relatively few cases and established no major new precedents, and thus the legacy in this area of the law will likely be minimal. In sharp contrast, the legacy of the Rehnquist Court seems likely to be substantial in regard to some of the other guarantees of the Sixth Amendment. The Rehnquist Court established an impressive line of precedents regarding the impartial selection of jurors, and this may continue as an important area for the future Supreme Court. Stemming from the *Crawford* case, the future Supreme Court is also likely to confront additional right of confrontation cases involving hearsay evidence. The area that seems most likely to occupy the attention of the future Supreme Court involves the controversial issue of the sentencing discretion of state and federal judges. The landmark cases of *Blakely* (2004) and *Booker* (2005) seem destined to occupy the agenda of the Supreme Court as the country and courts debate the role of judges in the sentencing process. Whatever the outcome, the Rehnquist Court will have left a lasting legacy by bringing into question the validity of existing sentencing rules.

The Eighth Amendment Protection against Cruel and Unusual Punishments

Did the Rehnquist Court engage in a dramatic conservative shift in regard to Eighth Amendment jurisprudence? The answer to this question is no. In both capital and non-capital cases involving the Cruel and Unusual Punishments Clause, the Rehnquist Court established a moderate record void of the creation of new conservative decisions replacing previous liberal precedents. Indeed, in two death penalty cases involving the mentally retarded and minors who are sixteen or seventeen years of age, the Rehnquist Court justices created new liberal precedents overturning their own earlier conservative precedents.

Capital punishment cases present a somewhat unusual area to analyze because the Warren Court did not engage in a constitutional revolution regarding the death penalty. The Warren Court heard only three capital punishment cases because the social movement against the death penalty did not manifest itself in a stream of court cases until the seventies. Thus, it was the Burger Court that established the leading capital punishment precedents. After initially finding all existing death penalty laws to be unconstitutional, in the 1976 case of *Gregg v. Georgia*, the Burger Court justices established the two-stage process for death penalty cases in an attempt to ensure fairness in the process. The Burger Court was confronted with numerous additional death penalty cases, and a moderate voting record emerged, with 47 percent of the cases being decided in favor of the individual.

The Rehnquist Court followed closely the pattern of the Burger Court, and thus it is not possible to argue that the Rehnquist Court justices engaged in a conservative counterrevolution in this area. The Rehnquist Court remained committed to the key precedent of *Gregg*, and the overall voting record in death penalty cases was 41 percent liberal, slightly more conservative than the record of the Burger Court. It appeared early in the Rehnquist Court era that a conservative majority might move capital punishment jurisprudence sharply to the right, but in recent years the Rehnquist Court moved in quite a different direction by explicitly overturning two of its own conservative precedents. In *Atkins v. Virginia* (2002), the Court reversed its 1989 decision of *Penry v. Lynaugh* in ruling that the Eighth Amendment prohibits the execution of the mentally retarded. The Court similarly in *Roper v. Simmons* (2005) reversed another 1989 precedent, *Stanford v. Kentucky*, ruling that the Eighth Amendment prohibits the execution of youth sixteen or seventeen years of age.

Just as they did not engage in a conservative shift in capital punishment cases, so too the Rehnquist Court did not reinterpret the Eighth Amendment in regard to non-capital cases. Although noncapital cases are relatively rare for the Supreme Court, the statistical evidence revealed that the Rehnquist Court was as liberal as the Warren

Court and substantially more liberal than the Burger Court. The Rehnquist Court decided 50 percent of its noncapital cases liberally, the same as the Warren Court and significantly more liberally than the Burger Court, at 17 percent. Furthermore, the Rehnquist Court did not introduce in this area any new conservative precedents that have overturned earlier liberal precedents.

The legacy of the Rehnquist Court seems likely to be minimal in regard to both capital and noncapital Eighth Amendment cases. In capital cases, the Rehnquist Court followed closely the pattern of the Burger Court, and it seems probable that the next era of Supreme Court history will see a similar pattern of continuity characterized by a commitment to the two-step process of *Gregg* and decisions that closely balance liberal and conservative outcomes. A similar pattern seems likely regarding noncapital cases; relatively few cases are likely to appear on the agenda of the future Court, and past doctrines and precedents are likely to be followed, although the use of the proportionality principle in noncapital cases could be eliminated.

Despite the probability that the Rehnquist Court's legacy may be limited in regard to interpreting the Eighth Amendment, a possibility exists that Court watchers might look back to the decisions in *Atkins* and *Roper* as the foundation for a radical reversal of death penalty jurisprudence, finding the death penalty unconstitutional. This possible development stems not so much from any language in *Atkins* or *Roper* but rather from the numerous criticisms that exist of the death penalty, including arguments that it is racially biased, it discriminates on the basis of economic status, it is highly related to poor legal representation, it allows the innocent to be executed, and it is opposed throughout the Western world. Despite these criticisms, however, the future Supreme Court seems unlikely to abolish the death penalty because of the language of the Constitution, the intent of the writers, powerful precedent, and public opinion.

Takings Clause

Although it initially appeared that the Rehnquist Court might dramatically alter existing jurisprudence regarding the Takings Clause, recent decisions suggest that the Rehnquist Court can best be characterized by continuity rather than change. Throughout history, the Court has been highly supportive of the government against individuals' claims of Takings Clause violations. The Warren Court established an 88 percent liberal record, and the Burger Court was also strongly supportive, at 76 percent liberal. The Rehnquist Court was less liberal, but the Rehnquist Court justices decided a majority—52 percent—of these cases in favor of the government. In a series of conservatively decided cases early in the Rehnquist Court era—*Nollan v. California Coastal Commission* (1987), *Lucas v. South Carolina Costal Council* (1992), and

Dolan v. City of Tigard (1994)—it appeared that the Rehnquist Court might be on the verge of fundamental change in Takings Clause jurisprudence. However, in the 2004–2005 term, the Rehnquist Court handed down three important decisions, all of which favored the government: *Kelo v. City of New London* (2005), *Lingle v. Chevron* (2005), and *San Remo Hotel v. City and County of San Francisco* (2005). It is difficult to assess exactly what these recent decisions will mean for future Takings Clause jurisprudence, but they certainly support the view that the Rehnquist Court did not engage in fundamental conservative change in this area of constitutional law.

The legacy of the Rehnquist Court in regard to the Takings Clause is somewhat ambiguous. However, the Rehnquist Court's decisions were largely consistent with those of the Warren and Burger Courts. This means that the Supreme Court of the future is most likely to continue interpreting the Takings Clause in a manner supportive of the government.

Race and Equal Protection

The Rehnquist Court will certainly not be remembered for its bold leadership regarding the achievement of racial equality in American society, but it is surely not possible to suggest that the Rehnquist Court has engaged in a conservative counterrevolution in regard to the issue of racial equality. Both our quantitative and qualitative analyses provide support for this conclusion.

The quantitative data revealed significant differences among the Warren, Burger, and Rehnquist Courts, but these differences are not strong enough to argue that the Rehnquist Court engaged in a radically conservative shift. The Warren Court was exceptionally liberal in racial equality cases, deciding 94 percent of these cases in favor of the individual bringing a claim of racial discrimination. The Burger Court was also strongly liberal, at 67 percent, although the Burger Court may have faced more difficult situations than the cases of blatant discrimination before the Warren Court. The overall record for the Rehnquist Court was also liberal, but it was more moderate, with 57 percent of the decisions favoring the individual. Although more moderate than the two preceding Court eras regarding racial equality, the Rehnquist Court did have a liberal voting record and hence cannot be considered to have engaged in a conservative counterrevolution.

The quantitative data also revealed a significant difference in the attention given to racial equality cases by the three Courts. The Warren Court and Burger Court heard sixty-nine and forty-nine cases, respectively, but the Rehnquist Court ruled on only fourteen racial equality cases through the 2004–2005 term, and only five such cases were decided in the natural court period since Breyer joined the Court. This is clearly not accidental given the Court's control over its agenda and suggests strongly that the

Rehnquist Court saw a somewhat limited role for the federal courts in the struggle for racial equality in American society.

The analysis of the major racial equality cases of the Rehnquist Court support the conclusion from the quantitative analysis that the Rehnquist Court has been moderately liberal in regard to racial equality cases. In addition to the 57 percent liberal voting record, the liberalism of the Rehnquist Court can be seen in its opposition to various forms of *de jure* discrimination, its continuing commitment to the use of strict scrutiny in race cases, and its strong support of eliminating racial bias in jury selection procedures. But evidence also exists beyond the voting data to show that the Rehnquist Court was more conservative than either the Warren or Burger Courts. The Rehnquist Court certainly did not give any hint of overturning *Brown*, but neither did the Rehnquist Court justices show any great support for *Brown*'s central concern of achieving racially integrated schools. The Rehnquist Court decided only one *Brown* case liberally, and that was in 1990, thus largely leaving this important issue to state and local communities. The Rehnquist Court was also conservative in the redistricting cases concerned with enhancing the likelihood of electing minority citizens to Congress. In addition, the Court rejected the challenge to the racial bias of Georgia's death penalty system. Finally, as we discuss shortly, the Rehnquist Court introduced a more conservative standard for evaluating affirmative action cases.

Assessing the legacy of the Rehnquist Court in regard to equal protection and race is a difficult challenge. It does seem clear that the future Supreme Court will be constrained by several liberal developments that were continued by the Rehnquist Court from the decisions of the Warren and Burger Courts. These include a strong opposition to any forms of *de jure* discrimination, a commitment to the use of the strict scrutiny test in deciding racial equality cases, and the elimination of racial discrimination in the jury selection process.

A conservative Rehnquist Court legacy will likely also be seen in the decisions of the future Supreme Court. Most importantly, the limiting of *Brown* seems likely to continue, with future Supreme Courts being content to allow state and local governments to deal with the issue of school integration, although *de jure* segregation will not be tolerated. It is uncertain what the orientation of the future Supreme Court will be in regard to legislative redistricting and to the issue of racial bias in the death penalty process, but the conservative precedents of the Rehnquist Court seem likely to remain controlling law.

Equal Protection and Gender

The Rehnquist Court certainly did not engage in a conservative constitutional revolution in regard to equal protection and gender. To the contrary, the justices of the Rehnquist Court extended the liberal revolution of the Burger Court. Unlike so many other areas, the Warren Court was not involved in a liberal revolution in the area of gender discrimination, deciding only one case and deciding it conservatively. The activities of the women's movement that began in the sixties brought a flood of litigation to the Burger Court, which did engage in a liberal revolution by deciding 64 percent of forty-seven cases liberally and creating a heightened scrutiny standard under the important government objective test. The Rehnquist Court established a record that is even more liberal than the Burger Court, deciding 75 percent of twenty-four gender cases in a liberal manner. The Rehnquist Court justices have maintained support for the intermediate scrutiny standard, and they have extended several of the liberal precedents of the Burger Court, especially in regard to the area of sexual harassment.

The legacy of the Rehnquist Court is likely to be significant. Even though it was the Burger Court that set the key liberal precedents in regard to gender discrimination, the Rehnquist Court extended this liberal legacy but did not add major new precedents. It seems likely that the future Supreme Court will continue to use the important government objective test as the appropriate approach to gender discrimination cases, but the possibility exists that the future Supreme Court could adopt the strict scrutiny approach in some future case. Justice Ginsburg's opinions provide a foundation for this development, and support for this position was expressed by the Justice Department in the VMI case. This development would probably be associated with the addition of more women to the Court, although O'Connor's record in gender discrimination cases reveals that the sex of a justice is far from a perfect predictor of voting behavior in gender discrimination cases. Statutory cases are likely to be even more frequent in the gender discrimination cases of the future Supreme Court, especially cases involving sexual harassment and Title IX. The liberal precedents of the Rehnquist Court will constitute an important legacy affecting the future Supreme Court.

Affirmative Action

Did the Rehnquist Court engage in a conservative constitutional counterrevolution in the area of affirmative action? This is a difficult judgment to make because the Rehnquist Court created major new conservative precedents regarding affirmative action that have required affirmative action programs to be reviewed under the strict scrutiny standard, and these decisions seemed to invalidate virtually all governmental affirmative action programs. In a major 2003 case involving the University of Michigan Law School, however, the Court found constitutional an affirmative action program using the strict scrutiny test. Thus, although the Rehnquist Court definitely shifted affirmative action jurisprudence in a conservative direction, this shift was not radical enough to consider it a constitutional revolution.

As was the case with gender discrimination, it was the Burger Court, not the Warren Court, that heard the initial affirmative action cases. Indeed, the Warren Court did not hear a single affirmative action case. The Burger Court, in contrast, decided sixteen cases, ruling liberally in 62 percent of these cases. The Burger Court was thus generally supportive of affirmative action programs, but the Court rejected programs with strict quota systems or that resulted in the loss of jobs for white workers. The Burger Court, however, was never able to achieve a majority consensus on the proper test for affirmative action programs.

The more conservative orientation of the Rehnquist Court can be seen in both the quantitative and qualitative analysis of the Court's affirmative action cases. The Rehnquist Court decided eleven affirmative action cases through the 2004–2005 term, ruling conservatively in 54 percent of the cases, a somewhat more conservative record than the Burger Court. As the Rehnquist Court's membership changed, the Court became increasingly conservative, with Kennedy's replacement of Powell and Thomas's replacement of Marshall being the key changes. In the 1989 *City of Richmond v. J. A. Croson Co.* case, the Rehnquist Court for the first time achieved majority agreement on the use of the strict scrutiny test in state affirmative action cases, thus making it extremely difficult for the government to defend affirmative action cases. In the 1990 case of *Metro Broadcasting, Inc. v. FCC*, the liberal justices prevailed in applying the intermediate standard to federal affirmative action programs, but in the 1995 *Adarand Constructors, Inc. v. Pena* case, the conservative coalition of Rehnquist, Scalia, Thomas, O'Connor, and Kennedy overturned *Metro* and established the strict scrutiny test as controlling in federal programs as well as state ones.

With *Croson* and *Adarand* as the controlling precedents, it appeared that few if any affirmative action programs could survive constitutional review, but two 2003 cases from the University of Michigan gave new hope to advocates of affirmative action programs. The key case was *Grutter v. Bollinger*, in which a five-person majority of O'Connor, Stevens, Ginsburg, Souter, and Breyer found that the affirmative action program of the University of Michigan's Law School met the tough standards of the strict scrutiny test because the school had a compelling interest in achieving a diverse student body, and the holistic consideration of many factors including race met the requirement of being narrowly tailored means. The undergraduate admissions affirmative action program in *Gratz v. Bollinger*, however, failed strict scrutiny because the twenty points automatically awarded to minority students was a type of quota that made race the decisive factor in the admissions process. The *Grutter* and *Gratz* decisions thus provide the foundation for the constitutionality of affirmative action programs that allow race to be considered among the factors in a decision without the use of rigid quotas and numeric standards.

The legacy of the Rehnquist Court in affirmative action is likely to be stronger than in any area we have thus far discussed. Unlike the previous areas we have examined, the Rehnquist Court set the major controlling precedents in *Croson* and *Adarand,* and the future Supreme Court seems likely to follow these strict scrutiny precedents. *Grutter* and *Gratz* will also be major precedents for the future Supreme Court, and they raise important questions that will have to be confronted. *Grutter* leaves open the issue of what constitutes a governmental compelling interest. Diversity in higher education is such a compelling interest, but is diversity a compelling interest in other fields as well? Similarly, the future Supreme Court will need to address difficult questions regarding what means are sufficiently narrowly tailored to meet the strict scrutiny test.

Other Equal Protection Cases

The Rehnquist Court's equal protection cases have not been limited to race, gender, and affirmative action, important as these areas may be. The Rehnquist Court has also dealt with cases involving members of such groups as the aged, the mentally ill, the poor, and homosexuals. The justices of the Rehnquist Court era have generally followed past Court precedent in deciding these cases, but in one area—homosexuality—the justices have created a major new liberal precedent, *Lawrence v. Texas* (2003). Thus, in the area of other equal protection cases, the Rehnquist Court certainly did not engage in a conservative counterrevolution; quite the contrary, the Court engaged in a liberal revolution, at least in regard to equal protection and homosexuality.

In analyzing the other equal protection cases of the Rehnquist Court, it is helpful to recall the equal protection doctrinal framework we have discussed. Under this framework, the Court subjects most cases to the minimal scrutiny or rational basis test. The only exceptions are for gender and illegitimacy, where intermediate scrutiny is applied, and for race, alienage, and affirmative action, where strict scrutiny applies. This framework was developed before the Rehnquist Court period, and the Rehnquist Court adhered closely to it, with the exception of affirmative action. The Rehnquist Court resisted efforts by other groups to achieve higher levels of protection, applying the rational basis test to cases involving the poor (*Kadrmas v. Dickerson Public Schools,* 1988), the aged (*Gregory v. Ashcroft,* 1991), and the mentally retarded (*Heller v. Doe,* 1993). All of these cases were decided conservatively, which is normal under the rational basis test, but they certainly do not involve the creation of new conservative precedents overturning prior liberal precedents.

The Rehnquist Court did, however, introduce a major new liberal precedent in regard to homosexuality. Before the Rehnquist Court era, the Supreme Court had never found a law to violate the Equal Protection Clause based upon discrimination against homosexuals. In *Romer v. Evans,* however, the Rehnquist Court in a 6–3 decision ruled that Colorado's Amendment 2 violated the Equal Protection Clause based upon the rational basis test. Although advocates for homosexual rights had hoped that the Court would apply either the intermediate or strict scrutiny test in the case, the decision was nonetheless a major development that at least promised protection for homosexuals against the most blatant types of discrimination.

The legacy of the Rehnquist Court in regard to other equal protection rights will probably be most profound in regard to the *Romer* decision. The Rehnquist Court did not issue any new precedents in regard to such groups as the aged, the poor, or the mentally ill, and it seems reasonable to assume that the future Supreme Court is unlikely to alter this pattern. The *Romer* decision, however, opens the door for future cases involving claimed discrimination based upon sexual orientation, and it seems most likely that the future Supreme Court will be called upon to decide emotionally charged cases involving homosexuality, including the constitutionality of laws prohibiting gay marriage.

The future Court will undoubtedly face the continuing question of the proper level of scrutiny to apply in cases involving homosexuality, and the eventual outcome of this struggle is unclear. Gay rights supporters hope that *Romer* will come to play a role similar to *Reed* in the area of gender discrimination, that is, establishing the rational basis test but setting the stage for the eventual introduction of a higher level of scrutiny. The key question in this issue seems to be whether homosexuality is genetic in nature, and public attitudes on this will be strongly affected both by developments in science as well as in popular culture. Regardless of the outcome, this will certainly be one of the major battlefields in the ongoing culture war.

Privacy and Abortion

The culture war is at its zenith in regard to the closely related topics of privacy and abortion, and the Rehnquist Court has outraged conservatives by its liberal rulings, which not only supported the abortion decision of *Roe v. Wade* but also brought homosexual conduct under the protection of the Fourteenth Amendment in *Lawrence v. Texas* (2003). Thus, we can conclude that the Rehnquist Court certainly did not engage in a conservative counterrevolution in regard to privacy and abortion but instead created a major new liberal precedent.

Both the quantitative and qualitative analyses supported the argument that the Rehnquist Court did not move the Court sharply to the right in the area of abortion. The Warren Court heard no abortion cases, although it did establish the right to privacy in the 1965 *Griswold* case. The Burger Court created the liberal revolution in its landmark *Roe* decision and eventually established a voting record of 50 percent liberal in twenty-four abortion cases. The Rehnquist Court has been slightly more liberal in its abortion jurisprudence, deciding liberally 53 percent of the time in its fifteen abortion-related cases. Despite O'Connor's retirement, the Court still has five justices—Kennedy, Stevens, Souter, Ginsburg, and Breyer—who support *Roe*, although Kennedy has generally supported government regulation of abortion. The key abortion case during the Rehnquist Court era was the 1992 *Planned Parenthood of Southeastern Pennsylvania v. Casey* decision. Kennedy was ready to join Rehnquist, Scalia, Thomas, and White in overturning *Roe*, but he changed his mind and joined O'Connor and Souter in a joint opinion upholding *Roe* but in a modified form that introduced the undue burden standard. Under this new standard, if the government regulation does not present an undue burden to a woman seeking an abortion, then the government only needs to meet minimal scrutiny standards. If, however, an undue burden is found, then the government must meet the much tougher standards of the strict scrutiny test. The Court used this test in the 2000 *Stenberg* case to strike down a Nebraska law prohibiting partial-birth abortions. Thus, the Rehnquist Court maintained the core of the 1973 *Roe* decision against substantial pressure to overturn it, and we can conclude that the Rehnquist Court provided a conservative modification to *Roe* but did not engage in a conservative counterrevolution.

The Rehnquist Court handed down several major privacy cases in addition to those dealing with abortion, including a major, new liberal precedent regarding homosexuals. In *Lawrence v. Texas* (2003), the Rehnquist Court explicitly overturned the 1986 Burger Court precedent of *Bowers v. Hardwick*, ruling unconstitutional by a 6–3 vote a Texas law that criminalized homosexual conduct because such activity is protected by the liberty guarantee of the Fourteenth Amendment Due Process Clause. This was a remarkable decision that revealed dramatically changing views regarding the acceptance of homosexuality, and it also added fuel to the fire of the culture war. The Rehnquist Court ruled conservatively in two other important privacy cases, one involving the standards needed to be met to halt life-sustaining procedures for the critically ill and the other upholding a law against physician–assisted suicide. Although both of these decisions were conservative, they did not involve the overturning of existing liberal precedent.

The legacy of the Rehnquist Court is likely to be greater in regard to privacy and abortion than in any other area of the law. In examining the impact of the Rehnquist Court thus far, we have generally seen that the Rehnquist Court followed the precedents of the earlier Warren and Burger Courts, and thus the legacy of the Rehnquist Court per se seems to be modest. In the area of privacy and abortion, however, the Rehnquist Court has clearly placed its own unique mark on constitutional law that will strongly shape the decision making of the future Supreme Court.

In the area of abortion, the undue burden standard set forth in the Rehnquist Court's *Casey* decision will be the key controlling precedent for the future Court. Efforts will undoubtedly be made to overturn both *Roe* and *Casey*, but at this point these precedents seem secure because only Scalia and Thomas oppose them. Even if

Roberts and Alito oppose *Roe*, the opponents still lack a majority. This will undoubt-edly remain a highly contentious area of constitutional law, and the future Court will probably allow greater room for abortion restrictions and regulations than existed under the original *Roe* decision.

The future Supreme Court is also likely to be strongly affected by the Rehnquist Court's other privacy decisions. The 2003 *Lawrence* case may be the foundation for numerous cases involving claimed unconstitutional invasions of privacy by homosex-uals. The *Lawrence* case must be considered in conjunction with the 1996 *Romer* case, which found a Colorado constitutional amendment to violate the Equal Protection Clause. Thus, attorneys for gay and lesbian persons have two avenues to pursue, pri-vacy and equal protection. It is difficult to predict which area will be pursued most vig-orously, but both avenues will undoubtedly be utilized in what will be one of the future Supreme Court's most contentious topics in the country's ongoing culture war.

Federalism

The Rehnquist Court established an ambiguous record in regard to federalism. Despite conflicting evidence, the Rehnquist Court does not appear to have engaged in a con-servative constitutional counterrevolution. Throughout history, the Supreme Court has fluctuated between two schools of thought on federalism. Dual federalism empha-sizes the limited role of the federal government and the more powerful role of the state governments, whereas cooperative federalism calls for close interactions between the stronger national government and the more subordinate state governments. Coopera-tive federalism was the dominant approach to federalism beginning with the New Deal era and extending through the Warren and Burger Court periods. The Rehnquist Court dramatically changed this to a dual federalism philosophy in a series of decisions in the nineties, but more recent decisions suggest a return to cooperative federalism.

This shift from cooperative to dual federalism in the nineties did not occur imme-diately. A critical development was the replacement of Justice Marshall by Justice Thomas. Thomas strongly supported dual federalism, and his addition to the Court created a five-person bloc consisting of Justices Thomas, Rehnquist, Scalia, Kennedy, and O'Connor. The "federalism five" introduced dual federalism interpretations to three major provisions of the Constitution: the Commerce Clause, the Tenth Amend-ment, and the Eleventh Amendment.

Since the constitutional revolution of 1937, with the "switch in time that saved nine," the Supreme Court has given Congress wide latitude to regulate the states under the Commerce Clause. The Rehnquist Court, however, was willing to draw the line by declaring various acts of Congress invalid because they went beyond the acceptable limits of the Commerce Clause. In *United States v. Lopez* (1995), for example, the

Court overturned the Federal Gun-Free Zones Act, and in *United States v. Morrison* (2000), the Court overruled on Commerce Clause grounds part of the Violence against Women Act passed by Congress.

The dual federalism philosophy also manifested itself in federalism cases involving the Tenth Amendment. The Rehnquist Court used the Tenth Amendment in *New York v. United States* (1992) to rule against provisions of the Low-Level Radioactivity Policy Act. Similarly, in the 1997 *Printz v. United States* case, the conservative coalition ruled unconstitutional under the Tenth Amendment a provision of the 1993 Brady Handgun Violence Protection Act.

Finally, the Rehnquist Court handed down several important decisions that have a dual federalism approach to the Eleventh Amendment. Although this amendment specifically prohibits only the suit against a state by citizens of another state, the Rehnquist Court frequently interpreted this amendment to prohibit a wide range of suits against a state. For example, in *Seminole Tribe of Florida v. Florida*, in 1996, the Court ruled that a Native American tribe could not sue Florida for its refusal to negotiate in good faith over the regulation of gaming. This case explicitly overturned the Rehnquist Court's own 1989 precedent of *Pennsylvania v. Union Gas Company.*

Despite these dual federalism decisions, the Rehnquist Court in more recent federalism cases seemed to back away from dual federalism and to move toward a philosophy of cooperative federalism. In *Tennessee v. Lane* (2004), for example, a majority of the Rehnquist Court justices ruled that states can be sued by handicapped persons in wheelchairs. Two additional major 2005 cases also supported the federal government: *Gonzales v. Raich* and *Granholm v. Heald.*

The legacy of the Rehnquist Court is difficult to predict in regard to the subject of federalism. The future Supreme Court may view itself as bound by a series of precedents involving the Rehnquist Court's dual federalism approach to the Commerce Clause, the Tenth Amendment, and the Eleventh Amendment. These decisions cannot easily be reversed, and they are the creation of the Rehnquist Court. The possibility does exist, however, that the future Supreme Court could challenge or minimize these decisions. The Court has fluctuated over time in its interpretation of federalism, and cooperative federalism could emerge again as the dominant paradigm. Furthermore, the current lineup of dual federalists consists of a bare majority of five justices even assuming that Justices Roberts and Alito support dual federalism, and membership change could significantly alter the existence of the current majority.

Government Powers

Government powers cases do not lend themselves to easy distinctions along liberal and conservative lines, but they constitute an important area of constitutional law during any era of Supreme Court history, including the Rehnquist Court period. We suggested in chapter 3 that an important theme in the Rehnquist Court's government powers cases was the assertion and preservation of its own power within the federal system of government. Thus, when the Court was faced with challenges to its power of judicial review in cases like *City of Boerne v. V. P. F. Flores* (the Free Exercise Clause) and *Dickerson v. United States* (the *Miranda* warnings), the Court did not hesitate to rule unconstitutional these direct challenges to the Court's authority to interpret the Constitution. The Rehnquist Court was also willing to challenge executive branch authority as seen in the 2004 terrorism cases, where the Court rejected the Bush administration's arguments that prisoners captured in the War on Terror were enemy combatants who had no access to the federal courts. The Rehnquist Court also ruled strongly against President Clinton's claim of immunity regarding being sued while in office for private conduct. The legacy of the Rehnquist Court regarding these government powers cases is difficult to assess because the Supreme Court typically hears so few of these types of cases each term. It does seem safe to suggest, however, that the future Supreme Court will follow the pattern of the Rehnquist Court in asserting and preserving the power of the Court in the American political system.

Conclusions

The central question of this study has been whether the Rehnquist Court engaged in a conservative constitutional revolution. The conclusion we have reached is to answer this question negatively. Despite the efforts of Republican Presidents Ronald Reagan and George H. W. Bush, the Rehnquist Court—like its predecessor, the Burger Court—was moderately rather than strongly conservative. In most areas of constitutional law, continuity rather than change characterized the Rehnquist Court's decision making. The Rehnquist Court moved constitutional law in a substantially conservative direction in a few areas, but even in these areas the Court developed policies that were moderately rather than radically conservative. And very importantly, the Rehnquist Court created several major, new liberal precedents that may prove to be the most important legacy of the Rehnquist Court.

In most areas of constitutional law, the Rehnquist Court adhered closely to the precedents established by the Warren and Burger Courts. Continuity, not change, characterized the Rehnquist Court's decision making in regard to freedom of expression; obscenity; the Fourth Amendment, including search and seizure and the exclusionary rule; the Fifth Amendment, including the protections against self-incrimination and double jeopardy; the Eighth Amendment's protection against cruel and unusual punishments involving both capital and noncapital punishments; the Takings Clause;

racial equality; gender equality; other equal protection areas; privacy; federalism; and government powers.

In a few areas, the Rehnquist Court altered existing precedent to move constitutional law in a significantly more conservative direction. The most salient areas are the free exercise of religion and affirmative action. Free exercise jurisprudence was significantly altered in the 1990 *Oregon v. Smith* case, which dramatically undercut the 1963 *Sherbert* test, replacing *Sherbert's* strict scrutiny approach with a minimal scrutiny orientation under *Smith*. In the area of affirmative action, the Rehnquist Court's decisions in *City of Richmond v. J. A. Croson Co.* (1989) and *Adarand Constructors, Inc. v. Pena* (1995) brought affirmative action cases under the Court's toughest standard, the strict scrutiny test.

Even in the areas of the free exercise of religion and affirmative action, however, the Rehnquist Court's record was not radically conservative because subsequent decisions provided liberal interpretations to these new precedents. In regard to the free exercise of religion, the Court in *Church of the Lukumi Babalu Aye v. City of Hialeah* (1993) found the government guilty of infringing the First Amendment rights of a minority religion. And in the 2003 affirmative action case of *Grutter v. Bollinger*, the Rehnquist Court found the University of Michigan Law School's affirmative action admissions program to meet the demands of the strict scrutiny test.

Four other areas can be identified in which the Rehnquist Court appeared to be on the verge of radical change but did not go that far. These areas are the Establishment Clause, the Takings Clause, abortion, and federalism. In regard to the Establishment Clause, the Rehnquist Court seemed poised to reject the liberal neutrality approach and the *Lemon* test, but that did not occur. Despite two Rehnquist Court cases—*Agostini v. Felton* (1997) and *Mitchell v. Helms* (2000)—that overturned previous Establishment Clause cases, the Rehnquist Court justices did not reach a majority consensus on how to interpret the Establishment Clause, as seen vividly in the 2005 Ten Commandments cases in which a badly fragmented Court allowed one display but found the other display to be unconstitutional.

The Rehnquist Court's Takings Clause jurisprudence initially promised to alter radically existing precedents that strongly favored the government, but a series of 2005 cases found a majority of the Rehnquist Court justices willing to support governmental efforts to use the power of eminent domain. The three key cases in 2005 were *Kelo v. City of New London, Lingle v. Chevron,* and *San Remo Hotel v. City and County of San Francisco.*

The Rehnquist Court's federalism cases exhibited a similar pattern to the Takings Clause decisions. When Thomas replaced Marshall, it appeared that Thomas would be part of a majority bloc with Rehnquist, Scalia, O'Connor, and Kennedy that would embrace a dual federalism that placed great emphasis on states' rights and sovereignty.

However, a series of cases—*Tennessee v. Lane* (2004), *Gonzales v. Raich* (2005), and *Granholm v. Heald* (2005)—favored the national government and brought into question the Rehnquist Court's commitment to dual federalism.

Abortion is the final area in which the Rehnquist Court appeared to be on the verge of radical change but did not go that far. In *Planned Parenthood of Southeastern Pennsylvania v. Casey* (1992), the Rehnquist Court was asked to overturn *Roe v. Wade* (1973). The Court refused to do this, although *Roe* was modified by introducing the undue burden standard, which provides for strict scrutiny only if the government regulations place an undue burden on the woman. This was a significant modification of the original *Roe* formulation, but O'Connor, Kennedy, and Souter emphasized in their controlling opinion that the essence of *Roe* remained intact.

Perhaps the most unexpected development during the Rehnquist Court era was the new liberal precedents that were introduced. Numerous cases can be cited. In *Romer v. Evans* (1996), the Rehnquist Court for the first time in the Court's history ruled a government policy unconstitutional under the Equal Protection Clause because it violated the rights of homosexuals. In another major case involving homosexuals, the Rehnquist Court in *Lawrence v. Texas* (2003) explicitly overturned the 1986 case of *Bowers v. Hardwick* in ruling unconstitutional a Texas law that criminalized homosexual activity.

In the area of the rights of the criminally accused, the Rehnquist Court introduced two new liberal precedents involving the Sixth Amendment. In *Ring v. Arizona* (2002), the Rehnquist Court justices overruled one of their own precedents, *Walton v. Arizona* (1990), ruling that only juries and not judges can determine the facts that would constitute the presence of an aggravating factor in death penalty cases. In *Crawford v. Washington* (2004), the Rehnquist Court overturned the 1980 case of *Ohio v. Roberts*, establishing the principle that an accused has the right to confront a hostile witness in the courtroom instead of allowing clearly reliable hearsay testimony to be introduced without the presence of the witness.

The Rehnquist Court also decided two major capital punishment cases that overturned their own decisions. In *Atkins v. Virginia* (2002), the Court ruled that it is unconstitutional to execute the mentally retarded, thus overturning the 1989 precedent of *Penry v. Lynaugh*. Similarly, a majority of the Rehnquist Court justices in the 2005 case of *Roper v. Simmons* prohibited the execution of persons who commit murder at sixteen or seventeen years of age, thus overturning the 1989 decision of *Stanford v. Kentucky*.

Several factors can be identified in an attempt to explain why the Rehnquist Court established a record that is characterized as moderately rather than radically conservative. Justice Souter's shift from a moderate conservative to a moderate liberal was certainly a key development. Justice O'Connor also played a major role in the Court's direction with her emergence as the key swing vote on a closely divided Court.

Similarly, but to a somewhat lesser extent, Justice Kennedy was also a moderating influence on the Court. Yet another critical personnel issue was President Clinton's opportunity to appoint two moderately liberal justices, Ginsburg and Breyer, with Ginsburg's appointment being especially critical because she replaced the conservative White.

Several additional factors can also be suggested. The Supreme Court has historically been in line with the views of the American public, and public opinion during the Rehnquist Court era favored moderate policies regarding the contentious issues facing the Court. In addition, the justices of the Rehnquist Court, like previous Supreme Court justices, took seriously the principle of *stare decisis*, thus reducing the overturning of existing precedent. It may also be that the Rehnquist Court felt the need to rein in conservative lower-court judges who were willing to engage in radical change in constitutional law.

We can thus conclude that the Rehnquist Court did not engage in a conservative constitutional counterrevolution. The battles of the culture war continue to rage, however, and the Supreme Court will undoubtedly be involved in these battles. This is a good thing. Throughout U.S. history, the Supreme Court has served the American people well, and the era of the Rehnquist Court is an important part of that proud tradition.

PART TWO

Reference Materials

Key People, Laws, and Events

School District of Abington Township v. Schempp, 374 U.S. 203 (1963)

In this case, the Warren Court considered the practice of reading Bible verses and reciting the Lord's Prayer as opening exercises for the public school day against a challenge that this practice violated the First Amendment prohibition against government establishment of religion. The case involved a 1959 Pennsylvania law that required "at least ten verses from the Holy Bible" to be read without comment. The opening exercises also included a reading of the Lord's Prayer, in which students stood and recited the prayer in unison. Students were allowed to opt out of the exercises with parental permission. Schempp brought the case on behalf of his children. Schempp argued that student participation was effectively compulsory, given the compulsory nature of public school attendance and concerns about ostracism if an exception were made.

In an 8–1 decision, the Court found that compulsory reading of Bible verses and of the Lord's Prayer were in violation of the Establishment Clause of the First Amendment. In determining whether the government actions were permissible, the Court established a two-prong standard for evaluation. First, the activity had to advance a secular legislative purpose; second, the activity could neither advance nor inhibit religion. The Court found that the practices in *Schempp* amounted to a state-sanctioned religious ceremony and breached the "wholesome neutrality" that was to guide the government in all matters pertaining to religious freedoms. The *Schempp* standard established the foundation for later Court analysis of Establishment Clause issues, including the *Lemon* test.

Affirmative Action Plans

An affirmative action plan is a documented system of policies, procedures, and programs intended to overcome the effects of past discrimination against members of minority groups. The term has its genesis in Executive Order 11246, signed by President Lyndon B. Johnson in 1965. Initially a concept applied to federal contracts, affirmative action was viewed as necessary to overcome many established employment practices such as seniority systems and aptitude tests that acted as barriers to equal employment opportunity for minorities. Affirmative action compliance for federal contracts is monitored through the Office of Federal Contract Compliance (OFCC). Affirmative action plans (AAPs) strive to achieve minority representation in the workforce that reflects the minority composition of the population from which the workforce is drawn. AAPs take many forms, and they typically include goals and timetables against which hiring, promotion, and other employment activities are assessed.

Affirmative action has extended to state and local governments, graduate and professional schools, and across the private sector. Attitudes on preferential treatment for minorities remain divided, however. Some remain committed to the principle that affirmative action is needed to remedy past discriminatory practices. A growing contingency argues that affirmative action is itself a racial preference prohibited by the Fourteenth Amendment and that affirmative action more accurately constitutes reverse discrimination against nonminorities. This sentiment found expression in the 1996 adoption by California voters of Proposition 209. This referendum banned the use of racial or gender preferences in public hiring, contracting, and education.

American Civil Liberties Union

The American Civil Liberties Union (ACLU) is a nonprofit organization that seeks to support persons who think that their rights have been violated. The ACLU began in 1920 with a focus on First Amendment issues, but the organization has grown significantly both in terms of covering all civil rights and liberties issues and in terms of organizational size. The ACLU currently has a national office in Washington, D.C., and affiliate chapters in all fifty states. Although the ACLU employs a few staff attorneys, most affiliates operate with private attorneys who provide "pro bono," or free, services.

The ACLU has been at the forefront of civil rights and liberties cases since its beginning. The organization not only files amicus briefs but also on occasion becomes a direct party in a suit. The ACLU is involved in more than 5,000 cases each year, and it files briefs in as many as 30 U.S. Supreme Court cases a year.

The ACLU is certainly a controversial organization. For example, the ACLU became a focal point in the 1988 presidential election, with Michael Dukakis declaring himself a "card-carrying member of the ACLU," a position that George H. W. Bush used effectively against Dukakis. The organization officially maintains a position of political neutrality, but conservative groups reject this argument because of the ACLU's frequent support of liberal causes.

Americans with Disabilities Act of 1990

The Americans with Disabilities Act of 1990 protects disabled people from discrimination by private employers. It also requires that public buildings and transportation be made accessible to disabled individuals and that telephone communications systems provide technological interface mechanisms to allow those with speech or hearing impediments to place and receive telephone calls. The ADA is arguably the most sweeping federal legislation to impact places of public accommodation and the private workplace since the Civil Rights Act of 1964; litigation prompted by the ADA continues to grow, and major questions are far from resolved.

Under the ADA, the notion of a disability is broadly defined as any condition that substantially impacts a major life activity. Upon demonstration of a disability, private employers must make reasonable accommodations for employees and may not discriminate in hiring or other employment practices with respect to a disability. Changes in job assignments, hours of work, and special ergonomic equipment have all been considered to be reasonable accommodations under the ADA. This deliberately sweeping approach to disability has prompted waves of litigation regarding specific conditions not included under previous statutes concerning the disabled, such as alcohol and chemical dependencies and some mental conditions. The public access requirements have spurred considerable modification of public and private buildings across the country, including immediately apparent changes in restrooms and sidewalks.

The ADA is the third major piece of federal legislation passed to assist those with disabilities. The Rehabilitation Act of 1973 prohibits unfair treatment of the disabled in federally funded programs and activities, and the act imposes hiring requirements on federally funded businesses. The Education for All Handicapped Children Act of 1975 requires the states to provide free education for school-aged children regardless of disability

Baker v. Carr, 369 U.S. 186 (1962)

This landmark decision of the Warren Court established the jurisdiction of federal courts over the legality of state apportionment schemes. The case was brought by Tennessee residents of urban areas, who claimed that the distribution of state legislative representation violated the Equal Protection Clause of the Fourteenth Amendment. Baker and others claimed that the state population had shifted significantly from rural to urban areas since the last apportionment, in 1901. They sought to compel state reapportionment, claiming that the inequitable distribution of legislative representation constituted discriminatory state action against urban residents.

Initially, federal jurisdiction was denied. However, the 7–2 opinion authored by Justice Brennan held that this question was properly within the purview of federal courts under the Fourteenth Amendment. This decision reversed earlier opinions of the Court that had held that redistricting and reapportionment were "political questions." The denomination of activities as "political questions" had effectively removed certain decisions from judicial scrutiny. *Baker v. Carr* represented significant retreat from the political questions doctrine established with Chief Justice Marshall's decision in *Martin v. Mott* (1827) and his interpretation of federalism and the separation of powers.

In *Baker v. Carr*, the Court held that Tennessee's failure to reapportion state legislative districts diluted the voting rights of its citizens in violation of the Equal Protection Clause. *Baker v. Carr* opened the door for subsequent Court rulings, which established the "one person, one vote" principle. This concept requires that all congressional districts be "substantially equal." This notion has been extended to state legislative districts and to local government districts as well.

Bork, Robert Heron

Born March 1, 1927, in Pittsburgh, Pennsylvania, Robert Heron Bork received a bachelor's degree from the University of Chicago in 1948. He received his law degree from the University of Chicago in 1953 and served two tours in the U.S. Marine Corps before returning to Chicago to specialize in antitrust law with a large firm. Bork joined the faculty at Yale University teaching antitrust and constitutional law in 1962.

At Yale, Bork's conservative scholarship reflected the free market philosophy of the Chicago school and drew political attention as well. Bork was appointed by President Richard M. Nixon to the position of solicitor general in 1973. On Nixon's order, Bork fired special prosecutor Archibald Cox at the height of the Watergate investigation into the Nixon administration, in what became known as the "Saturday Night Massacre." After returning to Yale in 1977, Bork joined private practice in 1981 and was then appointed in 1982 by President Ronald Reagan to the U.S. Court of Appeals, District of Columbia Circuit.

Reagan nominated Bork to replace retiring justice Lewis F. Powell Jr. in 1987. Bork's history of conservative scholarship included his published criticism of many Supreme Court decisions and doctrines. Among the legal interpretations that Bork strongly criticized were the right of privacy in *Griswold v. Connecticut* (1965) and its progeny, *Roe v. Wade* (1973). Bork also criticized many Warren Court decisions, including the principle of "one person, one vote," and he supported the reintroduction of prayer into the public schools.

Bork's confirmation hearing was contentious, reflecting a deep national divide on civil rights and civil liberties issues. Bork's nomination was opposed by a broad coalition, including the National Association for the Advancement of Colored People (NAACP), Common Cause, People for the American Way, the National Organization of

Women (NOW), the National Abortion Rights Action League (NARAL), and the American Civil Liberties Union (ACLU). Similarly, his nomination was praised by conservative religious leaders such as the Reverend Jerry Falwell and Pat Robertson. The Senate Judiciary Committee rejected Bork's nomination by a vote of 9–5; the full Senate rejected Bork's nomination to the Supreme Court by a margin of 58–42.

Brandenburg v. Ohio, 395 U.S. 444 (1969)

In this landmark case, the Warren Court upheld the rights of the Ku Klux Klan (KKK) to advocate for its goal of white supremacy. As the leader of a southern Ohio affiliate of the Klan, Clarence Brandenburg invited news reporters and camera crews to a rally to gain publicity for KKK views. Film of the rally showed hooded figures gathered around a burning cross, with several holding weapons. Brandenburg stated that if government officials did not respond to the concerns of the Klan that they might have to take matters into their own hands. He was subsequently charged with violating the Ohio Criminal Syndicalism Act, which was passed in 1919 to prevent the spread of unpatriotic views. Similar to other antisedition statutes adopted in that era, the Ohio statute was broadly drawn to prohibit acts of advocacy and voluntary assembly for the purposes of teaching or advocating the doctrine of "criminal syndicalism."

In 1927, the Court upheld a California statute with similar language in *Whitney v. California,* 274 U.S. 357. However, intervening decisions established the principle that state proscription on free expression could not prohibit advocacy of the use of force, or of violating the law, except when the expression was likely to result in such action. The *Brandenburg* decision was issued *per curiam* and overruled *Whitney,* holding that the Ohio Criminal Syndicalism Act violated the First and Fourteenth Amendments' free expression guarantees. The Court held that "mere advocacy" and "assembly with others merely to advocate" are protected forms of expression within the meaning of the First Amendment. Subversive or seditious speech could not be restrained unless the speech was a direct incitement to imminent lawless action. This standard of review thus replaced the "clear and present danger" test, which had been the Court's guidepost since the 1919 decision in *Schenck.*

Brown v. Board of Education of Topeka, Kansas, 347 U.S. 483 (1954)

In this unanimous ruling of the Warren Court authored by Chief Justice Earl Warren, the Court held that racially segregated public schools violated the Equal Protection Clause of the Fourteenth Amendment. This case overturned the historic doctrine of "separate but equal" established in *Plessy v. Ferguson* (1896), as separate educational facilities for blacks and whites were declared "inherently unequal." *Brown* thus declared *de jure* racial segregation, or the segregation of races by law, to be illegal. This ruling was interpreted to prohibit segregation in other public facilities as well, and it fostered the integration of hotels, transportation systems, stores, and recreational facilities.

Brown was brought by the National Association for the Advancement of Colored People (NAACP) on behalf of Linda Brown, who was denied permission to attend an all-white elementary school near her home. The chief counsel for the NAACP was Thurgood Marshall, who later was appointed by President Lyndon B. Johnson to become the first African American justice on the Supreme Court.

The *Brown* decision (*Brown I*) was amplified by the Court the following year in *Brown v. Board of Education of Topeka, Kansas* (*Brown II*) (1955); *Brown II* held that desegregation must proceed with "all deliberate speed." *Brown I* and *Brown II* were vigorously opposed in southern states, to the extent that progress toward integration in the public schools was essentially nonexistent for more than a decade. Many states took the position that state law superseded federal law on segregation matters and enacted statutes of "interposition" and "nullification."

Burger, Warren Earl

Warren Earl Burger (1905–1995) was the fifteenth chief justice of the U.S. Supreme Court. Burger was born on September 17, 1905, in St. Paul, Minnesota, and graduated from the University of Minnesota and the St. Paul College of Law. For more than twenty years, Burger was in private practice in St. Paul, in both civil and criminal law. He also participated actively in Republican politics.

Burger entered government practice in 1953 as an assistant attorney general in charge of the civil division of the U.S. Department of Justice. In 1956, Burger was appointed by President Dwight D. Eisenhower to the U.S. Court of Appeals for the District of Columbia. After establishing an extensive record as a conservative jurist, Burger was tapped by President Richard M. Nixon to succeed Earl Warren as chief justice of the U.S. Supreme Court. The Court under Burger's leadership evolved into a far more conservative Court than its predecessor, under Earl Warren. However, the Burger Court was highly divided between liberal and conservative views on many issues.

Notable Burger Court decisions included cases involving free speech arising from criticism of the Vietnam War (the *Pentagon Papers* case) and the exercise of executive privilege by then president Nixon during the Watergate scandal, which led to Nixon's resignation from office. The Burger Court determined that abortion was legal and that existing death penalty laws in 1972 constituted cruel and unusual punishment, leading to sweeping reform in state capital punishment statutes. Warren Burger resigned in 1986 and was replaced by Chief Justice William H. Rehnquist.

Bush, George Herbert Walker

The forty-first president of the United States, George Bush was born on June 12, 1924, in Milton, Massachusetts. Bush served in World War II as a carrier pilot, and he graduated from Yale University in 1948 with a degree in economics. He moved to Texas and prospered in the oil business before pursuing a career in Republican politics.

Initially unsuccessful in the 1964 campaign for U.S. Senate, Bush was elected from Texas to the U.S. House of Representatives in 1966. After a second unsuccessful Senate bid in 1968, he was appointed as ambassador to the United Nations by President Richard M. Nixon. Bush went on to serve in a series of administrative appointments, including chairman of the Republican National Committee, chief liaison officer in Beijing, and director of the Central Intelligence Agency. He lost the Republican presidential nomination in 1980 to Ronald Reagan and became his running mate; Bush became vice-president in 1981.

Bush won reelection with Reagan in 1984 and won the Republican nomination for the presidency in 1988. Bush won the election against the Democratic candidate, Massachusetts Governor Michael Dukakis. Bush lost his bid for reelection as president to Bill Clinton in 1992.

During his presidency, Bush was active and popular for his handling of foreign policy matters. His appointments to the Supreme Court include current justices David H. Souter in 1990 and Clarence Thomas in 1991. Souter was confirmed by the Senate in a 90–9 vote and replaced retiring liberal Democrat William J. Brennan. Thomas, an African American, was nominated to replace retiring justice Thurgood Marshall, the first African American justice on the Supreme Court. Thomas was finally confirmed with a 52–48 vote, after a confirmation process that was bitterly partisan and divisive, during which Thomas was accused of sexual harassment by lawyer Anita Hill. These appointments continued the conservative tradition of appointments by former president Ronald Reagan.

Central Hudson Gas v. Public Service Commission, 447 U.S. 557 (1980)

In this case dealing with the parameters of commercial speech, the Court found that state regulations that completely ban an electric utility from advertising to promote the use of electricity violated the First and Fourteenth Amendments. In December 1973, the New York Public Service Commission (NYPSC) ordered electric utilities to cease all advertising that "promotes the use of electricity." The order was based on an NYPSC finding that the utility system in New York did not have sufficient fuel stock to meet all customer demands for the 1973–1974 winter, in the face of a worldwide oil crisis.

The Burger Court held that, although the Constitution affords lesser protection to commercial speech than to other forms of expression, the First Amendment still provided protection against unwarranted government regulation. The Court had previously given only minimal protection to commercial speech, but in *Hudson* they elevated it to intermediate scrutiny. In *Hudson*, the Court established a four-step test for evaluating commercial speech falling within the ambit of First Amendment protection. First, commercial speech must concern lawful activity and must not be misleading. Second, the government interest advanced as the rationale for regulation must be substantial. Third, the state regulation must directly advance the claimed interest. Finally, the regulation must not be more extensive than necessary to serve that substantial state interest.

In *Hudson*, the NYPSC argued that the regulation was necessary to enforce the necessary degree of energy conservation, as advertising would encourage consumption in "off-peak" periods, which, if successful, would ultimately result in increases in overall usage. In applying the four-step test, the Court found that, although the state interest in energy conservation was substantial, complete suppression as called for under the regulation was not appropriate. The Central Hudson advertisements dealt with lawful activity and were not misleading. The regulation was not sufficiently related to the stated objective, as advertising could be employed to reduce consumption. Further, the NYPSC did not show that less-restrictive means could have been employed to accomplish what were acknowledged to be legitimate state objectives.

Chaplinsky v. New Hampshire, 315 U.S. 568 (1942)

In this case, the Court held that the state could lawfully punish an individual for the use of "fighting words" without violating federal law. Chaplinsky, a member of the Jehovah's Witness sect, was convicted for violating a state statute that prohibited the public address of another with offensive, derisive, or annoying words. Chaplinsky was distributing literature on the streets of Rochester on a busy Saturday afternoon. In response to citizen complaints against his activity, Chaplinsky was under forcible escort to the city police station when he encountered the city marshall and, in argument, denounced the marshall as "a God damned racketeer" and "a damned fascist." For those words, Chaplinsky was arrested under the ordinance.

Chaplinsky argued that the fact that speech was likely to cause violence was not grounds for suppression. The state argued that its legislative purpose was to preserve pubic order, and the state court found that the statute was specifically directed at "fighting words," which ordinary persons know are likely to cause a fight. In a unanimous decision, the Court upheld the state court's conclusions. The Court held that state police power included the ability to prohibit the use in a public place of words likely to cause a breach of the peace. The Court also established the broader principle that some forms of speech—fighting words, the libelous, the obscene, and the profane—were so lacking in social value that they were beyond the protection of the First Amendment.

Civil Rights Act of 1964

This landmark federal civil rights legislation bans discrimination on the basis of a person's color, race, national origin, religion, or sex. First proposed by President John F. Kennedy in 1963, the Civil Rights Act passed in 1964 with the strong support of President Lyndon B. Johnson after Kennedy's assassination in 1963.

The Civil Rights Act protects the right to seek employment, to vote, and to use hotels, parks, restaurants, and other places of public accommodation. The Civil Rights Act also prohibits discrimination by any program that receives federal funds; violations carry a potential penalty of debarment from federal contracts. The act effectively required public facilities to open their doors to African Americans, who had been systematically excluded on the basis of race and color.

In the landmark case of *Heart of Atlanta Motel v. United States* (1964), discussed later in this section, the act was upheld as constitutional. The owner of the Heart of Atlanta Motel contended that the operation of a hotel was a matter of "local" character and thus outside the purview of the antidiscrimination provisions of the act. The facts of the case, however, disclosed that the majority of customers at this hotel were from outside the state of Georgia. The United States relied on the Commerce Clause in making its case in support of African Americans and others denied by the Heart of Atlanta Motel. The government successfully argued that the unavailability of public accommodations interfered with the right to travel throughout the fifty states, which was protected by the Commerce Clause.

Enforcement of the Civil Rights Act is carried out by the Equal Employment Opportunity Commission (EEOC) and the Department of Justice. The EEOC investigates complaints of employment discrimination, and the Department of Justice handles other potential cases.

Clinton, William Jefferson

William Jefferson Clinton served two terms as the forty-second president of the United States (1993–2001). He was born on August 19, 1946, in Hope, Arkansas. He graduated from Georgetown University with a major in international affairs. He received a Rhodes Scholarship to the University of Oxford in England, and in 1970 he entered Yale University Law School. While at Yale, he met his wife, Hillary Diane Rodham.

After graduation in 1973, Clinton returned to Arkansas, where he taught at the University of Arkansas Law School. He first ran for office in 1974 and lost a race for a congressional seat. He was successful in the 1976 race for Arkansas attorney general, and he ran successfully for governor in 1978. Clinton lost his bid for reelection but returned as the winner in 1982, and he went on to serve a total of five terms as governor of Arkansas. With Tennessee Senator Al Gore as his vice-presidential running mate, Clinton was elected president in 1992 in a successful campaign against incumbent George H. W. Bush.

Clinton's terms as president were controversial. They were marked by innovation in social policy, including an unsuccessful attempt to provide universal access to health care and a successful initiative to reform the federal welfare system. Clinton also championed free trade in an increasingly global market environment, and he was heralded for success in foreign affairs initiatives. Clinton appointed more women and minorities to department-head and cabinet-level posts than any other president, including the appointment of the first woman, Janet Reno, as attorney general. Clinton also appointed two associate justices to the Supreme Court: Ruth Bader Ginsburg, to replace Byron R. White, and Stephen Breyer, to replace Harry Blackmun.

Throughout his presidency, Clinton was dogged by damaging accusations about his personal life. A liaison with a White House intern, Monica Lewinsky, resulted in the institution of impeachment proceedings against him. Although the House of Representatives voted out several articles of impeachment, the Senate did not vote to convict or to otherwise sanction him, and Clinton remained in office to finish his term.

Colorado Amendment 2

This amendment to the Colorado state constitution sought to prohibit the state and its subdivisions from "adopting or enforcing any law or policy which provides that homosexual, lesbian, or bisexual orientation, conduct or relationship constitutes or entitles a person to claim any minority or protected status, quota, preferences, or discrimination." This amendment sought to abolish city ordinances that banned discrimination on the basis of sexual orientation in the areas of employment, welfare, housing, public accommodation, education, and health services. Several cities, including Denver, Boulder, and Aspen, adopted such ordinances.

Placed on the statewide ballot for the November 4, 1992, election, the amendment was sponsored by conservative religious groups under the banner of "Colorado for Family Values." The campaign position of Colorado for Family Values was elemental: special rights could not be based upon sexual orientation. This approach proved to be stunningly successful. Voters approved Amendment 2 by a 53–47 percent margin, remarkable in a state in which polling data suggested that equal rights for gays were favored by approximately 70 percent of residents.

The adoption of Amendment 2 led to a legal challenge by Colorado and cities that had adopted nondiscrimination ordinances. The trial court and Colorado Supreme Court struck down the ordinance. On appeal, the Supreme Court also found Amendment 2 to be invalid in a 6–3 decision in *Romer v. Evans* (1996). In striking down Amendment 2, the *Romer* decision marked the first time that the Court employed the Equal Protection Clause in support of equal rights on the basis of sexual preference.

Communications Decency Act of 1996

The Communications Decency Act of 1996 (CDA) demonstrates the tension between freedom of speech and federal attempts to protect minors from harmful sexual material on the Internet, an international network of connected computers in which millions of people communicate and assess information. Title 47, USCA Section 223(a), criminalized the "knowing" transmission of "obscene or indecent" messages to anyone under eighteen years of age. Section 223(d) of the CDA prohibited "knowing sending or display to minors of any message that is patently offensive as measured by contemporary community standards in the depiction of sexual or excretory activities or organs."

Both of these provisions were successfully challenged in *Reno v. American Civil Liberties Union* (1997) by the American Civil Liberties Union (ACLU) as overbroad restrictions on speech under the First Amendment. Applying the strict scrutiny standard to the Internet, the Supreme Court recognized the legitimacy and importance of the congressional goal of protecting children from harmful material. The Court, however, found the legislative support for these two provisions to be less than persuasive when measured against the extensive congressional hearing record and research supporting the Telecommunications Act of 1996, which encourages the broadest access possible to the Internet. The provisions challenged in this case were added as Senate floor amendments, and the ACLU filed suit immediately upon the signing of the bill into law by President Clinton.

In holding in *Reno* that these provisions of the CDA were too vague to meet constitutional standards, the Supreme Court refused to extend doctrine from a long line of cases, including *Ginsberg v. New York* (1968), *F.C.C. v. Pacifica Foundation* (1978), and *Renton v. Playtime Theatres, Inc.* (1986). The Court cited the chilling effect of criminal standards and the lack of internal consistency in the language of the statute. Further, any application of contemporary community standards was essentially meaningless in a global medium. Protection of children was an important objective but could not be accomplished under the First Amendment through unnecessarily broad suppression of adult speech.

Exclusionary Rule

The exclusionary rule is a rule of evidence that prohibits the use of items obtained from a search or seizure by law enforcement officials in violation of the Fourth

Amendment protection against unreasonable and warrantless searches and seizures. Under the exclusionary rule, evidence so obtained must be excluded. This rule is not explicitly stated in the Fourth Amendment or elsewhere in the Constitution; it has evolved as a matter of judicial construction. The exclusionary rule was first established in 1914 in the case of *Weeks v. United States*. In *Weeks*, the Supreme Court held that the Fourth Amendment had no real meaning without this restriction of evidence obtained in violation of its protective language. The rule was not viewed as critical enough to be applied to state practices, however, until 1961, in the case of *Mapp v. Ohio*.

The exclusionary rule remains controversial today. Proponents argue that it creates incentives for police to adhere strictly to guidelines that protect individual liberties and to refrain from abuse or misconduct during the search process. Critics respond that application of the rule often results in criminal conduct going unpunished and that frequently reliable evidence is suppressed simply because it was obtained in violation of a judicial rule. Opposition to the rule and the sometime perverse consequences of its application have fostered many exceptions that continue today. Notable exceptions include use of tainted evidence when its discovery was inevitable, use of tainted evidence in grand jury proceedings and for impeachment of criminal defendants who take the stand at trial, and use if based upon good faith reliance upon a warrant later determined to be defective, although apparently properly issued by a neutral magistrate.

Executive Order 11246

Signed into law by President Lyndon B. Johnson in 1965, Executive Order (EO) 11246 imposes affirmative action obligations on federal government contractors. Under EO 11246, a government contractor or subcontractor regardless of tier, with a contract or subcontract in excess of $10,000, must not discriminate against any employee or applicant because of race, color, religion, sex, or national origin. Such a contractor or subcontractor must also take affirmative action to ensure that applicants and employees are treated without regard to race, color, religion, sex, or national origin in employment matters. If a contractor or subcontractor has fifty or more employees, and has a contract of $50,000 or more, it must also develop and keep on file at each business establishment a written affirmative action plan (AAP). The AAP details specific measures that the contractor must take to guarantee equal employment opportunity by addressing specific problems or needs of members of minority groups and women.

Together with the Civil Rights Act of 1964, Executive Order 11246 marked the beginning of government imposition of a wide range of socioeconomic obligations on federal contractors as a key method of motivating compliance with antidiscrimination policies and furtherance of affirmative action objectives.

Furman v. Georgia, 408 U.S. 238 (1972)

In this landmark case, the Burger Court held that the imposition and execution of the death penalty constituted cruel and unusual punishment in violation of the Eighth Amendment and the Fourteenth Amendment, in the circumstances set forth in three specific cases. In *Furman*, the Court consolidated three cases in which the death penalty had been imposed by juries under Georgia state law, one for murder and two for rape; each of the defendants was African American. The Court issued a one-paragraph *per curiam* opinion setting forth its 5–4 decision. Justices Douglas, Brennan, Marshall, Stewart, and White voted in the majority, and Justices Blackmun, Powell, and Rehnquist joined Chief Justice Burger in dissenting. Each justice wrote a separate opinion.

Prior to *Furman*, every state that authorized capital punishment had abandoned a mandatory death penalty and instead permitted juries to impose the death penalty without guidance from the judge or other statutory restriction. Although such discretionary sentencing had not been declared per se unconstitutional by the Court at the time of the *Furman* ruling, the opinions expressed within the *per curiam* decision led to a nearly immediate restructuring of state capital punishment statutes and practices. At issue were the notions of due process, equal protection, and the very real likelihood of inequitable application of capital punishment against the poor and minorities. Many states adopted mandatory death penalty statutes for specific crimes. The large majority of states attempted to provide specific "aggravating circumstances" that had to be proved as separate criminal elements to trigger the death penalty. Some states bifurcated the sentencing process from the adjudication of guilt and provided juries with specific sets of instructions to follow in imposing sentence; still others restricted the imposition of a capital sentence to judges.

The Burger Court resolved many of these uncertainties in *Gregg v. Georgia* (1976). In this case, the Court gave approval to a two-stage process in capital cases, with the first trial to determine guilt or innocence and, if guilty, a second sentencing hearing.

Gideon v. Wainwright, 372 U.S. 335 (1963)

In this landmark decision, the Supreme Court addressed the rights of indigent criminal defendants to appointed counsel in state proceedings. Here, defendant Gideon was charged with a noncapital felony by the state of Florida. Gideon's request for appointed counsel was denied on the basis that Florida law only appointed counsel for indigent defendants in capital cases. After representing himself, Gideon appealed his conviction on the basis that the Sixth Amendment guarantee to counsel and principles of a fair trial should extend to state proceedings in felony cases.

In an opinion authored by Justice Hugo Black, the Court held that the right of indigent defendants in a criminal trial to have assistance of counsel is a fundamental right essential to a fair trial. Gideon's conviction was therefore in violation of the Sixth and Fourteenth Amendments. Notably, the Court's ruling was limited to felony cases and did not extend to misdemeanors. In *Gideon*, the Court overruled the decision it handed down just twenty-one years earlier in *Betts v. Brady* (1942). In *Betts*, the Court had addressed essentially the same issues and had ruled that the Sixth Amendment guarantee of appointed counsel for indigent defendants did not extend to state court proceedings by way of the Fourteenth Amendment. In the *Gideon* decision, the Court expressly rejected the reasoning of *Betts* as an "anachronism when handed down."

Ginsburg, Douglas Howard

A federal circuit judge for the District of Columbia Circuit, Douglas Howard Ginsburg was nominated by President Ronald Reagan to the U.S. Supreme Court in 1987. Ginsburg's nomination was unsuccessful because of extensive publicity surrounding questions about his personal life and allegations of inexperience.

Ginsburg was born in Chicago, Illinois, on May 25, 1946. He graduated from the Latin School in 1963 and received a bachelor's degree from Cornell in 1970 after establishing the nation's first computerized dating service. Ginsburg returned to Chicago to earn his law degree from the University of Chicago, in 1973. Ginsburg clerked for U.S. Circuit Judge Carl McGowan from 1973 to 1974 and for Associate Justice Thurgood Marshall of the Supreme Court from 1974 to 1975. He joined the faculty of Harvard Law School in 1975 and served as assistant professor and was promoted to professor in 1981. From 1983 through 1986, Ginsburg held various appointments within the Reagan administration's Justice Department and Office of Management of Budget.

In 1986, Reagan named Ginsburg to the U.S. Court of Appeals for the District of Columbia Circuit and then in 1987 named Ginsburg to replace retiring associate justice Lewis F. Powell Jr., following the acrimonious public failed confirmation of Reagan's nominee, Robert H. Bork. Ginsburg had less than one year of judicial service at the time of his appointment, and thus his record lacked the substantial documentation of legal views that had been the subject of intense scrutiny plaguing the Bork nomination.

In the absence of a record of judicial scholarship, Ginsburg's inexperience itself became the subject of controversy. Further, his personal history and that of his wife sounded an unfavorable chord in some sectors. Ginsburg's wife, a physician, was rumored to have performed abortions. Ginsburg was challenged with conflict of interest questions concerning investment holdings in a company involved in a case he had handled while at the Justice Department. Further, Ginsburg admitted that he had smoked marijuana "on a few occasions" while a student and while on the faculty at

Harvard Law School. At the request of the White House, Ginsburg withdrew his name from consideration during the publicity surrounding this last item. To replace Justice Powell, Reagan was finally successful in his nomination of Anthony M. Kennedy.

Green v. School Board of New Kent County, 391 U.S. 430 (1968)

Following the landmark decisions of the Supreme Court in *Brown v. Board of Education* (*Brown I*) (1954), and *Brown v. Board of Education* (*Brown II*) (1955), school districts throughout the southern states struggled to identify plans that would satisfy local custom and also pass constitutional muster. In New Kent County, Virginia, the school board maintained two schools, on the east and west sides of the county. Approximately half of the county population was black, and no residential segregation existed. Despite *Brown I* and *Brown II*, New Kent County continued to operate segregated schools in keeping with Virginia state law. In response to a suit for injunctive relief filed in 1965, the New Kent County School Board developed a "freedom of choice" plan for desegregation in its schools. The plan permitted students to choose annually between the two county schools and required students to make firm choices in the first and eighth grades. Both the District Court and the Circuit Court of Appeals approved the freedom of choice plan.

The Supreme Court, however, struck down the freedom of choice plan in 1968 as failing to "dismantle the dual system approach as mandated by *Brown II*." The Court acknowledged the possibility that a freedom of choice plan could show real promise of achieving a unitary school system. However, a freedom of choice plan alone was not acceptable, as there were other reasonably available mechanisms, such as zoning, that promised "speedier and more effective conversion." Significantly, in the three years since the New Kent County freedom of choice plan had been operating, no white students had chosen to attend the black school, and only 15 percent of the black students had chosen to attend the white school.

Griswold v. Connecticut, 381 U.S. 479 (1965)

This decision overturned a Connecticut statute that criminalized the dissemination of birth control drugs or devices. Under the statute, the executive director of the Planned Parenthood League of Connecticut and its medical director, a licensed physician, were convicted for giving married couples information and medical advice on how to prevent conception and for prescribing contraceptives to the wives of the couples.

This landmark decision was authored by Justice Douglas and grounded in a right of privacy recognized explicitly by the Court for the first time. The Court found a fundamental right of privacy in the "penumbra" of rights emanating from the Bill of Rights taken as a whole. Specific mention was made of the embedded nature of the right to privacy within the freedom to associate (First Amendment), the prohibition against quartering soldiers "in any house" in time of peace without the consent of the owner (Third Amendment), the "right of the people to be secure in their persons, houses, papers, and effects, against unreasonable searches and seizures" (Fourth Amendment), and the ability of a citizen to create a zone of privacy within the protection against self-incrimination (Fifth Amendment) that "government may not force him to surrender to his detriment." The Court also relied upon the Ninth Amendment provision that enumeration of rights in the Constitution "shall not be construed to deny or disparage others retained by the people."

The relationship of husband and wife and the role of a physician in that relationship were found to be within the "zone of privacy" created by these various constitutional guarantees, and the Court noted that this right was older than the Bill of Rights itself. This right of privacy paved the way for many crucial decisions on personal freedoms, such as abortion in *Roe v. Wade* (1973).

The plurality opinion denotes the difficulty that many members of the Court had with advancing a right of privacy not explicitly stated in the language of the Constitution. This lack of explicit language remains a contemporary concern for the Court.

Heart of Atlanta Motel v. United States, 379 U.S. 241 (1964)

In this critical decision, the Court upheld the constitutionality of Title II of the Civil Rights Act of 1964, which prohibits discrimination in places of public accommodation. This decision had important implications for the practical extension of civil rights to everyday activities and also extended the Court's interpretation of the Commerce Clause.

The owner of the Heart of Atlanta Motel, located in Atlanta, Georgia, sought an injunction to prevent the enforcement of Title II of the Civil Rights Act of 1964, seeking to maintain the hotel's practice of providing services only to white clients. The motel owner argued that the act exceeded Congress's powers under the Commerce Clause, because operation of the hotel was of a primarily "local" character. The government argued that the unavailability of public accommodations effectively interfered with the rights of African Americans to travel throughout the fifty states. The evidence established that approximately 75 percent of the guests who stayed at the Heart of Atlanta Motel were from outside Georgia. Appearing on behalf of the United States was attorney Thurgood Marshall, who later was appointed to the Supreme Court as its first African American justice.

The Court upheld the constitutionality of Title II of the Civil Rights Act of 1964. In considering the implications for interstate commerce, the Court held that the interstate movement of persons constituted "commerce," whether or not the purposes for travel were commercial. In reaching this conclusion, the Court found that some federal restrictions on local commercial activities could be justified under the Commerce Clause, where the federal restrictions furthered some central and legitimate government purpose such as ending racial discrimination.

The Hyde Amendment

Named for its author, Henry J. Hyde, an Illinois congressman and an outspoken opponent of abortion rights, the Hyde Amendment prohibits the use of federal funds to perform abortions except in a situation when the life of the woman would be endangered if the fetus were carried to term. The Hyde Amendment was first offered as an amendment to the Labor-HEW appropriation bill for fiscal 1977, and it passed the House with a vote of 199–165.

Since its passage, versions of the Hyde Amendment have severely limited the use of federal funds to reimburse the costs of abortion through Medicaid, a program established in 1965 under Title XIX of the Social Security Act to provide federal assistance to states that choose to reimburse certain costs of medical treatment for poor persons. The constitutionality of the limitations placed on reimbursement by the Hyde Amendment, and the far-reaching interplay of the Hyde Amendment on social policy, are illustrated in *Harris v. McCrae* (1980).

Specifically, *Harris v. McCrae* addressed whether Title XIX required states that participated in Medicaid to fund the cost of medically necessary abortions for which federal reimbursement is unavailable under the Hyde Amendment. The argument was made that the Hyde Amendment, by withholding federal funds from certain medically necessary abortions, infringed on the constitutional principles of *Roe v. Wade*. The Supreme Court held that relief from indigency was not a constitutionally protected right. The Court held that "in encouraging childbirth except in the most urgent circumstances," the Hyde Amendment was rationally related to a legitimate governmental objective of protecting potential life. The Supreme Court found it constitutional for federal legislation to make childbirth a "more attractive option than abortion for persons on Medicaid." The application and enforcement of the Hyde Amendment continues today throughout the federal budget and across social service programs.

Independent Counsel

The Independent Counsel Statute is found in Title VI of the Ethics in Government Act of 1978 (29 U.S.C. 49, Section 591 et seq.). The Ethics in Government Act was prompted by the Watergate scandal surrounding President Richard M. Nixon and

Nixon's firing of Archibald Cox, the special prosecutor charged with responsibility for investigating allegations of misconduct in the Nixon administration.

The statute provides that the attorney general of the United States may appoint an independent counsel to investigate, and if warranted, prosecute, certain high-level federal officials. Whether or not to appoint an independent counsel is within the discretion of the attorney general. The selection and actual appointment of independent counsel is made by the Special Division, a division of the U.S. Court of Appeals for the District of Columbia Circuit. The Special Division is defined in the statute as a three-member panel of judges or justices appointed by the chief justice of the United States. One judge must be a member of the U.S. Court of Appeals for the District of Columbia Circuit, and no two judges of the same court may be appointed.

The Independent Counsel Statute was challenged in *Morrison v. Olson* (1988). Constitutional challenges were brought on the grounds that the statute violated the Appointments Clause (Article II, Section 2, Clause 2), Article III, and the principle of separation of powers articulated under Article II. The Court rejected each of these challenges.

However, the Independent Counsel Statute became increasingly controversial in its application over the next twenty years. Charges were leveled by both political parties that its use was unduly motivated by partisan concerns. The statute was allowed to expire in 1999 in the wake of independent counsel Kenneth Starr's $40 million investigation into the conduct of President Clinton. Critics argued that the Independent Counsel Statute disrupted the constitutional balance of powers, embroiling the federal judiciary in political disputes between Congress and the president.

Lemon v. Kurtzman, 403 U.S. 602 (1971)

In this case, the Burger Court found unconstitutional a Pennsylvania statute authorizing reimbursement to nonpublic schools under the First Amendment prohibition against the establishment of religion and its application to the states through the Fourteenth Amendment. The statute allowed the state to enter into contracts with nonpublic schools for the purchase of "secular educational services" under which the state directly reimbursed nonpublic schools for teacher salaries, textbooks, and instructional materials limited to secular subjects. Contracts under the statute represented more than 20 percent of the students in the state, and the majority of the students covered under the contracts were Roman Catholic. The complaint alleged that this arrangement with church-affiliated schools had the effect of propagating religion and was therefore unconstitutional.

In an opinion authored by Chief Justice Burger, the Court held that the cumulative impact of the entire relationship arising out of the statute constituted an "excessive entanglement" between government and religion, citing among other aspects the continuing and intimate relationship between church and state that was embedded in the government's power to audit expenditures under the statute. The *Lemon* opinion reiterated the understanding that absolute separation of church and state was not required by the Establishment Clause and that some relationship between government and religion was inevitable. A new three-part test was established by the Court to evaluate church-state relations, based on consideration of cumulative criteria that the Court had acknowledged over the years. The *Lemon* test requires that (1) the statute itself must have a secular purpose, (2) the principal or primary effect must be one that neither advances nor inhibits religion, and (3) the statute must not foster an "excessive entanglement" with religion.

Louisiana Creationism Act

The Louisiana Creationism Act, a Louisiana state law, was officially titled "Balanced Treatment for Creation-Science and Evolution-Science in Pubic School Instruction" (Creationism Act, La. Rev. Stat. Ann. Sections 17:286.1–17.286.7). The Creationism Act prohibited the teaching of the theory of evolution in public elementary and secondary schools unless accompanied by instruction in the theory of "creation science." In contrast to the theory of evolution, creation science is based on the Bible's book of Genesis, representing the biblical belief in the abrupt appearance of life in complex form. Under the statute, no school was required to teach either evolution or creation science; however, if either was taught, then the other must also be taught.

The constitutionality of the Creationism Act was tested in *Edwards v. Aguillard* (1987). Louisiana officials charged with implementing the act argued that its purpose was to protect the legitimate secular interest of academic freedom through teaching the sciences of both evolution and creation. In a 7–2 decision, the Supreme Court rejected the assertion that the statute could be supported on those grounds. Rather, the Court saw the statute as intending to discredit evolution and having therefore a preeminently religious purpose. Writing for the majority, Justice Brennan stated that "it is not happenstance that the legislature required the teaching of a theory that coincided with [a particular] religious view." Brennan noted testimony from the act's sponsor, Louisiana State Senator Keith, in which Keith expressed that his "disdain for the theory of evolution resulted from the support that evolution supplied to views contrary to his own religious beliefs. . . . The legislation therefore sought to alter the science curriculum to reflect endorsement of a religious view that is antagonistic to the theory of evolution." The Court's decision in *Edwards v. Aguillard* was consistent with its decision regarding state attempts to prohibit teaching of evolution, for example, *Epperson v. Arkansas* (1968).

Mapp v. Ohio, 367 U.S. 643 (1961)

This case extended the application of the exclusionary rule to state criminal proceedings. In *Mapp,* police conducted a warrantless search of Mapp's residence, seeking materials incident to bombing and gambling. Obscene materials were found instead, in the bottom of a closed dresser drawer. Mapp was prosecuted and convicted for their possession. Mapp appealed primarily on grounds that Ohio's obscenity law violated the First Amendment. An amicus brief filed by the ACLU argued that the 1949 decision in *Wolf v. Colorado,* which refused to extend the exclusionary rule to the states, should be overturned and that the evidence against Mapp should be excluded as obtained in violation of the Fourth Amendment.

The 6–3 decision held that the state was required to exclude the evidence. The majority based its decision on the protection of privacy and the historic inadequacy of other safeguards as protection against police abuse of constitutional guarantees. The Court opined that the application of the exclusionary rule to the states appeared to be the only viable method of protecting Fourth and Fifth Amendment rights of citizens.

The *Mapp* decision was highly controversial and has been attacked by the law enforcement community, courts, and scholars alike. The purpose for the exclusionary rule was originally couched in terms of preserving judicial integrity. Since *Mapp,* this expression has given way to the prevailing notion that the purpose of the rule is to deter police misconduct. In turn, this construction now supports a balancing approach, in which the Court weighs the cost and benefits of excluding evidence within a particular context. Most often, this balance is resolved in favor of government conduct.

Miller v. California, 413 U.S. 15 (1973)

In this landmark obscenity case, the Supreme Court sought to articulate more clearly a set of standards to provide greater assistance for triers of fact in identifying obscenity. Here, the Burger Court applied standards from *Roth v. United States* (1957) to evaluate the California laws and fashioned a new standard against which to assess the obscene. In writing for the 5–4 majority and allegedly to forge consensus, Chief Justice Warren Burger set forth the following guidelines, which represent the most detailed set of parameters that had yet been issued by the Court on this subject: (1) whether the average person, applying contemporary community standards and judging the dominant theme of the work taken as a whole, determined that the work appealed to prurient interest; (2) whether the work depicts or describes in a "patently offensive way" sexual conduct specifically defined by state law; and (3) whether the work, taken as whole, lacks "serious artistic, political or scientific value."

The Court rejected the standard previously used in *Roth* and *Memoirs v. Massachusetts* (1966), which was that material be "utterly without redeeming social value."

The *Miller* opinion further rejected the notion of a national standard for measuring obscenity, holding that contemporary community standards were by definition subject to local determination. *Miller* has remained the controlling standard throughout the Rehnquist Court era.

Miranda v. Arizona, 384 U.S. 436 (1966)

This landmark ruling of the Warren Court established parameters for police conduct in the interrogation of criminal suspects. The 5–4 decision reversed several criminal convictions in which suspects had made confessions during police interrogations without first being advised by a law enforcement officer of their rights under the Constitution. In the opinion authored by Chief Justice Earl Warren, the Court held that such confessions were obtained in violation of the Fifth Amendment protection against self-incrimination. The ruling established minimum procedural safeguards for criminal suspects. Specifically, *Miranda* holds that a criminal suspect in custody must be advised of his right to remain silent and his right to consult with legal counsel. In addition, he must be advised that any statements made may be used against him and that counsel will be assigned to represent him if he is unable to afford to retain an attorney. The rationale for the decision was that, to protect the constitutional rights guaranteed under the Fifth Amendment, these parameters were required as a necessary counterweight to the possibility of police abuse.

The *Miranda* decision expanded upon an earlier ruling by the Warren Court, *Escobedo v. Illinois* (1964). *Escobedo* established that a suspect must be advised of the right to counsel prior to interrogation, but it failed to establish specific procedures to ensure the protection of a suspect's constitutional rights. The *Miranda* decision was highly controversial and sparked sweeping changes in law enforcement practices. Within the next two years, *Miranda* also prompted a change in federal law (18 U.S.C., Section 3501) that established the voluntary nature of a confession as the key element in a "totality of the circumstances" approach; however, this was overturned in *Dickerson v. United States* (2000), and *Miranda* has never been overruled.

NAACP Legal Defense Fund

The Legal Defense Fund is an organization that is closely related to the National Association for the Advancement of Colored People (NAACP). The NAACP was created in 1909 as an organization dedicated to improving the lives of African Americans. An important component of this program involved legal advocacy, and this has been provided largely through the Legal Defense Fund. In the initial years of the NAACP, the organization relied on volunteer attorneys. Beginning in the 1920s, however, the NAACP hired Charles Hamilton Houston as its first full-time staff attorney. In 1939, two major events occurred: (1) the Legal Defense Fund was incorporated as a separate entity from the NAACP to preserve the parent organization's tax-exempt status, and (2) Thurgood Marshall was picked to replace Houston as director of the fund.

Building on past successes, Marshall and his associates developed a long-range plan to attack legally segregated public schools in the southern and border states. This strategy was eventually successful when, in 1954, the Supreme Court in *Brown v. Board of Education* and its companion cases declared unconstitutional public schools that were segregated by law. *Brown* overturned *Plessy v. Ferguson* (1896) and the concept of separate but equal.

The Legal Defense Fund continued to be active in seeking to use the courts to confront racial inequality, and it continues this work today. The organization is still involved in school desegregation but has expanded to tackle racial discrimination in many areas of American law, including housing, employment, and capital punishment.

New York Times v. Sullivan, 376 U.S. 254 (1964)

In this landmark decision, the Supreme Court determined for the first time the extent to which constitutional protections for speech and press limit state powers to award damages in a defamation action brought by a public official against the media for criticism of public conduct.

Sullivan was one of three elected commissioners of the city of Montgomery, Alabama. He sued the *New York Times* and four black clergymen for libel on the basis of statements contained in a full-page advertisement in the *New York Times* on March 29, 1960. The advertisement was titled "Heed Their Rising Voices" and was signed by "Committee to Defend Martin Luther King and the Struggle for Freedom in the South" along with the names of individuals. The advertisement did not mention Sullivan by name but rather described many events that occurred across Alabama aimed at preventing racial integration. Some of these events took place in Montgomery, and some of the statements pertaining to those events contained factual errors. At trial in state court, Sullivan was awarded $500,000 in damages based on instructions to the jury that the statements were "libelous per se" and thus entitled to a presumption of damage.

In a unanimous opinion by Justice Brennan, the Court reversed, holding that the First and Fourteenth Amendments prohibited the state from awarding damages to a public official for false defamatory statements unless "actual malice" was proven. In establishing this separate standard of review, the Court relied on the fundamental nature of freedom of expression in the American experience on "public questions," holding that a standard of simple falsity for libel per se of a public official would restrict vigorous public debate over those very questions.

Further, the Court found that the constitutional guarantees of free speech and press were not inapplicable simply because the expression was in the form of a paid advertisement. The Court framed the advertisement as an expression of "grievance and protest on one of the major public issues of our time" and as such clearly qualified for constitutional protection. Negligent factual errors did not erase this protection, as erroneous statements are "inevitable in free debate."

New York Times v. United States, 403 U.S. 713 (1971)

In a *per curiam* opinion issued at the height of the Vietnam War, the Burger Court rejected the demands of the U.S. government to halt publication of classified government reports about military activities in Southeast Asia, known as *The Pentagon Papers*. Several installments of the documents were published by the *New York Times* and *Washington Post*. The government argued that the reports were classified as top secret and as such would cause "irreparable injury" to national security. The *Times* and the *Post* argued that the government's injunction was an attempt at prior restraint of free press in violation of the First Amendment.

The magnitude of this issue within the context of the intense public controversy surrounding the war effort was demonstrated in the manner in which the case was expedited through the judicial system. The case moved from the district court to the Supreme Court in less than two weeks, and the Court extended its regular session to hear the matter. The *per curiam* decision rejected the government's claim to a national security exemption from prior restraint on free speech, stating that any prior restraint on free expression "comes to this Court bearing a heavy presumption of invalidity." The separate concurring opinions reflect great diversity of legal reasoning but arrive at the same conclusion: prior restraint on free press can rarely be justified.

The Pentagon Papers

Officially titled *History of U.S. Decision-Making Process on Viet Nam Policy*, the so-called *Pentagon Papers* were a 1968 top secret classified report on U.S. foreign policy in Vietnam. The documents contained a history of U.S. involvement in Vietnam and other countries in Southeast Asia. In 1971, a former federal official, Daniel Ellsberg, obtained the forty-seven-volume report and secretly copied it. He then provided portions of it to the *New York Times* and the *Washington Post*, which published several installments of it. The articles disclosed the extent of U.S. involvement in the conflict as greatly in excess of that which had been provided to the public to date. *The Pentagon Papers* were highly controversial in light of the nation's active military engagement in the Vietnam War at the time.

The United States sought an injunction against the publication, claiming that the articles would cause "irreparable injury" to American national security. The case came before the Supreme Court in 1971 in *New York Times v. United States*. The Supreme Court ruled 6–3 that publication could continue and refused to grant the injunction. In a *per curiam* opinion, the Court held that prior restraint on publication carries a heavy presumption that it is unconstitutional and that the government had not met its burden in demonstrating that prior restraint was justified.

Physician-Assisted Suicide

Physician-assisted suicide is a controversial concept supported by those who believe that new approaches are needed to address care at the end of life. In the procedure, a doctor helps a patient die painlessly and with dignity. The issue is hotly contested in the United States and around the world. Reasons offered in support of physician-assisted suicide include the proliferation of life-extending medical techniques and the belief that individuals should be able to receive medical assistance in dying if they are able to think clearly and can freely request or decline assistance.

Opponents, including the majority of mainstream medical professionals, believe that physicians are morally, ethically, and professionally obligated to use all means possible to preserve life. Opponents believe that physician-assisted suicide is a form of "active" euthanasia, in which the fatally ill are put to death with or without consent. Opponents also fear that legalizing physician-assisted suicide would open the door to less-consensual forms of physician assistance.

The concept of physician-assisted suicide is inextricably linked with opinions about a "right" to die. Proponents of a right to die argue that dying patients and physicians should have the right to suspend treatments that will only temporarily extend life. They also argue that a patient's family and physician should be able to stop such treatment in the event that the patient becomes incompetent to do so.

The Court has upheld principles of personal choice in this area but has declined to decriminalize the conduct of either doctors or others who terminate the life of another under terminal medical circumstances. In 1990, the Supreme Court upheld a patient's right to "passive" euthanasia, in cases in which a patient's wishes to suspend life-extending treatment are clearly expressed, in the case of *Cruzan v. Director, Missouri Department of Health*. Most states have laws that permit such expression through a document known as a "living will."

Attempts to enact permissive physician-assisted suicide statutes have been unsuccessful in several states. Recent Court decisions involved challenges to such laws in the states of Washington and New York. In both *Washington v. Glucksberg* (1997) and *Vacco, Attorney General of New York, v. Quill* (1997), physicians sought to have state criminal statutes that prohibited assisted suicide declared unconstitutional infringements upon Due Process and Equal Protection Clauses of the Fourteenth Amendment. Their argument was that the laws did not

> treat equally all competent persons who are in the final stages of fatal illness and wish to hasten their deaths because those in the final stages of terminal illness who are on life support systems are allowed to hasten their deaths by directing the removal of such systems; but those who are similarly situated, except for the previous attachment of life sustaining equipment, are not allowed to hasten death by self administering prescribed drugs.

In both *Quill* and *Glucksberg*, the Court found the state legislative classifications bore a rational relation to some legitimate end and explicitly refused to extend the principles of *Cruzan* as a basis declaring the states' laws unconstitutional. The Court summarized its support for the states' interests in *Quill*, holding that the "difficulty in defining terminal illness and the risk that a dying patient's request for assistance in ending his or her life might not be truly voluntary justifies the prohibitions on assisted suicide we uphold here."

Reagan, Ronald

Ronald Reagan was the fortieth president of the United States, serving from 1981 to 1989. Elected on a conservative Republican platform, he was succeeded by his vice-president of two terms, George H. W. Bush.

Reagan was born on February 6, 1911, in Tampico, Illinois. He graduated from Eureka College and worked as an announcer in radio broadcasting, which led to a long career in movies under contract with Warner Bros. He was also active in the actors' union, the Screen Actors Guild, and served as its president for several years. He began his political life as a Democrat and switched to the Republican Party in 1962.

Reagan was elected governor of California in 1966 and attempted unsuccessfully to gain the Republican nomination for president in 1968 and 1976. In 1980, a conservative wave carried Reagan to the nomination and to successful election along with many other conservative Republicans. His foreign policies favored strong national defense. Reagan's domestic policies centered around reducing the size of government, and he implemented economic policies that cut domestic spending and provided tax reductions to stimulate economic growth. The national debt rose steeply during his two terms in office.

Reagan's appointments to the Supreme Court had a profound influence in setting the tone of the contemporary conservative Court. Four nominations of fellow

Republicans were confirmed by the Senate, including Sandra Day O'Connor, in 1981, as the first female justice on the Court, to replace liberal justice Potter Stewart. In 1986, Reagan nominated William H. Rehnquist, then an associate justice, to replace retiring chief justice Warren Burger; for Rehnquist's seat, Reagan nominated Antonin Scalia.

Not all of Reagan's appointments were without controversy. Reagan's first and second nominees to replace retiring justice Lewis Powell were not confirmed. Robert H. Bork's nomination was rejected by the Senate by a vote of 48–52 for what were perceived to be archly conservative views. A second nominee, Douglas Ginsburg, withdrew from consideration after reports that he had used marijuana while a professor at Harvard Law School. Anthony M. Kennedy was nominated and confirmed by unanimous vote in 1988 to fill Powell's seat.

Religious Freedom Restoration Act

This federal legislation was signed into law by President Clinton on November 16, 1993, after unanimous passage by the House of Representatives and a 97–3 vote of passage in the Senate. The Religious Freedom Restoration Act (RFRA) required governments to (1) refrain from limiting religious freedom unless they had a compelling reason to do so and (2) to select the least intrusive methods to their goal, if they needed to restrict religious freedom. In reaction to the 1990 *Employment Division, Department of Human Resources of Oregon v. Smith* decision, the purposes of the RFRA were to (1) to restore the compelling interest test of *Sherbert v. Verner* (1963) and *Wisconsin v. Yoder* (1972), and to guarantee its application in all cases where the free exercise of religion was substantially burdened, and (2) to provide a claim or defense to persons whose religious exercise was substantially burdened by government.

In 1997, the Supreme Court found the RFRA to be an unconstitutional limitation on the sovereign powers reserved to the states under the Tenth Amendment in the case of *City of Boerne v. P. F. Flores* (1997). Here, the Roman Catholic archdiocese of San Antonio, Texas, sought a construction permit from the city of Boerne to expand its church into a historical district in the city. The permit was denied, and the archdiocese filed suit under the RFRA.

In a 6–3 opinion authored by Justice Kennedy, conservative justices Rehnquist, Scalia, and Thomas joined liberals Ginsburg and Stevens in the majority opinion. In striking down the statute, the Court cited the emphasis in RFRA legislative hearings on laws that placed an incidental burden on religion. The hearings did not disclose instances of religious bigotry or animus or widespread patterns of discrimination regarding the free exercise of religion. RFRA was found to be out of proportion to a remedial objective and instead a proscription on state conduct, in conjunction with the most demanding test known under constitutional law. In *Flores*, the Court considered the RFRA to be an intrusion into the traditional prerogatives of state governance and therefore was in violation of the Tenth Amendment.

Reynolds v. United States, 98 U.S. 145 (1879)

This case represents the first attempt of the Supreme Court to define religion for First Amendment purposes. Reynolds was prosecuted for violating a federal statute that criminalized polygamy; he was fined $500 and sentenced to two years of hard labor. Reynolds was the head of the Church of Jesus Christ of Latter-day Saints, also known as the Mormon Church. Reynolds argued that his polygamy was protected by the Free Exercise Clause of the First Amendment as a fundamental tenet of religious practice. In a unanimous opinion issued by Chief Justice Waite, the Court disagreed.

The Court had few prior opportunities to consider the dimensions of religion under the First Amendment and relied heavily upon two principles. The first was the notion that polygamy had always been regarded as a highly offensive practice and one that had always been void under common law. Thus, the government was within its legislative powers to prohibit such a practice. Second, the Court relied upon the notion that the Free Exercise Clause was targeted at beliefs and not at practices; practices could therefore be subject to valid restriction through laws not intended to affect religion generally but that impacted religious practices. Notably, the Mormons were widely persecuted across the developing United States at the time of this prosecution.

Reynolds remains good law today, and Chief Justice Waite's opinion fashioned a framework that has been employed by the Court in contemporary times in *Smith*. For example, in *Oregon v. Smith* (1990), the Court held that the practice of using illegal drugs was not immune from employer or state sanction simply on the basis of drug use as a religious practice.

Roe v. Wade, 410 U.S. 113 (1973)

In this watershed decision, the Supreme Court struck down as unconstitutional state criminal abortion laws. In a class action filed in the name of a pregnant single woman (Roe), the constitutionality of a Texas statute was challenged. The statue criminalized abortion except to save the life of the mother.

In his opinion for the Court, Justice Blackmun relied upon a woman's right to privacy, which had been recently established in *Griswold v. Connecticut* (1965). The Court found that the right to privacy included a qualified right to terminate pregnancy and established a balancing test based upon the right of the state to protect the health of women and the potentiality of human life. Based upon the trimesters of pregnancy, the test left the abortion decision to the woman and her physician during the first trimester of pregnancy. In the second trimester, any state regulations must be reasonably related to maternal health. Subsequent to viability, which was at the time considered to begin about the beginning of the third trimester, states were permitted to regulate abortion except where medically necessary to preserve the life or health of the woman. This decision also resolved an important question in the area of judicial standing. *Roe* was held to have presented the Court with a "case or controversy" under Article III, although the state argued that the circumstances did not yet present a justiciable question.

The trimester structure of this opinion has shaped decisions about reproductive rights since its adoption. As medical science has advanced, the date of viability has been argued to occur much earlier than the end of the second trimester. Although *Roe v. Wade* is still the law of the land, it also remains a politically divisive decision. An opinion on *Roe* has become a critical consideration for appointment for the Supreme Court, with conservatives and religious fundamentalists in favor of overturning the decision.

In recent decisions regarding abortion, the Court has increasingly recognized the right of states to impose restrictions on the right to choose to abort. In *Planned Parenthood of Southeastern Pennsylvania v. Casey* (1992), the Court introduced a new undue burden standard that triggers strict scrutiny only if a regulation creates an undue burden on the woman seeking an abortion; absent an undue burden, the minimal scrutiny test is employed. In *Casey*, the Court upheld requirements for parental notification of minors seeking to terminate a pregnancy, for waiting periods in which patients are required to obtain information, and the requirement that information about abortion must be provided by a doctor rather than by a nonphysician counselor.

Roth v. United States, 354 U.S. 476 (1957)

In this landmark case, the Supreme Court determined that obscenity was not speech protected by the First Amendment. In reaching its decision, the Court relied upon a historical analysis of the First Amendment and concluded that its "unconditional" phrasing was not intended to protect every utterance. Rather, the Court found that protection given to speech and to the press was intended to ensure the "unfettered exchange of ideas" for the accomplishment of political and social change. Ideas with any redeeming social importance were to be protected, however provocative. *Roth* drew upon the notion of "redeeming social value" as the standard against which to measure speech and held that implicit in the history of the First Amendment was the "rejection of obscenity as utterly without redeeming social importance."

Having thus placed obscenity outside the purview of constitutional protection, the Court was forced to define *obscenity*. In establishing parameters for obscene speech, the Court noted that obscenity was not synonymous with sex but was rather that which appealed to the "prurient interest." The Court noted a clear "distinction of difference" between the two, which could be discerned by the average person. The standard to be applied in determining whether speech was obscene, and therefore outside the protection of the First Amendment, was set forth: whether the average person, applying contemporary community standards and judging the dominant theme of the work taken as a whole, determined that the work appealed to prurient interest. *Roth* was subsequently modified by the Warren Court, especially the *Memoirs* case of 1966, to provide strong protection for sexual expression. The Burger Court modified the *Roth* and *Memoirs* test in *Miller v. California* (1973), and *Miller* was the controlling doctrine in the Rehnquist Court era.

Schenck v. United States, 249 U.S. 47 (1919)

This landmark decision by the Holmes Court established the "clear and present danger" test as the permissible standard against which to evaluate prior restraint by the government on free expression. Defendants Schenck and others were convicted of violating the Espionage Act of 1918, one of the Sedition Laws, by mailing pamphlets to men eligible for the draft that urged them to avoid conscription. Defendants argued that this expression was protected by the First Amendment and that the Espionage Act amounted to restraint upon free speech.

Justice Holmes authored the unanimous opinion of the Court, which held that the context and circumstances of speech must be considered in an examination of First Amendment guarantees. Holmes wrote by way of example that one's right to announce falsely a fire in a crowded theater and cause panic would not be speech protected by the Constitution. The Court held that, in the context of a law that imposes prior restraint upon the freedom of speech, speech must be examined in its circumstances to determine whether a clear and present danger is created such that the words will produce the very conduct that the law had been enacted to prevent. The clear and present danger test was used to uphold the convictions of Schenck and the other defendants.

Historic events and political context are fundamental to an understanding of the *Schenck* decision and the creation of the "clear and present danger" test. The war effort of the day placed more than four million Americans in uniform and sent more than one million troops to Europe. Opposition to selective service was simply unpatriotic; the antidraft pamphlets constituted a clear and present danger to military recruiting during that time. The Court noted that speech uttered outside the context of a time of war might well receive different treatment.

Sherbert v. Verner, 374 U.S. 398 (1963)

This case tested a dimension of the right to free exercise of religion under the First Amendment, in the context of employment. Here, appellant was a member of the Seventh-day Adventist Church and worked at a textile mill. Initially, her employment was scheduled in a five-day workweek and posed no conflict with the proscription of her church against working on Saturday. When her employer changed the workweek to a mandatory six days for all employees on each of three shifts, she was discharged because she was unable to work on Saturdays. Upon her application for unemployment benefits, she was also denied by the state of South Carolina on the basis that she was not "able to work . . . and available for work" as required by the state unemployment laws, again because her religious beliefs forbade Saturday work.

In an opinion authored by Justice Brennan, the Supreme Court found the South Carolina unemployment law to violate the First Amendment right to free exercise of religion. As the acts of the appellant posed no substantial threat to public safety, peace, or order, the incidental burden that the South Carolina law presented to the free exercise of religion could only be justified through a showing of a compelling state interest. South Carolina argued that the Employment Security Commission's decision did not interfere with the exercise of religion, but the Court held that such reasoning did not rise to a "compelling" level. Significantly, the South Carolina law did not deny unemployment compensation for individuals who were unavailable for work on Sundays, in recognition of the practice of Christianity, and the Court distinguished the state interest in this law from the state's interest (albeit one of administration) in establishing a single uniform day of rest from work.

The Court found that the disqualification for unemployment benefits solely on the basis of a refusal to accept Saturday work grounded in a religious belief was an unconstitutional restriction of the free exercise of religion and prohibited by the First and Fourteenth Amendments. This holding reaffirmed the Court's position in *Everson v. Board of Education* (1947) that no state may "exclude individual Catholics, Lutherans, Mohammedans, Baptists, Jews, Methodists, Non-believers, Presbyterians, or the members of any other faith, because of their faith, or lack of it, from receiving the benefits of public welfare legislation."

Takings Clause

The Takings Clause is a section of the Fifth Amendment that reflects a significant guarantee of the sanctity of private property. The Takings Clause states "nor shall private property be taken for public use, without just compensation." This clause reflects the tension between private property rights and the government's need to acquire private property to complete important government objectives, such as the construction of roads and other public works.

The Takings Clause was designed to force an equitable distribution of the cost of acquiring private property by mandating that property owners be compensated by the government for the taking. As with other aspects of the Bill of Rights, the Takings Clause was originally applied only against action by the federal government. The Takings Clause was extended to state and local governments in *Chicago, Burlington, and Quincy Railroad Company v. Chicago* (1897).

The power of the government to take private property for public purposes is no longer disputed. Issues involving the Takings Clause now primarily concern the parameters of just compensation and the extent to which government action constitutes a "taking." The concept of taking has been expanded to include government action that severely restricts use or enjoyment of private property in addition to actual appropriation or physical entry onto the land. In *United States v. Causby* (1946), the Court found that the construction of a federal airfield for daily use by military aircraft constituted a taking of private property; the end of the airport was only 2,200 feet from property used for both residential and commercial purposes and significantly interfered with use of the property as a commercial chicken-farming operation. Other interpretations of the Takings Clause have upheld state historic landmark preservation laws as serving a broader public benefit that does not diminish an owner's value to the extent of a taking of property requiring compensation.

Contemporary interpretations of the Takings Clause reflect the tension between strong advocacy for the protection of private property rights in the face of state and local protective land use regulations and permitting requirements related to flood control, soil erosion, and other environmental concerns. State regulations that fostered broader public access to Pacific Coast beaches were found to constitute a compensable taking when home-building permits were made contingent upon the grant of public rights of access from one public beach to another in *Nollan v. California Coastal Commission* (1987). Compensable state action has also been found in cases in which regulations effectively prohibit the use of property for any purpose, as in *Lucas v. South Carolina Coastal Council* (1992). In a series of 2005 cases, however, the Rehnquist Court ruled in favor of the government, leaving uncertain the future of Takings Clause cases.

Term Limits

Term limits restrict the number of terms that elected officials may serve in office. The Twenty-second Amendment establishes the president's term limit at a maximum of two four-year terms. Many state constitutions also prescribe term limits for the governor's office. Some term limit provisions require a break in service, and others prohibit all service in a particular office after the limit is reached.

Over the last decade, public sentiment in favor of establishing term limits has become quite pronounced. Proponents of term limits argue that incumbents are not responsive to their constituents, as the high reelection rates for incumbents amount almost to an unfair electoral advantage, and that elected service was not intended to be a lifelong career. Proponents suggest that term limits would shift legislators' priorities from raising money for reelection back to legislative business. Finally, by generating more electoral contests between nonincumbents, term limits would open greater opportunities for minority and female candidates. Opponents argue that term limits are an unnecessary restriction on democratic choice and that the electoral process itself establishes term limitation for every office. Opponents also argue that term limits remove experience from the electoral process and actually work to shift power away from elected officials to executive and agency staff positions and to lobbyists. Many states have enacted term limits for state and local elected offices and have sought to limit the terms for congressional representatives as well. In *U.S. Term Limits v. Thornton* (1994), the Supreme Court ruled that it was unconstitutional for states to establish term limits for members of Congress. This decision has prompted some critics to call for a constitutional amendment to allow voters to limit congressional terms through state legislation.

Terry v. Ohio, 392 U.S. 1 (1968)

This case marks the first attempt by the Supreme Court to delineate circumstances under which it was appropriate for law enforcement officers to engage in the practice of "stop and frisk." Here the Court upheld the conviction of Terry, who had been approached and frisked by police for suspicious behavior falling short of the probable cause necessary for an arrest. The frisk produced a gun, which was introduced as evidence at trial. In an opinion authored by Chief Justice Earl Warren, the Court held that citizens were entitled to the protection of the Fourth Amendment during on-the-street encounters with police. Forcible detainment for questioning was determined to constitute a seizure, and frisking was held to constitute a search within the meaning of the Fourth Amendment.

In balancing individual freedoms against community safety needs, the Warren Court opinion established the standard as one of reasonableness rather than probable cause. Law enforcement officers were directed that a stop and frisk was permissible if a "reasonably prudent" officer, under the circumstances, is warranted in the belief that his safety or that of others is in danger.

Terry reflects the continuing interpretation that Fourth Amendment protections are not absolute and that situational demands make compliance with its warrant requirement either impractical or impossible.

Title I of the Elementary and Secondary Education Act of 1965

The entanglement between state action and religion in the execution of the state's public education function is illustrated in the implementation of provisions of Title I of the

Elementary and Secondary Education Act of 1965. Title I authorized the U.S. secretary of education to distribute financial assistance to local educational institutions to meet needs of children from low-income families. Some states have used federal funds to pay salaries of public employees who teach in parochial schools.

In New York, such a program was established, which included remedial reading, reading skills, English as a second language, and remedial mathematics. These programs were carried out by public school employees including teachers, guidance counselors, psychologists, psychiatrists, and social workers who volunteered to teach in parochial schools. Materials and supplies were provided by public funds, and employees remained public school employees under the sole control of the public school system.

In *Aguilar v. Felton* (1985), the New York program was challenged on the grounds that it violated the Establishment Clause of the First Amendment. The Supreme Court found that the supervisory system in place in New York presented a classic application of the *Lemon* test as an example of excessive entanglement between church and state. Theoretically, the Court left open the possibility that a supervisory system could have been utilized to prevent Title I programs from being used either "intentionally or unwittingly to inculcate religious beliefs." Dissenters included Chief Justice Burger and Justices Rehnquist and O'Connor. Justice Rehnquist called the reasoning a "Catch 22 paradox of its own creation," in that financial aid must be supervised to ensure that excessive religious entanglement does not occur, but the very act of supervision itself was found in this case to create the prohibited entanglement. The *Aguilar* decision was reversed in 1997, however, in *Agostini v. Felton*.

Title VII of the 1964 Civil Rights Act

As part of the larger Civil Rights Act of 1964, Congress in Title VII prohibited employers with more than twenty-five employees, unions with more than twenty-five members, and employment agencies from discrimination based upon race, national origin, color, gender, or religion in regard to hiring, classification, training, or promotion. Title VII was subsequently extended to employers and unions with fifteen or more persons and also extended both to state and local governments and educational institutions. This legislation has been one of the most important factors in the struggle for equality for all Americans, but the Supreme Court has given a variety of interpretations to the law.

The Court's initial consideration of Title VII was on the 1971 case *Griggs v. Duke Power Company*, which involved a claim that a North Carolina power company discriminated against African Americans by requiring qualifications that went beyond those needed for employment. The Burger Court unanimously supported the plaintiffs in giving a broad interpretation to Title VII.

The Court's support for a liberal reading of Chapter VII continued throughout most of the Burger Court era, but the early Rehnquist Court gave more narrow, conservative interpretations to Title VII. The most publicized case was *Wards Cove Packing Co. v. Atonio* (1989), in which the Court ruled that statistical disparities alone were inadequate to establish employment discrimination. Congress, however, passed a law in 1991 that had the effect of overturning the ruling in *Wards Cove* as well as related cases. Title VII remains an important piece of legislation in the struggle for equality.

Title IX of the Education Amendments of 1972

Title IX of the Education Amendments of 1972 is the cornerstone of a package of education amendments to the Civil Rights Act of 1964, passed to remedy specific discrimination practices in higher education. Title IX states that "no person in the United States shall, on the basis of sex, be excluded from participation in, be denied benefits, or be subjected to discrimination under any educational program or activity receiving federal assistance." Title IX had considerable leverage in forcing compliance with federal antidiscrimination regulations, and it required organizations receiving federal financial assistance to file forms with the federal government to demonstrate the absence of discriminatory practices.

In its early application, Title IX was applied on an institution-wide basis. However, the scope of the amendment was narrowed considerably during the Reagan era in *Grove City College v. Bell* (1984). As an institution that did not receive direct federal financial assistance, Grove City College challenged the application of Title IX to the college as the result of admitting students who received federal financial assistance from Basic Educational Opportunity Grants. The *Grove City* decision was unanimous and established two important interpretations of Title IX. The first was that there was no meaningful distinction to be made between direct and indirect federal aid; thus Grove City College was fully within the purview of Title IX. However, the Court also acted to apply Title IX on a program-specific basis rather than across the institution as a whole. Thus, compliance requirements were limited only to those programs that received federal support.

This ruling provoked further legislation regarding gender discrimination in higher education institutions, with specific concerns about discriminatory impacts continuing in athletic programs. Subsequently, the Civil Rights Restoration Act of 1988 was passed to overturn the effects of the *Grove City* decision.

United States v. O'Brien, 391 U.S. 367 (1968)

This decision upheld the criminal conviction of O'Brien for burning his draft card in violation of federal law. Amendments in 1965 to the Universal Military Training and Service Act made knowing destruction or mutilation of draft cards a crime. On March 31, 1966, O'Brien and others burned their draft cards on the steps of the South Boston Courthouse in front of a sizable crowd that included several agents of the Federal Bureau of Investigation. At trial, O'Brien acknowledged that he knowingly burned his draft card and testified that he burned the card publicly to influence others to adopt antiwar beliefs. O'Brien challenged the constitutionality of the federal law on the grounds that it abridged his right to free speech under the First Amendment, arguing that the symbolic act of burning the card amounted to protected speech.

Chief Justice Warren authored the opinion, which held that the 1965 amendment to the act did not abridge free speech on its face. Further, the Court established the standard for evaluating legislation that may suppress symbolic speech as a variant within the range of free expression. The Court held that when "speech" and "nonspeech" elements are combined in the same course of conduct, a sufficiently important government interest in regulating nonspeech conduct can justify an incidental imitation on First Amendment freedoms. Here, the governmental function of maintaining a military force in the national defense was facilitated by the use of draft cards. The opinion validated the law as having an important or substantial government interest unrelated to suppression of free expression.

The statute was determined to be drawn narrowly and to place restrictions necessary to the continuing availability of conscription information necessary to the ability of Congress to raise armies. In 1971, the conduct of the conscription system was changed to a lottery. In 1973, the Selective Service system was abolished and service in the U.S. military became voluntary. The *O'Brien* test established the framework within which many symbolic speech acts would be evaluated, including protests against the Vietnam war, burning the American flag, and other forms of political demonstration.

Virginia Military Institute

Virginia Military Institute (VMI) is the oldest state military college in the United States. A state-supported baccalaureate institution of higher education, VMI is located in Lexington, Virginia. VMI provides mandatory military education and training across the various branches of the U.S. armed services, including a rigorous and extensive program of physical and mental preparation. Its distinctive mission is to produce "citizen-soldiers," and many of its graduates receive military commissions upon completion of their degrees. Until 1996, VMI admitted only male students.

In *United States v. Virginia* (1996), VMI's admissions practices were challenged by the United States in response to a letter of complaint by a female high school student. The suit against VMI and the Commonwealth of Virginia claimed that denial of the unique educational opportunity provided by VMI was a violation of the Equal Protection Clause of the Fourteenth Amendment. VMI argued that the character of its educational process would be damaged through gender integration of its mental and physical preparedness strategies. The District Court ruled in favor of the state, concluding that single-sex schools added diversity of opportunity to the range of educational opportunities provided by the Commonwealth. The court of appeals reversed, holding that the state could not justify provision of unique educational opportunities to men but not to women. Reminiscent of the efforts of southern states seeking to forestall racial integration, VMI established a separate program for females, the Virginia Women's Institute for Leadership (VWIL). VWIL was found to be an insufficient remedy for VMI's violation of the Equal Protection Clause. As a result, in 1997, VMI became the last publicly funded military service institution of higher education to admit women on an equal basis.

Writing for the 7–1 majority, Justice Ruth Bader Ginsburg specifically addressed gender stereotypes, noting that discriminatory admissions practices could not be supported with general claims about "the way women are." "Neither the goal of producing citizen-soldiers nor VMI's implementation methodology is inherently unsuitable to women," she wrote, stating that "there is no reason to believe that the admission of women capable of all the activities required of VMI cadets would destroy the institute rather than enhance its capacity to serve the more perfect union."

Voting Rights Act of 1965

The Voting Rights Act of 1965 was signed into law by President Lyndon B. Johnson. Perhaps the most sweeping electoral reform legislation of the century, the Voting Rights Act eliminated state election laws and practices that discriminated against minorities. The Voting Rights Act provided for the automatic suspension of literacy tests and other voter qualification devices, all of which had been widely used to limit the exercise of voting rights by blacks, especially in southern states. The Voting Rights Act gave federal authorities the ability to register voters in areas that were not meeting a 40 percent registration level and to assign federal examiners to list and entitle qualified applicants to vote in all elections. Also, the act authorized the U.S. attorney general to investigate the validity of poll taxes still in use by some states. The act further required that any new state voting laws be subjected to federal review for discriminatory impact. Under the act, interference with the legal exercise of the right to vote became a criminal offense.

In 1965, states that were subject to the greatest scrutiny under the Voting Rights Act included Alabama, Alaska, Georgia, Louisiana, Mississippi, South Carolina, and Virginia as well as portions of Arizona, Hawaii, Idaho, and North Carolina. As voter qualifications had been historically within the reserved powers of the states, the constitutionality of this broad federal intervention was challenged. In *South Carolina v. Katzenbach* (1996), the act was upheld, as was its use of specific remedies.

Implementation of the Voting Rights Act was bolstered by the passage of the Civil Rights Act of 1964, earlier in the Johnson administration. The Voting Rights Act was extended in 1970 and the voting age was lowered from twenty-one to eighteen, although the Court struck down this extension for state and local elections in *Oregon v. Mitchell* (1970). Congress subsequently abrogated the Court's ruling in *Oregon v. Mitchell* with the Twenty-sixth Amendment in 1971.

The Voting Rights Act has been amended twice, in 1975 and in 1982. Key provisions of those amendments include the addition of bilingual requirements in some locations and a permanent ban on the use of literacy tests as a voting requirement. The ability to exercise the right to vote has also been enhanced for those with disabilities, who now have the right to be accompanied and assisted in the voting process by a person of their choosing.

Warren, Earl

Earl Warren was appointed as the fourteenth chief justice of the Supreme Court in 1953 and served until his retirement, in 1969. He presided over the liberal "Warren Court," which under his leadership handed down numerous decisions of consequence in the areas of individual liberties, including civil rights, rights for the accused in criminal proceedings, religious freedoms, and censorship. He authored landmark opinions that declared unconstitutional racial segregation in public schools (*Brown v. Board of Education of Topeka, Kansas*, 1954) and ruled that criminal suspects had to be informed of the right to remain silent and the right to counsel before questioning (*Miranda v. Arizona*, 1966). Other landmark decisions dealt with legislative apportionment (*Baker v. Carr*, 1962) and limited the use of libel laws (*New York Times v. Sullivan*, 1964).

Warren was born in Los Angeles on March 19, 1891, and educated at the University of California. He was admitted to the bar in 1914 and practiced in the San Francisco area. Warren had a long political career as a liberal Republican, beginning with various offices in local government, including three terms as district attorney of Alameda County. Warren was elected attorney general of California in 1938. In 1942, he was elected governor of California and was reelected in 1946 and 1950 with bipartisan support. Warren only failed on one occasion to be elected, as the Republican candidate for vice-president in the unsuccessful 1948 presidential campaign of Thomas E.

Dewey. In 1963, Warren was appointed by President Lyndon B. Johnson to head the commission formed to investigate the assassination of President John F. Kennedy. *The Warren Commission Report*, issued by the commission, found no evidence of conspiracy and concluded that a single assassin killed Kennedy. Warren remained chief justice until June 23, 1969, when he was succeeded by Warren Earl Burger, who was appointed by President Richard M. Nixon.

West Virginia Board of Education v. Barnette, 406 U.S. 205 (1943)

In this case, the Supreme Court struck down state regulations that required the daily saluting of the American flag and recitation of the Pledge of Allegiance in public schools. The challenge to this law was brought by the Jehovah's Witnesses on behalf of the Barnette family, members of the church whose children had been disciplined and expelled for failure to comply. Notably, expulsion was grounds for delinquency under West Virginia law, and parents of delinquent children were also subject to criminal fines and incarceration.

The Court held that the state law infringed upon the First Amendment right of free speech, stating that "no official . . . can prescribe what shall be orthodox in politics, nationalism, religion or . . . force citizens to confess by word or act their faith therein." The Court thus affirmed an individual's freedom from government compulsion to express views that the individual does not espouse and reinforced the strength of religious freedoms as immune from government interference.

This case overruled the Court's holding only three years earlier in *Minersville School District v. Gobitis* (1940). In *Gobitis*, the Court upheld virtually identical flag-saluting regulations against a claim that the regulations violated the right of free exercise of religion, also under the First Amendment. In *Barnette*, however, the claim was made in part on free speech grounds, which may account for the change of mind by three justices. Further, the composition of the Court had changed with the addition of three new justices appointed by President Roosevelt, two of whom voted in the majority in *Barnette*.

Wisconsin v. Yoder, 406 U.S. 476 (1972)

In this decision of the Burger Court, compulsory school attendance laws were invalidated as applied to Amish parents who refused on religious grounds to send their children to school. The Yoders and others respondents were members of the Old Amish Order religion and the Conservative Amish Mennonite Church. They were convicted of violating Wisconsin law, which requires a child's school attendance until age sixteen, by declining to send their children to public or private school after they had grad-uated from the eighth grade.

In an opinion authored by Chief Justice Burger, the Court upheld the respondent's claim that application of this law to them violated the Free Exercise Clause of the First Amendment, applicable to the states under the Fourteenth Amendment. The Court explicitly recognized the Old Amish Order as a religion and relied upon evidence pre-sented at trial that demonstrated the respondents' sincere belief that high school atten-dance was contrary to the Amish religion and way of life and that they would endanger their own salvation and that of their children by complying with the Wisconsin law. The Court held that the state's interest in universal education must be balanced against other fundamental rights, such as those specifically protected by the Free Exercise Clause of the First Amendment and the traditional interest of parents with respect to the religious upbringing of their children. The Court held that Wisconsin could not demonstrate a compelling interest in keeping the Amish in school for the last year or two before their sixteenth birthdays, at which time attendance was no longer compul-sory under school attendance laws. *Wisconsin v. Yoder* arguably opened the door to challenges that states were required to grant special exemptions for those who opposed educational laws and regulations on religious grounds.

Chronology

1986   June   President Ronald Reagan appoints Associate Justice William H. Rehnquist to replace retiring Chief Justice Warren Burger.

Antonin Scalia appointed by President Ronald Reagan to fill the Rehnquist vacancy as associate justice.

September   William Rehnquist is confirmed to replace Chief Justice Warren Burger (65–33); Antonin Scalia is confirmed to fill the Rehnquist vacancy (98–0).

Antonin Scalia is sworn in as associate justice to fill the vacancy created by William Rehnquist's confirmation as chief justice.

1987   March   *Johnson v. Agency of Santa Clara County, California*, approving the application of affirmative action to women.

April   *McCleskey v. Kemp*, rejecting the argument that Georgia's death penalty system is racially biased.

June   *Edwards v. Aguillard*, rejecting Louisiana legislation prohibiting the teaching of evolution in public schools.

Nollan v. California Coastal Commission, finding a compensable taking when building permits are made contingent on the grant of a public right of access to the beach.

South Dakota v. Dole, upholding congressional legislation requiring states to have twenty-one as the drinking age or lose federal highway funds.

Justice Lewis Powell announces his retirement.

July   Robert H. Bork nominated by President Ronald Reagan to replace retiring Justice Lewis Powell.

October   Robert H. Bork is rejected by the Senate (42–58).

Douglas Ginsburg nominated by President Reagan to replace Justice Lewis Powell.

Ginsburg withdraws from consideration.

November   Anthony M. Kennedy appointed by President Ronald Reagan to replace retiring Justice Lewis Powell.

1988   February   Anthony M. Kennedy is confirmed to replace retiring Justice Lewis Powell (97–0).

Anthony M. Kennedy is sworn into office.

Hustler Magazine v. Falwell, supporting the right of *Hustler Magazine* to use parodies of famous people.

June   *Morrison v. Olson,* upholding the constitutionality of the independent counsel provisions of the Ethics in Government Act of 1978.

November   Republicans George Herbert Walker Bush and J. Danforth Quayle are elected to the offices of president and vice-president, defeating the Democrats Michael S. Dukakis and Geraldine Ferraro in the general election.

1989   January   George Herbert Walker Bush is inaugurated as the forty-first president of the United States.

City of Richmond v. J. A. Croson Co., rejecting Richmond, Virginia's affirmative action plan for minority-owned businesses and requiring strict scrutiny for the first time in affirmative action cases.

March   *National Treasury Employee Union v. Von Raab* and *Skinner v. Railway Labor Executives' Association,* approving federal drug-testing programs without a warrant or any degree of probable cause.

June   *Texas v. Johnson*, ruling that the First Amendment protects burning the American flag in political protest.

Stanford v. Kentucky, permitting the death penalty for persons sixteen and seventeen years of age.

Penry v. Lynaugh, approving the death penalty for the mentally retarded.

Webster v. Reproductive Health Services, allowing states to place various restrictions on the abortion process.

1990   February   *Michigan v. Sitz*, upholding sobriety roadblocks.

April   *Employment Division, Department of Human Resources of Oregon v. Smith*, holding that the practice of using illegal drugs as a part of a religious practice is not immune from employer or state sanction.

June   *Cruzan v. Director, Missouri Department of Health*, ruling against parents who wished to take their daughter off of life-sustaining hospital machines.

Metro Broadcasting, Inc. v. FCC, ruling that a federal affirmative action program regarding radio licensing is constitutional under the intermediate scrutiny test.

July   Justice William Brennan announces his retirement.

David H. Souter is nominated by President George H. W. Bush to replace retiring Justice William Brennan.

October   David H. Souter is confirmed to replace retiring Justice William Brennan (90–9).

1991   May   *Rust v. Sullivan*, approving requirement that counselors not discuss abortion in federal programs funding birth control clinics.

June   *Florida v. Bostick*, approving police randomly inquiring in public places if they can search through belongings.

Payne v. Tennessee, allowing victim impact statements to be made in capital punishment cases, overturning two earlier Rehnquist Court cases.

Justice Thurgood Marshall announces his retirement.

July   Clarence Thomas is nominated by President George H. W. Bush to replace retiring Justice Thurgood Marshall.

October   Clarence Thomas is confirmed to replace retiring Justice Thurgood Marshall (52–45).

November   Clarence Thomas is sworn in as associate justice.

1992   June   *Planned Parenthood of Southeastern Pennsylvania v. Casey*, upholding the core principles of *Roe v. Wade* (1973) but approving state procedural restrictions on the right to abortion that are rationally related to a permissible state objective and not "unduly" burdensome, including informed consent and parental consent for minors.

Lucas v. South Carolina Coastal Council, finding that state action that effectively prohibits the use of property for any purpose is a compensable taking.

Lee v. Weisman, finding prayer at public school graduation activities violates the Establishment Clause.

November   Democrats William Jefferson Clinton and Albert Gore Jr. are elected president and vice-president in the general election, defeating a Republican ticket led by incumbent George H. W. Bush and an Independent ticket let by H. Ross Perot.

1993   January   William Jefferson Clinton is inaugurated as the forty-second president of the United States.

June   *Church of the Lukumi Babalu Aye v. City of Hialeah*, finding unconstitutional under the Free Exercise of Religion Clause Hialeah's animal sacrifice law.

Justice Byron White announces his retirement.

Ruth Bader Ginsburg is nominated by President Clinton to serve as the second woman on the Court, to replace retiring Justice Byron White.

August   Ruth Bader Ginsburg is confirmed to replace retiring Justice Byron White (96–3).

Ruth Bader Ginsburg is sworn in as associate justice.

1994   June   *U.S. Term Limits v. Thornton*, finding state attempts to limit congressional terms to be unconstitutional.

Dolan v. City of Tigard, holding that under the Takings Clause, cities cannot attach conditions to building permits that constitute the taking of private property without just compensation.

Justice Harry Blackmun announces his retirement.

Stephen G. Breyer is nominated by President Clinton to replace retiring Justice Harry Blackmun.

July   Stephen G. Breyer is confirmed to replace retiring Justice Harry Blackmun (87–9).

August   Stephen G. Breyer is sworn in as associate justice.

1995   April   *United States v. Lopez*, deciding that Congress exceeded its power under the Commerce Clause in regard to the Gun-Free School Zone Act.

June   *Adarand Constructors, Inc. v. Pena*, holding that a federal affirmative action program to encourage minority businesses was unconstitutional and that federal affirmative action programs should be viewed under strict scrutiny.

1996   May   *Romer v. Evans*, striking down Colorado Amendment 2, marking the first time the Court had used the Equal Protection Clause to support homosexuals.

June   *United States v. Virginia*, finding unconstitutional Virginia Military Institute's policy of prohibiting women from attending.

November   Democrats Clinton and Gore are reelected in the general election, defeating a Republican ticket headed by Bob Dole and the Independent ticket led by H. Ross Perot.

1997   January   Clinton is inaugurated for his second term as president.

May   *Reno v. American Civil Liberties Union*, finding unconstitutional provisions of the Communications Decency Act of 1996 as overbroad restrictions on free speech.

June   *City of Boerne v. P. F. Flores*, finding the Religious Freedom Restoration Act of 1993 to be an unconstitutional intrusion on the powers of the judiciary.

Agostini v. Felton, overturning a previous case and finding no Establishment Clause violation in allowing public school teachers to instruct in remedial programs under Title I.

Washington v. Glucksberg, approving Washington's ban on physician-assisted suicide.

Clinton v. Jones, ruling against President Clinton's argument that the president is immune from private civil suits while in office.

1998   January   Independent Counsel Kenneth Starr opens grand jury inquiry into allegations against President Clinton made by White House intern Monica Lewinsky.

June   *Clinton v. City of New York*, ruling unconstitutional the line item veto power for the president.

Knowles v. Iowa, finding that the Fourth Amendment prohibits police from searching a car if only a citation is given.

September   Independent Counsel Kenneth Starr issues report to the House of Representatives on the investigation of President Clinton.

October   House of Representatives approves an open-ended impeachment inquiry of President Clinton by a vote of 258–176.

November   In midterm elections, Democratic candidates score upset victories.

The House Judiciary committee releases four articles of impeachment against President Clinton.

December   The House of Representatives approves two of four articles of impeachment against President Clinton, for perjury and obstruction of justice.

1999   January   The Senate impeachment trial begins, with Chief Justice Rehnquist presiding.

February   The Senate acquits the president on charges of perjury (45–55) and obstruction of justice (50–50).

June   *Alden v. Maine*, placing limits on Congress's authority to require non-consenting states to be subject to private suits.

2000   May   *United States v. Morrison*, finding unconstitutional under the Commerce Clause part of a 1994 federal law allowing women rape victims to bring suit in federal court.

June   *Dickerson v. United States*, ruling unconstitutional an attempt by Congress in the sixties to replace the *Miranda* warnings with a test asking if testimony was given voluntarily.

November   Republicans George W. Bush and Richard Cheney are elected to the offices of president and vice-president even though they received fewer popular votes than Democratic candidates Albert Gore and Joseph Lieberman.

December   *Bush v. Gore*, finding that a proposed recount of key Florida votes would violate the Equal Protection Clause, resulting in George W. Bush becoming president.

2001   January   George W. Bush is inaugurated as the forty-third president of the United States.

March   *Ferguson v. City of Charleston*, finding unconstitutional under the Fourth Amendment a program that required certain women to be drug tested.

June   *Kyllo v. United States*, ruling that federal agents could not use a heat-sensing device to determine if a person was growing marijuana in his home unless the agents obtained a search warrant.

September   Terrorist attacks on the United States in New York City and Washington, D.C., by al Qaeda.

October   USA Patriot Act passed by Congress and signed into law by President Bush.

2002   June   *Zelman v. Simmons-Harris*, ruling that the Cleveland, Ohio, school-voucher program does not violate the Establishment Clause.

Atkins v. Virginia, holding that it is unconstitutional to execute the mentally retarded, overturning one of the Rehnquist Court's own precedents.

Ring v. Arizona, ruling that any facts must be determined by a jury in a capital case, not a judge, in regard to increasing a maximum sentence.

November   In midterm elections, Republicans win majorities in both the House and Senate.

2003   March   *Ewing v. California*, approving as constitutional California's three-strike law.

June   *Lawrence v. Texas*, ruling unconstitutional a Texas law criminalizing homosexual sodomy and overturning *Bowers v. Hardwick* (1986).

Grutter v. Bollinger, ruling constitutional the affirmative action program of the University of Michigan Law School.

Gratz v. Bollinger, ruling unconstitutional the affirmative action program used for undergraduate admission to the University of Michigan.

2004   March   *Crawford v. Washington*, ruling that defendants have the right to confront hostile witnesses in the courtroom even if a deposition is highly reliable.

May   *Tennessee v. Lane*, ruling that states can be sued under the Americans with Disabilities Act for not providing access to courtrooms for people in wheelchairs.

June   *Blakely v. Washington*, holding that Washington's sentencing scheme gave too much authority to judges rather than juries.

Hamdi v. Rumsfeld, holding that a U.S. citizen captured in Afghanistan and held at Guantanamo Bay has a right to challenge his detention in U.S. courts.

Rasul v. Bush, finding that captives taken during the U.S. invasion of Afghanistan and held at Guantanamo Bay were entitled to access to U.S. courts.

November   Incumbent president George W. Bush defeats Democratic candidate John Kerry, and Republicans win majorities in both the House and Senate.

2005   January   George W. Bush begins his second term as president.

March   *Roper v. Simmons*, ruling unconstitutional the execution of minors age sixteen and seventeen when the crime was committed, overturning a previous Rehnquist Court case.

June   *Gonzales v. Raich*, ruling that Congress can criminalize the use and possession of marijuana even though California law allows this for medical purposes.

Kelo v. City of New London, allowing the city to exercise its power of eminent domain for an economic development program.

McCreary v. ACLU, ruling that the display of the Ten Commandments in a public courthouse violates the Establishment Clause.

Van Orden v. Perry, holding that the display on the grounds of the state capitol in Texas of a six-foot-high monument containing the Ten Commandments is constitutional.

July   Justice Sandra Day O'Connor announces her resignation.

President Bush nominates federal circuit judge John Roberts to replace retiring Justice Sandra Day O'Connor.

September   Chief Justice Rehnquist dies, and President Bush nominates Roberts to become chief justice replacing Rehnquist.

Senate confirms Roberts as chief justice by a vote of 78–22.

Roberts sworn in as chief justice.

October   President Bush nominates Harriet Meiers to replace Justice Sandra Day O'Connor, but Meiers withdraws in the face of intense pubic outcry.

President Bush nominates federal circuit judge Samuel Alito to replace O'Connor.

2006   January   Alito is confirmed by the Senate to replace Justice O'Connor.

February   Alito is sworn into office.

List of Cases

Abington Township, School District of, v. Schempp, 374 U.S. 203 (1963)

Adamson v. California, 332 U.S. 46 (1947)

Adarand Constructors, Inc. v. Pena, 515 U.S. 200 (1995)

Agins v. City of Tiburon, 447 U.S. 255 (1980)

Agostini v. Felton, 521 U.S. 203 (1997)

Aguilar v. Felton, 473 U.S. 402 (1985)

Akron v. Akron Center for Reproductive Health, 462 U.S. 416 (1983)

Alabama v. Shelton, 535 U.S. 654 (2002)

Alden v. Maine, 527 U.S. 706 (1999)

Alexander v. Holmes Board of Education, 396 U.S. 19 (1969)

Alexander v. Sandoval, 532 U.S. 275 (2001)

Allegheny, County of, v. ACLU, 492 U.S. 573 (1989)

American Library Association; United States v., 539 U.S. 194 (2003)

Apodaca v. Oregon, 406 U.S. 404 (1972)

Apprendi v. New Jersey, 530 U.S. 466 (2000)

Argersinger v. Hamilton, 407 U.S. 25 (1972)

Arizona v. Fulminante, 499 U.S. 279 (1991)

Arizona v. Roberson, 486 U.S. 675 (1988)

Ashcroft v. American Civil Liberties Union, 535 U.S. 564 (2002)

Ashcroft v. Free Speech Coalition, 535 U.S. 564 (2002)

Associated Press v. Walker, 388 U.S. 130 (1967)

Atkins v. Virginia, 536 U.S. 304 (2002)

Baker v. Carr, 369 U.S. 186 (1962)

Ballew v. Georgia, 435 U.S. 223 (1978)

Barron v. Baltimore, 7 Pet. 243 (1833)

Batson v. Kentucky, 476 U.S. 79 (1986)

Beal v. Doe, 432 U.S. 438 (1977)

Benton v. Maryland, 395 U.S. 784 (1969)

Berman v. Parker, 348 U.S. 26 (1954)

Bethel School District v. Fraser, 478 U.S. 675 (1986)

Betts v. Brady, 316 U.S. 455 (1942)

Bigelow v. Virginia, 421 U.S. 809 (1975)

Blakely v. Washington, 124 S. Ct. 2531 (2004)

Blockberger v. United States, 284 U.S. 299 (1932)

Board of Directors of Rotary International v. Rotary Club of Duarte, 481 U.S. 537
    (1987)

Board of Education v. Allen, 392 U.S. 236 (1968)

Board of Education of Oklahoma City Public Schools v. Dowell, 498 U.S. 237 (1991)

Board of Education of Pottawatomie County v. Earls, 536 U.S. 822 (2002)

Board of Trustees of the University of Alabama v. Garrett, 531 U.S. 356 (2001)

Bob Jones University v. United States, 461 U.S. 574 (1983)

Bond v. United States, 529 U.S. 334 (2000)

Booker v. United States, 543 U.S. _____ (2005)

Booth v. Maryland, 482 U.S. 496 (1987)

Bowen v. Roy, 476 U.S. 693 (1986)

Bowers v. Hardwick, 478 U.S. 186 (1986)

Bradwell v. Illinois, 16 Wall. 130 (1873)

Brandenburg v. Ohio, 395 U.S. 444 (1969)

Braunfeld v. Brown, 366 U.S. 599 (1961)

Brewer v. Williams, 430 U.S. 387 (1977)

Brown v. Board of Education of Topeka, Kansas, 347 U.S. 483 (1954)

Brown v. Board of Education of Topeka, Kansas, 349 U.S. 294 (1955)

Brown v. Mississippi, 297 U.S. 278 (1936)

Calandra; United States v., 414 U.S. 338 (1974)

California Federal Savings and Loan Association v. Guerra, 479 U.S. 272 (1987)

Cantwell v. Connecticut, 310 U.S. 296 (1940)

Carroll v. United States, 267 U.S. 132 (1925)

Central Hudson Gas v. Public Service Commission, 447 U.S. 557 (1980)

Chandler v. Miller, 520 U.S. 305 (1997)

Chaplinsky v. New Hampshire, 315 U.S. 568 (1942)

Chicago, Burlington, and Quincy Railroad Company v. Chicago, 166 U.S. 226
    (1897)

Chimel v. California, 395 U.S. 752 (1969)

Church of the Lukumi Babalu Aye v. City of Hialeah, 508 U.S. 520 (1993)

City of Boerne v. P. F. Flores, 521 U.S. 507 (1997)

City of Erie v. Pap's A.M., 529 U.S. 277 (2000)

City of Richmond v. J. A. Croson Co., 488 U.S. 469 (1989)

Clark v. Jeter, 486 U.S. 456 (1988)

Clinton v. City of New York, 524 U.S. 417 (1998)

Clinton v. Jones, 520 U.S. 681 (1997)

Fullilove v. Klutznick, 448 U.S. 448 (1980)

Furman v. Georgia, 408 U.S. 238 (1972)

Gaines v. Canada (See *Missouri ex rel. Gaines v. Canada*)

Garcia v. San Antonio Metropolitan Transit Authority, 469 U.S. 578 (1985)

Gault, In re, 387 U.S. 1 (1967)

Gebseret v. Lago Vista Independent School District, 524 U.S. 274 (1998)

Georgia v. McCollum, 505 U.S. 42 (1992)

Gertz v. Welch, Inc., 418 U.S. 323 (1974)

Gideon v. Wainwright, 372 U.S. 335 (1963)

Gitlow v. New York, 268 U.S. 652 (1925)

Goldman v. Weinberger, 475 U.S. 503 (1986)

Good News Club v. Milford Central School, 533 U.S. 98 (2001)

Grady v. Corbin, 495 U.S. 508 (1990)

Grand Rapids School District v. Ball, 473 U.S. 373 (1985)

Gratz v. Bollinger, 539 U.S. 244 (2003)

Green v. School Board of New Kent County, 391 U.S. 430 (1968)

Gregg v. Georgia, 428 U.S. 153 (1976)

Gregory v. Ashcroft, 501 U.S. 452 (1991)

Griffin v. Wisconsin, 483 U.S. 868 (1987)

Griswold v. Connecticut, 381 U.S. 479 (1965)

Grutter v. Bollinger, 539 U.S. 306 (2003)

Hamdi v. Rumsfeld, 542 U.S. 508 (2004)

Hammer v. Dagenhart, 247 U.S. 251 (1918)

Harmelin v. Michigan, 501 U.S. 957 (1991)

Harris v. Forklift Systems, Inc., 510 U.S. 17 (1993)

Harris v. McCrae, 448 U.S. 297 (1980)

Harris v. New York, 401 U.S. 222 (1971)

Harris v. United States, 331 U.S. 145 (1947)

Hawaii Housing Authority v. Midkiff, 467 U.S. 229 (1984)

Heart of Atlanta Motel v. United States, 379 U.S. 241 (1964)

Heath v. Alabama, 474 U.S. 82 (1985)

Heller v. Doe, 509 U.S. 312 (1993)

Helling v. McKinney, 509 U.S. 25 (1993)

Hernandez v. Commissioner of Internal Revenue Service, 490 U.S. 680 (1989)

Hester v. United States, 265 U.S. 57 (1924)

Hobbie v. Unemployment Appeals Commission of Florida, 480 U.S. 136 (1987)

Hoyt v. Florida, 368 U.S. 57 (1961)

Hudson v. McMillian, 503 U.S. 1 (1992)

Hurley v. Irish-American Gay, Lesbian, and Bisexual Group of Boston, 515 U.S. 557 (1995)

Hustler Magazine v. Falwell, 485 U.S. 46 (1988)

Illinois v. Krull, 480 U.S. 340 (1987)

Illinois v. Lidster, 540 U.S. 419 (2004)

Illinois v. Perkins, 496 U.S. 292 (1990)

Illinois v. Rodriguez, 497 U.S. 177 (1990)

In re. See name of party

Indianapolis v. Edmond, 531 U.S. 32 (2000)

International Union, United Auto., Aerospace and Agr. Implement Workers of America, UAW v. Johnson Controls, Inc., 499 U.S. 189 (1991)

Jacobellis v. Ohio, 378 U.S. 184 (1964)

James v. Illinois, 493 U.S. 307 (1990)

Janis; United States v., 428 U.S. 433 (1976)

J.E.B. v. Alabama ex rel. T.B., 511 U.S. 127 (1994)

Jimmy Swaggart Ministries v. Board of Equalization of California, 493 U.S. 378 (1990)

Johnson v. Eisentrager, 339 U.S. 763 (1950)

Johnson v. Transportation Agency of Santa Clara County, California, 480 U.S. 646 (1987)

Johnson v. Zerbst, 304 U.S. 458 (1938)

Kadrmas v. Dickinson Public Schools, 487 U.S. 450 (1988)

Katzenbach v. McClung, 379 U.S. 294 (1964)

Kelo v. City of New London, 545 U.S. _____ (2005)

Keyes v. School District No. 1, Denver, 413 U.S. 189 (1973)

Kimel v. Florida Board of Regents, 528 U.S. 62 (2000)

Klopfer v. North Carolina, 386 U.S. 213 (1967)

Knowles v. Iowa, 525 U.S. 113 (1998)

Korematsu v. United States, 323 U.S. 214 (1944)

Lamb's Chapel v. Center Moriches Union Free School District, 508 U.S. 385 (1993)

Lawrence v. Texas, 539 U.S. 558 (2003)

Lee; United States v., 345 U.S. 252 (1982)

Lee v. Weisman, 505 U.S. 577 (1992)

Lemon v. Kurtzman, 403 U.S. 602 (1971)

Leon; United States v., 468 U.S. 897 (1984)

Lingle v. Chevron, _____ U.S. _____ (2005)

Locke v. Davey, 540 U.S. 713 (2004)

Lopez; United States v., 514 U.S. 549 (1995)

Lucas v. South Carolina Coastal Council, 505 U.S. 1003 (1992)

Lujan v. Defenders of Wildlife, 504 U.S. 555 (1992)

Lynch v. Donnelly, 465 U.S. 668 (1984)

Lyng v. Northwest Indian Cemetery Protective Association, 485 U.S. 439 (1988)

Wisconsin v. Yoder, 406 U.S. 205 (1972)

Witherspoon v. Illinois, 391 U.S. 510 (1968)

Wolf v. Colorado, 338 U.S. 25 (1949)

Wolman v. Walter, 433 U.S. 229 (1977)

Wygant v. Jackson Board of Education, 476 U.S. 267 (1986)

Wyoming v. Houghton, 526 U.S. 295 (1999)

Yates v. United States, 354 U.S. 298 (1957)

Zadvydas v. Davis, 533 U.S. 678 (2001)

Zelman v. Simmons-Harris, 536 U.S. 639 (2002)

Zobrest v. Catalina Foothills School, 509 U.S. 1 (1993)

Glossary

absolutism   An approach to interpreting the First Amendment that emphasizes the language stating that Congress shall pass *no* laws interfering with First Amendment rights, thus meaning that any form of governmental interference with these guarantees is unconstitutional.

actual malice   A standard used in libel cases that requires that material must be published with knowledge that it was false or with a reckless disregard of the truth.

adversary proceeding   A legal process that involves a contest between two opposing parties. Formal notice is served on the party against whom an action has been filed to allow that party an opportunity to respond. This system is generally regarded as the most effective means for the evaluation of evidence.

advisory opinion   An opinion of a court indicating how it would rule on an issue if the issue were presented in an actual case—although no real case exists to present the legal question; an interpretation of law without binding effect.

affirmation   An appellate court ruling that upholds the judgment of a lower court—that maintains the judgment of the lower court is correct and should stand.

affirmative action   A concept embodied in programs that seek to address the effects of discriminatory practices against minority groups and women. These programs can take a wide variety of forms but can only be justified if the government is pursuing a compelling interest through narrowly tailored means.

amicus curiae (lit., "friend of the court")   A person or group not a party to a case that submits a brief detailing its views on a case. The purpose of an amicus brief is to direct a court's attention to an issue or argument that might not be developed in the same way by the parties themselves.

appeal   A process by which a final judgment of a lower court ruling is reviewed by a higher court.

appellant   The party that appeals a decision of a lower court to a higher court. Because most of the Supreme Court's cases arrive via a petition for a writ of certiorari rather than an appeal, the first-listed party who brought the case to the Supreme Court is usually the petitioner. The appellant's name appears first in the title of the case.

appellate jurisdiction   Authority of a superior court to review decisions of inferior courts. Appellate jurisdiction empowers a higher court to conduct such a review and affirm, modify, or reverse the lower-court decision. Appellate jurisdiction is conveyed through constitutional or statutory mandate. Federal appellate jurisdiction is granted by Article 3 of the Constitution, which says that the Supreme Court possesses such jurisdiction "both as to law and fact, with such exceptions and under such regulations as the Congress shall make."

appellee   The party who prevails in a lower court and against whom an appeal of the judgment is sought; in some situations called a "respondent."

arguendo   For the sake of argument; assuming something is so, without accepting its truth, to extend further a line of argument.

arraignment   An early step in the criminal justice process where formal charges are read to the defendant and the defendant enters a plea of "guilty" or "not guilty."

assembly, right to   A fundamental right provided by the First Amendment that the people are entitled peaceably to gather and petition the government for "redress of grievances." It includes the right to protest governmental policies as well as to advocate particular, even distasteful, views. The government can impose regulations on the time, place, and manner of assembly, provided that substantial interests, such as preventing threats to public order, can be shown.

balancing test   A judicial decision-making approach where interests on one side are weighed against interests on another, based on the traditional idea that individual freedoms and governmental authority must be kept in equilibrium. This approach is used most frequently where courts are reviewing individual rights issues.

bench trial   A trial conducted by a judge alone without a jury. A bench trial occurs when a defendant waives the constitutional right to a trial by jury for serious charges or when the defendant is charged with petty offenses and therefore has no right to a jury trial.

bill of attainder   A statutory law that imposes a penalty upon an individual without a hearing or trial. This is prohibited by Article III, Section 9, of the Constitution.

Brandeis brief   A written document presented by an attorney to a court that emphasizes social science rather than or in addition to citation to legal authority.

brief   A document containing arguments on a matter under consideration by a court. A brief submitted to a court by an attorney typically contains, among other things, points of law from previous rulings.

capital offense   A crime that is punishable by the death penalty.

capital punishment   Imposition of the death penalty upon a criminal defendant found guilty of a crime for which death can be imposed.

case   A legal dispute brought before a court for resolution involving parties with a live controversy.

case law   Precedent created as courts resolve disputes. Case law is made by judges as they rule on a specific set of facts. Common law is similar to case law but judicially incorporates accepted traditional community values, usages, and customs into court decisions. Statutory law, by contrast, is enacted by a legislative body.

case or controversy   A constitutional requirement that disputes or controversies be definite and concrete and involve parties whose legal interests are truly adverse. This requirement, contained in Article 3 of the Constitution, establishes a bona fide controversy as a precondition for adjudication by federal courts.

censorship   An action by the government that prevents expression from occurring. This is also called prior restraint. The government can engage in censorship only under the most extreme circumstances.

certiorari (lit., "to be informed of, to be made certain in regard to")   A writ or order to a court whose decision is being challenged on appeal to send up the records of the case to enable a higher court to review the case. The writ of certiorari is the primary means by which the U.S. Supreme Court reviews cases from lower courts.

circuit courts   Thirteen courts in the federal judicial system that constitute an intermediate system between the federal district courts of original jurisdiction and the Supreme Court. Most states also have an intermediate system of appellate courts, but these are not always called "circuit courts" as in the federal judicial system.

citizenship   A legal status that entitles a person to all the rights and privileges guaranteed and protected by the Constitution of the United States. All persons born in the United States or to parents who are U.S. citizens possess U.S. citizenship. Others may obtain citizenship through naturalization, a process established by Congress.

civil law   The body of law that deals with the legal relationships, rights, and duties of private persons. Civil law is distinguished from criminal law, which deals with crimes against the government.

civil liberties   Those liberties spelled out in a bill of rights or a constitution that guarantee the protection of persons, opinions, and property from the arbitrary interference of governmental officials. Civil liberties create immunities from certain governmental actions that interfere with an individual's protected rights.

civil rights   Positive acts of government designed to protect persons against arbitrary and discriminatory treatment by government or individuals. Civil rights guarantees may be found in constitutions but more frequently take the form of statutes.

class action   A legal action in which one or more persons represent both themselves and others who are similarly situated. All members of a class must share a common legal interest and meet particular requirements to proceed as a class or collective action.

commerce clause   Provision found in Article I, Section 8, of the U.S. Constitution that empowers Congress to "regulate commerce with foreign nations, and among the several states, and with the Indian tribes." Since the 1930s the commerce power has been the basis for extensive federal regulation of the economy and, to a limited extent, federal criminal law.

commercial speech   Another name for advertising, a form of expression that is protected under the First Amendment through intermediate scrutiny.

common law   A body of principles that derive their authority from court judgments that are grounded in common customs and usages. Common law consists of principles that do not have their origin in statute and as such are distinct from law created by legislative enactments.

compelling state interest   A test that requires the government to show an extremely important objective achieved through narrowly tailored means to interfere with a constitutional right or liberty. This test is used in a variety of areas, especially in freedom of expression and equal protection cases. It is also called the strict scrutiny test.

concurrent jurisdiction   Authority that is shared by different courts and may be exercised at the same time over the same subject matter.

concurring opinion   An opinion by a judge that agrees with the decision of the majority but disagrees with the majority's rationale—in other words, has arrived at the same conclusion but for different reasons.

conference A closed meeting of Supreme Court justices in which the justices conduct all business associated with deciding cases—determining which cases to review, discussing the merits of cases after oral argument, and deciding by vote which party to a case will prevail.

consent decree A court order in which the parties to the decree agree to act in accordance with the term set by the order, generally used to settle lawsuits before they go to trial.

conspiracy An agreement or association created for criminal purposes.

constitutional court A federal court created by Congress under authority conveyed by Article 3. Judges of constitutional courts serve for the duration of good behavior (life tenure) and are protected from having their salaries reduced by the legislature.

contempt An act that in some way shows disrespect for a court or obstructs the activities of the court. Contempt can occur in both civil and criminal law and is usually a punishable offense.

criminal law The body of law that is concerned with enforcing laws defined as crimes by the state and with punishing those persons who are found guilty of violating these laws. Criminal law is contrasted with civil law, which deals with the legal relationships between private persons.

de facto (lit., "from the fact") Something that exists or is actual but, unlike *de jure*, is not caused by any official or state action. For example, racial segregation that is not legally mandated, but exists nonetheless, is referred to as *de facto* segregation.

de jure (lit., "by right") A *de jure* action occurs as a result of law or official government action.

declaratory judgment A ruling of a court that clarifies rights of the parties or offers an opinion or a legal question and is invoked when a plaintiff seeks a declaration of his or her rights. It differs from a conventional action in that no specific order is issued nor is any relief or remedy granted.

decree A judgment or order of a court.

defamation The harming of a person's reputation. This is one of the elements that must be proven in a libel action.

defendant The party who is sued in a civil action or charged in a criminal case; the party responding to a civil complaint. A defendant in a criminal case is the person formally accused of criminal conduct.

dicta   See obiter dictum.

dissenting opinion   The opinion of a judge that disagrees with the result reached by the majority.

diversity jurisdiction   Authority conveyed by Article 3 of the Constitution empowering federal courts to hear civil actions involving parties from different states.

docket   A listing of all the cases filed in a court.

double jeopardy   The trying of a person twice for the same offense. This is prohibited by the Fifth Amendment.

due process   Government procedures that follow principles of essential or fundamental fairness. Provisions designed to ensure that laws will be reasonable both in substance and in means of implementation are contained in two clauses of the Constitution. The Fifth Amendment prohibits deprivation of "life, liberty, or property, without due process of law." It sets a limit on arbitrary and unreasonable actions by the federal government. The Fourteenth Amendment contains parallel language aimed at the states. Due process requires that actions of government occur through ordered and regularized processes.

eminent domain   The principle that the government may take private property for public use if just compensation is paid. This principle is stated in the Fifth Amendment.

en banc (lit., "on the bench")   A proceeding in which all the judges of an appellate court participate, as distinguished from a proceeding heard by a panel of three judges.

enjoin   To require to perform or refrain from a specified action. A party is enjoined by a court issuing an injunction or a restraining order.

error, writ of   An order sent from an appellate court to a lower court that asks for the record in a case, which can be reviewed for error.

ex parte (lit., "on one side")   Done for, on behalf of, or on the application of one party only.

ex post facto law   A law that makes something a crime that was not illegal at the time when the action occurred. This is prohibited by Article I, Section 9, of the Constitution.

exclusionary rule   A rule that any evidence obtained in violation of a constitutional guarantee for the criminally accused must be excluded from the trial.

exclusive power Authority that is assigned to either the national or state level of government but not exercised by both.

executive order A regulation issued by the president, a state governor, or some other executive authority for the purpose of giving effect to a constitutional or statutory provision. An executive order has the force of law and is one means by which the executive branch implements laws.

executive privilege The exemption of the executive from disclosure requirements that exist for ordinary citizens based upon the executive's need for confidentiality in undertaking the duties of office.

federal preemption The exclusive power of the federal government to override state authority in certain areas, for example, interstate commerce.

federal question An issue arising out of provisions of the Constitution, federal statutes, or treaties. A federal court has authority to hear federal questions under powers conferred by Article 3.

federalism A political system in which a number of sovereign political units join together to form a larger political unit that has authority to act on behalf of the whole. A federal system or federation preserves the political integrity of all the entities that compose the federation. Federal systems are regarded as weak if the central government has control over very few policy questions and strong if the central government possesses authority over most significant policy issues. Authority that is not exclusively assigned may be shared by the two levels and exercised concurrently. The supremacy clause of the Constitution requires that conflicts arising from the exercise of federal and state power are resolved in favor of the central government. Powers not assigned to the national government are "reserved" for the states by the Tenth Amendment.

felony A serious criminal offense usually involving a penalty of at least one year in state or federal prison.

gerrymander Redrawing the boundaries of a legislative district to maximize certain advantages.

grand jury A panel of twelve to twenty-three citizens who review prosecutorial evidence to determine if there are sufficient grounds to formally accuse an individual of criminal conduct. The charges a grand jury issues are contained in a document called an indictment.

habeas corpus (lit., "you have the body") Habeas corpus was a procedure in English law designed to prevent the improper detention of prisoners. The habeas process forced jailers to bring a detained person before a judge who would examine the justification for the detention. If the court found the person was being improperly held, it could order the prisoner's release by issuing a writ of habeas corpus.

harmless error   A decision by an appellate court that a mistake made by a lower court did not sufficiently affect the rights of a party alleging the error to justify a reversal of the judgment.

immunity   A grant to a person of exemption from prosecution on the condition that testimonial evidence is provided.

implied power   Authority that is possessed by inference from expressed provisions of a constitution and deduced from circumstances, general language, or the conduct of parties rather than conveyed by explicit language.

in camera (lit., "in a chamber")   In private; a hearing conducted with no spectators present.

in forma pauperis   A Latin term meaning in the manner of a pauper. This is a mechanism by which a poor person can file papers before a court without any costs being involved. Prisoners frequently use this method to appeal cases to the Supreme Court.

in re (lit., "in the matter of")   The usual manner of entitling a judicial proceeding in which there are no adversarial parties as such but some issue requiring judicial action.

incorporation   The question of whether the federal Bill of Rights extends as a limitation on state governments. The issue has been largely resolved, and most federal Bill of Rights provisions now operate at the state as well as the federal level. Several differing schools of thought on incorporation have existed historically.

indictment   A written accusation presented by a grand jury to a court, charging that a person has done some act or omission that by law is a punishable offense.

injunction   An order prohibiting a party from acting in a particular way or requiring its specific action. An injunction allows a court to minimize injury to a person or group until the matter can otherwise be resolved, or it may prevent injury altogether. Failure to comply with an injunction constitutes contempt of court. Once issued, an injunction may be annulled or quashed, and it may be temporary or permanent. Temporary injunctions, known as interlocutory injunctions, are used to preserve a situation until the issue is resolved through normal processes of litigation. A permanent injunction may be issued upon completion of full legal proceedings.

intermediate scrutiny   A judicial test used in both freedom of expression and equal protection cases that provides heightened but not the highest level of protection. When this test is used, the government must establish that it has an important government objective that is being pursued through means that are substantially related to this objective. This is also called the important government objective test.

interpretivism   A theory of interpreting the Constitution that seeks to control the influence of justices' personal attitudes and values by requiring that decisions be based upon the language of the Constitution, the intent of the framers, and the original understanding of the provisions of the Constitution.

judgment of the court   The final conclusion reached by a court—the outcome as distinguished from the legal reasoning supporting the conclusion.

judicial activism   An interventionist approach or role orientation for appellate decision making that has the appellate courts playing an affirmative policy role. Judicial activists are inclined to find more constitutional violations than those who see a more restrained role for courts; activists are more likely to invalidate legislative and executive policy initiatives. Critics regard judicial activism as legislating by justices to achieve policy outcomes compatible with their own social priorities.

judicial review   The power of a court to examine the actions of the legislative and executive branches with the possibility of declaring those actions unconstitutional. Judicial review was discussed extensively at the Constitutional Convention in 1787, but it was not included in the Constitution as an expressly delegated judicial function. The Supreme Court first asserted the power of judicial review in *Marbury v. Madison* (1803).

judicial self-restraint   A role view of appellate court decision making that minimizes the extent to which judges apply their personal views to the legal judgments they render. Judicial self-restraint holds that courts should defer to the policy judgments made by the elected branches of government.

jurisdiction   The boundaries within which a particular court may exercise judicial power, the power of a court to hear and decide cases. The jurisdiction of federal courts is provided in Article 3 of the Constitution in the case of the Supreme Court and in acts of Congress in the case of the lower federal courts. Federal judicial power may extend to classes of cases defined in terms of substance and party as well as to cases in law and equity stemming directly from the federal Constitution, federal statutes, treaties, or those cases falling into the admiralty and maritime category. Federal judicial power also extends to cases involving specified parties; regardless of the substance of the case, federal jurisdiction includes actions where the federal government itself is a party, between two or more states, between a state and a citizen of another state, between citizens of different states, between a state and an alien, between a citizen of a state and an alien, and where foreign ambassadors are involved. State constitutions and statues define the jurisdiction of state courts.

jurisprudence   A legal philosophy or the science of law; the course or direction of judicial rulings. Jurisprudence draws upon philosophical thought, historical and political analysis, sociological and behavioral evidence, and legal experience; it is grounded in the view that ideas about law evolve from critical thinking in a number of disciplines. Jurisprudence enables people to understand how law has ordered both social institutions and individual conduct.

justiciable   Appropriate for a court to hear and decide.

laissez-faire   An economic theory that advocates the government ought not interfere with the dynamics of a free market economy—government should stay out of economic matters. The decisions of the U.S. Supreme Court from the 1890s through 1937 frequently reflect laissez-faire values.

libel   Harming the reputation of another person through written material that is false and that was written with a knowledge of its falseness or with a reckless disregard of the truth.

liberty of contract   A laissez-faire doctrine used to free private agreements from governmental regulation. The liberty of contract concept holds that individuals have a right to assume contractual obligations affecting their personal affairs. This includes the right of employers and employees to agree about wages, hours, and conditions of work without government interference. The concept was a central element of substantive due process, in which the courts closely examined the reasonableness of governmental regulations. The liberty of contract concept was used to strike down laws establishing minimum wages and maximum work hours.

litigant   A party to a lawsuit.

majority opinion   An opinion in a case that has the support of a majority of the members of the court and thus becomes controlling precedent for future cases.

minimal scrutiny test   Also called the rational basis test, this test is used in numerous areas of constitutional law and usually results in the government prevailing against individuals' claimed violations of constitutional rights and liberties. The government is required under this test only to show that it is pursuing a legitimate objective through means that are rationally related to the objective.

misdemeanor   A criminal act that is considered to be less serious, usually punishable by less than a one-year period of incarceration.

moot   A situation in which a legal question has already been resolved, the situation has changed so that the legal issue no longer exists, or a hypothetical issue is under consideration.

mootness doctrine   A principle that applies if a question presented in a lawsuit cannot be answered by a court because the issue has resolved itself or conditions have so changed that the court is unable to grant the requested relief.

motion   A request made to a court for a certain ruling or action.

natural law   Laws considered applicable to all nations and people because they are basic to human nature. Contrasts with positive law.

natural rights   Rights based not upon statutory law but based instead upon a higher law transcending human sources, whether it be nature, a deity, or some other source.

naturalization   Legal procedure by which an alien is admitted to citizenship. Congress is authorized by Article 1, Section 8, of the Constitution to establish uniform rules for naturalization. An individual over eighteen may be naturalized after meeting certain qualifications, including residence in the United States for five years; ability to read, write, and speak English; and proof of good moral character. The residence requirement is lowered for spouses of citizens and for aliens who serve in the armed services. Minors become citizens when their parents are naturalized.

obiter dictum (lit., "something said in passing")   Statement contained in a court's opinion that is incidental to the disposition of the case. Obiter dicta often are directed to issues upon which no formal arguments have been heard; thus, the positions represented there are not binding on later cases.

obscenity   Sexual expression that is beyond the protection of the First Amendment. The Court has struggled to achieve a precise definition of *obscenity*, and the three-part *Miller* test embodies the Court's current criteria.

opinion of the court   The statement of a court that expresses the reasoning, or *ratio decidendi*, upon which a decision is based. The opinion summarizes the principles of law that apply in a given case and represents the views of the majority of a court's members. Occasionally, the opinion of a court may reflect the views of less than a majority of its members; it is then called a plurality opinion.

order   A written command issued by a judge.

original intent   The purpose or intended meaning of a constitutional provision by those who wrote it.

original jurisdiction The authority of a court to hear and decide a legal question before any other court. Original jurisdiction typically is vested with trial courts rather than appellate courts, although Article 3 of the Constitution extends very limited original jurisdiction to the Supreme Court. Trial courts are assigned specific original jurisdiction defined in terms of subject matter or party.

overbreadth A freedom of expression doctrine that stipulates that any government regulation of expression must not extend beyond the legitimate authority to control expression.

***per curiam* opinion** (lit., "by the court") An unsigned written opinion issued by a court.

peremptory challenge During the process of jury selection, the discretionary removal of a prospective juror that does not require any reason for the removal. In contrast, removal for cause requires a showing as to why a juror would not be impartial.

petit jury A jury that hears a trial. A petit jury is contrasted with a grand jury, which determines if there is sufficient evidence to bring charges against a defendant.

petitioner A party seeking relief in court.

plaintiff The party who brings a legal action to court for resolution or remedy.

plea bargain An agreement reached between a defendant and a prosecutor in which the defendant pleads guilty in exchange for a reduced charge or a lesser sentence. The Court has ruled that plea bargains are consistent with the requirements of the Sixth Amendment.

plenary review The process by which the Supreme Court agrees to hear a case and then requires attorneys for both sides to prepare written briefs and to present oral arguments to the justices.

plurality opinion An opinion announcing a court's judgment and supporting reasoning in a case but not endorsed by a majority of the justices hearing the case.

police power Authority that empowers government to regulate private behavior in the interest of public health, safety, and general welfare. In the U.S. constitutional system, police power resides with the state, not the federal government. It is a comprehensive power, and states possess substantial discretion for its exercise, but it is limited by various provisions of the U.S. Constitution and state constitutions and must conform to the requirements of due process.

political question   An issue that is not justiciable, or appropriate for judicial determination, because it is primarily political or involves a matter directed toward either the legislative or executive branch by constitutional language. The political question doctrine is sometimes invoked by the Supreme Court, not because the Court is without power or jurisdiction but because the Court adjudges the question inappropriate for judicial response. In the Court's view, to intervene or respond would be to encroach upon the functions and prerogatives of one of the other two branches of government.

pornography   A rather general and imprecise term referring to sexual expression that is constitutionally protected, whereas the obscene is beyond constitutional protection because it is lacking in any significant social value.

precedent   A previous court decision that is applicable to a new case before a court. The doctrine of *stare decisis* maintains that judicial officials should be guided in their decision making by adherence to precedent.

preemption doctrine   The notion that federal laws supersede, or preempt, state laws in certain policy areas. Grounded in the Supremacy Clause of Article 6, the preemption doctrine applies where the federal regulatory interest is so dominant or pervasive as to allow no reasonable inference that room is left for states to act. Congress may state explicitly such a preemptive interest, or the courts may interpret the intent of Congress fully to occupy the field.

preferred position doctrine   The concept that legislative enactments that affect First Amendment rights must be scrutinized more carefully than legislation that does not because they affect fundamental rights such as free speech. The burden is clearly on the state to demonstrate justification for limiting a preferred position freedom. The preferred position doctrine is attributed to Justice Stone, who said in a footnote to his opinion in *United States v. Carolene Products Co.* (1938) that a lesser presumption of constitutionality exists when legislation "appears on its face to be within a specific prohibition such as those of the first ten amendments."

prior restraint   A restriction placed on a publication before it can be published or circulated. Prior restraint typically occurs through a full prohibition on publication or a licensure or censorship process that involves the state's review of materials for objectionable content. Prior restraint poses a greater threat to free expression than after-the-fact prosecution because government restrictions are imposed in a manner that precludes public scrutiny. The First Amendment therefore prohibits prior restraint in most instances, though it may be justified if the publication threatens national security, incites overthrow of the government, is obscene, or interferes with the private rights of others.

probable cause　A term contained in the Fourth Amendment of the Constitution that sets the standard for judicial officials to determine if a warrant should be issued in a criminal case. Probable cause exists if a reasonable person would believe based upon the totality of the circumstances that a crime has occurred and that evidence could be discovered.

probation　A status in which a person convicted of a crime is freed from incarceration before finishing a complete sentence, although the person remains under supervision.

procedural due process　Fundamental fairness in the means by which governmental actions are executed. Procedural due process demands that before any deprivation of liberty or property can occur, a person must be formally notified and provided an opportunity for a fair hearing. Procedural due process—including access to legal counsel, the ability to confront witnesses against the accused, and a trial by jury—must also be accorded persons accused of crimes. This is in contrast to substantive due process.

rational basis test　A test used to interpret the constitutionality of government legislation and actions in cases involving freedom of expression, the free exercise of religion, and equal protection. This test places a strong burden of proof on the individual claiming a government violation of a constitutional right or liberty because the government only needs to establish that it is pursuing a legitimate objective through means that are rationally related to the objective. This is also called the minimal scrutiny test.

reapportionment　An alteration in the boundaries of electoral districts based upon changes in the population. The principle of "one person, one vote" is supposed to guide the reapportionment process.

recusal　The process by which a judge is disqualified from hearing or reviewing a case when such participation might be inappropriate because of self-interest or bias. Disqualification may be initiated by a party to a case or by the judge himself or herself.

remand　To send a case back to an inferior court for additional action, such as correcting a specified error.

respondent　The party against whom a legal action is filed.

reversal　An action by an appellate court setting aside or changing a decision of a lower court. The opposite of an affirmation.

right　A power or privilege to which a person is entitled. A right is legally conveyed by a constitution, statutes, or common law and may be absolute, such as one's right to believe, or conditional so that the acting out of one's beliefs will not injure other members of a political community.

ripeness   A condition in which a legal dispute has evolved to the point where the issue(s) it presents can be determined by a court.

search warrant   A term specified in the Fourth Amendment that is an authorization by a judicial official who believes probable cause exists to allow a law enforcement officer to search and seize evidence relating to a crime. The search warrant must be specific in regard to the place to be searched and the items to be seized.

self-incrimination   Giving testimony that could implicate oneself in a crime. The Fifth Amendment guarantees protection against self-incrimination.

separation of powers   The principle of dividing the powers of government among several coordinate branches to prevent excessive concentration of power. Separation of powers is designed to limit abusive exercise of governmental authority by partitioning power and then assigning that power to several locations. In distributing powers, the U.S. Constitution functionally distinguishes between the government and the people and between legislative, executive, and judicial branches. Although the Constitution creates three separate branches, it also assigns overlapping responsibilities, which makes the branches interdependent through the operation of a system of checks and balances.

slander   Causing harm to the reputation of another through the spoken word that contains false statements.

speech plus conduct   Freedom of expression that involves activities by groups of people, such as demonstrations, protests, rallies, and so forth. The government can issue reasonable time, place, and manner restrictions in regard to speech plus conduct.

standing to sue   Sometimes simply called standing, this is the condition in which a party meets the required conditions to initiate a lawsuit. This typically includes having a personal interest in the controversy and its outcome.

stare decisis (lit., "to let the decision stand")   The doctrine that once a principle of law is established for a particular fact situation, courts should adhere to that principle in similar cases in the future. The case in which the rule of law is established is called a precedent. Precedents may be modified or abandoned if circumstances require, but the expectation is that rules from previously adjudicated cases will prevail, creating and maintaining stability and predictability in the law.

state action   An action taken by an agency or official of government. The state action concept is used to determine whether an action complained of has its source in state authority or policy. The concept is critically important in cases presenting allegations of discrimination, as the Equal Protection Clause typically cannot be applied to private acts of discrimination but only to conduct that occurs "under color" of governmental authority.

statute   A written law enacted by a legislative body.

strict scrutiny   The highest level of protection that the Court applies in civil rights and liberties cases, this test requires the government to show that it is pursuing a compelling government interest through narrowly tailored means. This is also known as the suspect classification test in equal protection cases.

subpoena   A judicial order to appear before a grand jury, a court, or a legislative hearing.

substantive due process   Fundamental fairness in the content or substance of government policy. Substantive due process review requires courts to examine the reasonableness of legislative enactments—that laws be fair and reasonable in substance as well as application. Substantive due process is distinguished from procedural due process.

summary decision   An action by the Supreme Court issuing a decision in a case without receiving written briefs or hearing oral arguments.

suspect classification test   A doctrine associated with equal protection cases that requires any government law or action involving race or alienage to be justified by a compelling governmental interest achieved through narrowly tailored means. This is also called the strict scrutiny test.

symbolic speech   A form of freedom of expression that involves the use of symbols, such as a flag, to communicate ideas. Symbolic expression is generally given an intermediate level of protection.

Tenth Amendment   Provision added to the U.S. Constitution in 1791 that retains, or "reserves," for the states powers not assigned to the federal government. The Tenth Amendment has frequently been used to limit the actions of the federal government.

vacate   To set aside or annul the decision of a lower court.

vagueness   A doctrine that requires any government law to be sufficiently precise and clear so that a reasonable person can understand what is prohibited and what is permitted.

venue   The place where a trial is held.

vested right   A right that so completely applies to a person that it cannot be impaired by the act of another person. Such rights must be recognized and protected by the government.

voir dire   A French term meaning "to speak the truth"; this is the process by which a jury is selected.

war power   The grant of authority in the Constitution to the national government to declare and wage war.

warrant   A judicial order authorizing an arrest or search and seizure.

writ   A written order of a court commanding the recipient to perform certain specified acts.

Annotated Bibliography

Aliotta, Jilda M. "Justice O'Connor and the Equal Protection Clause: A Feminine Voice?" *Judicature*, 78 (1995): 232–235.

This article notes the arguments made by some that increasing numbers of female lawyers and judges would inject uniquely feminine qualities into the law. However, the case of Justice O'Connor, as well as many less-prominent examples, does not support this expectation. Aliotta presents O'Connor's positions as much the same as her male colleagues on forty Equal Protection Clause cases. Aliotta speculates that such a feminine approach might exist out of public view but that this cannot be documented without access to private papers.

Baugh, Joyce A. *Supreme Court Justices in the Post-Bork Era: Confirmation Politics and Judicial Performance.* New York: Peter Lang, 2002.

The author examines the confirmation process of the nominees after the fiasco of the Bork battle. Baugh concludes that only the nomination of Clarence Thomas was controversial because of whom he was to replace, his views, and the Anita Hill controversy. Otherwise, writes Baugh, nominations tend to be unique events, only generating controversy if a nominee's views threaten to upset the balance of the Court.

Belsky, Martin H., ed. *The Rehnquist Court: A Retrospective.* New York: Oxford University Press, 2002.

This collection of conference-based academic papers examines various aspects of the record and impact of the Rehnquist Court.

Bland, Randall W. *Private Pressures on Public Law: The Legal Career of Justice Thurgood Marshall, 1934–1991.* Lanham, MD: University Press of America, 1993.

Bland's evaluation of Marshall is that he was a great man but not a great justice. The advocacy that made Marshall such a great civil rights lawyer did not serve him well on the Court. Whether Marshall was unusual in being guided by his central concern (fairness) or not, Bland feels that Marshall needed to subordinate his advocacy to the broader needs of the Supreme Court and often did not. Hence, this is a respectful but critical biography.

————. *Justice Thurgood Marshall: Crusader for Liberalism: His Judicial Biography, 1908–1993.* Bethesda, MD: Academica Press, 2001.

This book updates the earlier biography with new material concerning Marshall's years on the Supreme Court. Bland is unwilling to characterize Marshall as "great," noting that his jurisprudential interest was limited outside the field of civil rights and liberties.

Brenner, Saul. "The Memos of Supreme Court Law Clerk William Rehnquist—Conservative Tracts, or Mirrors of His Justice's Mind?" *Judicature,* 76 (1992): 77–81.

Brenner analyzes two types of memos drawn from the files of Justice Robert Jackson to answer this question. He concludes that Rehnquist was usually mirroring Jackson's mind. He looks briefly at the Rehnquist memo defending the *Plessy* decision, but he essentially brushes it off as inconsequential.

Brisbin, Richard. "Antonin Scalia, William Brennan, and the Politics of Expression: A Study of Legal Violence and Repression." *American Political Science Review,* 87, no. 4 (1993): 912–927.

This article is based upon analysis of Justice Brennan's and Justice Scalia's First Amendment opinions. Justices Brennan and Scalia could be viewed as opposites on the Court's political spectrum. There is, in fact, more freedom envisioned by Brennan, but Brisbin notes the potential of even Brennan's opinions (and obviously Scalia's) to constrain individuals and maintain social order.

————. *Justice Antonin Scalia and the Conservative Revival.* Baltimore: Johns Hopkins Univ. Press, 1997.

An analysis of Justice Antonin Scalia's record on both the U.S. Court of Appeals for the District of Columbia and the U.S. Supreme Court. The study examines both Scalia's voting records and his written opinions, presenting an important analysis of Scalia's judicial philosophies.

————. "The Reconstitution of American Federalism? The Rehnquist Court and Federal-State Relations, 1991–97." *Publius: The Journal of Federalism,* 28, no. 1 (1998): 189–215.

A study of the Rehnquist Court's federalism decisions in the nineties. The article argues that the justices have reinterpreted American federalism in fundamental ways.

Brown, Judith Olans, Wendy E. Parmet, and Mary E. O'Connell. "The Rugged Feminism of Sandra Day O'Connor." *Indiana Law Review*, 32, no. 4 (1999): 1219–1246.

The authors assess the level of O'Connor's feminism, but their use of the word *rugged* refers neither to the persistence of her feminist approaches nor to the connection of her youth on a ranch to her judicial values. The authors assert that a kind of feminism might come into play if the human issue in a case is close enough to O'Connor's experience, as a comfortable white woman with early encounters with gender discrimination, to evoke her empathy.

Caldiera, Gregory A., and Charles E. Smith Jr. "Campaigning for the Supreme Court: The Dynamics of Public Opinion on the Thomas Nomination." *Journal of Politics*, 58, no. 3 (1996): 655–681.

This article examines the process of Thomas's confirmation battle as a political campaign. Looking at shifts of opinion within particular groups as the battle proceeded, the authors measure partisanship and racial, gender, and informational differences in their quest to gauge the public impact of the campaign.

Chemerinsky, Erwin. "The Supreme Court 1988 Term: Forward—The Vanishing Constitution." *Harvard Law Review*, 103 (1989): 43–104.

A major study that is highly critical of the Rehnquist Court during its early years, especially the 1988 term. The dire warning and predictions in the article did not fully materialize in subsequent years, but the article shows the passionate views held by some about the direction of the early Rehnquist Court.

Conlan, Timothy J., and Francois Vergniolle De Chantal. "The Rehnquist Court and Contemporary American Federalism." *Political Science Quarterly*, 116 (2001): 253–276.

The authors examine the Court's record to see if it constituted a "second front" in the "devolution" battles of the nineties—the first having stalled in Congress. They conclude that despite the amount of overturned legislation, the record falls short of successful "devolution" because of philosophical and political constraints, narrow majorities, lack of public support, and the perceived need for "balance."

Danforth, John C. *Resurrection: The Confirmation of Clarence Thomas*. New York: Viking, 1994.

The title's biblical allusion runs through Danforth's sympathetic portrayal of Thomas's confirmation experience. As Thomas's early mentor, Danforth was the senator closest to him throughout the process. Danforth's close relationship is reflected by his repeated reference to the future justice as "Clarence."

Davis, Derek. *Original Intent: Chief Justice Rehnquist and the Course of American Church/State Relations*. Buffalo, NY: Prometheus Books, 1991.

This book examines early Rehnquist Court jurisprudence on the Establishment and Free Exercise Clauses, focusing on Chief Justice Rehnquist's emphasis on original intent. Davis maintains, in criticism of Rehnquist, that the chief justice's views do not wholly reflect the intent of the framers and that they have moved the Court away from an earlier and sounder separatist interpretation.

Davis, Sue. *Justice Rehnquist and the Constitution*. Princeton, NJ: Princeton University Press, 1989.

This book examines Rehnquist's record on the Court by analyzing the interaction of his judicial philosophy with his assertion of strict constructionism. The combination of Rehnquist's democratic model, moral relativism, and emphasis on original intent guarantees that he will seek judicial restraint, deference to majorities, and narrow constitutional interpretations.

———. "Power on the Court: Chief Justice Rehnquist's Opinion Assignments." *Judicature*, 74 (1990): 66–72.

This article asks to what extent Rehnquist has used his power to assign opinions to carry out his policy preferences. Davis finds that Rehnquist did not exercise that power fully, although the reader must keep in mind that the research might now be dated. She suggests that given Rehnquist's conservative base on the Court, the power was simply not needed.

———. "The Voice of Sandra Day O'Connor." *Judicature*, 77 (1993): 134–139.

Davis observes that O'Connor began her tenure on the Court by largely mirroring the views of William Rehnquist, but since then she has become a much more independent swing vote. Skeptical of assertions of a feminine perspective in O'Connor's votes, Davis's analysis points more to the occasional influence of her personal experiences with discrimination in some cases involving equality.

Decker, John F. *Revolution to the Right: Criminal Procedure Jurisprudence during the Burger-Rehnquist Court Era*. New York: Garland Press, 1992.

An analysis of both the Burger Court and the early years of the Rehnquist Court in the area of criminal procedure. The argument is made that the Rehnquist Court has followed in the footsteps of the Burger Court in cutting back dramatically the pro-defendant decisions of the Warren Court.

Devins, Neal, and Davison M. Douglas, eds. *A Year at the Supreme Court*. Durham, NC: Duke University Press, 2004.

This collection of essays focuses upon the 2002–2003 term of the Rehnquist Court. Four cases are emphasized: *Lawrence v. Texas*, the two University of Michigan affirmative action cases, *Lockyer v. Andrade*, and *Virginia v. Black*. The pivotal roles of Justices O'Connor and Kennedy are emphasized.

Dinan, John. "Congressional Responses to the Rehnquist Court's Federalism Decisions." *Publius*, 32 (2002): 1–25.

Noting that Congress generally has the power by which essentially to reenact legislation invalidated by the Supreme Court, Dinan nevertheless concludes that it has not done so in the majority of federalism-based cases. Dinan sees this fact as caused by a combination of shifts in balances of political power, tactical retreats on the part of legislative sponsors, and strategic shifts of support from key interest groups.

Dionne, E. J., and William Kristol, eds. *Bush v. Gore: The Court Cases and the Commentary*. Washington, DC: Brookings Institution Press, 2001.

This collection of Court cases and commentary is most useful as a balanced reference source. The editors disagreed about what ought to happen and what was appropriate, but they agreed that the "Florida Moment" was historic and in need of compilation in book form.

Domino, John C. *Civil Rights and Liberties in the 21st Century*. 2d ed. New York: Longman, 2003.

An examination of the civil rights and liberties decisions of the Rehnquist Court through the 2000–2001 term. The book presents a balanced assessment of the Rehnquist Court, arguing that the Court's three most conservative justices——Rehnquist, Scalia, and Thomas——have generally not been successful in achieving a conservative counterrevolution.

Dworkin, Ronald, ed. *A Badly Flawed Election: Debating Bush v. Gore, the Supreme Court, and American Democracy*. New York: Free Press, 2002.

A range of essays not only about the election aftermath and the court cases but also about other courses of possible action and possible consequences of what was done or not done.

Flax, Jane. *The American Dream in Black and White: The Clarence Thomas Hearings.* Ithaca, NY: Cornell University Press, 1998.

A detailed analysis of the confirmation hearings before the Senate Judiciary Committee involving Clarence Thomas. A central theme of the book is that Thomas benefited from the dominant American cultural values of male supremacy as well as rugged individualism.

Friedelbaum, Stanley H. *The Rehnquist Court: In Pursuit of Judicial Conservatism.* Westport, CT: Greenwood Press, 1994.

A balanced assessment by a British scholar of the initial years of the Rehnquist Court through the early nineties, focusing primarily upon constitutional rights and liberties cases but also including an analysis of the Court's federalism cases.

Gerber, Scott Douglas. *First Principles: The Jurisprudence of Clarence Thomas.* New York: New York University Press, 2002.

An examination of Justice Clarence Thomas's general judicial philosophy as well as an analysis of his opinions in civil rights, civil liberties, and federalism cases. Only brief attention is given to Thomas's background before coming to the Court and his Senate confirmation process.

Gerber, Scott Douglas, and K. Park. "The Quixotic Search for Consensus on the U.S. Supreme Court: A Cross-Judicial Empirical Analysis of the Rehnquist Court Justices." *American Political Science Review,* 91 (1997): 390–408.

The authors examine the behavior of those Rehnquist Court justices who have appellate court backgrounds. Gerber and Park find less consensus (and more concurrences and dissents) on the Supreme Court. They suggest that this could be inevitable because of the unique, ultimate nature of the Court.

Gillman, Howard. *The Votes That Counted: How the Court Decided the 2000 Presidential Election.* Chicago: University of Chicago Press, 2001.

The author is clearly of the opinion that the Court's involvement in *Bush v. Gore* was not one of its greatest hours. The book is based on a wide variety of both primary and secondary sources and is one of the best studies of the case.

Goldman, Roger, and David Gallen. *Thurgood Marshall: Justice for All.* New York: Carroll and Graf, 1992.

Several leading scholars reflect on the career of Thurgood Marshall's jurisprudence and his life as a civil rights advocate. The collection includes a compilation of Justice Marshall's major written opinions and a brief doctrinal analysis by Goldman and Gallen.

———. *Justice William J. Brennan: Freedom First.* New York: Carroll and Graf, 1994.

A collection of reflections on the career of William Brennan, combined with Goldman and Gallen's brief doctrinal analysis of Brennan's career and a compilation of a few of his major written opinions.

Goldstein, Robert Justin. *Flag Burning and Free Speech: The Case of Texas v. Johnson.* Lawrence: University Press of Kansas, 2000.

Goldstein presents the history and context of *Texas v. Johnson,* its outcome, and the reaction to it. Although he makes clear his agreement with the Court's decision in the case that flag burning is protected symbolic speech, he presents the logic and arguments of both sides of the controversy.

Gottlieb, Stephen E. *Morality Imposed: The Rehnquist Court and the State of Liberty in America.* New York: New York University Press, 2000.

For Gottlieb, there are no moderates on the Rehnquist Court. According to Gottlieb, the Rehnquist Court lacks a center, and opinions are philosophically based and extremely political, having little in common because of the lack of a balancing force.

Hensley, Thomas R., and Christopher E. Smith. "Membership Change and Voting Change: An Analysis of the Rehnquist Court's 1986–1991 Terms." *Political Research Quarterly,* 48 (1995): 837–856.

An analysis of the relationship between membership change and voting change on the Rehnquist Court in civil rights and liberties cases for the period of the 1986–1991 terms. The study reports that the Rehnquist Court was more liberal in this period than the Burger Court was in its last decade. Voting changes on the Rehnquist Court were influenced by membership change as well as by changes in the voting behavior of continuous members of the Court and issue change.

Hensley, Thomas R., Christopher E. Smith, and Joyce A. Baugh. *The Changing Supreme Court: Constitutional Rights and Liberties.* Minneapolis/St. Paul: West/Wadsworth, 1997.

A textbook on the constitutional rights and liberties opinions of the U.S. Supreme Court. This text has the unique feature of focusing on the question of whether the Rehnquist Court has engaged in a conservative constitutional counterrevolution. Using both extensive voting data and the Court's written opinions, the argument is advanced that fundamental conservative change has occurred in only a few areas: the free exercise of religion, warrantless searches, and affirmative action.

Higginbotham, A. Leon, Jr. "An Open Letter to Justice Clarence Thomas from a Federal Colleague." *University of Pennsylvania Law Review*, 140 (1992): 1005–1028.

This is a slightly revised version of a letter sent to Justice Thomas in late November 1991. Concerned about Thomas's conservative ideas, Higginbotham calls upon the justice to consider the impact of the civil rights legacy on his own success and to choose to "preserve," not "dilute," the social and legal progress that helped Thomas achieve his position.

Hutchinson, Dennis J. *The Man Who Was Once Whizzer White: A Portrait of Justice Byron White*. New York: Free Press, 1998.

Justice White refused to cooperate with this biography by one of his former law clerks. Hutchinson reveals that White, regrettably, destroyed many of his Court papers. Despite these problems, the book is the most definitive study of Justice White.

Irons, Peter. *Brennan vs. Rehnquist: The Battle for the Constitution*. New York: Knopf, 1994.

This highly readable book analyzes the experience and impact of Brennan and Rehnquist as contending Court leaders between 1972 and 1990. Irons contrasts the very different constitutional views of these liberal and conservative spokesmen through 100 opinions in Bill of Rights cases. Irons readily admits his own preference for Brennan's concern with "dignity" over Rehnquist's concern with "deference."

Jeffries, John C., Jr. *Justice Lewis F. Powell, Jr.* New York: Charles Scribner's Sons, 1994.

Unlike Byron White's main biographer, this scholar had the cooperation of both Powell and his family in his work. The result is a rich combination of primary research and interviews. The latter part of the book, which deals with Powell's Court years, concentrates on school desegregation, Watergate, abortion, the death penalty, affirmative action, and gay rights. Perhaps the best part of the book recounts Powell's uncomfortable encounter with the case of *Bowers v. Hardwick*. Torn between his belief in privacy rights and his repulsion by the gay lifestyle, Powell, by nature a moderating voice on the Court, looked for a compromise position but could find none.

———. *Justice Lewis F. Powell, Jr.* New York: Fordham University Press, 2001.

This updated biography includes Powell's role in abortion, death penalty, affirmative action, and gay rights cases as well as Powell's involvement in the Watergate tapes case.

Jenkins, John A. "A Candid Talk with Justice Blackmun." *The New York Times Magazine,* February 20, 1983: 20ff.

Several characteristics stand out in the almost unprecedented interview: Blackmun's evolution from conservative to liberal (and his gradual alienation from Warren Burger), his high level of sensitivity, and his apparent mistrust of ideology. Jenkins asserts that Blackmun moved left mainly because of the impact of Justice O'Connor and that his votes are tied to a sense of fairness, not any legal theory.

Johnson, Scott P., and Christopher E. Smith. "David Souter's First Term on the Supreme Court: The Impact of a New Justice." *Judicature,* 75 (1992): 238–243.

One of the few published studies on Justice David Souter, this article analyzes Souter's first term on the U.S. Supreme Court by examining both his voting record and his written opinions. Souter is characterized as a cautious newcomer to the Court, decidedly more conservative than his predecessor, Justice William Brennan, but hardly a doctrinaire conservative.

Kairys, David. *With Liberty and Justice for Some: A Critique of the Conservative Supreme Court.* New York: New Press, 1993.

A highly critical examination of the civil rights and liberties decisions of the early Rehnquist Court that argues that the Court's conservative decisions favored the rich and powerful. The study is an important critique of the early Rehnquist Court, but it is now dated.

Kan, Liang. "A Theory of Justice Souter." *Emory Law Journal,* 45 (1996): 1373–1427.

Although Souter is seen as a disappointment to President Bush (who hoped he would be more conservative), Kan sees the justice as more concerned with the legitimacy of the judicial process than any activist liberalism. Souter's concerns lead him to oppose what he views as too many reversals of precedent based on the Rehnquist Court's "originalism." Souter has used originalism himself—but he has a much different reading than the frequent Rehnquist majority.

Kannar, George. "The Constitutional Catechism of Antonin Scalia." *Yale Law Journal*, 99 (1990): 1297–1357.

The title of this article reflects the combined influence of traditional Catholicism and conservative legal theory on Justice Scalia. Kannar sees a combination of "original meaning" textualism and Catholic habits of learning in Scalia's efforts to "codify reality and capture it in rules."

Karkkainen, Bradley C. "Plain Meaning: Justice Scalia's Jurisprudence of Strict Statutory Construction." *Harvard Journal of Law and Public Policy*, 17, no. 2 (1994): 401–477.

Karkkainen asserts that Scalia's "new textualism" is neither new nor textualism. He feels that Scalia's critics oversimplify his method, but that method is hardly the objective one that Scalia claims. Karkkainen believes, nonetheless, that Scalia has done well to bring a discussion of judicial interpretation to center stage.

Keck, Thomas. *The Most Activist Supreme Court in History: The Road to Modern Judicial Conservatism.* Chicago: University of Chicago Press, 2004.

Keck analyses the Supreme Court from 1937 to the present, arguing that the Court took a distinctively conservative turn beginning in 1969 and continuing through 1994 but that judicial conservatism has splintered in the period since 1994.

Kloppenberg, Lisa A. *Playing It Safe: How the Supreme Court Sidesteps Hard Cases and Stunts the Development of Law.* New York: New York University Press, 2001.

This study is critical of the Court, examining cases it avoids. The cases are often in sensitive areas like race, disability, gender discrimination, and environmental degradation. Kloppenberg asserts that the Court is wrongly refusing to take responsibility to adjudicate conflicting lower-court rulings or to make critical decisions interpreting the application of the Constitution and current law to major individual and/or public policy issues.

Koby, Michael. "The Supreme Court's Declining Reliance on Legislative History: The Impact of Justice Scalia's Critique." *Harvard Journal on Legislation*, 36, no. 2 (1999): 369–395.

Koby concludes that, whatever other justices think of Scalia's conclusions in cases, his usual rejection of any kind of legislative history as a judicial tool has had a major impact on them. His quantitative research, detailed in the article, shows a clear reduction in reliance on history—and a return to a similar and older Court tradition.

Lazarus, Edward. *Closed Chambers: The First Eyewitness Account of the Epic Struggles inside the Supreme Court.* New York: Times Books, 1998.

A book by a former U.S. Supreme Court clerk who worked for Justice Harry Blackmun during the 1988 term of the Court. Focusing on three controversial issues—abortion, affirmative action, and the death penalty—the book presents an interesting and controversial account of how the Supreme Court operates. This book was updated with a new chapter in 2005.

Lee, E. G., III, et al. "Context and the Courts: Sources of Support for Civil Liberties on the Rehnquist Court." *American Politics Quarterly*, 24 (1996): 377–395.

Lee finds a surprisingly high level of support for civil liberties on the Rehnquist Court but not because of ideological shifts to the left. Lee determines that the efforts of Presidents Reagan and Bush to nominate conservatives to district and appellate courts was so successful that the Rehnquist Court sometimes feels the need to rein in the lower courts' ultraconservative decisions.

Long, Carolyn N. *Religious Freedom and Indian Rights: The Case of Oregon v. Smith.* Lawrence: University Press of Kansas, 2000.

Long's study of the Rehnquist Court's most significant free exercise decision details the legal and political aspects of the case and the impact of drug enforcement laws on traditional American Indian religious practices. Long provides detailed background information on the key participants in the case as well as an evaluation of the impact of the decision—both on constitutional doctrine and American politics.

Lubbers, Jeffrey S. "Justice Stephen Breyer: Purveyor of Common Sense in Many Forums." *Administrative Law Journal of American University*, 8 (1995): 775–787.

The article is a commentary on Justice Breyer's legal expertise: administrative law. Lubbers argues that this has helped him develop a moderate perspective.

Maltz, Earl M., ed. *Rehnquist Justice: Understanding the Court Dynamic.* Lawrence: University Press of Kansas, 2003.

This is a balanced analysis of the Rehnquist Court, with major Court scholars presenting detailed analyses of the nine justices who served continuously since 1994: Breyer, Ginsburg, Kennedy, O'Connor, Rehnquist, Scalia, Souter, Stevens, and Thomas. Contrasting overviews of the Rehnquist Court are presented by Maltz in an introduction supportive of the Court and by Mark Silverstein in a more critical concluding chapter.

Maltzman, F., and P. J. Wahlbeck. "May It Please the Chief? Opinion Assignment in the Rehnquist Court." *American Journal of Political Science*, 40 (1996): 421–443.

The authors examine the patterns for Rehnquist's opinion assignments and find that organizational needs, not ideological preferences, generally guide Rehnquist's decisions. They see Rehnquist seeking equitable opinion distribution, expertise and area specialization, composition efficiency, and harmony in general. The only exceptions to this policy come when his majority cannot afford to loose any votes.

Marcosson, Samuel A. *Original Sin: Clarence Thomas and the Failure of the Constitutional Conservatives*. New York: New York University Press, 2002.

This book, as its title suggests, is a major critique, not only of Thomas but also of Antonin Scalia and allied members of the judiciary. Marcosson contends that originalists are inconsistent about their applications and constrict their own ability to make sound rulings by ignoring changes to the Constitution, congressional intent behind social legislation, and the evolution of American society since 1789.

Massaro, J. "President Bush's Management of the Thomas Nomination: Four Years, Several Books, Two Videos Later (and Still More to Come!)." *Presidential Studies Quarterly*, 26 (1996): 816–827.

This article focuses on President George H. W. Bush's role in Thomas's confirmation strategy, when Bush emphasized Thomas's race, character, and accomplishments while playing down his ideology and lack of judicial experience. The article gives Bush some credit for a shrewd initial choice, but it observes that Thomas gained more from self-defense and the poor performance of Judiciary Committee Democrats than he did from any key Bush management role. The article ends with an open-ended question as to the negative long-term effects of the confirmation on Bush, the Court, and the American public.

Maveety, Nancy. *Justice Sandra Day O'Connor: Strategist on the Supreme Court*. Lanham, MD: Rowman and Littlefield, 1996.

Maveety feels O'Connor's work on the Court has been overshadowed in most analyses by her position as the first female justice. Therefore, the author seeks to provide analytical balance to previous gender-based studies of O'Connor's ideas. Maveety argues that pragmatic realism is a more useful predictor of O'Connor's positions than gender-based attitudinal models for assessing her philosophy and impact.

Melone, Albert P. "Revisiting the Freshman Effect Hypothesis: The First Two Terms of Justice Anthony Kennedy." *Judicature*, 74 (1990): 6–13.

An examination of Justice Kennedy's first two terms on the U.S. Supreme Court. An analysis of both Kennedy's voting patterns and his opinions reveals a cautious new member of the Court and a justice with distinctive conservative leanings.

Michelman, Frank I. *Brennan and Democracy*. Princeton, NJ: Princeton University Press, 1999.

This book is composed of two reworked papers, one focusing on Brennan's idea of the appropriate role of a constitutional judge, the other focusing on Brennan's underlying political ideas. The analyses are enriched by Michelman's experience as a clerk for Brennan in the early sixties.

O'Brien, David M. "The Supreme Court from Warren to Burger to Rehnquist." *PS: Political Science and Politics*, 25 (1987): 492–495.

An interesting review of the policies of the Warren Court and the Burger Court with predictions about the possible directions of the Court with William Rehnquist as the new chief justice.

———. *Animal Sacrifice and Religious Freedom: Church of Lukumi Babalu Aye v. City of Hialeah*. Lawrence: University Press of Kansas, 2004.

O'Brien presents a detailed case study of the Rehnquist Court's free exercise of religion case involving the unsuccessful attempts by the city of Hialeah, Florida, to prevent an unpopular religious minority from practicing animal sacrifice as part of their religious activities. This book complements Carolyn Long's book, *Religious Freedom and Indian Rights* (2000), on *Oregon v. Smith* (1990) as part of the excellent series by the University Press of Kansas on major Supreme Court decisions.

O'Connor, Karen. "The Effects of the Thomas Nomination on the Supreme Court." *PS: Political Science and Politics*, 25 (1992): 492–495.

The author asserts that Thomas ultimately formed a new bloc to the Right of Rehnquist, typically voting most frequently with Scalia. The author writes that the Thomas confirmation hearings have had a bigger impact, with many judicial figures foresee-ing future credibility problems and damage to the prestige of the Court.

O'Connor, Sandra Day. "Our Judicial Federalism." *Case Western Reserve University Law Review*, 35 (1985): 1–12.

The article explains her perspective on the history of the Supreme Court's federalist doctrine, especially the role of Justice Black. Justice O'Connor defends the role of state courts in the constitutional framework.

————. *The Majesty of the Law: Reflections of a Supreme Court Justice.* Craig Joyce, ed. New York: Random House, 2003.

This book focuses reflectively on O'Connor's progression to the Supreme Court and tenure upon it, touching on various issues and events and her reaction to them. The nar-rative reflects her faith in the "rule of law" as the best way for societies to progress.

O'Connor, Sandra Day, and H. Alan Day. *Lazy B: Growing Up on a Cattle Ranch in the American Southwest.* New York: Random House, 2002.

This family memoir, written by Justice O'Connor and her younger brother, is useful in evoking the environment in which O'Connor grew up and the values that have helped to mold her judicial opinions.

Ogundele, A., and Linda Camp Keith. "Reexamining the Impact of the Bork Nomina-tion to the Supreme Court." *Political Research Quarterly*, 52, no. 2 (1999): 403–420.

The authors ask whether a marked change occurred in the level of questions raised during the Bork nomination. They find a raised level in scrutiny—but determine that the change can be traced to the Rehnquist nomination. They note that questions are also affected by individual qualities, closeness to the president, and whether a given president is in the fourth year of his term of office.

Perry, Barbara A. *"The Supremes": Essays on the Current Justices of the Supreme Court of the United States.* New York: Peter Lang, 1999.

In this extremely useful book, Perry provides analyses of the nine 1999 members of the Supreme Court, summarizing the major influences, values, and rationales of each justice.

Perry, Barbara A., and Henry J. Abraham. "A 'Representative' Supreme Court? The Thomas, Ginsburg, and Breyer Appointments." *Judicature*, 81, no. 4 (1998): 158–165.

The authors address the issue of diversity on the Court by recounting how the nominees were chosen and then looking into their voting records and written opinions once on the Court. Perhaps their most interesting comments have to do with the civil liberties sympathies of Ginsburg and Breyer as a quite self-conscious legacy of their Jewish backgrounds.

Pickerill, J. Mitchell, and Cornell W. Clayton. "The Rehnquist Court and the Political Dynamics of Federalism." *Perspectives on Politics*, 2, no. 2 (2004): 233–248.

This article evaluates the federalism decisions of the Rehnquist Court, in which the "federalist five"—Justices Kennedy, O'Connor, Rehnquist, Scalia, and Thomas—invalidated a wide range of congressional statutes and have reinterpreted constitutional doctrine regarding federalism. The authors examine both normative theories of federalism and a historical-empirical theory they label "political regimes," arguing that the Court's decisions not only reflect trends in the national political regime but also the dominant normative theories.

Pierce, Richard J. "Justice Breyer: Intentionalist, Pragmatist, and Empiricist." *Administrative Law Journal of American University*, 8 (1995): 747–754.

The article extols Justice Breyer's pragmatic streak while noting that, before coming to the Court, he was better known for his narrow technical expertise in the fields of administrative law, government regulation, and antitrust law than for any knowledge of constitutional law.

Powell, Jeff. "The Compleat Jeffersonian: Justice Rehnquist and Federalism." *The Yale Law Journal*, 91 (1991): 1317–1370.

Powell examines the validity of Rehnquist's assertion of a constitutional "first principle" of federalism. He concludes that Rehnquist cannot claim an objective reading of the framers' original intent in this area because his position is much closer to the anti-federalists than it is to the federalists.

Pressman, Carol. "The House That Ruth Built: Ruth Bader Ginsburg, Gender and Justice." *New York Law School Journal of Human Rights*, 14, no. 1 (1997): 311–337.

The author recounts the events that led Ruth Bader Ginsburg to become an advocate for gender equality. Ginsburg's brief in *Reed v. Reed* became a template for arguments that changed the legal landscape in America.

Rabkin, Jeremy A. "The Supreme Court in the Culture Wars." *The Public Interest*, 125 (1998): 3–26.

The author argues that America is engaged in a struggle over the direction of its society, and the Supreme Court is an ally of the most antitraditional elements in that culture war.

Ragan, Sandra L. *The Lynching of Language: Gender, Politics, and Power in the Hill-Thomas Hearings.* Urbana: University of Illinois Press, 1996.

This collection focuses on the nature of the discourse during the Hill-Thomas hearings and its political and cultural ramifications. Using Thomas's claim of a "high-tech lynching" as a starting point for her communications analysis, the author contends that the positions of victim and accused harasser were reversed by language. This, in turn, contributed to the continuing controversy about Thomas's credibility and the appropriateness of his confirmation.

Rehnquist, William H. *The Supreme Court.* New York: Knopf, 2001.

An update on the 1987 original, this book combines historical commentary with operational observations. It is equally interesting in its indications of Rehnquist's views of the Court's past and of his perceptions of how and why the Court functions as it does.

"The Rehnquist Years: A Supreme Court Retrospective [Symposium]." *Nova Law Review*, 22, no. 3 (2001): 667–761.

A review of the Rehnquist Court and contemporary issues in constitutional law with commentaries on abortion, the role of the solicitor general, and an introduction by National Public Radio correspondent Nina Totenberg.

Rosche, Staci. "How Conservative Is the Rehnquist Court? Three Issues, One Answer." *Fordham Law Review*, 65 (1997): 2685–2745.

Rosche argues that the Rehnquist Court has been very unsympathetic to the interests of minorities. Although the article explains that the Court's decisions can be explained by its majoritarian bent, this does not change the fact that minorities are increasingly aware that the Court is not a place to find redress.

Rowan, Carl T. *Dream Makers, Dream Breakers: The World of Thurgood Marshall.* Boston: Little, Brown, 1993.

Although based on the author's research, this biography is an informal and partisan tribute to Marshall by one of the justice's oldest friends. At its best, however, the book provides both great detail and insight into Marshall's experiences, values, and interpretations of the Constitution.

Savage, David G. *Turning Right: The Making of the Rehnquist Supreme Court.* New York: Wiley, 1993.

An analysis by a journalist assigned to the U.S. Supreme Court, the book provides a highly readable study of the early years of the Rehnquist Court, emphasizing the impact of the Reagan and Bush appointments in making the Court a more conservative institution.

Scalia, Antonin. *A Matter of Interpretation: Federal Courts and the Law.* Princeton, NJ: Princeton University Press, 1998.

A relatively brief work authored by Justice Antonin Scalia in which he sets forth key elements of his judicial philosophy, arguing that judges should interpret regulatory, statutory, and constitutional law through textual analysis and original meaning. Notable scholars Gordon Wood, Laurence Tribe, Mary Ann Glendon, and Ronald Dworkin offer commentaries about Scalia's views.

Schultz, David A., and Christopher E. Smith. *The Jurisprudential Vision of Justice Antonin Scalia.* Lanham, MD: Rowman and Littlefield, 1996.

The authors see a clear pattern in Justice Scalia's jurisprudence, which is a mixture of the political and the legal. Its main features are deference to executive authority, respect for the majority, questioning of legislative policy, and dislike of the Court in a social protection role.

Schwartz, Herman, ed. *The Rehnquist Court: Judicial Activism on the Right.* New York: Hill and Wang, 2002.

While predictably critical of the Rehnquist Court in general (its essays, for the most part, originally appeared in the left-of-center *Nation*), this collection is especially well written and strongly supported in its arguments. Major attention is devoted to the Court's use of the Commerce Clause, Section 5 of the Fourteenth Amendment, and federalism to attack and/or undermine social legislation.

Sickels, Robert J. *John Paul Stevens and the Constitution: The Search for Balance.* University Park: Pennsylvania State University Press, 1988.

This book focuses on Steven's pragmatism and independence, whether about the Constitution or the role and process of judicial review. Sickels's 1988 contention that Stevens is equally aligned with both the liberal and conservative justices is now dated, because his more recent votes have put him among the most liberal justices.

Simon, James F. *The Center Holds: The Power Struggle inside the Rehnquist Court.* New York: Simon and Schuster, 1995.

Simon analyzes the power struggle on the Rehnquist Court in four areas of constitutional interpretation: racial discrimination, abortion, criminal law, and First Amendment freedoms. Simon's theme is that the widely expected conservative turn only partially materialized. Instead, "the center held," as liberal justices frequently won the support of moderates to outvote the conservative wing of the Court.

Smith, Christopher E. *Critical Judicial Nominations and Political Change: The Impact of Clarence Thomas.* Westport, CT: Praeger, 1993.

In a republication of earlier articles, Smith uses the Thomas nomination as a case study to look at the Supreme Court nominating process. He argues that controversial nominations are often "catalysts" for unplanned political change.

―――. *Justice Antonin Scalia and the Supreme Court's Conservative Moment.* Westport, CT: Praeger, 1994.

Smith explores the reasons behind Justice Scalia's failure to influence the Court to the degree that both his supporters and detractors predicted. According to Smith, the legal reasoning that Scalia used was different from that of his fellow conservatives. Likewise, his personality was not conducive to coalition building.

Smith, Christopher E., and Joyce A. Baugh. *The Real Clarence Thomas: Confirmation Veracity Meets Performance Reality.* New York: Peter Lang, 2000.

Smith and Baugh compare Thomas's testimony during his confirmation hearings to his subsequent opinions and conclude that Thomas was somewhat less than honest about his views. Aside from the serious questions raised by Anita Hill, the gaps between his assertions in the hearing and later opinions lead the authors to wonder about Thomas's fitness to be on the Court.

Smith, Christopher E., and Thomas R. Hensley. "Assessing the Conservatism of the Rehnquist Court." *Judicature,* 76 (1993): 83–89.

An article using voting data to argue that the Rehnquist Court had not been as conservative as many critics had contended and that the replacements of Justice Brennan with Justice Souter and Justice Marshall with Justice Thomas had not shifted the Court radically to the Right. Justices O'Connor and Kennedy were identified as key figures in slowing the Court's conservative counterrevolution.

Smith, Christopher E., and Scott P. Johnson. "The First-Term Performance of Justice Clarence Thomas." *Judicature*, 76 (1993): 172–178.

This analysis of Justice Clarence Thomas's first year on the U.S. Supreme Court reveals a justice with a strongly conservative voting record but also a justice who wrote few opinions and gave little insight into his jurisprudential philosophies.

Smith, Christopher E., Joyce A. Baugh, and Thomas R. Hensley. "The First-Term Performance of Justice Stephen Breyer." *Judicature*, 79 (1995): 74–79.

The article evaluates the performance of Justice Stephen Breyer in his initial term, replacing conservative-turned-liberal Harry Blackmun. The article notes that Breyer is a moderate who can go to either side, depending upon the issue. The authors compare Breyer to President Clinton insofar as he generally supports moderate positions but becomes more liberal when pushed on some issues.

Smith, Christopher E., Joyce A. Baugh, Thomas R. Hensley, and Scott P. Johnson. "The First-Term Performance of Justice Ruth Bader Ginsburg." *Judicature*, 78 (1994): 74–80.

A quantitative and qualitative analysis of Ruth Bader Ginsburg's first term on the U.S. Supreme Court, arguing that Ginsburg was a moderate liberal in her first year on the Court.

Smolla, Rodney A., ed. *A Year in the Life of the Supreme Court*. Durham and London: Duke University Press, 1995.

Using nine representative cases, this collection of decisions provides a sample of a typical year on the Rehnquist Court. Two special strengths of the collection are its detailed explanations of case contexts and its companion portraits of individual justices' behavior.

Stith, K. "Byron R. White: Last of the New Deal Liberals." *Yale Law Journal*, 103, no. 1 (1993): 19–35.

Stith writes of the influence of New Deal thinking on Justice White, especially his acceptance of far-reaching congressional authority. Given that White tended toward judicial conservatism, it is somewhat surprising to note his liberal positions on issues such as set asides and his dissent in *Rodriguez* on grounds of financial equity in education. However, both attitudes fit within the context of economic fairness and deference to Congress from the New Deal.

Strum, Philippa. *Women in the Barracks: The VMI Case.* Lawrence: University Press of Kansas, 2002.

Another book from the University Press of Kansas on landmark Supreme Court cases, this is an authoritative account of *United States v. Virginia* (1996), in which the Court ruled against the exclusion of women from the Virginia Military Institute (VMI).

Sunstein, Cass R. *One Case at a Time: Judicial Minimalism on the Supreme Court.* Chicago: University of Chicago Press, 1999.

An important book on the overall jurisprudence of the Rehnquist Court that argues that the Court has purposely avoided broad rulings on numerous controversial issues and has instead focused on one case at a time. Sunstein supports this approach, which he characterizes as "minimalism," arguing that it enhances rather than limits public debate.

Sunstein, Cass R., and Richard A. Epstein, eds. *The Vote: Bush, Gore, and the Supreme Court.* Chicago: University of Chicago Press, 2001.

This is a collection of essays about *Bush v. Gore*, ranging from positive to negative evaluations. Perhaps the most interesting is the mixed reaction from editor Sunstein. To some extent, he views the decision as a positive example of "minimalism" while questioning other aspects of it. Further, the editors puzzle over the sharp political division of opinions, even among academics, about the ruling, noting that law and politics overlap strongly.

Tucker, D. F. B. *The Rehnquist Court and Civil Rights.* Aldershot, UK: Dartmouth University Press, 1995.

Tucker favors the Rehnquist Court's effort to reverse the direction of the Warren and Burger Courts. In praise of Justice Scalia, Tucker asserts that the earlier Courts were misguided by a dualist belief that the "liberal elite" judiciary needed to balance the majority. Tucker supports the view that the Court should defer to the values of popular majorities as enacted by the elected governmental branches.

Tushnet, Mark. *The New Constitutional Order.* Princeton, NJ: Princeton University Press, 2003.

Tushnet presents a sweeping analysis of America since the late 1930s. He argues that the New Deal–Great Society constitutional order has been replaced by a new constitutional order that embodies a much more restrictive view of the ability of government to solve problems.

————. *A Court Divided: The Rehnquist Court and the Future of Constitutional Law.* New York: Norton, 2005.

Tushnet makes the argument that the Supreme Court has a long history of following closely prevailing public opinion. He argues that this has been true for the Rehnquist Court and is likely to hold true regardless of the Court's membership.

Urofsky, Melvin I. *Affirmative Action on Trial: Sex Discrimination in Johnson v. Santa Clara.* Lawrence: University Press of Kansas, 1997.

Urofsky presents an in-depth analysis of *Johnson v. Santa Clara*, in which the Rehnquist Court ruled for the first time in support of an affirmative action plan benefiting women.

Van Sickel, Robert W. *Not a Particularly Different Voice: The Jurisprudence of Sandra Day O'Connor.* New York: Peter Lang, 1998.

An analysis of Justice Sandra Day O'Connor. Although some attention is given to O'Connor's early life and career before joining the U.S. Supreme Court, the primary focus is on O'Connor's jurisprudence, which is characterized as "marginalist," emphasizing adherence to precedent, principles of states' rights, and deference to the popularly elected branches of government.

Wise, Charles R. "Judicial Federalism: The Resurgence of the Supreme Court's Role in the Protection of State Sovereignty." *Public Administration Review*, 58, no. 2 (1998): 95–98.

Wise sees the Court's move in the nineties back to federalism as a positive change. He views the shift as a return to an earlier and better role of balancing the interests of the federal and the state governments instead of heavily favoring the federal government.

Yarbrough, Tinsley E. *The Rehnquist Court and the Constitution.* New York: Oxford University Press, 2000.

Yarbrough asserts that, despite the best efforts of Presidents Reagan and G. H. W. Bush, the Rehnquist Court has not broken nearly as much with its predecessors as hoped.

————. *Race and Redistricting: The Shaw-Cromartie Cases.* Lawrence: University Press of Kansas, 2002.

This is a case study of three related redistricting suits decided between 1993 and 2001, determining the limits to state discretion in the redrawing of congressional districts meant to assure fair racial representation. Particular interest centers on the background of the initiator of the two *Shaw* suits, a self-made "southern liberal" who found discrimination and race-conscious preferential treatment equally objectionable.

Index

Note: t. indicates table; italic page numbers indicated pictures.

425

About the Authors

Thomas R. Hensley is Professor Emeritus of Political Science at Kent State University. He has written over 100 books, articles, reviews, and professional papers, and he has also won numerous teaching awards including Ohio Professor of the Year.

Kathleen Hale is currently teaching full-time in the Political Science Department at Kent State University, where she recently earned her PhD. She will begin teaching in a tenure-track position at Auburn University in the fall of 2006.

Carl Snook is currently a PhD candidate at Michigan State University. He earned his BA and MA in political science at Kent State University. His interests include judicial decision making and the role of political institutions in determining public policy.